P9-DWY-130

DATE DUE

NO 8'00		
JA 31 01		
JE 10 02		

DEMCO 38-296

INTERNATIONAL ENVIRONMENTAL LAW, POLICY AND ETHICS

International Environmental Law, Policy and Ethics

ALEXANDER GILLESPIE

CLARENDON PRESS · OXFORD
1997

Riverside Community College
Library
SEP '98
4800 Magnolia Avenue
Riverside, CA 92506

K 3585.4 .G55 1997

Gillespie, Alexander.

International environmental
law, policy, and ethics

Great Clarendon Street, Oxford OX2 6DP
Oxford New York
Athens Auckland Bangkok Bogota Bombay
Buenos Aires Calcutta Cape Town Dar es Salaam
Delhi Florence Hong Kong Istanbul Karachi
Kuala Lumpur Madras Madrid Melbourne
Mexico City Nairobi Paris Singapore
Taipei Tokyo Toronto
and associated companies in
Berlin Ibadan

Oxford is a trade mark of Oxford University Press

Published in the United States
by Oxford University Press Inc., New York

© Alexander Gillespie 1997

All rights reserved. No part of this publication may be reproduced,
stored in a retrieval system, or transmitted, in any form or by any means,
without the prior permission in writing of Oxford University Press.
Within the UK, exceptions are allowed in respect of any fair dealing for the
purpose of research or private study, or criticism or review, as permitted
under the Copyright, Designs and Patents Act, 1988, or in the case of
reprographic reproduction in accordance with the terms of the licences
issued by the Copyright Licensing Agency. Enquiries concerning
reproduction outside these terms and in other countries should be
sent to the Rights Department, Oxford University Press,
at the address above

British Library Cataloguing in Publication Data
Data available

Library of Congress Cataloging in Publication Data
Gillespie, Alexander.
International environmental law, policy, and ethics/Alexander
Gillespie.
p. cm.
Includes bibliographical references and index.
1. Environmental law, International. 2. Environmental protection—
Moral and ethical aspects. I. Title.
K3585.4.G55 1997
341.7'62—dc21 97–19430
ISBN 0–19–826562–X

1 3 5 7 9 10 8 6 4 2

Typeset by Cambrian Typesetters, Frimley, Surrey
Printed in Great Britain on acid-free paper by
Bookcraft Ltd., Midsomer Norton, Somerset

Acknowledgements

THIS book was made feasible by support from Rotary International, the Spencer Mason Trust in New Zealand, and the Nottingham University Law School in the United Kingdom. All three of these bodies made generous contributions which enabled me to complete my studies without having to live in Sherwood Forest.

This book was also greatly assisted by a multitude of people, comparable to the Merry Men who traditionally stalked this area. There are far too many people to list individually, who talked me through, round, and over cliffs in attempting to help reach the end of this project. All the help and support from the folks at the Law School (especially Mike), and the students and friends in both New Zealand and Nottingham is gratefully appreciated.

However, the absolute thanks must go to Rachel. She has been the true Robin Hood in this story. The real hero, without whom none of this would have been possible. This book is dedicated to her.

Contents

Table of Important Laws, Declarations, and Decisions,
in Chronological Order   xi

Introduction   1

I. Anthropocentricism   4

1. Foundations, Theories, and Positions   5

    A.   The Physical and the Mental   5
    B.   The Individual Nature of Existence   6
    C.   The Dichotomies Between Humanity and Nature   9
    D.   The Use and Value of Nature   11
    E.   The Control of Nature   12

2. The Anthropocentric Basis of International Environmental
Law   15

II. The Self-Interest Justification for Environmental Protection

1. Self-Interest in the International Environmental Context   19

2. Self-Interest and Current Environmental Argument   20

3. The Problems of the Anthropocentric Self-Interested Approach   22

4. Self-Interest and International Environmental Law   23

    Self-Interest and Climate Change   25

III. The Use of Economic Rationale as a Justification for Environmental Protection

1. The Background   28

2. The Reasons for the Economic Emphasis within Environmental
Policy   33

    The Total Economic Value of Tropical Forests   36

3. Acceptance of the Argument   37

The Problems with Economic Justifications for Environmental
Protection   38

1. The Question of Values   38

A. The Problem of Value   38
    Sustainable Whaling   45
B. The Location of Values   47

2. The Social Problems of Economic Considerations   50
3. Political Problems   54
4. Market Problems   57

IV. Religious Justifications for Environmental Protection

1. International Law and Religion   62
2. Environmental Protection, Law, and Religion   63
3. Environmental Protection and Religion   65
4. The Environmental Argument in a Biblical Context   67

The Problems with Religiously Inspired Conservation as a Suitable
Source of Environmental Protection   71

1. Differing, Changing, and Failing Interpretations   71
2. Religious Hostility, Indifference, and Motivational Concerns
    with Regard to Environmental Protection   76
    Population and Theology   77
3. The Limited Role of Religion in a Secular Society   80

V. Aesthetic, Cultural, and Recreational Justifications

1. Aesthetic Justifications for Environmental Protection   82

    A. Aesthetics and International Environmental Law   82
    B. The Arguments for Aesthetic Environmental
        Considerations   84
        Sealing and Aesthetics   85
    C. The Problems with Aesthetics as a Basis for
        Environmental Concern   87

        (i)   Subjectivity   87
        (ii) Collective Aesthetics   90
        (iii) Residual Problems with Aesthetics   91

2. The Cultural Justification for Environmental Protection   92

    A. Culture and International Environmental Protection   92
        Maori, Culture, and Environmental Protection   94
    B. The Cultural Argument   95
    C. Initial Difficulties with the Cultural Exception   97
        Rhinoceros and Culture   97

   D. The Defence of Environmentally Destructive Cultures   99
   E. The Final Refutations   101
3. Recreational Values and the Importance of Wilderness as
    Justifications for Environmental Protection   102
   A. The Problems of Wilderness and Recreation   104

**VI. The Rights of Future Generations as a Justification for
          Environmental Protection**

1. International Law and the Rights of Future Generations   107
2. The Moral Considerability of Future Generations:
    Past and Present   110
    Nuclear Waste and Future Generations   112
3. Theories of the Rights of Future Generations   114
   A. John Rawls and the Ideal Observer   114
   B. The Cross-Temporal Argument   115

The Problems with the Future Generations Argument   117
1. Motivational and Practical Problems   117
2. Theoretical Problems   119
   A. Knowledge, Distance, and Cost   119
   B. Interests and Existence   122
   C. The Anthropocentric Assumptions Within the Theories
       for the Moral Consideration of Future Generations   124

**VII. The Growth of New, Non-Anthropocentric Ideals within
            International Environmental Law**

1. The Change of Values   127
    The Philosophical Problems of Protecting Endangered Species   131
2. The Change of Objectives   133
3. The Possibilities of the Non-Anthropocentric Approaches   135

VIII. The Moral Considerability of Animals

1. The Utilitarian Approach   137
   A. Problems with the Utilitarian Approach   139
2. Inherent Value   141
3. Further Philosophical Challenges   144
4. The Moral Considerability of Animals and Environmental Ethics   145

IX. Respect for Life

1. The Proposal   150
2. Reverence for Life   152
3. The Difficulties of the Life Approach   152

X. The Land Ethic

1. The Basis and Objective   159
2. Philosophical Problems   162
3. Problems with Ecological Theory   164
4. Misanthropic Tendencies   168
5. Strategies for Progress   174
       The Problem of Poverty   174

XI. Conclusion   176

Bibliography   179

Index   211

Table of Important Laws, Declarations, and Decisions, in Chronological Order

Convention Relative to the Preservation of Fauna and Flora in Their Natural State. 1933. 1 LNTS Vol. 172 (No. 3995), 241.

Convention on Nature Protection and Wildlife Preservation in the Western Hemisphere. UNTS Vol. 161 (No. 11: 485), 193.

International Convention for the Regulation of Whaling. 161 UNTS 72. TIAS No. 1849.

Convention For The Protection Of Cultural Property In The Event Of Armed Conflict. 14 May 1954. 249 UNTS 240.

Convention Concerning the Protection of Indigenous and Other Tribal Populations in Independent Countries of the International Labour Organisations. 1957. ILO 107.

Declaration on the Elimination of Religious Intolerance and Discrimination. UNGA Res. 1781, 17 UN GAOR Supp. (no. 17), at 33. UN Doc. A/517. (1962).

Charter for African Unity. 25 May 1963, 479 UNTS, 39.

Problems of the Environment. UNGA Res. 2398 (XXIII) 1968.

African Convention on the Conservation of Nature and Natural Resources. 1968. Algiers. 15 September. UNTS Vol. 1001 (No. 14689). 3.

International Convention for the Conservation of Atlantic Tuna. UST Vol. 20 (1969), 2887–2940. TIAS 6767.

UNESCO Convention on the Means of Prohibiting and Preventing the Illicit Import, Export, and Transfer or Ownership of Cultural Property 1970. 14 November. 10 ILM. 1970. 1.

Convention on Wetlands of International Importance. UNTS Vol. 996. 244. 11 ILM 1972. 963.

Agreement on the Conservation of Polar Bears. TIAS. No. 8409.

OECD's *Guiding Principles on the Environment*. US Dept. of State Release. No. 130. 1972. 1 June. 11 ILM. 1972. 1172.

Declaration of the United Nations Conference on the Human Environment. 1972. UN Doc. A/CONF 48/14/Rev. 1. 11 ILM. 1972. 1416.

Convention on International Trade in Endangered Species of Wild Fauna and Flora. TIAS. No. 8249; 12 ILM. 1085.

Convention Concerning the Protection of the World Cultural and Natural Heritage. 1921. 27 UST, 37, TIAS. No. 8226. 1972.

Convention for the Conservation of Antarctic Seals. British Command Paper Cmnd. 5302, Misc. II (1973); Cmnd. 7209 Treaty Series 45 (1978).

Declaration of the Council of European Communities on the Program of

Action of the European Community on the Environment. 1973. *Official Journal of the European Communities.* Volume 16. No. 6. 112. 22 December 1973.

Nordic Convention. 1974. ILM 13 (1974). 591.

Charter of Economic Rights and Duties of States. UNGA Res. 3281 (XXIX). 1974.

International Covenant on Economic, Social and Cultural Rights. United Nations Resolutions on the Importance of Cultural Values. UNGA Res. 31/39. 1976.

Convention on the Conservation of Nature in the South Pacific. 1976. Apia. 12 June.

European Convention for the Protection of Animals During International Transport. 1979. ETS 103. 22 IPE 387.

Convention on Long Range Transboundary Air Pollution on the Reduction of Sulphur Emissions. 18 ILM. 1979. 144.

Convention on the Conservation of Migratory Species of Wild Animals. British Command Paper Cmnd. 7888, Misc. 11 (1980) and Cm. 1332 TS 87 (1990) 19 ILM 1980. 15.

Historical Responsibility of States for the Preservation of Nature for Present and Future Generations. UN Doc A./RES/35/8. 1980. 30 October.

Convention on the Conservation of European Wildlife and Natural Habitats. UKTS No. 56. 1982. Cmnd. 8738. Europ. TS No. 104.

World Charter for Nature. GA Res. 7, 36 UN GAOR Supp. (No. 51) at 17, UN Doc. A/51 (1982).

Berne Convention on the Conservation of European Wildlife. Europ TS No. 104. UKTS No. 56 (1982) Cmd. 8738.

Convention on Future Multilateral Cooperation in North Atlantic Fisheries. British Command Paper 8474 Misc. 2 (1982).

Nairobi Declaration, 18 May 1982, UNEP report. 37 UN. GAOR Annex 2, Supp. (no. 25) at 49, UN Doc. A/37/25 (1982).

Convention on the Conservation of European Wildlife and Natural Habitats. UKTS. No. 56 (1982). Europ TS No. 104.

Declaration of the World's National Park Congress. Environmental Policy and the Law, 10 (1983), 62.

European Council Directives on the Protection of Animals Used for Experimental Purpose. Official Journal of the European Communities 29, No. L. 358. (18 December), 1–13.

Convention for the Protection, Management and Development of the Marine and Coastal Environment of the East African Region. 1985. (French) Journal Official 1989, 7729.

Declaration on the Right to Development. UNGA Res. 41/18.

Declaration of Fontainebleau. IUCN Bulletin. 20. 7.

Additional Protocol of the European Convention for the Protection of Pet Animals. ETS 125.

Directive on the Protection of Laying Hens in Battery Cages. Official *Journal of the European Communities.* 29, No. L. 95. (10 April), 45–48.

Convention for the Co-operation in the Protection and Development of the Marine and Coastal Environment of the West and Central African Region. 1981. *International Legal Materials.* 20 (1988). 746–761.

Convention on Conservation of Antarctic Marine Living Resources. International Legal Materials, 27 (1988), 868.

Decision of Economic Commission of Europe; Declaration of Environmental Usage. Reprinted in *Environmental Law and Policy.* 18 (1988). 132.

Wellington Convention on the Regulation of Antarctic Mineral Resource Activities. UN Doc. AMR/SCR/88/78. (1988). 28 ILM 1988. 686.

Protection of the Global Climate for Present and Future Generations of Mankind. A/Res./43/53. A/44/86. 1989.

Kampala Declaration on Sustainable Development in Africa. Declared at the First African Regional Conference on the Environment and Development. 1989. Kampala, Uganda. 12–16 June.

Bergen Ministerial Declaration on Sustainable Development in the EEC Region. Reprinted in *Environmental Policy and the Law,* 20 (1990), 104.

Decision of the Interparliamentary Conference on the Global Environment. Environmental Policy and the Law. 20 (1990). 112.

Protocol on Environmental Protection to the Antarctic Treaty. 30 ILM. 1991. 1462.

Rio Declaration on Environment and Development. A/CONF 151/5. 1992. 3–14 June.

Report of the United Nations Conference on Environment and Development. A/CONF 151/26.

Agenda 21. A/CONF 187/26 (Vol. III). 1992. 14 August.

Statement of Principles for a Global Consensus on the Management, Conservation and Sustainable Use of all Types of Forests. 1992. UNCED Doc. A/CONF 151/6/Rev. 1. 31. ILM. 1992. 881.

United Nations Convention on Biodiversity. UNCED. 1992. UNEP. Bio. Div./CONF L2. 1992.

Cartagena Commitment, Environmental Policy and the Law, 22 (1992), 189.

Lucerne Declaration. In *Environmental Policy and the Law.* (1993), 185.

Draft Program of Action for the Sustainable Development of Small Island States. A/CONF 167/9. 1994. 18 March.

Draft Declaration on the Rights of Indigenous Peoples. UN Doc. E/CN 4/ Sub.2/1994/2 (5 April 1994).

Conference on Straddling and Highly Migratory Fish. A/CONF 164/22. 1994. 23 August.

Report of the International Conference on Population and Development. A/CONF 171/13. 1994. 18 October.

Declaration and Programme of Action of the World Summit for Social Development. A/CONF 166/L 3/Add. 1. 1995. 10 March.

Report of the World Summit for Social Development. A/CONF 166/9. 1995. 19 April.

Introduction

> Humanity stands at a defining moment in history. We are confronted with a perpetuation of disparities between and within nations, a worsening of poverty, hunger, ill health and illiteracy, and the continuing deterioration of the ecosystems on which we depend for our well-being.
>
> (*Agenda 21*, Chapter 1, Preamble, Paragraph 1.1.)

At the end of the twentieth century, the problems affecting the international environment are of common concern. Terms like ozone hole, greenhouse effect, biodiversity, deforestation, population growth, 'third world' debt and poverty, and sustainable development are universal linguistic currency. However, the remedies to these problems are not as obvious as the problems themselves.

In an attempt to confront the international environmental *problematique*, a combination of political, economic, and philosophical paradigms and subsequent agendas have been presented. These intellectual mind-sets and the programmes that flow from them have been largely incorporated into international environmental law and policy. It is the central submission of this book that currently these are misplaced and ultimately contradictory to the objective of protecting the environment.

To prove this argument I will examine the reasons *why* the environment is protected and how these ideas are represented in the international environmental arena of policy and law. This will be juxtaposed against what is broadly known as the theories of 'radical ecology'.[1]

Radical ecology devolves into two parts. The first is known as 'deep ecology'[2] and the second as 'social ecology'.[3] Very briefly, deep ecology is concerned with *why* the environment is protected, whereas social ecology is concerned with *how* to achieve this end.[4] This book will only be working primarily with the theories of deep ecology, or more specificially, the idea of anthropocentric and non-anthropocentric justifications—of which deep ecology is only one perspective, to protect the environment.

Deep ecology is also known as 'land ethics' or holistic environmental ethics. By virtue of the fact that deep ecology has evolved from the works of a number

---

[1] See generally, Merchant, C., *Radical Ecology: The Search for a Livable World* (Routledge, London, 1992).

[2] See Devall, B. and Sessions, G., *Deep Ecology: Living As If Nature Mattered* (Gibbs Smith, Utah, 1985). Fox, W., *Towards a Transpersonal Ecology: Developing New Foundations for Environmentalism* (Shambhala, London, 1990), 83–144.

[3] See Bookchin, M., *The Ecology of Freedom* (Cheshire Books, California, 1982), 16–43.

[4] See Goodin, R. E., *Green Political Theory* (Polity, Cambridge, 1992), 15–18.

of theorists it is not a theory that is rigidly defined. There is however one common feature that is often agreed by all the relevant theorists,[5] namely that environmental protection must be based upon the inherent (or intrinsic)[6] value of non-human Nature.

This is in contrast to what is known as 'shallow environmentalism' which justifies environmental protection on the grounds that Nature has instrumental value for humans. This position, which revolves around anthropocentricism, proclaims that only humanity has inherent value.[7] It is this shallow environmentalism that forms the predominant basis of international environmental law and policy, and as I will demonstrate, this creates distinct problems and contradictions in the search for a justification to protect the environment.

From this point I will examine how non-anthropocentric justifications for environmental protection have arrived with a growing presence in international environmental law and policy. However, these too are also besieged by a number of faults and limitations that will prevent deep ecology, in its present form, from being the panacea for all environmental considerations.

The objective of this book is not to find answers to the current contradictions. Rather, it is to demonstrate the limitations of both current and alternative paradigms as justifications to protect the environment. Any 'answers' will be provided by pointing to routes we should not be pursuing, rather than routes that we should be.

---

[5] Ibid. Note, this is by no means a rule. Indeed, certain theorists have attempted to move to non-anthropocentric positions which involve ontological arguments that 'extend the self', as opposed to ethical arguments which grant inherent value in non-anthropocentric entitites. See e.g. Fox, W., *Towards a Transpersonal Ecology: Developing New Foundations for Environmentalism* (Shambhala, Boston, 1990).

[6] Note that the labels inherent and intrinsic value are often used interchangeably. See Devall, B., *Simple in Means, Rich in Ends: Practising Deep Ecology* (Green Print, Surrey, 1990), 15. Sylvan, R. 'On the Core Value of Deep Green Theory', in Oddie, G. and Perrett, R. (eds.), *Justice, Ethics and New Zealand Society* (Oxford University Press, Oxford, 1992), 222. Goodin loc. cit, 26. For a criticism of the synonymous usage of these terms, see Hargrove, E. (ed.), *The Animal Rights and Environmental Ethics Debate: The Environmental Perspective* (Sunny, New York, 1992), xvii–xviii.

[7] Naess, A., 'The Shallow and the Deep, Long Range Ecology Movement', *Inquiry*, 16 (1973), 95–100. Devall, ibid. 5–38.

... I grieve, when on the darker side
Of this great change I look; and there behold
Such outrage done to nature as compels
The indignant power to justify herself;
Yea, to avenge her violated rights ...

(William Wordsworth.
'Outrage done to Nature.'
The Excursion. 1814. Book VIII. 151)

I

Anthropocentricism

People have seen themselves as placed, not just at the relative centre of a particular life, but at the absolute, objective centre of everything. The centrality of MAN [*sic*] has been pretty steadily conceived, both in the West and in many other traditions, not as an illusion of perspective, imposed on us by our starting-point, but as an objective fact, and indeed an essential fact, about the whole universe.

(Mary Midgley. 'The End of Anthropocentricism?'[1])

An anthropocentric outlook is one which regards humanity as the centre of existence. Such a paradigm that has been built up over thousands of years of human existence. For example, Protagoras proclaimed 'Man is the measure of all things.'[2] Sophocles in his tragedy *Antigone* asserted:

Wonders are many on earth, and the greatest of these is man . . . He is master of ageless Earth, to his own will bending . . . He is lord of all things living; birds of the air, Beasts of the field, all creatures of sea and land.[3]

Ficino, the Italian Renaissance author proclaimed, 'Man not only makes use of the elements, but also adorns them . . . man who provides generally for all things, both living and lifeless, is a kind of God.'[4] Manetti stated, 'Nothing in the world can be found that is worthy of more admiration than man.'[5] Kant suggested that, 'Man . . . is the ultimate purpose of creation here on Earth.'[6] While Marx proposed that, 'The whole of what is called world history is nothing but the creation of man by human labour.'[7] Nietzsche philosophized that humanity was near 'perfect', and that the position of humanity with regard to other animals had to be reconsidered. He even went so far as to suggest that 'man' would progress 'into a God'.[8] Mao proclaimed, 'Of all the things in the world, people are most precious.'[9]

[1] Midgley, M., 'The End of Anthropocentricism?', in Attfield, R. (ed.), *Philosophy and the Natural Environment* (Cambridge University Press, Cambridge, 1994).

[2] Protagoras, quoted in Rodman, J., 'The Dolphin Papers', *North American Review*, (1974), 12, 16.

[3] Sophocles, 'Antigone', in the *Theban Plays* (Harmondsworth, 1947).

[4] Ficino, M., 'The Soul of Man', in Ross, J., (ed.), *The Portable Renaissance Reader* (Harmonsdworth, Penguin, 1977), 387.

[5] Manetti, *The Dignity and Excellence of Man* (Cambridge University Press, Cambridge 1901), 54.

[6] Kant, I., *Critique of Judgement* (Macmillan, London, 1914).

[7] See Parson, H., *Marx and Engels on Ecology* (Greenwood Press, Connecticut, 1977), 10.

[8] Nietzsche, F., *The Gay Science* (Penguin, Harmondsworth, 1975), 115, 285.

[9] Mao Tsetung, 'The Bankruptcy of the Idealist Conception on History', in Mao Tsetung, *Selected Works* (New York, 1954), 451, 454.

This sample of views represents the anthropocentric position. Anthropocentricism is basically simple human chauvinism, with a narrowness of sympathy that is comparable to sexual, racial or national chauvinism. The paradigm in this context involves the core of beliefs that underpins the human relationship with the natural world.[10] These intellectual mind-sets lead to discourse and judgements that initiate actions, create preferences, and cement attitudes. The overall problem here is that if these are misplaced then an entire intellectual investment in a mode of thinking and judging evaporates. This problem is the starting point of this book. However, before moving on and discussing the derived arguments from the anthropocentric position, it is useful to understand some of the ideas which have helped lead to the creation of anthropocentricism, and to see how these have been reflected in international environmental law and policy.

1. FOUNDATIONS, THEORIES, AND POSITIONS

A. The Physical and the Mental

It is my contention that there are five main strands in the development of the anthropocentric position. The first strand derives from the early rationalists. Here, Pythagoras and Plato laid part of the foundations for the separation of humanity from Nature via two belief systems. First, both of these philosophers believed in the separation of the (immortal) soul from the (mortal) body.[11] Following from this belief, the physical world was considered as ultimately a trap for the soul.[12] Secondly, Pythagoras and Plato were both distrustful of sensation and empirical observation as a source of knowledge. Rather, they both preferred to rely on the use of abstract reason to gain knowledge.[13]

These approaches are in contrast with other great thinkers such as Aristotle and Kant, who valued both the importance of the senses and the connection between the philosopher and the world within which they exist(ed).

[10] Murdy, W. H., 'Anthropocentricism: A Modern Version', in Scherer, D. (ed.), *Ethics and the Environment* (Prentice Hall, New Jersey, 1983), 12, 13–15, 19–20. Sterling, S., 'Towards an Ecological World View', in Engel, J. R. and J. G. (eds.), *The Ethics of Environment and Development: Global Challenge, International Response* (Belhaven, London, 1990), 77, 78.

[11] Wheelwright, H., *The PreSocratics* (Indianapolis, 1960), 132.

[12] Rodman, J., 'The Other Side of Ecology In Ancient Greece', *Inquiry*, 19 (1976), 111. Callicott, J. B., 'Traditional American Indians and Traditional Western European Attitudes Towards Nature: An Overview', in Elliot, R. and Gare, A. (eds.), *Environmental Philosophy* (Queensland University Press, Queensland, 1982), 231, 236–7. Sherrard, P., *The Rape of Man and Nature*. (Golgonooza, Suffolk, 1987), 31–2. Oelschlaeger, M., *The Idea of Wilderness: From Prehistory to the Age of Ecology* (Yale University Press, New York, 1991), 57–60.

[13] Cottingham, J., *Rationalism* (Paladin, London, 1984), 18. Sessions, G., 'Spinoza and Jefferson Man in Nature', *Inquiry*, 20 (1977), 481, 482, 487. Hargrove, E., *The Foundations of Environmental Ethics* (Prentice Hall, New Jersey, 1989), 22-3, 35-7. Heisenberg, W., *Physics and Philosophy* (Harper and Rowe, New York, 1962), 59.

Nevertheless, it was Plato's view of the physical world which came to be dominant in early Western society after the birth of Christ. The idea of a spirit separated from a material world became common currency and was not even questioned until Aquinas raised the issue in the thirteenth century.[14]

The dichotomy between the mental and the physical world was completely cemented with Descartes and his philosophical method of radical doubt.[15] With this theory he could only establish his own identity by his ability to think ('I think, therefore I am'). Everything outside of his own identity had a questionable existence. He added to this belief that 'outside' surroundings were not important to his material dependence. As a result Descartes divided the world into two metaphysically different and hierarchical orders: mind and matter.[16] Additionally, like Plato, Descartes came to believe that anything that could not be validated scientifically, in the wider sense, did not exist. Consequently, when the question arose, 'what is nature made of?' he suggested that Nature consisted of only tangible qualities, like size and weight.[17] Intrinsic values and other non-quantifiable values (such as beauty) were denied importance.

B. The Individual Nature of Existence

Descartes's views of philosophical method and the assumptions he derived from his enquires have helped support the next important idea in this area. This concerns the belief that everything consists of insular understandable parts.[18] However, the importance of conceptual individualism predates Descartes by over fifteen hundred years. Pythagoras asserted that all things were numbers. Democritus and the Atomists expanded upon this theory by suggesting that not only were all things composed by numbers, but they were also isolated, individual units.[19] Thus, according to Leucippus and Democritus, everything was made of atoms which were solid, and insular.[20] The concept reappeared with the Greek and Roman period of Stoicism. Here Lucretius proposed his argument that the universe was made up of 'absolutely solid' and insular atoms.[21]

---

[14] Cottingham, ibid. 27–8, 98. Sherrard, *supra* n. 12, 57–62. Oelschlaeger, *supra* n. 12, 62–7.

[15] See 'The Meditations on First Philosophy. Meditation One (Concerning Those Things That Can Be Called Into Doubt)', in Descartes, R., *Philosophical Writings* (Routledge, London, 1985), vol. 1.

[16] 'Meditation Two, (That the Mind is More Known than the Body)' and 'Meditation Six (The Real Distinction of the Mind from the Body)', in Descartes, ibid.

[17] 'Meditations' One, Two (especially ss. 30–3), 'Meditation Five', (Concerning the Essence of Material Things), and ss. 71, and 74 of 'Meditation Six', all in Descartes, ibid.

[18] Descartes, R., *Principles of Philosophy* (Reidel, London, 1983), 51st section.

[19] See Marshall, P., *Nature's Web: An Exploration of Ecological Thinking* (London, Simon and Schuster, 1992), 69–71.

[20] O'Sullivan, M., *The Four Seasons of Greek Philosophy* (Efstathiadis, Cyprus, 1982), 67–70. Heisenberg, *supra* n. 13, 47.

[21] Lucretius, *On the Nature of the Universe* (Penguin, London, 1951), 28–45.

The concept of individualism took on a much larger relevance with Augustine, and, somewhat independently, the general precepts of Christianity which elevated the importance of the individual.[22] The concept reappeared again with a religious emphasis during the Reformation. After this period, the idea of abstract individualism spilled over into other aspects of social and scientific life.[23] In the social arena Thomas Hobbes picked up on the idea of society comprising nothing more than self-interested atomistic individuals.[24] In the domain of science, atomism was at the heart of the new metaphysics of Nature conceived in the seventeenth century, founded upon the achievements of Newton and Galileo.[25] This is discussed shortly.

Despite the importance of the new scientific methods in the seventeenth century, it was Descartes who came to represent the highest point for philosophical individualism. He built this up from his philosophical *cogito*. This provided verification for his own existence as a separate entity. Everything existed outside of him, and he believed himself to be truly insular.[26] The importance of individualism continued with Locke who interpreted natural law as a claim on innate, indefeasible rights inherent in each individual.[27] Next, Rousseau borrowed heavily from the 'systematic individualism' of Locke.[28] Leibniz also worked with the concept of individuality, or at least the importance to view in abstract.[29]

These perspectives on the importance of the individual became and remain of central importance to liberalism. This is in distinct contrast to earlier, more holistic, social theories. The importance of abstracted individualism also became a central feature of both the French and Scottish Enlightenment. It dominated the English eighteenth century, the American Constitution and the French encyclopedists. Hegel adopted the importance of individualism as did Kant, Nietszche, and Kierkegaard. It then spilt over into the twentieth century via a multitude of different and diverse disciplines. Contemporary liberal philosophers such as John Rawls,[30] Ronald Dworkin,[31] and Robert Nozick[32] all continue to stress the importance of the individual. Variations of this view also permeate contemporary political debates. For example, Margaret Thatcher asserted in 1987 that, 'There is no

[22] Russell, B., *A History of Western Philosophy* (Allen and Unwin, 1946), 240.
[23] Sabine, G. H. and Thorson, T. L., *A History of Political Theory* (Dryden, Illinios, 1973), 424–5. See also Whitehead, A. N., *Science and the Modern World* (Macmillan, 1925), 65, 93, 167.
[24] Hobbes, T., *Leviathian* (Penguin, Harmondsworth).
[25] See Scott, W., *The Conflict Between Atomism and the Conservation Theory* (MacDonald, London, 1970), 3.
[26] Descartes, 'Meditations'1–3. *Supra* n. 15.
[27] Sabine and Thorson, *supra* n. 23, 485.
[28] Ibid. 533–5.
[29] Russell, *supra* n. 22, 565.
[30] Rawls, J., *A Theory of Justice* (Oxford University Press, Oxford, 1972).
[31] Dworkin, R., *Taking Rights Seriously* (Duckworth, London, 1977); 'Liberalism', in Hampshire, S. (ed.), *Public and Private Morality* (Cambridge University Press, Cambridge, 1979), 113.
[32] Nozick, R., *Anarchy, State, Utopia* (Oxford University Press, Oxford, 1974).

such thing as society. There are individual men and women and there are families.'[33]

The philosophical positions outlined above were paralleled by the revolutionary changes in physics and astronomy in the sixteenth and seventeenth centuries. Galileo Galilei started this process with his mathematical descriptions of Nature, which have remained an important foundation of scientific theories up to the present day. To make it possible to describe Nature mathematically, Galileo (like Descartes) postulated that studies should be restricted to the essential properties of shapes, numbers, and movements which could be measured and quantified as 'irreducible and stubborn facts'.[34] Thus, the rationalization of knowledge was rooted in an understanding of the physical world that defined reality as a set of observable and predictable regularities. Properties like colour, taste, sound, smell or more intangible qualities like life itself, were seen as merely subjective elements and were consequently to be left out of the domain of science.[35]

Isaac Newton completed the scientific revolution. Newton proposed a theory that was able to explain the motion of the planets, moons, and comets down to the smallest details, as well as the flow of tides and various other phenomena related to gravity. The elements of the Newtonian world which moved in absolute space and absolute time via linear causation were material particles: small, solid, and indestructible objects of which all matter was made.[36] Thus, the Newtonian model of matter was atomistic.

Newton's mathematical system captured the intellectual world. Many disciplines and individual academics from this point onwards have drawn directly from his atomistic approach, as it became a central piece in the Enlightenment period.[37] Consequently it can be asserted that 'the history of philosophy runs curiously parallel to that of science'.[38] However this is no mere fact of history. Rather, the same tendency continues largely unabated today.[39]

Aside from the sciences, this methodology can also be seen in all disciplines that draw on positive methodologies such as certain areas of law and

---

[33]   Thatcher, M., cited in *Observer*, 27 Dec. 1987, 4.

[34]   Gallileo Gallilei, *The Assayer* (1621). Clarke, J. J. (ed), *Nature in Question: An Anthology of Ideas and Arguments* (Earthscan, London, 1993), 85–8. Whitehead, *supra* n. 23, 19.

[35]   Capra, F., *The Turning Point, Science, Society and the Rising Culture* (Simon and Schuster, London, 1982), 54–5. Sheldrake, R., *The Rebirth of Nature: The Greening of Science and God* (Rider, London, 1990), 44. Skolimowski, H., *Living Philosophy: Eco-Philosophy as a Tree of Life*. (Arkana, London, 1992), 223–5. Merchant, C., *The Death of Nature: Women, Ecology and the Scientific Period* (Wildwood, London, 1982), 275–80. Heisenberg, *supra* n. 13. Whitehead, *supra* n. 23, 21, 67. Sherrard, *supra* n. 12, 96–100.

[36]   Westfall, R., *A Biography of Isaac Newton* (Cambridge University Press, Cambridge, 1980), 292. See also Whitehead, *supra* n. 23, 62–3.

[37]   Capra, *supra* n. 35, 67. Oelschlaeger, *supra* n. 12, 89–92.

[38]   Whitehead, *supra* n. 23, 172.

[39]   See Koskenniemi, P., *From Alienation of Reason: A History of Positivist Thought* (UCL Press, London, 1969), 8.

philosophy. The apex of this adoption is found in the discipline of economics.[40]

An important concept that flowed from the rationalist approach is the application of the metaphor of 'the machine' to Nature. The idea of Nature, and specifically animals, as machines happened because the question arose of how isolated entities (such as animals) work. The answer to this first appeared with the German astronomer Kepler who put forward the analogy that nature was a machine.[41] Descartes adopted the machine metaphor and went on to suggest that movements and actions of animals can be attributed to 'nature which acts in them according to the disposition of their organs, [like] . . . a clock'.[42] According to this metaphor, the material world operates like any machine according to fixed and unvarying rules, with laws that have been built into the machine from the start. It has no creativity or spontaneity of its own.[43]

As a consequence of the machine metaphor humanity adopted an instrumentalist rationality.[44] This assumes a mandate to experiment, operate, or to manipulate Earthly Nature as humans see fit. The former image of the organic unity of Earthly Nature was replaced by the notion of the world as a machine with dimensions susceptible to measurement and control. Additionally, the inertness of matter, the asserted lack of sentience and lack of inherent value in all that is not human, absolves humanity of any guilt regarding the apparent damage that humans may inflict upon individual animals or complete ecosystems.[45]

C. The Dichotomies Between Humanity and Nature

A third element in the creation of anthropocentric thinking has to do with the alleged dichotomies between humanity and non-human Nature. The traditional

---

[40] See Koskenniemi, P., *From Apology to Utopia: The Structure of International Legal Argument* (Finnish Lawyers Publishing, Helinski, 1989), 101–30. Norton, B. G., 'Why Environmentalists Hate Mainstream Economists', *Environmental Ethics*, 13 (1991), 235, 247. Capra, *supra* n. 35, 191–4.

[41] Kepler, J. 'Harmonise Mundi', quoted in Pepper, D., *The Roots of Modern Environmentalism* (Routledge, London, 1990), 47.

[42] Descartes, *supra* n. 15, VI. 49. See also s. 84 of 'Meditation Six'. Pointers towards this position can be traced to Aquinas who postulated that, 'Dumb animals and plants are devoid of the life and reason whereby to set themselves in motion, they are moved, as it were, by another, by a kind of natural impulse.' Aquinas, T., *Summa Theologica* (Burns and Oates, London, 1992), Vol. 2. Q64. 1.

[43] See Abram, D., 'The Mechanical and the Organic: Epistemological Consequences of the Gaia Hypothesis', in Bunyard, P and Goldsmith, E. (eds.), *GAIA. The Thesis, the Mechanisms and the Implications* (Wadebridge, Cornwall, 1988), 119. Smith, S. 'The Messes Animals Make In Metaphysics', Journal of Philosophy, 46 (1949), 833, 851. Goldsmith, E., *The Way: Towards an Ecological World View* (Rider, London, 1992), 52, 119–22.

[44] O'Neill, J., *Ecology, Policy and Politics: Human Well-Being and the Natural World* (Routledge, London, 1993), 152–5. Short, J. R., *Imagined Country: Society, Culture and Environment* (London, Routledge, 1991), 18. Nasr, S. H. (1968), *Man and Nature: The Spiritual Crisis in Modern Man* (Allen and Unwin, London, 1988), 70. Thomas, K., *Man and the Natural World: Changing Attitudes in England 1500–1800* (Penguin, 1984), 32–4. Marshall, *supra* n. 19, 168–72.

[45] Note, it is uncertain whether Descartes himself actually denied pain in animals. See Cottingham, R. G., 'A Brute to the Brutes? Descartes' Treatment Of Animals', *Philosophy*, 53 (1978), 551.

distinction between humans and the rest of Nature, has been based on humanity's supposed unique rationality.[46] This suggestion has been put forward by Aristotle,[47] Aquinas,[48] Ficino,[49] Locke,[50] Schopenhauer,[51] Pascal,[52] Pufendorf,[53] Rousseau,[54] and Kant.[55] Linked to the assertion that only humans are rational, is the assumption that only humans can communicate. Hobbes,[56] Descartes,[57] Hegel,[58] Nietszche,[59] and Wittgenstein[60] were all advocates of this position.

Another common justification for the division between humanity and the rest of the natural world concerns moral behaviour. From one perspective of this argument, theriophobia is the rule. This is the fear and hatred of beasts as wholly or predominantly irrational, physical, insatiable, violent or vicious beings which humans resemble when they are wicked. In Hobbes' philosophical settings 'man is a wolf'; or with Plato a society founded on the satisfaction of desires is 'a city of pigs'. This is similar to Socrates' argument that the most virtuous human being is, 'the one who most fully transcends their animal and vegetative nature'.[61]

The trepidation of Nature was particularly strong between the sixteenth and

---

[46] Note that not all theorists who believe in a distinction in rationality between humanity and everything else from the natural world use it for a justification for human dominance. Rather, some reverse this situation. For examples see Bookchin in Schwarz, W. 'Anatomy of an Eco-Anarchist', *Guardian,* 15 May 1992, 29. Eckersley, R., 'Divining Evolution: The Ecological Ethics of Murray Bookchin', *Environmental Ethics*, 11 (1989), 99, 724–6. Brophy, B., *The Rights of Animals* (Sphere, London, 1989), 134. Devall, B., *Simple in Means, Rich in Ends: Practising Deep Ecology* (Green Print, Surrey, 1990), 178. See also ch. 10 of this book.

[47] Aristotle, *Ethics* (Harmondsworth, Penguin, 1963), 83.

[48] Aquinas, *Basic Writings* (New York, 1945), Vol. 2, 220. Aquinas, *supra* n. 42, vol. 2, 64. 1, 65. 3.

[49] Ficino, M. 'Letters', in Casserirer, E. (ed.), *The Renaissance Philosophy of Man* (Chicago University Press, Chicago, 1948), 2:1.

[50] Locke, J., *An Essay Concerning Human Understanding*, (Thomas Tegg, London, 1972), Book II, 88–91.

[51] Schopenhaur, A., *The World as Will and Representation*, (Kegan Paul, New York, 1969), 228–30.

[52] Pascal, B., *Lettres Provincials*, (Cambridge University Press, Cambridge, 1928), 148.

[53] Pufendorf, S, *The Law of Nature and of Nations* (Oceana, New York, 1931), vol. II., 147–8, 180–3, 526–7, 530–31.

[54] Rousseau, H., *The Social Contract and Discourses* (Dent, London, 1913), 184–6.

[55] Kant, I., *Lectures on Ethics: Duties Towards Animals and Spirits*, (Harper and Rowe, Oxford, 1963), 239; *Fundamental Principles Of Metaphysics And Morals* (Bobbs-Merril, London, 1973), 345–6.

[56] Hobbes, T., 'De Cive', in Molesworth, D. (ed.), *The English Works of Thomas Hobbes of Malmsbury* (John Bohn, London, 1841), vol. 2. 63–75, 113–14.

[57] Descartes, 'Letter to Henry Moore', in Chomsky, N., *Cartesian Linguistics* (Harper and Rowe, New York, 1966), 6; 'Discourses', in *Philosophical Writings*, *supra* n. 15, 80–1, 116–17.

[58] Hegel, F., *Lecture on the Philosophy of World History* (Cambridge University Press, Cambridge, 1975), 48–51.

[59] Nietzsche, F., *Human, All Too Human* (Oxford University Press, Oxford, 1886); 11, *The Joyful Wisdom* (Foulis, London, 1910), 296–300.

[60] Wittgenstein, L., *Philosophical Investigations* (Blackwell, Oxford, 1953), Part 1, ss. 25, 495, 647. Part 2, 174e, 184e, 223e, 229e.

[61] Socrates, quoted in Eckersley, R., *Environmentalism and Political Theory: Towards an Ecocentric Approach* (UCL Press, London, 1992), 50.

nineteenth centuries when wilderness was feared because of the belief that evil elements resided within it. This apprehensiveness was common throughout society from the Puritans in America through to folk tales (that continue today) like Little Red Riding Hood, and to beliefs of the devil being half animal and half human.[62]

Another supposed characteristic justifying human chauvinism in this area is the ability to use tools or modify and change the environment. Marx and Engels alleged humanity was different as 'only man produces when he is free from physical need'.[63] The creation of art is also supposed to be a distinctive human characteristic.[64]

Finally, a number of historically important thinkers have based the distinction between humanity and other animals on religious grounds. For example, Aquinas argued that 'man alone was created in the image of God'.[65] Descartes argued that only 'man' had an immortal soul.[66] Others, from Plato and Aristotle to Augustine, Hooker, Bacon, and Leibniz have also based the alleged difference on this ground.[67] Accompanying this perspective was the belief in the 'Great Chain of Being' that put God at the apex of the universe, with humanity second, and the natural world below humanity.

D. The Use and Value of Nature

A fourth factor in the creation of the anthropocentric position derives from the theories of social processes involving the use of the natural world by humanity. This is evident in the belief that labour is the only valuable factor in production. This theory of value in property goes back to Aquinas. It became solidified with the near identical positions of liberal and Marxist theory. For example, Marx argued, 'The purely natural material in which no human labour is objectivised . . . has no value'.[68] Despite the obvious anomalies inherent in such a perspective it has remained popular socialist theory.[69]

---

[62] Short, *supra* n. 44, 5–6. Thomas, *supra* n. 44, 36–7.

[63] Engels, F., 'Dialects of Nature', in Marx, K. and Engels, F., *Collected Works* (Lawrence and Wishart, Oxford, 1987), 48, 404–5. Marx, K., *Economic and Social Manuscripts* (London, 1956), vol. 3. 275–7, 329; *Capital* (Foreign Publishing, Moscow, 1981), vol. 3, 812. And see also McLean, D. (ed.), *Karl Marx: Selected Writings* (Oxford University Press, Oxford, 1978), (early writings) 82, (history) 160, (notes) 581.

[64] Diamond, J., *The Rise and the Fall of the Third Chimpanzee* (Radius, London, 1991), 152. For earlier attempts at finding differences, see Thomas, *supra* n. 43, 30–2.

[65] Aquinas, Thomas., 'Summa Contra Gentiles', in *The English Dominion Fathers*, (Burns and Oates, London, 1928), 3:2:112.

[66] Descartes, 'Meditation Three' (Concerning God, That He Exists). See also 65, 129, 139 of Descartes, R., *Discourse on Method and the Meditations* (Penguin, Harmondsworth, 1976).

[67] Leibniz, G. W., *Monadology* (Lowe and Brydone, London, 1898), 259–71. Hooker, R., *Laws of Ecclesiastical Policy* (Dent, 1907), 166–7. See also ch. 4 of this book.

[68] Marx, K., *Capital* (Foreign Publishing, Moscow, 1981), vol. 1, 206–7, vol. 3, 745. McLean, (ed.), *supra* n. 74, 443. Barber, W. J., *A History of Economic Thought* (Penguin, Harmondsworth, 1967), 129. Cf. Marx's writings in McLean, 81–2, 104.

[69] Schmidt, A., *The Concept of Nature in Marx* (New Left, London, 1971), 152.

In the opposite political camp, the father of modern liberalism, John Locke, suggested that, in its natural state, Nature was almost worthless. Locke placed almost no value on 'raw' land until it was improved. Even after the improvement, he still held that labour was the chief factor in any value assessment.[70] Likewise, Adam Smith proposed that, 'Labour, . . . is the real measure of the exchangeable value of all commodities'.[71] This type of view of labour helps establish property rights over land by making it seem that it is primarily the individual's labour mixed with the land, rather than the land itself, that is where the value is located.

Both Marxist and liberal views of these conceptions meant that property (Nature) is near worthless on its own. Therefore, Nature remains only valuable for instrumental purposes, as it is without inherent value.[72]

E. The Control of Nature

A fifth consideration that helps establish the concept of anthropocentricism is drawn from the self-fulfilling conclusions from all the previous positions. Namely the belief in the mastery of Nature. This position is primarily attributed to Francis Bacon, whose importance and influence stretches from the Enlightenment to the present day.[73]

However, this line of thought actually predates Bacon by around fifteen hundred years. For example, Aristotle suggested 'nature . . . has made all animals for the sake of man'.[74] Epictetus held very similar views.[75] Lucretius 'longed to smash the constraining locks of nature's door',[76] and Cicero made the Stoic Balbus declare, 'The produce of the Earth was designed for those who make use of it, and though some beasts may rob us of a small part, it does not follow that the earth produced it also for them'.[77] Despite these precedents, it was Bacon who fully defined the idea, and it was Bacon who was in the right place (England) at the right time (prior to the industrial revolution) to advocate it and receive credit for it.

Bacon became known for portraying the arts and sciences as encouraging invention so that Nature could be changed and made more adaptable to human

---

[70] Locke, J., *Two Treatises of Civil Government* (Dent, London, 1936), ss. 37, 42–3, 304, 305, 314, 316, 308.

[71] Smith, A., *An Enquiry Into the Nature and Causes of the Wealth of Nations* (Methuen, London, 1904), vol. 1. 32–3.

[72] See Daly, H. E. and Cobb, J., *For the Common Good: Redirecting the Economy Towards the Community, the Environment and a Sustainable Future* (Beacon Press, Boston, 1989), 111–13.

[73] Leiss, W., *The Domination of Nature* (Brazillier, New York, 1972), 45–71; Oelschlaeger, *supra* n. 12, 80–7.

[74] Aristotle, *Politics* (Everyman, New York, 1972), 10.

[75] Epictetus, *Discourses* (Everyman, London, 1910), ch. 10.

[76] Lucretius, *On the Nature of the Universe* (Penguin, London, 1951), 229.

[77] Cicero, *On the Nature of the Gods*, quoted in Passmore, J., *Man's Responsibility for Nature* (Duckworth, London, 1980), 14.

purposes. He placed an emphasis upon 'new and useful knowledge'. This in turn would, 'stretch the deplorably narrow limits of man's dominion over the universe to their promised bound'. This is what Bacon called knowledge 'for the benefit of man, for the relief of man's estate'. He argued, 'Our main object is to make nature serve the business and conveniences of man'. Nature must be 'bound into service'. He also became known for his focus upon science and his basic argument that 'scientific knowledge is technological power over nature'. Finally, he hoped humanity would subdue 'nature with all her children, to bind her to service, and to make her a slave'.[78] These views were very similar to those of Descartes who sought to, 'find a practical philosophy to . . . render ourselves the masters and possessors of nature'.[79]

This desire for the mastery of Nature became the call of the period. This belief went on to become incorporated in the mainstream philosophies of the coming ages.[80] For example, Leibniz proclaimed that the progress of humanity consisted in gaining control over nature and improving on the Earth's design.[81] Ficthe argued:

I will be the Lord of Nature, and she shall be my servant. I will influence her according to the measure of my capacity, but she will have no influence on me.[82]

When speaking of the equality of peoples, Locke stated:

There can not be subordination among us . . . as if we were made for one another's uses, as the inferior ranks of creatures were made for ours. . . . God who hath given the world to men in common, hath also given them reason to make use of it to best advantage of life and convenience.[83]

Kant argued that because non-human Nature is not self-conscious then it is 'merely a means to an end. That end is man'.[84] John Dewey argued that 'nature is just raw materials to be used by us for the application of ideas'.[85] Engels hoped that:

The idea of solidarity could finally . . . grow to a point where it will embrace all mankind and oppose it, as a society of brothers living in solidarity, the rest of the world—the world of minerals, animals and plants.[86]

---

[78] Bacon, F., *Novum Organum* (1620), Book 1, XV; *Essays; The Wisdom of the Ancients and the New Atlantis* (Oldham Press, London, 1977), 134, 166; 'The New Atlantis', in Spedding, J. (ed.), *The Works of Francis Bacon* (London, 1857), vol. 4, 517; 'The Great Instauration', also in Spedding, vol. 4. 15, 20; Farrington, G., *The Philosophy of Francis Bacon* (New York, 1970), 62, 83, 92, 93, 129, 130.

[79] Descartes, 'Discourses', in *Philosophical Writings*, supra n. 15, 78.

[80] Leiss, *supra* n. 73, 23, 40, 87–94.

[81] Leibniz, G. W., *Monadology* (Lowe, London, 1714), 259–71.

[82] Fichte, J. G., *The Vocation of Man* (Routledge, London, 1946), 29.

[83] Locke, J., *supra* n. 70, 118, 119, 122, 129, 131.

[84] Kant, I., *Metaphysics and Morals*, *supra* n. 55, 70, 76, 96.

[85] Dewey, discussed in Sessions, *supra* n. 13, 481, 491.

[86] Engels, *supra* n. 63. XV, 330–1.

Marx held similar aspirations.[87] J. S. Mill proposed that:

It is the duty of man to co-operate with the beneficent powers, [of Nature] not by imitating but by perpetually striving to amend the course of nature.[88]

The social Darwinist, William Sumner, suggested in 1896:

It is legitimate to think of Nature as a hard mistress against whom we are maintaining a struggle for existence. All our science and art are victories over her, but when we quarrel amongst ourselves we lose the fruits of our victory just as certainly as we would if she was a human opponent.[89]

Freud suggested that the right way to sublimate human aggression was to direct it away from other people against the rest of the biosphere:

combining with the rest of the human community and taking up the attack on nature, thus forcing it to obey human will, under the guidance of science.[90]

Similar ideas have continued largely unchallenged throughout the twentieth century. For example, in 1961 the former Socialist Communist Party stated with approval in its Programme, 'Communism elevates man to a tremendous level of supremacy over nature and makes possible a greater and fuller use of its inherent forces'.[91]

It should be noted here that complete human control is not what Bacon, Descartes or Newton had intended. This is because all three were devoutly religious men, who believed that humanity would ultimately be controlled by God. However, Descartes's method of doubt soon came to be used to question God's existence. As God's existence could not be objectively proved, the Christian God 'died' and as a result Christian metaphysics had lost much of its former power by the nineteenth century. Consequently, the religious casing in which Bacon and other Enlightenment thinkers embedded their ideas gradually fell away under the onslaught of subsequent scientific and philosophical endeavour. Additionally, following the logic of Descartes's theory, the only thing left in control was the 'purely terrestrial man who became the measure of all things'.[92] The human will simply filled the void and left Nietzche proclaiming 'the age of human will as the centre of reality'.[93]

From this point onwards, everything was to be determined from the viewpoint

---

[87]   Marx, noted in McMellan, D. (ed.), *Early Texts*. (Blackwell, Oxford, 1971), 139, 141.
[88]   Mill, J. S., *Nature, The Utility of Religion and Theism* (London, 1858), 9–10.
[89]   Sumner, Quoted in Jung, C., 'The Splendour of the World', *Atlantic Naturalist*, 29 (1974), 9.
[90]   Freud, quoted in Midgley, *supra* n. 1.
[91]   Noted in Singleton, J., 'Do the Greens Threaten the Reds?', *World Today*, 46 (1986), 160. See also Webb, B. and S., *Soviet Communism: A New Civilisation* (Longman, London, 1941), vol. 2. 928–9.
[92]   See McGinn, T., 'Ecology and Ethics', *International Philosophical Quarterly*, 14 (1974), 154. See also Ponting, C., *A Green History of the World* (Sinclair Stevenson, London, 1991), 159–60. Nasr, *supra* n. 44, 68–9.
[93]   Nietzsche, *supra* n. 8, 125; *Daybreak* (Oxford, 1886), 23.

of unrestricted human interest. With the help of the new science and philosophies, the only role left to humanity was to conquer and dominate the perceived
machine of Nature and make it serve its needs.[94]

2. THE ANTHROPOCENTRIC BASIS OF INTERNATIONAL
ENVIRONMENTAL LAW

All of the above ideas—of a division between the physical and mental worlds, of
humanistic atomism, of dichotomies between humanity and Nature, considerations of how Nature is valued, and a belief in the right to control and conquer
Nature—have helped culminate in anthropocentric outlooks. This belief system
has been implicitly or explicitly accepted by many (if not most) of the world's
dominant cultures. Accordingly, anthropocentric views have permeated all types
of activities, including environmental legislation on both the domestic and international levels.

However, this is not to claim that all environmental policy is exclusively
anthropocentric. Within the last twenty years there has been a slow growth
within environmental policy of the belief that Nature should be protected because
of its own inherent value. This area is discussed in chapters seven to ten.
Nevertheless, despite this growing trend anthropocentricism currently remains
central to contemporary environmental policy. This means that the environment
is protected because of instrumental human considerations.

This view of the primacy of humanity is standard within international envi-
ronmental law. For example Article II, which is entitled the 'Fundamental
Principle' of the 1968 *African Convention on the Conservation of Nature and
Natural Resources*, states that the parties:

shall undertake to adopt the measures necessary to ensure conservation, utilisation and
development of the soil, water, flora and faunal resources in accordance with scientific
principles and with due regard to the best interests of the people.[95]

The 1972 *Declaration of the United Nations Conference on the Human
Environment* reflected its anthropocentric basis in its very title. This was
strengthened further with the emphasis upon protecting the environment for
present and future [human] generations. Additionally, the Declaration emphasized (as Mao had done earlier) that 'of all things in the world, people are the
most precious'.[96] In 1973 the Council of Europe declared that, 'As befits the

---

[94]   See Horkheimer, M., *The Eclipse of Reason* (Oxford University Press, Oxford, 1947), 20–1,
93, 97.

[95]   Art. 22: *African Convention on the Conservation of Nature and Natural Resources*. 3 UNTS
1001.

[96]   (1972), Para. 7, Ch. 1. *Declaration of the United Nations Conference on the Human
Environment*, UN Doc. A/CONF 48/14. 1972. Maurice Strong continued this theme in his opening
address at Stockholm with the suggestion that the international community must 'put man and his
plight at the centre of our concerns'. Text of *Opening Statement* by Maurice Strong. 5 June 1972.

genius of Europe, particular attention will be given to intangible values and to protecting the environment so that progress may really be put at the service of mankind'.[97] The 1980 *World Conservation Strategy*, which advocated sustainable development, defined development as:

the application of human, financial, living and non-living resources to satisfy human needs and to improve the quality of human life.[98]

The Strategy also stated that conservation in the modern sense means:

The management of human use of the biosphere so that it may yield the greatest sustainable benefit to present generations while maintaining its potential to meet the needs and aspirations of future generations.[99]

In 1980 the first Brandt report, *North-South: A Program For Survival*, defined development as leading to the 'self fulfilment' of 'full human potential'.[100] The 1982 *World Charter for Nature* recognized that:

Ecosystems and organisms, as well as the land, marine and atmospheric resources that are utilised by man, shall be managed to achieve and maintain optimum sustainable productivity.[101]

In 1987 the World Commission on Environment and Development stated:

Sustainable development . . . is a process . . . that is designed to enhance both current and future potential to meet human needs and aspirations.[102]

This 'resources' type view of the WCED has been interpreted as implying that 'other species do not have intrinsic value in their own right, but are considered 'resources' for human use'.[103] This same position was reflected in the 1986 United Nations *Declaration on the Right to Development*, which recognized that:

The human person is the central subject of the development process and that development policy should therefore make the human being the main participant and beneficiary of development.[104]

---

[97]   Official Journal of the European Communities (1973), Part 1. Introduction of the *Declaration of the Council of the European Communities on the Program of Action of the European Community on the Environment*, vol 16, no. 6, 112, 20 Dec.

[98]   See paras. 4 and 5 of Strategy 1, IUCN (1980), *World Conservation Strategy*: 'conservation, like development is for people'. (Switzerland). Reprinted in Rusta, B. and Simma, B. (eds.), *International Protection of the Environment* (Oceana, New York), vol. XIII, 427.

[99]   Para. 4, Strategy 1, ibid.

[100]   Brandt Commission, *North-South: A Programme For Survival* (Pan Books, London, 1980), 223.

[101]   General Principle 4. *World Charter for Nature*. 35 UN GAOR. Annex 2. Or UN Doc. A/35/141. 1982.

[102]   The World Commission on Environment and Development, *Our Common Future* (Oxford University Press, Oxford, 1987), 23, 46.

[103]   Merchant, C., *Radical Ecology: The Search for a Livable World* (Routledge, London, 1992), 229–30.

[104]   Para. 13, and Art. 4, United Nations (1986), *Declaration on the Right to Development*. UNGA Res. 41/18.

Likewise, the 1992 *Rio Declaration on Environment and Development* stated, 'Human beings are at the centre of concerns for sustainable development'.[105] This was reiterated at the 1994 International Conference on Population and Development,[106] the Program of Action for the Sustainable Development of Small Island Developing States,[107] and the World Summit for Social Development in 1995.[108] Such perspectives, implicitly, continue to accept the proposition that the 1994 Report of the International Commission on Peace and Food suggested, namely 'Human beings are the most creative, productive and precious resource'.[109]

Anthropocentric terminology also appears in a number of international environmental documents and texts in the designation of Nature as resources rather than attributing to it intrinsic value of its own accord.[110] This type of classification can be found in the 1972 *Declaration of the United Nations Conference on the Human Environment*[111] and the 1992 *Rio Declaration on Environment and Development*.[112] It is also common within a number of specific international agreements, such as the 1983 *International Tropical Timber Agreement*,[113] the *Convention on the Conservation of Antarctic Marine Living Resources*,[114] and a number of fishery conservation agreements[115] including the *International Convention for the Regulation of Whaling*.[116]

Once it is asserted that humanity is at the centre of environmental policy, and that everything non-human is to be regarded as resources, then all justifications for environmental protection must come from anthropocentric considerations. This means that Nature, within the anthropocentric paradigm, will only be conserved on account of the instrumental values attributed to it by humans, rather

---

[105] Principle 1, UNCED (1992): United Nations Conference on Environment and Development, *Rio Declaration on Environment and Development*. A/CONF 151/5/Rev. 1. 13.

[106] Principle 2; *Report of the International Conference on Population and Development*. A/CONF 171/13. 1994. 18 October.

[107] Para. 56. *Draft Program of Action for the Sustainable Development of Small Island States*. A/CONF 167/9. 1994. 18 March.

[108] See paras. 8, 24, 26 (a), *Report of the World Summit for Social Development*. A/CONF 166/9. 1995. 19 April.

[109] Report of the International Commission on Peace and Food, *Uncommon Opportunities: An Agenda for Peace and Equitable Development* (Zed, London, 1994), 27. See also point 14 of the executive summary with the demands for a 'human centred theory of development'. At 201.

[110] Devall, *supra* n. 46, 30.

[111] UN Doc. A/CONF 48/14/Rev. 1.

[112] UN Doc. A/CONF 151/5/Rev. 1.

[113] See Art. 2, definitions. Geneva, 18 November, 1983. British Command Paper Cmnd. 9240, Misc. 11 (1984).

[114] As portrayed in its very title. *Convention on Conservation of Antarctic Marine Living Resources. International Legal Materials*, 27 (1988), 868.

[115] e.g., Art. 8 of the *International Convention for the Conservation of Atlantic Tuna*. UST Vol. 20 (1969), 2887–2940. TIAS 6767. Preamble, *International Convention for the High Seas Fisheries of the North Pacific Ocean*. UNTS Vol. 205 (No. 1 2770) 65. *Convention on Future Multilateral Cooperation in North Atlantic Fisheries*. British Command Paper 8474 Misc. 2 (1982).

[116] Para. 1, preamble. *International Convention on the Regulation of Whaling*. 1946. 161. UNTS. 72; TIAS no. 1849.

than being protected because of its own intrinsic value. There are seven common forms of arguments that exemplify this central precept. These are self-interest through health considerations arguments, economic proposals, religious, aesthetic, cultural, and recreational justifications, and finally arguments that work on the idea of preserving the environment for future generations.

It is these seven areas which will make up the basis of the following chapters. In each one of these, the specific anthropocentric justification will be shown as an idea, and how it fits into international environmental law and policy. Each area will then be juxtaposed against the difficulties with it.

II

The Self-Interest Justification for
Enviromental Protection

1. SELF-INTEREST IN THE INTERNATIONAL ENVIRONMENTAL CONTEXT

Many forms of anthropocentric environmental protection are derived from some form of self-interest. However, in this instance, anthropocentric self-interest is restricted to the more specific idea that the survival and prospering of humanity is linked to the health of the biosphere and its interdependent ecosystems.[1] That is—humanity protects Nature, because Nature protects humanity.

This form of self-interest as a justification for environmental protection has been recognized in a number of international documents. For example, in 1968 the United Nations General Assembly passed a resolution expressing concern about the deterioration of the environment and the effect it was having on humanity.[2] In 1969 the Pearson Commission based part of its appeal for additional finance for Southern countries on 'enlightened and constructive self-interest'.[3] In 1972 the United Nations Conference on the Human Environment recognized that:

The natural resources of the earth, . . . must be safeguarded for the benefit of present and future generations through careful planning or management.[4]

In 1973, UNEP stated that its first policy objective was 'to anticipate and prevent threats to human health'.[5] In 1980 the Palme Commission on *Disarmament and Security Issues* argued that humanity was facing a possible apocalyptic future, which the recognition of self-interest could avert.[6] The Brandt Reports of 1980 (*A Program For Survival*) and 1983 (*Common Crisis*) both recognized that human survival may be at stake. Additionally, even without an apocalypse, it was forcefully argued that it would be beneficial for nations to work together.[7] The first Brandt Report stated:

[1] Ehrenfeld, D., *The Arrogance of Humanism* (Oxford University Press, Oxford, 1978), 184. Eckersley, R., *Environmentalism and Political Theory: Towards An Ecocentric Approach* (UCL Press, London, 1992), 37. It is important to note that this self-interest argument should not be seen as assuming that it is somehow 'humans v. Nature'. Indeed, it is commonly believed the two goals, i.e. protecting Nature for the good of humanity, and the overall protection of Nature, are quite complementary. However, my argument is to suggest that this is not necessarily so.
[2] *Problems of the Environment*. UNGA Res. 2398 (XXIII) 1968.
[3] Pearson Commission, *Partners in Development* (Pall Mall Press, London, 1969), 9.
[4] Principle 2, *Stockholm Declaration*. UN Doc. A/CONF 48/14.
[5] UNEP, 'Policy Objectives', in Rusta, B. and Simma, B. (eds.), *International Protection of the Environment* (Oceana, New York, 1975), vol. 1. 184.
[6] Palme Commission, *Disarmament and Security Issues* (Oxford University Press, Oxford, 1980), 52.
[7] Brandt Commission, *North-South: Common Crisis* (Oxford University Press, Oxford, 1983), 9.

We believe that nations, even on grounds of self-interest, can join in the common task of ensuring survival, to make the world more peaceful and less uncertain.[8]

In 1982 the *World Charter for Nature* enunciated that:

Lasting benefits from nature depend upon the maintenance of essential ecological processes and life support systems, and upon the diversity of life forms.[9]

In 1987 the World Commission on Environment and Development stated that:

There are environmental trends that threaten to radically alter the planet, that threaten the lives of many species upon it, including the human species . . . we must be ever mindful of the risk of endangering the survival of life on Earth.[10]

The report states specifically that 'mutual self-interest' is 'essential to human progress'.[11] Very similar conclusions were echoed in 1990 by the South Commission's, *Challenge of the South* report.[12] Finally, the 1995 Report of the Commission on Global Governance, *Our Global Neighbourhood,* suggested that it was essential to address the international environmental problems as:

they pose a danger to the very survival, not just the well-being, of whole societies. In this sense, together with nuclear war, they constitute the ultimate security risk.[13]

2. SELF-INTEREST AND CURRENT ENVIRONMENTAL ARGUMENT

In parallel with recognitions in the international environmental field, there has been a growing recognition by many environmental theorists that prudent self-interest provides powerful reasons for the protection of the environment.[14] For example, John Passmore suggested:

An ethic dealing with man's relation to land, and to the plants and animals growing on it would not only be about the behaviour of human beings, as is sufficiently obvious, but would have to be justified by reference to human interests.[15]

---

[8] Brandt Commission, *North-South: A Programme For Survival* (Pan, London, 1980), 47, 77.

[9] Preamble, *World Charter for Nature*. GA Res. 7, 36 UN GAOR Supp. (No. 51) at 17, UN Doc. A/51 (1982).

[10] World Commission on Environment and Development, *Our Common Future* (Oxford University Press, Oxford, 1987), 32–3, 148.

[11] Ibid. 90.

[12] South Commission, *The Challenge of the South* (Oxford University Press, Oxford, 1990), 212.

[13] Commission on Global Governance, *Our Global Neighbourhood* (Oxford University Press, Oxford, 1995), 83.

[14] Hooker, C. A., 'Responsibility, Ethics and Nature', in Cooper, D. E. and Palmer, J. A. (eds.), *The Environment in Question: Ethics and Global Issues* (Routledge, London, 1992), 147, 152. Cooper, D. 'The Idea of Environment', in the same volume, 165, 178–9. Katz, E., 'Utilitarianism and Preservation', *Environmental Ethics*, 1 (1979), 362. Wilson, E. O., *Biophilia* (Harvard University Press, Massachusetts, 1984), 138. Lewis, M. W., *Green Delusions: An Environmentalist's Critique of Radical Environmentalism* (Duke University Press, London, 1992), 176–9.

[15] Passmore, J., 'Removing the Rubbish: Reflections on the Ecological Craze', *Encounter*, (1974), 19.

In essence 'an inchoate sense of obligation towards natural objects then develops, which is flattened into an aspect of self-interest'.[16] The end conclusion of this approach is that in the field of environmental regulation, 'legislation is created which protects nature not for its own sake, but in order to preserve its potential value for man'.[17]

It is important to note here that there are two forms of self-interest that can lead to environmental protection. The most commonly used one, as above, focuses on anthropocentric self-interest. The other form of self-interest protection is derived from the discipline of deep ecology. This second position proceeds from a holistic base, and the belief that the individual is connected with all aspects of the natural world. From this precept it becomes logical to protect the environment, as to protect 'the larger self' (i.e. the environment) implicitly also means protecting the 'smaller self' (i.e. the individual).[18]

This holistic position should not be confused with anthropocentric self-interest which is the primary focus of this chapter. It is important to avoid confusing the two approaches as with the holistic approach the desire to protect the environment is not derived from the individual as such, but from the desire to protect the larger community on which the individual is dependent. In this sense, the individual is subservient to the environment ethic, and the individual's interests are secondary.[19] Additionally, the holistic approach recognizes that the 'larger whole' possesses independent inherent value aside from the 'smaller self'.[20] This is distinct from the anthropocentric self-interested position which only accords the environment instrumental value, and environmental considerations are freely traded against other anthropocentric considerations.[21]

---

[16]   Tribe, L. H., 'Ways Not to Think About Plastic Trees: New Foundations For Environmental Law', *Yale Law Journal*, 83 (1975), 1325. See also, Porritt, J. *Seeing Green* (Blackwell, Oxford, 1984), 117.

[17]   Tribe, ibid. 1325.

[18]   Fox, W., *Towards A Transpersonal Ecology: Developing New Foundations For Environmentalism* (Boston, Shambhala, 1990), 225–43. Devall, B., *Simple in Means, Rich in Ends; Practising Deep Ecology* (Green Print, Surrey, 1990), 35–72. Naess, A., *Ecology, Community and Lifestyle* (Cambridge University Press, Cambridge, 1989), 8–9, 85–6, 170–81. Mathews, F., 'Conservation and Self Realisation: A Deep Ecology Perspective', *Environmental Ethics*, 10 (1988), 351. Abram, D., 'The Perceptual Implication of Gaia', *Ecologist*, (1985), 103. Callicott, J. B., 'The Metaphysical Implications of Ecology', *Environmental Ethics*, 8 (1986), 301, 313. Fabel, A. J., 'Environmental Ethics and the Question of Cosmic Purpose', *Environmental Ethics*, 16 (1994), 303, 312–14. Curtin, D., 'Dogen, Deep Ecology and the Ecological Self', *Environmental Ethics*, 16 (1994), 195, 197, 203–5, 212–13. Cf. Plumwood, V., 'Nature, Self and Gender', *Hypatia*, 6 (1991), 1, 3–7, 10–22. O'Neill, J., *Ecology, Policy and Politics: Human Well-Being and the Natural World* (Routledge, London, 1993), 24–5, 149–51.

[19]   See Devall, B. and Sessions, G., *Deep Ecology: Living As If Nature Mattered* (Gibbs Smith, Utah, 1985), 11. Fox, ibid., 113.

[20]   Fox, *supra* n. 18, 240.

[21]   See Ash, M., *The Fabric of the World: Towards A Philosophy of Environment* (Green Books, Devon, 1992), 18–19. Fox, *supra* n. 18, 240.

3. THE PROBLEMS OF THE ANTHROPOCENTRIC
SELF-INTERESTED APPROACH

Enlightened anthropocentricism appears to have the best of both worlds, as it combines the good of humanity with the good of the biosphere. However in all such cases 'the reverence for Nature is not ultimate, and this has significant consequences'.[22] First, as Robyn Eckersly stated:

If we restrict our perspective to a human welfare ecology perspective we can provide no protection to those species which are of no present or potential use or interest to humankind.[23]

This is a significant problem as many parts of Nature cannot necessarily be demonstrated to have utilitarian value, either individually or as components of an ecosystem. Consequently, if utilitarian value is the only basis for preservation, then humanity may not need to preserve those species.[24]

This leads to a second problem. This is that once the preservation of a piece of Nature is justified solely by human self-interest, its protection is only required for as long as that need is believed to be present. Once the interest is gone, so too is the reason to preserve the environment.[25] This has implications for the no longer 'required' components of ecosystems which humans once depended upon. This area is elaborated upon in The Location of Economic Values in chapter three.

The final problem with the self-interest approach is primarily philosophical, but it has a very practical result. Plato in *The Republic* argued that the good of society coincided with the good of the individual. In effect this meant that the individual's pursuit of self-interest was beneficial not only to the individual, but also to society.[26] This is a view that is prevalent with the belief structure of neo-classical economics. For example, Adam Smith, in his most important work, the *Wealth of Nations*, wrote, 'It is not from the benevolence of the butcher, the brewer, or the baker, that we expect our dinner, but from their regard to their own interest'.[27] Today this ideal of mutual benefit for all, by the pursuit of individual self-interest is a fundamental pillar of modern economic ideology.[28]

---

[22] Livingston, J., *The Fallacy of Wildlife Conservation* (Toronto University Press, Toronto, 1981), 42.

[23] Eckersley, *supra* n. 1, 39. See also O'Neill, *supra* n. 18.

[24] Murdy, W. H., 'Anthropocentricism: A Modern Version', in Scherer, D. (ed.), *Ethics and the Environment* (Prentice Hall, New Jersey, 1983), 12, 15. Rodman, J. 'Four Forms of Ecological Consciousness Reconsidered', also in Scherer, 82–3. Doremus, H., 'Patching the Ark: Improving Legal Protection of Biological Diversity', *Ecology Law Quarterly*, 18 (1991), 265, 277.

[25] Livingston, *supra* n. 22, 46. Murdy, ibid. Rodman, ibid.

[26] *The Republic*, trans. F. Conford (Oxford University Press, Oxford, 1974), 2–7, 9–40, 42–66, 102–5, 119–43.

[27] Smith, A., *An Enquiry Into the Nature and Causes of the Wealth of Nations* (Methuen, London, 1904), Book 1, 14.

[28] Abolafia, M., 'Competitive Systems: A Sociological View', in Ekins, P. and Max-Neef, M. (eds.), *Real Life Economics: Understanding Wealth Creation* (London, 1992), 315.

However, there have been centuries of arguments raised against the ideal of self-interest as a guiding principle for ethics or society. For example, Kant argued from a deontological position that the highest moral choice is doing an act because it is right, not because it is in the actor's self-interest.[29] On the other hand, arguing from a utilitarian position, it has long been recognized that it is the greatest amount of happiness of the whole that must be maximized, not the maximum happiness of the individual, which is what an appeal to self-interest dictates. Consequently, as Henry Sidgwick concluded, 'the ultimate precept of reason cannot be both egoistic and universalistic'.[30] This problem is most aptly demonstrated by the fact that to pursue direct self-interest as a guiding principle can lead to inconsistent duties for different actors, and may consequently prompt conflict as different self-interests collide.[31] This problem is all the more evident when taken from an individual context to an international one.

4. SELF-INTEREST AND INTERNATIONAL ENVIRONMENTAL LAW

International relations, since their beginning, have been built upon the principle of self-interest.[32] Indeed, Thucydides recognized before the advent of the Roman Empire that the objective of self-interest is utmost. He even went so far as to advocate that justice is to be equated with self-interest.[33] This pursuit has continued throughout the centuries. For example, in the Middle Ages Machiavelli was forthright in his assertions that behind all forms of public policy were assumptions that human nature was essentially selfish, and that the most effective motives on which a statesman must rely are egoistic. He instructed the Prince

---

[29] Kant, I., *Critique of Practical Reason* (Routledge, London, 1981), Book II, Ch. ii, § 5; *Groundwork of the Metaphysics of Morals* (Hutchinson, London, 1948), 61–2, 64–7, 74, 80–92, 95–107.

[30] Sidgwick, H., *The Methods of Ethics* (Macmillan, London, 1893), xx. Additional philosophical problems with the pursuit of direct self-interest over other 'moral choices' that would not necessarily result in benefit to the actor concerned, involve problems of inconsistency in the actors' actions, lack of trustworthiness, and the loss of moral benefit for doing the morally right, as opposed to self-interested, actions. See Nozick, R., *Philosophical Explanations* (Clarendon Press, Oxford, 1981), 403–11, 507–15. Gauthier, D. 'Morality and Advantage', *Philosophical Review*, 76 (1967), 460–75. Singer, P., *Practical Ethics* (Cambridge University Press, Cambridge, 1993), 322–7.

[31] See Medlin, H., 'Ultimate Principles and Ethical Egoism', in Gauthier, D. (ed.), *Morality and Rational Self Interest* (Englewood Cliffs, New Jersey, 1970), 56.

[32] This statement is, of course, the matter of much debate amongst theoreticians of international politics, due to the differing realist, liberal and neo-liberal, and political economy perspectives. While accepting the insights of the liberal and Marxist perspectives I have chosen, for the specific purpose of this chapter, to utilize the realist position. For some introductory readings on this, see Kegley, C. W. and Wittkopf, E. R., *The Global Agenda: Issues and Perspectives* (McGraw, New York, 1995), 35–44, 119–231. Little, R. and Smith, R., *Perspectives on World Politics* (Routledge, London, 1993), 1–139, 405–69. Boyle, F. A., *World Politics and International Law* (Duke University Press, Durham, 1985), 3–16, 159–70, 171–6.

[33] Thucydides, *History of the Peloponnesian War* (Penguin, Harmondsworth, 1954), 80–1, 199, 214–15, 222, 402–3.

that human nature is profoundly aggressive and acquisitive. These tendencies lead to a situation of continual strife and competition as 'men' aim to keep what they have and to acquire more. Consequently, only the pursuit of self-interest matters, and the purpose of politics is to preserve and increase political power itself.[34] Thomas Hobbes added his weight to the perspective with his belief in the absolute 'state of nature' that existed if there was no common sovereign. In such a state, any action may be permissible if survival is obtained.[35] Therefore:

Every commonwealth has an absolute liberty to do what it shall judge, that is to say, what that assembly that representeth it, shall judge most conducing to their benefit.[36]

Centuries later, Nietzsche argued that justice is power and power seeks self-preservation.[37]

Advocates have continued to propound these views late into the twentieth century. Certain theorists still maintain that there is nothing but the pursuit of self-interest in the international arena.[38] However, despite the fact that this is the way that international relations are likely to work, this is not beneficial. For example, in the seventeenth century, in the *Leviathan*, Hobbes painted a grim picture of the lawless world in which people moved only by considerations of self-interest, without moral, political or social institutions to modify their behaviour. In such a world, people bent on their own preservation and well-being found themselves in competition for the scarce goods that enhance life. From this competition arises hostility. The end result is that each person finds themselves in constant competition with others all attempting to pursue their own, and somewhat different self-interests.[39] Garrett Hardin applied exactly the same theory in his famous essay 'The Tragedy of the Commons'.[40] The difference between Hobbes and Hardin, was that Hardin saw the continual pursuit of individual self-interest as resulting in the collapse of the environmental commons, and, thereafter, the disintegration of the lives of individuals. Hobbes, owing to his location in history, could not have foreseen the loss of the environment as a consequence. To him, the possibility of 'nasty, short and brutish' human life seemed the worst scenario.

[34] Machiavelli, *The Prince* (Quality Paperbooks, London, 1992), 37–9, 50–6, 82–3. See also Sabine, G. H. and Thorson, T. L., *A History of Political Theory* (Dryden, Hong Kong, 1973), 311–31. Boyle, *supra* n. 32.

[35] Hobbes, T., *Leviathan* (Penguin, Harmondsworth, 1976), 151, 160–1, 186, 189, 224.

[36] Hobbes, ibid. 189. This approach is a follow on from the Ch. XX which emphasizes, 'unlimited power'. Indeed, 'the sovereign power is as great as possibly men can be imagined to make it'.

[37] Nietzsche, F., *Human, All Too Human* (Penguin, Harmondsworth, 1978), 9.

[38] See Schwarzenberger, G., *Power Politics* (Stevens, London, 1964). James, A., 'Power Politics', in Sanders, B. L. (ed.), *Contemporary International Politics: Introductory Readings* (Wiley, New York, 1971), 113. Morgenthau, H., 'Positivism, Functionalism and International Law', *American Journal of International Law*, 34 (1940), 261. Weber, W., 'Morality and National Power in International Politics', *Review of Politics*, 26 (1964), 31.

[39] Hobbes, *supra* n. 35.

[40] Hardin, G., 'The Tragedy of the Commons', *Science*, 162 (1968), 1244.

The application of this theory to the international environmental arena suggests that the current sovereign set-up at the end of the twentieth century is (still) in the 'state of nature'. Thus nations pursue interests at the cost of other nations.[41] These conflicts in the arena of international environmental law can be well demonstrated in a multitude of international environmental problems. A particularly good example of this is with climate change.

Self-Interest and Climate Change

Climate change is one of the central international environmental concerns because 'humanity is conducting an unintended, uncontrolled, globally pervasive experiment whose ultimate consequences could be second only to a global nuclear war'. (UNEP; *Proceedings of the World Conference on the Changing Atmosphere*. 1988. Toronto. vii). The implications of this may be particularly acute for some States. For example, the *Action Plan from the Conference on the Sustainable Development of Small Island Developing States* in 1994 emphasized 'Small Island States are particularly vulnerable to global climate change, climate variability and sea-level rise . . . the very survival of certain low-lying countries would be threatened . . .'. (A CONF 167/9. 1994. Paragraphs 16 & 17). Due to such extreme possibilities, the 1992 *United Nations Framework Convention on Climate Change (FCCC)* (UNCED A/AC 237/18 (Part II) Add. 1. 1992) declared in Article 3 that, 'The parties should take precautionary measures to anticipate, prevent or minimise the causes of climate change and mitigate its adverse effects. Where there are threats of serious or irreversible damage, lack of full scientific certainty should not be used as a reason for postponing such measures . . .'.

It has been postulated by the body which is responsible for the scientific assessment of climate change—the Intergovernmental Panel on Climate Change (IPCC) that a 60% reduction in carbon dioxide emissions is necessary just to stabilize greenhouse emissions. (IPCC; The *Supplementary Report*. 1992.) However, the best that could be achieved with the 1992 *Framework Convention on Climate Change* was a promise by developed nations to 'aim' at stabilizing greenhouse emissions that are not already governed by the Montreal Protocol, by the year 2000 to 1990 levels (Article 4(2)). Such levels of commitment were not commensurate with the scale of the problem that the Convention attempted to address. Consequently, when the

---

[41] Ophuls maintains that 'international [environmental] politics is the epitome of the Hobbesian state of Nature'. Ophuls, W., *Ecology and the Politics of Scarcity* (Freeman, San Francisco, 1977), 208–10. See also Pirages, D., 'The Ecological Perspective on International Politics', Soroos, M., 'The Tragedy of the Commons in Global Perspective', Ophuls, W., 'The International State of Nature and the Politics of Scarcity'; all in Kegley, *supra* n. 32, 331–41, 422–36, 436–46. Cf. Walker, K. J., 'The Environmental Crisis: A Critique of Neo-Hobbesian Responses', *Polity*, 21 (1988), 67–88.

signatories met for their first Conference of the Parties in Berlin in 1995 a proposed protocol to the *FCCC* for a 20% reduction of carbon emissions by developed countries was mooted by Alliance of Small Island States (AOSIS). (INC A/AC/237/L 23. 1994. 27 September) This was not accepted by the parties, although they did agree to re-examine the problem in 1997 with the objective of setting specific reduction targets. (The *Berlin Mandate*. Decision 1/CP.1.)

Thus, it can be seen, that despite the absolute seriousness of the problem that is posed by climate change and the promise to act to avert it in accordance with the precautionary principle, there has not been an appropriate response to the dilemma. This has been because the international community has been pursuing individual self-interests and these do *not* coincide to provide environmental protection from climatic change.

This clash of interests, which was evident at the 1992 Earth Summit and the 1995 Conference of the Parties, developed because there is a combination of beneficial and detrimental effects associated with climate change. (IPCC; *Synthesis Report*. 1995. Paragraph 4.3.) Absolutely or relatively, there will be distinct winners and losers in the debate over climate change. At the extreme on one side there is the AOSIS whose foremost self-interest resides in stopping the climatic change which could threaten their very existence. On the other side of the self-interest debate are an unusual coalition of Southern and Northern countries who were, and remain, reluctant to take steps needed to reduce climatic change. This aversion can be attributed to three reasons.

First, despite the fact that global warming will be generally detrimental, not all nations will suffer to the same extent. For example, rainfall is expected to increase with global warming. This factor combined with an atmosphere richer in carbon dioxide and the associated longer frost-free growing seasons, is expected to be favourable to the growth of biomass. Thus, as global warming proceeds, some countries will actually have better conditions enabling them to have increased agricultural output.

The second consideration is that many Southern countries refuse/refused to be drawn into a strong treaty on climate change because they need to use fossil fuels to develop economically (preamble and articles 2 and 3 of the *FCCC*). This problem was accentuated for many Southern countries who correctly recognized that they have a very limited liability with regard to the historical causation of the problem (preamble, FCCC).

The final factor is that certain Northern countries, particularly the United States, were/are unprepared to make any form of substantial cut in the emissions that they produce which effect climatic change, as it was/is believed that such actions could have detrimental results on their economy. Thus, the *FCCC only* goes so far as to stipulate that actions taken in accordance with the precautionary principle should be cost-effective and at the lowest possible cost (article. 3.3), with a view to minimizing the adverse effects upon the economy (article 4 (1)(f)). The problem is, to truly address climatic change, adverse effects upon national economies may have to be accepted.

The practical result of this conclusion is that while the pursuit of self-interest may be beneficial for the odd coalition of Southern countries and some Northern ones, it could well be disastrous for the environment and the smaller island states. For a fuller discussion of this area and the specific case study of New Zealand, see Gillespie, A., *Burning Follies: The Failure of the New Zealand Response to Climate Change* (Dunmore Press. Palmerston, 1997).

The pursuit of nationalistic self-interest in the international environmental context does not always lead to environmental protection. This is because nationalistic self-interests do *not* always coincide in the production of outcomes that are good for both the global environment and the common good of the community of nations.[42]

---

[42] See Panjabi, R. K. L., 'Idealism and Self-Interest In International Law: The Rio Dilemma', *Californian Western International Law Journal*, 23 (1992), 189, 194–6. He concludes at 197 that 'nations must subsume their own perceived self interests to the greater interest of the entire planet'. For a similar analysis see Zamagni, S., 'Global Environmental Change, Rationality and Ethics', in Campiglio, L. et al. (eds.), *The Environment After Rio: International Law and Economics* (Graham and Trotman, London, 1994), 235, 244–7. Note that this type of conclusion is not shared by all commentators. See for example Weale, A. who stipulates that 'the existence of a complex variety of international resource regimes is a challenge to the Hobbesian picture of international relations'. *The New Politics of Pollution* (Manchester University Press, Manchester, 1992), 190. The problem with this analysis is the fact that although there may be international institutions, many are still fundamentally limited due to the pursuit of each nation's self-interest. For a much fuller discussion of this area, see Gillespie, A., *International Environmental Politics: Questions of Politics in International Environmental Law and Policy* (forthcoming).

III

The Use of Economic Rationale as a Justification for Environmental Protection

Economic justifications for the protection of the environment are probably the most popular protection rationales in environmental debates. However, before examining why this is so, it is helpful to see how this justification is reflected in international and domestic law and policy.

1. THE BACKGROUND

Since international environmental agreements have existed, it has been generally recognized in a number of preambles that it is worthy to protect the environment because of its economic importance. For example, in 1902 an international treaty for the protection of birds was justified on the grounds that certain birds provided economic benefits for agriculture.[1] Over the decades this rationale has become mainstream within international environmental law.[2] This has been evident within international environmental agreements concerning topics as diverse as endangered species,[3] wetlands,[4] air pollution,[5] and the protection of entire regions.[6]

---

[1] See the 1902 *Convention for the Protection of Birds Useful to Agriculture*. 102. BFSP 969. Discussed in Lyster, S., International Wildlife Law. (Grotius, Cambridge, 1985), 63–4.

[2] For a recent history of the use of modern economic instruments in the area of environmental preservation, see Hanemann, M., 'Preface', in Navrud, S. (ed.), *Pricing the European Environment* (Oxford University Press, Oxford, 1992), 9–37. For the historical development of the economic value of the environment as a justification for environmental protection in the UK, see Thomas, K., *Man and the Natural World: Changing Attitudes in England 1500–1800* (Penguin, Harmondsworth, 1984), 188–91.

[3] Preamble, *Convention on International Trade in Endangered Species of Wild Fauna and Flora*. 1973. UNTS. Vol. 973 (No. I. 14537), 243–438.

[4] Preamble of the *Convention on Wetlands of International Importance*. 1971. UNTS. Vol. 996, 244. Note that in 1984 it was suggested that when taking decisions of wetlands, 'quantifications of both direct (monetary) and indirect (non-monetary) values of wetlands and formation of criteria to enable all values to be taken into account in the planning of conservation projects' with regards to wetlands should be taken into account. See Recommendation 2.2 of Art. 5 of the Recommended Amendment. *Environmental Policy and the Law*, 12 (1984), 118.

[5] Preamble, Protocol to the 1979 *Convention on Long Range Transboundary Air Pollution on the Reduction of Sulphur Emissions*. 18 ILM. 1979. 144.

[6] Preamble, *Convention for the Protection of the Natural Environment of the South Pacific*. 1986. In Rummel-Bulsks, I. (ed.), *Multilateral Treaties in the Field of the Environment*. (Grotius, Cambridge, 1991), vol. 2., 372. Preamble, *Convention for the Protection, Management and Development of the Marine and Coastal Environment of the Eastern African Region*. In the same volume, 324.

Economic justifications achieved great prominence in 1987 with the publication of *Our Common Future*. Here, the World Commission on Environment and Development was explicit in its recognition of the role that economics should play.[7] The Commission stated that, 'Conservation pricing requires that governments take a long term view in weighing the costs and benefits of the various measures'.[8] Since then there has been much literature showing how to use economics to protect the environment and achieve sustainable development.[9] This literature, like the World Commission itself, has forcefully argued that the environment and the economy must be joined to achieve sustainable development. Therefore, as David Pearce suggested, 'Environmental concerns must be properly integrated into economic policy from the highest level to the most detailed level'.[10] Since then, environmental and economic problems have been perceived in conventional environmental literature as inseparable.

Consequently a number of new economic approaches have been developed which are intended to protect the environment by offering financial incentives to do so. This is to be achieved through market orientated approaches that use new institutional, monetary, and pricing policies. However, this chapter will not be directly discussing the larger ideological issues revolving around this. Rather, this section is only focusing upon the development of economic valuation or the redefinition of pricing policies for the environment, its justification, method, and difficulties.

The economic valuation of the environment proceeds largely from cost-benefit analysis (CBA). This is an economic technique that is derived from simple profit and loss accounting methods. Such an approach compares inherently different interests, values, and components, and attempts to overcome their dissimilarity by reducing everything to a common medium: money.[11] Once this is achieved, then 'elements of human welfare, such as health, spiritual and emotional well-being and social cohesion can be ranked'.[12] However, as noted, the catch is that they must be converted to a 'neutral value' to acquire a ranking. The central idea in this context is that everything can be reduced to monetary

---

[7] World Commission on Environment and Development, *Our Common Future* (Oxford University Press, Oxford, 1987), 13, 155–7.

[8] Ibid. 15.

[9] The foremost contemporary example of this was Pearce, D., Markandya, A., and Barbier, E. B., *Blueprint for a Green Economy* (Earthscan, London, 1989).

[10] Ibid. xiv.

[11] O'Neill, J., *Ecology, Policy and Politics: Human Well-Being and the Natural World* (Routledge, London, 1993), 115–18. Rodgers, W., 'Benefits, Costs and Risks: Oversight of Health and Decision Making', *Harvard Environmental Law Review*, 4 (1980), 191. Johansson, P., 'Valuing Environmental Damage', in Helm, D. (ed.), *Economic Policy Towards the Environment* (Blackwell, Oxford, 1992), 110. Pearce, D. and Barbier, E. W., *Sustainable Development: Economics and Environment in the Third World* (Earthscan, London, 1990), 57–60.

[12] Pepper, D., 'New Economics and the Deficiencies in Green Political Thought', *Political Quarterly*, 58 (1987), 334, 335. Edwards, S., 'In Defence of Environmental Economics', *Environmental Ethics*, 9 (1987), 73, 74, 76, 82–5. O'Neill, ibid. 62–4, 83, 102–3, 115–17.

valuations, and thus, a 'neutral value' can be acquired.[13] From here it is assumed that in principle everything can be traded against everything else in monetary terms through individual consumer preferences.[14] This position dispels the argument that any preferences are higher or lower than any others.[15] Human values are regarded as subjective wants or personal preferences.[16] This, of course, is a normative judgement in itself and is not value free. Yet it presents itself as such, and expects others to accept and follow this position.[17] The follow on from this is that everything other than humans can only be given instrumental value. Nothing non-human can possess inherent value.[18] Value is to be found solely in the satisfaction of human desires.[19] As Dallas Burtraw said:

Cost-benefit analysis recognises no inherent values that transcend individual valuations. Thus, neither trees nor birds nor micro-organisms have value unless some persons value them.[20]

These economic valuation principles have been used to justify the extensive use of CBA within environmental areas. Indeed, CBA is believed to be perfectly suited to creating a basis for environmental decision making.[21] This is especially so as the methods of the economic valuation of the environment have improved since their introduction in the early 1980s when former President Reagan passed Executive Order 12291, which ordered the Environmental Protection Agency (EPA) and other government agencies to prepare a 'Regulatory Impact Analysis' that included a cost-benefit evaluation of every proposed major regulation.[22] This policy has continued throughout the Reagan, Bush, and Clinton administrations.[23] Additionally, the objective of CBA and the method of choosing the most cost

[13] Baram, M. S., 'Cost-benefit Analysis: An Inadequate Basis for Health, Safety and Environmental Regulatory Decision-making', *Ecology Law Quarterly*, 8 (1980), 473, 483.

[14] Jacobs, M., *The Green Economy: Environment, Sustainable Development and the Politics of the Future* (Pluto, London, 1991), 203. Posner, R., 'Utilitarianism, Economics and Legal Theory', *Journal of Legal Studies*, 8 (1979), 103, 119. Johansson, *supra* n. 11, 111, 112.

[15] Daly, H. E. and Cobb, J. (1989), *For the Common Good: Redirecting the Economy Towards the Community, the Environment and a Sustainable Future* (Beacon Press, Boston, 1989), 92–3.

[16] Kennedy, D., 'Cost-Benefit Analysis: A Critique', *Stanford Law Review*, 33 (1981), 387.

[17] Daly and Cobb, *supra* n. 15, 94–5.

[18] Leiss, W., 'Instrumental Rationality, the Domination of Nature, and Why We Do Not Need an Environmental Ethic', in Hanson, S. (ed.), *Environmental Ethics: Philosophical and Political Perspectives* (Simon Fraser University Press, Toronto, 1986), 175, 178. Edwards *supra* n. 12, 73, 74, 76.   [19] Daly and Cobb, *supra* n. 15, 107.

[20] Burtraw, D., 'Environmental Policy in the United States', in Helm, *supra* n. 11, 289, 303.

[21] Freeman, A. M., 'Economics, Incentives and Environmental Regulation', in Vig, N. J. and Kraft, M. E. (eds.), *Environmental Policy in the 1990s* (Washington, 1990), 145, 149. Ruff, L. E., 'The Economic Common Sense of the Pollution', in Dorfman, D. and N. (eds.), *The Economics of the Environment: Selected Readings* (Toronto University Press, Toronto, 1972), 1, 9. Hueting, R., 'The Economic Functions of the Environment', in Ekins, P and Max-Neef, M. (eds.), *Real Life Economics: Understanding Wealth Creation* (Routledge, London, 1992), 61, 62.

[22] *Executive Order No. 12291*, 46 Fed. Reg. 13193 (1981).

[23] See Vig, N. J., 'Presidential Leadership: From the Reagan to the Bush Administration', in Vig and Kraft, *supra* n. 21, 33, 42–3. Hanemann, *supra* n. 2, 9, 28–31.

beneficial method when faced with a choice is spelt out in some American environmental legislation.[24] However, this is not a universal approach in the United States and in some environmental statutes this is not the rule. Nevertheless, the influence of CBA within the EPA remains considerable.[25]

CBA in an environmental context has also become a more common feature with environmental policy in Britain.[26] This has been due to a combination of internal economic ideology and external EC pressure.[27] CBA has also become increasingly recognized in other European and OECD countries.[28] Even in the post-perestroika former Soviet Union, CBA in an environmental context has been 'adopted enthusiastically by Soviet planners'.[29]

There have also been a number of international environmental initiatives that have spoken of the importance of a monetary value for the environment. For example, the *Bergen Ministerial Declaration on Sustainable Development* in 1990 stated that it is necessary to:

integrate environmental considerations with economic and sectoral planning . . . at present environmental goods are underpriced and even considered as free goods. This has in many cases led to over exploitation.[30]

This followed from the Group of Seven's 1989 Paris economic summit, where it was suggested that:

clear assessments of the costs, benefits and resource implications of environmental protection should help governments take the necessary decisions . . . [it is necessary to create] . . . price signals, reflecting where possible, the full value of natural resources.[31]

The 1992 *Statement of Principles for a Global Consensus on the Management, Conservation and Sustainable Development of Forests*, emphasized in Principle 13(c) that:

Incorporation of environmental costs and benefits into market forces and mechanisms, in order to achieve forest conservation and sustainable development, should be encouraged both domestically and internationally.[32]

---

[24] Burtraw, *supra* n. 20, 289, 296–301.
[25] Environmental Protection Agency, *EPA's Use of Cost Benefit Analysis* (Washington, 1987), 25. Burtraw, *supra* n. 20, 289, 304–5. Hanemann, *supra* n. 2, 9, 22–5.
[26] British Treasury, *Green Booklet* (London, 1984), 12. Waldegrave, W. 'The British Approach', *Environmental Policy and the Law*, 15 (1985), 112, 114. Department of the Environment, *This Common Inheritance. The Second Year Report.* 1992. CM 2068. 32, 34.
[27] Pearce, *supra* n. 9, 124–7.   [28] Navrud, *supra* n. 2.
[29] DeBardeleben, U., 'Economic Reform and Environmental Protection in the USSR', *Soviet Geography*, 31 (1990), 237, 245. Maggs, P. B. 'Marxism and Soviet Environmental Law', *Colombia Journal of Transnational Law* 23 (1984–5), 355, 361.
[30] Principle 6 (B). *Bergen Conference: Ministerial Declaration on Sustainable Development. Environmental Policy and the Law*, 20 (1990), 104.
[31] Paragraph 37, 1989 *G–7 Economic Summit*. Paris. 16 July. *International Legal Materials*. (28) 1989. 1293.
[32] *Statement of Principles for a Global Consensus on the Management, Conservation and Sustainable Use of all Types of Forests*. 1992. UNCED Doc. A/CONF 151/6/Rev. 1.

The Statement of Principles even went so far as to suggest that economic values, other than that provided by timber, should be taken into account when seeking to achieve the sustainable development of forests.[33] Section 11.21 and 11.22 of *Agenda 21* went on to advocate that to achieve the sustainable development of forest ecosystems it is necessary:

To improve recognition of the social, economic and ecological values of trees, forests and forest lands, including the consequences of the damage caused by the lack of forests . . . to promote methodologies with a view to incorporating social, economic and ecological values of trees, forests and forest lands into the national economic accounting systems.[34]

The same chapter also asserts that it is necessary to develop, adopt and strengthen national programmes for accounting the economic and non-economic value of forests.[35] *Agenda 21* also has a number of other provisions calling for a reassessment of economic pricing in other areas. For example, section 30.9 calls on governments and industries to:

work towards the development and implementation of concepts and methodologies for the internationalisation of environmental costs into accounting and pricing mechanisms.[36]

This position was also recognized in 1995 by the Commission on Global Governance which was emphatic in its suggestions that 'All governments should adopt policies that make maximum use of environmental taxes and the polluter pays principles of charging'.[37] This was seen as the best method to give 'a firm signal to individuals' that they are practising unsustainable lifestyles of production methods.[38]

The importance of a correctly priced environment is also a central part of current moves to liberalize trade. It is suggested that this is 'best achieved by a synthesis of economic instruments designed to correct distortions'.[39] This principle was recognized in the 1992 *Cartagena Commitment.*[40]

---

[33] See principles 12(a) and 16(e). Ibid.

[34] See also s. 11.20. *Agenda 21*. 1992. UNCED. Doc. A/CONF 151/4.

[35] Paragraph 11.23. Ibid.

[36] *Agenda 21*, ibid. S. 8.28 also suggests that it is necessary 'to incorporate environmental costs in the decisions of producers and consumers, to reverse the tendency to treat the environment as a free good, and pass these costs onto other parts of society, other countries and future generations'. See also ss. 8.31 and 8.37. Such actions are also deemed necessary because as 4.4 states, 'Without the stimulus of price and market signals that make clear . . . the environmental costs of the consumption of energy, materials and natural resources and the generation of wastes, significant changes . . . seem unlikely to occur in the near future.'

[37] The Commission on Global Governance, *Our Global Neighbourhood* (Oxford University Press, Oxford, 1995), 211.

[38] Ibid. 210.

[39] See *Business Council For Sustainable Development: Changing Course* (MIT Press, Massachusetts, 1992), xi, 16–17.

[40] See para. A, Subject 10 of the *Cartagena Commitment, Environmental Policy and the Law*, 22 (1992), 189, 190.

2. THE REASONS FOR THE ECONOMIC EMPHASIS
WITHIN ENVIRONMENTAL POLICY

Sophisticated methods have been evolving over the last twenty years which attempt to maximize the net economic value of the environment.[41] It is believed that in high economic valuations lies the justification for conserving the environment. This is not strictly a new idea. For example, in 1910, Gifford Pinchot, the Chief Forester of the United States, argued that if it could be shown that the net benefits to society from conservation were higher than any other form of land use, then there was a clear case for conservation. The weighing of these benefits, he concluded, must be through economic considerations. Consequently, if the net benefits of conservation are higher than those of alternative uses of investment, then a strong economic case for conservation has been established.[42]

This form of economic impetus for conservation has now reappeared eighty years later with a flurry. Such arguments are becoming common in many areas of environmental concern. This increasing trend can be partly attributed to the realization that traditional economic methods do not reflect the complete economic value of the environment. As Elizabeth Dowdeswell, the Executive Director for the United Nations Environment Program, explained in 1995:

Until recently, the language of mainstream economics has defined the economy in market terms, without giving much attention to non-market elements such as subsidies provided by eco-system services, subsistence activities, household labour or cultural aspects of human social services. This must change. From an ecological and an economic perspective, both poverty and environmental degradation are symptoms of a poorly functioning economic system.[43]

For example, conventional CBAs are typically biased towards the quantifiable aspects of decisions. Consequently, the costs and benefits that are more difficult to measure tend to be ignored.[44] This process is exacerbated by the fact that CBAs are often carried out in a short-term, myopic, economic climate that is typically insensitive to fragile, soft, and unquantifiable environmental and human values.[45]

---

[41] This is because 'it is essential that the authorities make accurate assessments . . . of the economic aspects of anti-pollution measures'. See Ch. 9, Annex, Part II. *Declaration of the Council of European Communities on the Program of Action of the European Community on the Environment.* 1973. *Official Journal of the European Communities.* Vol. 16. No. 6. 112. 22 Dec. 1973.

[42] Pinchot, G., *The Fight for Conservation* (Harcourt Brace, New York, 1910), 38–41; *Breaking New Ground* (Harcourt, New York, 1947), 263, 325–6.

[43] Dowdeswell, E. *Speech at the World Summit For Social Development.* 1995. 7 Mar. UNEP. Speech. 1995/3.

[44] See Munasinghe, M., *Environmental Economics and Sustainable Development* (World Bank, Washington, 1993), 4–5.

[45] See Leonard, H. and Zechauser, S. T., 'Cost-Benefit Analysis Applied to Risk: Its Philosophy and Legitimacy', in McLean, A. (ed.), *Values at Risk* (Random House, New York, 1986), 31, 43.

Additionally, conventional CBAs often fail to provide alternative scenarios against which the results can be compared. As the World Commission on Environment and Development explained, the environment has traditionally been seen as the provider of 'free services'. However, these are *not* free as the cost of damage to the environment is ultimately borne by someone other than the person who created the problem. This problem must be alleviated by both realizing the value of the environment and making those who pollute it, pay for it.[46] Since the Commission reported in 1987, this principle has been elaborated upon. For example, as David Pearce explained, when speaking of the economic problem of tropical deforestation in the Amazon:

In effect, what these policies call for is a new economic strategy that takes into account the total value of the Amazonian ecosystem. The current strategy underestimates this value by assuming that conversion of Amazonian forests is 'costless' . . . this strategy extends to include the inefficient and unsustainable mining of the Amazonian forests for timber, as well as conversion of water resources to hydroelectric generation . . . an alternative strategy for sustainable development must start with the proper economic analysis of its total values.[47]

The problem of conventional CBA is well illustrated with global warming. For example, William Nordhaus argued that:

the flow of damages identified with climate change is estimated to be [between] about one quarter of one percent . . . or at most 2% of total global output . . .[48]

He then concluded that it would cost substantially *more* than this to make large cuts in the emission of greenhouse gases.[49] Thus, under conventional CBA it is better to allow the majority of climatic change to take place and adapt to it, rather than pay 'disproportionate' costs to avert it.[50]

The implications of this type of calculation are shown in what the sum does

[46] World Commission, *supra* n. 7, 220.

[47] Pearce, D., 'An Economic Approach to Saving the Tropical Forests', in Helm, *supra* n. 11, 239. Pearce, *supra* n. 9, 4–5. See also Barbier, E. B., 'The Economic Framework For Natural Resource Management', in Polunin, N. and Burnett, J. H. (eds.), *Maintenance of the Biosphere. Proceedings of the Third International Conference on Environmental Future* (Edinburgh University Press, Edinburgh, 1990), 199–205. Barbier, E. B., 'Tropical Deforestation', in Pearce, D. (ed.), *Blueprint 2: Greening the World Economy* (Earthscan, London, 1991), 138, 147. Gillis, M., 'Economics, Ecology and Ethics: Mending the Broken Circle For Tropical Forests', in Bormann, F. H. and Kettert, S. R. (eds.), *Ecology, Economics, Ethics: The Broken Circle* (Yale University Press, New York, 1991), 155, 164–5. Ruitenbeek, H. J., *The Economic Analysis of Tropical Forest Conservation Initiatives: Examples From West Africa* (World Bank, Washington, 1992), 241, 251.

[48] Nordhaus, W. D., 'To Slow, or Not to Slow: The Economics of the Greenhouse Effect', *Economic Journal*, 101 (1991), 921–36. See also Bate, R. and Morris, J., *Global Warming: Apocalypse of Hot Air?* (Institute of Economic Affairs, London, 1994), 28–9, 41–2, 49.

[49] Nordhaus, ibid. Bate, ibid. 49.

[50] Wilfred Beckermann makes substantially the same case in 'Global Warming and International Action: An Economic Perspective', in Hurrell, A. and Kingsbury, B. (eds.), *The International Politics of the Environment* (Oxford University Press, Oxford, 1992), 253. Beckerman, W., 'Global Warming: A Sceptical Assessment', in Helm, *supra* n. 11, 52.

not consider. This means that Nordhaus's economic view, by focusing on human deaths and prima facie economic costs, largely ignored the damage caused to Nature, ecological, social welfare and intangible or non-utilitarian values. Consequently, global warming which is one of the foremost international environmental threats is not seen as a great risk and tends to be glossed over as unimportant.[51]

Positions like Nordhaus's were very influential with the Bush Administration at the 1992 Earth Summit. They argued that 'the sheer magnitude of the difference between the cost and the benefits meant that the evidence could not be ignored'.[52] Consequently, they believed they could not sign a strong Climate Change Convention, because the economic costs were too high. However, in reaching this conclusion, they substantially undervalued other less direct economic costs which would have suggested that it is actually economically beneficial (and not overtly detrimental) to combat climatic change.

The overall point here is that conventional CBA is flawed because the environment is substantially underpriced. To correct this problem it is suggested that the market must be righted.[53] As the World Bank stated in 1992:

The primary cause of environmental problems, is not the price-making market, but rather the failure of markets and governments to price the environment appropriately.[54]

By placing new and correct economic values upon the environment, then it is assumed that one of the main ingredients of environmental destruction will be removed.[55]

This position is consistent with the *Polluter Pays Principle*. This is a guiding principle of the OECD's environmental policy, which recognizes:

---

[51] Guruswamy, L. D., 'Global Warming: Integrating United States and International Law', *Arizona Law Review*, 3 (1990), 222, 225. Cooper, R. N. 'United States Policy Towards the Global Environment', in Hurrell and Kingsbury, ibid. 290, 305. MacNeil, J., Winsemius, P., and Yakushiji, T., *Beyond Interdependence: The Meshing Of The World's Economy And The Earth's Ecology* (Oxford University Press, Oxford, 1991), 95, 97. Foley, G., *Global Warming: Who Is Taking The Heat* (Panos, London, 1991), 53. Leggett, J., *'Anxieties and Opportunities in Climate Change'*, in Prins, G. (ed.), *Threats Without Enemies: Facing Environmental Insecurity* (Earthscan, London, 1993), 41, 58–9.

[52] Fish, A. L., 'Industrialised Countries and Greenhouse Gas Emissions', *International Environmental Affairs*, 6 (1994), 14, 33–4., Massey, S. C., 'UNCED Will Not Culminate in a Successful Preventive Global Warming Treaty Without the United States Support', *Georgia Journal of International and Comparative Law*, 22 (1992), 175, 195–9. Hayes, P. and Smith, K. R. (eds.), *The Global Greenhouse Regime: Who Pays?* (Earthscan, London, 1993), chs. 8–13.

[53] Pearce, D. and Turner, R. K., *The Economics of Natural Resources and the Environment* (Harvester, 1990), 41. Pearce, *supra* n. 9, 32. Pearce and Barbier, *supra* n. 11. Barbier, E., 'Economic Policy and Sustainable Natural Resource Management', in Holmberg, J. (ed.), *Policies for a Small Planet* (Earthscan, London, 1992), 65, 66. Cairncross, F., *Costing the Earth* (Economist Books, London, 1991), 91.

[54] World Bank, *World Development Report 1992: Development and the Environment* (Oxford University Press, Oxford, 1992), 71.

[55] Pearce, *supra* n. 9, 5–7, 154–5, 162–5. Rees, W. F., 'The Ecology of Sustainable Development', *Ecologist*, 20 (1990), 18, 20.

when the costs of [environmental] deterioration are not adequately taken into account in the price system, the market fails to reflect the scarcity of such resources . . . [consequently] . . . the polluter should bear the expenses of pollution . . . in other words, the costs of these measures should be reflected in the costs of goods and services which cause pollution and/or consumption.[56]

The principle was reiterated in Principle 16 of the 1992 *Rio Declaration,*[57] and again with the 1993 *Lucerne Declaration.*[58]

To achieve such objectives it is necessary to establish a method to value the environment correctly in an economic setting. This task has been accomplished by a new form of economic equation that seeks to establish the 'total economic value'.

Total Economic Value (TEV) consists of a total economic aggregate of three separate economic factors. These are consumptive or direct use values, non-consumptive or indirect use values, and existence and option values.[59] Consumptive use values can be assigned prices through such mechanisms as estimating market value if the product were sold on the market, instead of being consumed. Indirect use values correspond to the ecologist's concept of ecological functions. Option values relate to the amount that an individual would be willing to pay to conserve something for possible future use and existence values relate to how much people are willing to pay for the existence of parts of the environment, irrespective of its other uses or values.

When all three of these economic values are subsumed into the Total Economic Value, then economic logic should provide a strong justification for the conservation of the natural environment. These arguments have been forcefully applied for the protection of individual species, such as elephants,[60] or complete ecosystems, such as tropical forests.

The Total Economic Value of Tropical Forests

> The *total* economic value of tropical forests, as a justification for their preservation is vastly greater than the current economic values for which they are currently seen as possessing (i.e. the price of cut timber and created cattle pasture) which leads to their destruction.

---

[56] See principles 2 and 4 of the OECD's *Guiding Principles on the Environment.* US Dept. of State Release. No. 130. 1972. 1 June. 11 ILM. 1972. 1172. For the influence of this policy in the OECD and the EC, see Smets, H., 'The Polluter Pays Principle in the Early 1990s', in Campiglio, L. (ed.), *The Environment After Rio: International Law and Economics* (Graham and Trotman, London, 1994), 131–43.

[57] Principle 16, *Rio Declaration,* UN. Doc A/CONF 151/5. 1992. 7 May.

[58] *The Lucerne Declaration.* In *Environmental Policy and the Law* (1993), 185, 186.

[59] See Pearce, D. W. and Warford, J. J., *World Without End: Economics, Environment and Sustainable Development* (World Bank, Washington, 1993), 102–5. Pearce and Turner, *supra* n. 53. Pearce, 'Tropical Forests', *supra* n. 47, 239, 244. Johansson, *supra* n. 11, 111.

[60] See Barbier, E., Burgess, J., Swanson, T., and Pearce, D., *Elephants, Economics and Ivory* (Earthscan, London, 1990), 18–20,

Indeed, the latter valuation ignores other direct use values which are non-consumptive (i.e. not destructive) such as nuts, rattan, latex, and rubber, as well as the economic benefits that can be derived from medicinal plants and eco-tourism.

The indirect economic values of tropical forests lie in the environmental services they provide. These range from the ecosystem functions from pollination to overall stability, the maintenance of water cycles, regulation of climate, soil production and protection, storage and recycling of essential nutrients, the absorption and breakdown of pollutants through to the photosynthetic fixation of solar energy and the importance of this in the ecosystems. Of particular importance here is the global importance of tropical forests (most of the other benefits are local) as absorbers of carbon dioxide, and thus as pivotal considerations in the debate over climatic change *independent* of other economic valuations. This valuation alone has lead to postulated economic values of rainforest services at over thousands of dollars per hectare.

The third and final component of total economic value is generated via bequest, existence, and option values. This involves the giving of monies for conservation so that the object in question is preserved for the possible benefit of present and future generations. Additionally, this encompasses the ideal that people are willing to pay monies for their individual peace of mind that tropical forests will continue to exist, regardless of their possible other values.

The conclusion is that the balance sheet should show that when the non-consumptive direct use values, the indirect use values and the option values are added up the tropical forests are worth substantially more standing up, than they are by being turned into wood pulp and cattle pasture. (Global Environmental Facility; *Economics and the Conservation of Biodiversity.* 1993. 13, 16–19, 47–50. IUCN, WWF, WRI; *Conserving the World's Biodiversity.* 1990. 25, 28–34.)

3. ACCEPTANCE OF THE ARGUMENT

Environmental questions are becoming increasingly dominated by economics. Despite the fact that many of those involved in environmental protection are weary of economic rationales, many have nevertheless accepted the central message of this type of approach: namely that some form of economic analysis should control the level of environmental quality that society tries to achieve in practice. A primary justification for this change is because of the high economic values that can be attached to the environment through reformulated economic methods. These new methods can act as powerful stimuli for environmental protection.

Reformed CBA and monetary valuation has also been adopted by many because it indirectly avoids confrontation with fundamental and far reaching political[61] and ethical[62] questions. Additionally, philosophical arguments are seen as ineffective due to their fragmented, shifting, and hard-to-quantify basis.[63] Economic arguments are not believed to suffer from these deficiencies.

Finally, valuing the environment is also said to be useful because it gives decision makers 'an idea of what the polluters should have to pay' if they decide to let it be used for any such environmentally destructive practices.[64] This aspect leads to the supposedly beneficial results of governments having at least rough CBAs, so as to be able to make choices upon all the relevant economic considerations. Consequently, decision makers should not make decisions which are wrong from both environmental and economic points of view. It has also been suggested that correct economic values are beneficial as they 'speak in a language' that those concerned with economic development can understand.[65] Others have suggested that to speak this language is to act, 'realistically'.[66] Finally, the World Bank has argued that monetary valuation of the environment is necessary as, 'Measurement is essential since tradeoffs are inevitable'.[67] Consequently, decision makers will be able 'to determine which development option should take place'.[68]

THE PROBLEMS WITH ECONOMIC JUSTIFICATIONS FOR ENVIRONMENTAL PROTECTION

1. THE QUESTION OF VALUES

A. The Problem of Value

The first overall problem in this area concerns 'economism' which is a belief in the primacy of economic forces and values in human affairs. This is a foundation of modern Western society and contemporary government. Economic rationality postulates a theory of human behaviour that owes little to science and much to a deductive logic that interprets events on the basis of philosophical assumptions regarding human motivation and rationality.[69]

---

[61] Commoner, B., 'Economic Growth and Environmental Quality: How to Have Both', *Social Policy,* 16 (1985), 18, 25. Dawson, R. K., 'Environmental Policy in the Real World', *Environmental Forum,* 5 (1988), 21, 23.

[62] Pearce, *Tropical Forests, supra* n. 47, 239, 258.

[63] Norton, B. G., 'Environmental Ethics And Non Human Rights', *Environmental Ethics,* 4 (1982), 19, 21.

[64] Cairncross, *supra* n. 53, 20. Pearce, *supra* n. 9, 33–9.

[65] Porritt, J., 'Halting the G-7 Juggernaut', *Guardian,* 16 July 1991, 7. IUCN, WWF, *Conserving the World's Biodiversity* (Gland, 1990), 25.

[66] See Murray, M., 'The Value of Biological Diversity', in Prins, *supra* n. 51, 66, 81.

[67] World Bank, *supra* n. 54, 71.

[68] Barbier, *supra* n. 47, 138, 147.

[69] See Barry, N. P., *The New Right* (Croom Helm, New York, 1987), 34–5.

The difficulty is that the proponents of the economic position suggest that the theory of economic self-interest should not just underlie economics, but all aspects of social relations.[70] However, these propositions are threatened by two facts. Firstly, no credible evidence exists that people become happier, that is more satisfied, in some substantive sense when their desires, beyond their basic needs, are met.[71]

Secondly, and more importantly, other values exist that do not fit within economic logic. Indeed, Adam Smith himself noted on the first page of his book, *The Theory of Moral Sentiments*, that people do not always act out of economic self-interest.[72] Economic self-interest does not provide all the justifications for human activity. For example, many things that people cherish, admire or respect cannot be valued in monetary terms. Consequently, it is fair to say that often the worth of things is better measured by our unwillingness to pay for them. Consider love, or something that has to be worked for, such as a university degree. A degree that can be bought is not worth buying. However the fact that these things are not for sale does not make them worthless. These things have a dignity rather than a price.[73] Also, money values do not recognize integrative values like honour, respect and reverence that refer not to personal desires but to feelings orientated in other spheres of commitment.[74] This leads to the problem that some people would be disgusted at the thought of receiving money for certain events, i.e. in exchange for someone's life or betraying their own family, community or country.[75]

The recognition of social and ethical interests over economic factors has also been recognized in some early American environmental cases which stated that CBA could *not* be used to make a decision concerning endangered species.[76] This is because the American Endangered Species Act called for the preservation of endangered species on account of their aesthetic, ecological and educational values. The noteworthy point is that the American Congress did not initially include economic values as one of the reasons for preserving

---

[70] See Lux, K., *Adam Smith's Mistake* (Century, London, 1990), 202–3.

[71] For an illustration by way of historical analysis of trends and changing attitudes, see Rescher, T., *Welfare: The Social Issues in Philosophical Perspective* (1972), 36–59. Argyle, B., *The Philosophy of Happiness* (UCL Press, London, 1987), 102, 142–4, 207–8.

[72] Smith, A., *The Theory of Moral Sentiments* (Methuen, London), 1.

[73] See Sagoff, M., 'We Have Met the Enemy and He is Us, or Conflict and Contradiction in Environmental Law', *Environmental* Law, 12 (1982), 283, 306. O'Neill, J., *Ecology, Policy and Politics: Human Well-Being and the Natural World* (Routledge, London, 1993), 118–22.

[74] Baker, C. E., 'The Ideology of the Economic Analysis of Law', *Philosophy and Public Affairs*, 5 (1975), 3, 35.

[75] Adams, J. G. U., 'Unsustainable Economics', *International Environmental Affairs*, 2 (1990), 14, 21. O'Neill, *supra* n. 73, 119-120.

[76] 'Economic exigencies . . . do not grant courts a licence to rewrite a statute, no matter how desirable the purpose or result might be.' Re, *Hill* v. *TVA* 549 F 2d. 1064. (6th Cir. 1977), aff.d. 437 US 153. (1978). Quote at 1074.

species.[77] This was not because of their lack of such values, but because their preservation was not an economic issue. Thus, economic efficiency was initially placed below other anthropocentric environmental values.[78] However, the problem of attaching economic values to the environment is actually more complex than this. For example, as Elizabeth Dowdeswell, the executive director of UNEP stated:

we have to realise that we cannot put a price on everything. There is a limit to natural resource accounting. Can we price the value of the pristine mountains, the beauty of the sunset, the sound of the swirling brook?[79]

Such values derived from the environment are intangible and cannot be transferred into a neat economic equation. They involve moral, not economic, choices.[80] It is the same logic that is applied to social issues from abortion to labour policy. Such decisions cannot be made solely on economic grounds. The same deduction should include environmental debates.[81] The correct approach to this situation, in an environmental context, was stated by Holmes Rolston:

What we want to know about here, or ought to want to know about, are the citizens' convictions about goods in Nature and their appropriate response to them, their public conscience, and we only confuse those we interview when we ask about their desire to pay. The question is about principles, not pocketbooks. They are being asked if an ideology is for sale.[82]

---

[77]   *Endangered Species Act.* 16 USC § 1531 (b) (1988). The initial view was that the value of endangered species was 'incalculable'. See *TVA* v. *Hill* 437 US 153, 187. (1978). For useful discussions on the initial and subsequent approaches, see Yaffee, S. L., *Prohibitive Policy: Implementing the Federal Endangered Species Act* (MIT Press, Massachusetts, 1982). Sagoff, M., 'On The Preservation Of Species', *Colombia Journal Of Environmental Law*, 7 (1980), 33, 52, 53. Flevares, W. M., 'Ecosystems, Economics and Ethics: Protecting Biological Diversity at Home and Abroad', *Southern California Law Review*, 65 (1992), 2039, 2055.

[78]   Note, that in 1978 the American Congress authorized legislation which stated that in cases of 'irreconcilable conflict' federal projects could be exempted from the requirements of the Act after being reviewed by a high level inter-agency committee. In addition, proposals involving 'critical habitat' would now have to include an economic impact statement. PL 95–362, 10 Nov. 1978. 9 Stat. 3751.

[79]   Dowdeswell, E., *Speech at the World Summit on Social Development*, UNEP. 1995/3. 17 Mar. 1995. Al Gore earlier came to very similar conclusions with his statement that 'Past a certain point, however, it is impossible to put a price on the environmental effect of our economic choices. Clean air, fresh water, the sun rising through the mist on a mountain lake, an abundance of life on the land, in the air and in the sea — the value of these things is incalculable.' See Gore, A., *Earth in Balance: Forging A New Common Purpose* (Earthscan, London, 1992), 190–1.

[80]   Naess, A., *Ecology, Community and Lifestyle* (Cambridge University Press, Cambridge, 1989), 106, 112–23. Nash, R., 'Do Rocks Have Rights', *Centre Magazine*, 10 (1977), 1. Yaffee, *supra* n. 77, 27, 31.

[81]   Or as Aldo Leopold suggested, conservation should be seen 'in terms of decency rather than dollars'. A. Leopold, 'Conservation as a Moral Issue', *Environmental Ethics*, 1 (1979), 131. See also Devall, B. and Sessions, G., *Deep Ecology: Living As If Nature Mattered* (Gibbs Smith, Utah, 1985), 136.

[82]   Rolston, H., 'Valuing Wetlands', *Environmental Ethics*, 7 (1985), 38. See also O'Neill, J., *supra* n. 73, 68–76.

Unfettered economic logic could allow 'undesirable' consequences, such as the destruction of culturally important public spaces or socially repugnant practices such as child labour.[83] The objections to these propositions are obvious. Specifically, when only monetary variations are considered, to the exclusion of other considerations, then a misrepresentation of social and ethical values appears.

This economic approach easily disregards that which is ultimately important, by trivializing or reducing its ethical imperatives to mere dollars and cents.[84] Economic values are a different consideration, and should not be confused with ethical ones. Additionally, economic considerations must be recognized as being subservient to ethical considerations. As Ronald Coarse, the man who reintroduced the problem of economical social cost to a modern audience concluded, 'problems of welfare economics must ultimately dissolve into a study of aesthetics and morals'.[85]

An important problem here is the use of monetary values to measure political, ideological or moral convictions. This is what philosophers call a category mistake. This is because an attempt is made to describe an object in terms that do not apply to it. Hence, the idea that moral or ideological convictions should be forgotten unless they can be backed up with hard cash is problematic as it is trying to test the worth of an ideal by asking people what they are willing to pay for it.[86] In a very similar (yet ignored) sense, nobody asks economists how much they are willing to pay for their view that CBA should form the basis of regulatory policy. The problem is, as Mark Sagoff explained:

> An efficient criterion, as it is used to evaluate public policy, assumes that the goals of our society are contained in the preferences individuals reveal or would reveal in markets. Such an approach may appear attractive, even just because it treats everyone equally, at least theoretically, by according to each person's preferences the same respect and concern. To treat a person with respect, however, is also to listen and to respond intelligently to his or her views and opinions. This is not the same thing as to ask how much he or she is willing to pay for them. The cost-benefit analysis does not ask economists how much they are willing to pay for what they believe, that is that the workplace and the environment should be made efficient. Why, then, does the analyst ask workers and environmentalists, and others how much they are willing to pay for what they believe is right?[87]

---

[83] See Jean Dorst in Chisholm, A., *Philosophers of the Earth: Conversations with Ecologists* (Scientific Book Club, London, 1974), 158, 162. See also Ash, M., *The Fabric of the World: Towards A Philosophy of Environment* (Green Books, Devon, 1992), 35–6.

[84] Little, C. E., 'Has the Land Ethic Failed in America? An Essay on the Legacy of Aldo Leopold', *University of Illinois Law Review*, 2 (1986), 313, 316–19. Adams, *supra* n. 75, 14, 21, 26.

[85] Coarse, R., 'The Problem of Social Cost', *Journal of Law and Economics*, 3 (1960), 213.

[86] Redclift, M., 'Sustainable Development: Needs, Values, Rights', *Environmental Values*, 2 (1993), 1, 13. See also Soderbaum, P., 'Economics, Evaluation and Environment', in Hall, Myers and Maganis (eds.), *The Economics of Ecosystem Management* (Netherlands, 1985), 5, 8.

[87] Sagoff, M., 'At The Shrine Of Our Lady Fatima or Why Not All Political Questions Are Not All Economic', *Arizona Law Review*, 23 (1981), 1290–1. Santamaria, A. S., 'Economic Science and Political Democracy', in Ekins, P. and Max-Neef, M. (eds.), *Real Life Economics: Understanding Wealth Creation* (Routledge, London, 1992), 10, 17.

Proponents of the economic approach have not been able to respond adequately to the criticisms of why environmental policy ought to strive to satisfy preferences on a willingness-to-pay basis, without regard to the values those preferences express.[88] Nevertheless, they continue to propagate an approach value that has such fallacies and obvious ideological preferences within it.[89]

When ethical considerations like those above are recognised, people may choose not to participate within the ambits of the economic debate. For example, if an individual is asked to place a price on what they would be willing to accept as payment for the use of an environment, an individual may reply 'It's priceless', or 'I won't sell' or 'infinity'.[90] This type of position can be attributed to the argument that such alternatives are simply intolerable regardless of any amount of financial compensation. Yet the market approach is working on a presumption that a median, or midway point can be achieved. Additionally, it classifies responses such as, 'I won't sell', as illicit and irrational.[91]

This classification is unpersuasive. A decision may still be rational even if it is not based on an individualistic assumption of what someone is willing to pay or receive for the gain or loss of a certain thing. To object outright to environmental degradation and not accept payment for it in compensation should be seen as a rational response. In fact, it could be suggested that to refuse to discuss economic values for the environment is not 'irrational'. Rather, it is to recognize the illegitimacy of the debate.[92] This illegitimacy occurs because there are other values at stake. It is particularly apt here to demonstrate this point with environmental values.

Non-monetary environmental values have developed as a growing number of people have devised new ways of looking at environmental issues. These include theories such as the moral considerability of animals and environmental ethics which are discussed in chapters eight, nine, and ten. There is also the ethical theory of the 'rights' of future generations, which is discussed in chapter six. Only the future generation approach is taken into account by those advocating

---

[88] Norton, B. G., 'Economists' Preferences and the Preferences of Economists', *Environmental Values*, 3 (1994), 311, 318–19, 329–30. Sagoff, M., 'Reason and Rationality in Environmental Law', *Ecology Law Quarterly*, 14 (1987), 265, 272–3. Redclift, *supra* n. 86, 15.

[89] See Gillis, M., 'Economics, Ecology and Ethics: Mending the Broken Circle for Tropical Forests', in Bormann, F. H. and Kettert, S. R. (eds.), *Ecology, Economics, Ethics: The Broken Circle* (Yale University Press, New York, 1991), 155, 156. Myrdal, S., 'Institutional Economics', *Journal of Economic Issues*, 12 (1978), 6. Goodin, R. E., *Green Political Theory* (Polity, Cambridge, 1992), 20–2.

[90] Sagoff, M., *The Economy of the Earth* (Cambridge University Press, Cambridge, 1990), 81–8.

[91] Pearce, D., Markandya, A., and Barbier, E. B., *Blueprint for a Green Economy* (Earthscan, London, 1989), 55. Helm, D. (ed.), *Economic Policy Towards the Environment* (Blackwell, Oxford, 1991), 3.

[92] Sagoff, *supra* n. 88, 265, 301. Kelman, S., 'Cost-Benefit Analysis: An Ethical Critique', in Glickman, T. S. and Glough, M. (eds.) *Readings in Risk* (John Hopkins University Press, Washington, 1986), 129, 133. Sagoff, M., 'Four Dogmas of Environmental Economics', *Environmental Values*, 3 (1994), 285, 300–3.

the new economic values for the environment. However, with this factor alone, the focus still remains slanted as it is 'radically anthropocentric'.[93] This is an outcome which is totally unacceptable to those advocating non-anthropocentric views.

Both the perspective of the moral considerability of animals and that of environmental ethics share the belief that value exists independently of human instrumental use values. Additionally, it is argued that the reformulated economic instruments cannot even capture the complete and more developed anthropocentric environmental values, i.e. aesthetic considerations, that exist beyond direct economic self-interest.[94]

This type of realization was recorded in the 1990 *Bergen Ministerial Declaration on Sustainable Development* which recognized that:

Efforts to supplement accounting systems to reflect the importance of natural resources are laudable, but that should be tempered by an awareness that it is not possible to translate all environmental values into monetary terms.[95]

Perspectives that are not anthropocentric stipulate that Nature has more value than instrumental human values. It has value, in and of itself.[96] Yet monetary valuation through either conventional CBA or the enhanced methodology of the Total Economic Value, does not recognize this. The environment is still substantially recognized for the values that it provides to humans.[97] The problem here is that environmental questions cannot be resolved on the basis of a simple accounting exercise in which monetized human values are entered as data that can be registered against any other monetized human values. Environmental values and economic values are incommensurable: like apples and pears they cannot be added or subtracted from one another. Quite simply, as Henry Snodgrass said in 1910, and as Stuart McBurney elaborated upon in 1991, 'Ecology into economics won't go'.[98] Yet this is exactly what the economic valuation of the environment attempts to do by converting all values into monetary units and then comparing them as if they were simple commodities. This is an environmentally dangerous and intellectually deceptive exercise.[99]

---

[93] Fox, W., *Towards A Transpersonal Ecology: Developing New Foundations For Environmentalism* (Boston, Shambhala, 1990), 152–3. Devall, B. and Sessions, G., *Deep Ecology: Living As If Nature Mattered* (Gibbs Smith, Utah, 1985), 117. Turner, R. K., 'Environment, Economics and Ethics', in Pearce, D. (ed.), *Blueprint 2: Greening the World Economy* (Earthscan, London, 1991), 209, 214. O'Neil, *supra* n. 73, 46-7, 59-61.

[94] Norton, B., 'Why Environmentalists Hate Mainstream Economists', *Environmental Ethics*, 13 (1991), 235, 248–51.

[95] Point 6(c), *Bergen Conference: Ministerial Declaration on Sustainable Development. Environmental Policy and the Law*, 20 (1990), 104.

[96] Parker, K., 'The Values of a Habitat', *Environmental Ethics*, 12 (1990) 353, 357.

[97] Turner, *supra* n. 93, 209, 218.

[98] McBurney, S., *Ecology into Economics Won't Go* (Green Print, Devon, 1990), 168–75.

[99] Jacobs, M., *The Green Economy: Environment, Sustainable Development and the Politics of the Future* (Pluto, London, 1991), 202. Soderbaum, P., 'Neoclassical and Institutional Approaches to Environmental Economics', *Journal of Economic Issues*, 24 (1991), 481, 489.

The problem of the conflict between non-anthropocentric environmental values and the use of economic rationale is well illustrated by examining the purpose of economic rationales within environmental policy. These rationales work with two objectives in mind. Firstly, they intend to protect the environment, to the extent that its productivity is not endangered. Secondly, they aim to achieve utmost utilization, with minimum inefficiency or waste. The overall objective is that 'resources be optimally allocated to their best use'.[100] This is the classic conservationist position, whereby 'the goose that lays the golden egg is preserved'.[101] As Gifford Pinchot explained around the turn of the twentieth century:

The first duty of the human race on the material side is to control the use of the earth and all that therein is. Conservation means the wise use of the earth and its resources for the lasting good of men. Conservation is the foresighted utilisation, preservation and renewal of forests, waters, lands and minerals for the greatest good of the greatest number for the longest time.[102]

This 'wise use' ethic of conservation policy is the basis of the vast majority of environmental approaches on both domestic and international levels.[103] For example, the World Commission on Environment and Development suggests that States should observe, 'The principle of optimum sustainable yield in the exploitation of living natural resources and ecosystems'.[104] This form of idea is common throughout a number of international environmental documents.[105]

The central concept of this approach is the 'utilisation of species' or the 'rational use of resources'.[106] The environment is to be preserved primarily because it is useful, and in this context, economically useful. Preservation because it may be the ethically correct action to adopt, is a secondary consideration.[107] Thus environmental conservation proceeds from a purely economic and implicitly

---

[100] Pearce, D. and Barbier, E. B., *Sustainable Development: Economics and the Environment in the Third World* (Earthscan, London, 1990), 206. Oelschlaeger, M., *The Idea of Wilderness: From Prehistory to the Age of Ecology* (Yale University Press, New York, 1991), 286–9.

[101] Mabbott, G., 'Politics and the Environment', *Texas Quarterly*, 17 (1974), 9–12.

[102] Pinchot, G., *Breaking New Ground* (Harcourt, New York, 1947), 505. See also McConnell, G., 'The Conservation Movement: Past and Present', in Burton, I. and Kates, R. W. (eds.), *Readings in Resource Management and Conservation* (University of Chicago Press, Chicago, 1965), 189. Udall, S., *The Quiet Crisis and the Next Generation* (Gibbs Smith, Utah, 1988), 97–108, 118–25.

[103] Passmore, J., *Man's Responsibility For Nature* (Duckworth, London, 1974), 73–100. Birnie, P. and Boyle, A. E., *International Law and the Environment* (Clarendon Press, Oxford, 1992), 437–40. Udall, *ibid.* 69–109.

[104] World Commission on Environment and Development, *Our Common Future* (Oxford University Press, Oxford, 1987), 331.

[105] See pages 17–18 of this book.

[106] See Principles 1 and 2 Decision E. 43, of the 43rd *Decision of Economic Commission of Europe; Declaration of Environmental Usage*. Reprinted in *Environmental Law and Policy*, 18 (1988), 132.

[107] Norton, B. G., 'Conservation and Preservation: A Conceptual Rehabilitation', *Environmental Ethics*, 8 (1986), 195, 210, 211. Adams, W. A., *Green Development: Environment and Sustainability in the Third World* (Routledge, London, 1990), 47.

anthropocentric utilitarian standpoint, for as Gifford Pinchot stated, 'There are just two things on this material earth—people and natural resources'.[108] However, such an approach runs contra to a strong set of ethical value systems. This debate is well illustrated in the context of 'sustainable whaling'.

Sustainable Whaling

Whaling is one of the oldest known areas of over-exploitation of Nature. Indeed, as the preamble of the International Convention on the Regulation of Whaling (161 UNTS 72) notes, the 'history of whaling has seen the overfishing of one area after another and of one species of whale after another'. Consequently, it was necessary to establish an International Whaling Commission (IWC) to 'protect all species of whales from further overfishing'. While the IWC failed miserably in its objective to protect whales in the early years of its existence, in the last twenty it has come to the forefront of conservation concerns with the establishment of both moratoriums on commercial whaling and designated sanctuaries from scientific whaling. In doing so, the IWC has been instrumental in the protection and preservation of a number of threatened species of whales.

However, since the initial moratorium on whaling in 1982, comprehensive scientific research on the numbers of certain other species of whales, such as Minke whales, has been carried out. This research has shown that the Minke is not endangered (with approximately 112,000 in the North Atlantic and 750,000 around the Antarctic), and it is possible to take a sustainable harvest of these whales, in accordance with the Revised Management Plan (RMP). Under the RMP, it is presumed that whale populations that are stable should be harvested. If their numbers fall below what is considered biologically suitable (fifty-four per cent of their initial level) to long term stability, then they should be protected. In 1992 the IWC stressed that it was integral within this management process that ongoing population assessment and monitoring was achieved in coordination with effective international inspection and observers.

Given the above considerations being met, the scientific committee of the IWC recommended in 1992 and 1993 the establishment of a sustainable commercial whaling of the Minke. The IWC eventually accepted their proposals in 1994 for a revised management procedure if it was properly supervised.

This form of whaling, with a strong emphasis upon sustainability is in accordance with the objectives of the ICRW which was set up because 'increases in the size of whale stocks will permit increases in the number of whales that may be captured'. Indeed, the delegates to

---

[108] Pinchot, *Breaking New Ground, supra* n.102, 326. For a continuation of this perspective, see World Bank, *World Development Report 1992: Development and the Environment* (Oxford University Press, Oxford, 1992), 8.

the initial agreement 'decided to conclude a convention to provide for the proper conservation of whale stocks and thus make possible the orderly development of the whale industry' (preamble). Likewise, the powers of the IWC are for the purpose of the 'conservation, development, and *sustainable utilisation* of the whale resource'(re Section V.(2)).

This ideal, of the protection of both whales and whalers, within the rubric of sustainable utilization is what a number of countries, such as Norway, have been pursuing. However, opposing them have been a powerful coalition of countries who have objected to the resumption of commercial whaling—even if it is sustainable. Their objections have been on 'moral and ethical grounds'. (Committee of Foreign Affairs. (1993). *International Environmental Issues for the US House of Representatives.*) A good example of this perspective was encapsulated by the Australian government at the 1981 IWC meeting where it was stated, 'There has developed in some countries a strong view that whaling activities should not be carried on any longer because of the ethical implications of taking whales. They consider the method of killing is not humane and the industry cannot be justified as satisfying important human needs by killing animals of such special significance as the whale'. (IWC 1981. OS 31.) Similarly, New Zealand stated at the 1992 Earth Summit that whales are 'in a sense the equivalent in the marine environment of human beings in the land environment'. (UNCED Prep. Com. III. Working group II.)

This ethical approach has not been derived from an animal rights' perspective (as the implications would be contradictory from any non-vegetarian countries) but from angles that have focused upon the humaneness of killing whales, the (alleged) special qualities of whales and the necessity of watertight management regimes if whaling is to be reintroduced.

Norway's rejection of considerations such as the 'special qualities of whales' led it to announce in 1993 that it would restart commercial whaling. For them, it is not primarily a question of humaneness or the 'special qualities' of whales, but one of sustainability, the invoking of the precautionary principle, a focus upon the management of the whole ecosystem, and effective monitoring and control. (Norwegian Ministry of Foreign Affairs. 1993. *Management of Marine Resources.*) Thus, if whales can be culled in accordance with these principles, then they should be harvested like any other natural resource. They suggest that to do so is not only in line with the ICRW, but it is also in accordance with modern conservation practices and goes to the heart of what sustainable development should mean. As the prime minister of Norway, and Chairperson of the World Commission on Environment and Development, Gro Bruntland, has stated, if the overall existence of the Minke whale is not threatened by whaling, and a limited cull can be achieved without detrimental effects to the species, then they should be utilized. Thus, 'We have to base resource management on science and knowledge, not on myths that some specifically designated animals are different and should not be hunted regardless of the ecological justification for doing so. International co-operation is in danger if this kind of selective animal welfare consideration is allowed to dictate resource policies'. (Bruntland. 1993. in Vidal, J.,'Weeping and Whaling', *Guardian*, 7 May 1993.)

The distinct difficulty here is that those who advocate the 'sustainable utilization' of whales or any other species because of economic benefits can see no difference between a whale and a fish finger, or any other natural product that humanity uses. This type of approach may not provide a sufficient basis for a conservation ethic for many people today, as even if utilization is sustainable it may still not be ethical or an acceptable option to pursue. For these people the issue is not one of sustainable yields, but one of ethics. For a fuller discussion of this area, see Gillespie, A., 'The Ethical Question in the Whaling Debate', *Georgetown International Environmental Law Review* 9 (1997) 355–87.

B. The Location of Values

The second major area that is problematic with the economic valuation of the environment is that economic values cannot always be established and even if they are, they may change. Dealing with the first problem it can be asserted that if the environment is valued as an economic resource, then harmful species, or things which humanity has no value for in an economic context, can be exterminated with a clear conscience. On a wider scale this is a frightening precedent, for as Aldo Leopold noted:

Our basic weakness in a conservation system based wholly on economic motives is that most of the members of the land community have no economic value . . .[109]

This position can be extended by the fact that there are sections of Nature which also have no cultural, aesthetic, recreational or other anthropocentric self-interested values.[110]

Likewise, if the piece of Nature in question can be substituted by something else with a higher economic value, then under the economic approach this is a legitimate choice. For example, in New Zealand, introduced trout have resulted in the extinction of various types of indigenous trout. These new trout, however, are considered to be better fighters as sport fish, have the same food value as the

[109] Leopold, A., *A Sand County Almanac* (Oxford University Press, Oxford, 1949), 210–12, 214. See also Ehrenfeld, D., *The Arrogance of Humanism* (Oxford University Press, Oxford, 1978), 190.
[110] See Johnson, L., *A Morally Deep World: An Essay on Moral Significance and Environmental Ethics* (Cambridge University Press, Cambridge, 1991), 168–70. Evernden, N., 'Beyond Ecology; Self, Place and the Pathetic Fallacy', *North American Review*, 263 (1978), 16. Ehrenfeld, ibid. 210.

original trout, and also contribute to the New Zealand economy by attracting over-seas tourists who come to fish this super-hybrid.[111] Therefore, if economic utility is the sole ground for preservation, then it would seem economically rational to intro-duce species which are more useful, even at the expense of the original species.

This perspective is also troubled by the assumption that the 'biotic clock' will continue functioning without the pieces that cannot be given economic value. This is a distinct problem as modern conservation approaches are becoming increasingly aware that for success in their objectives, it may be essential that complete ecosystems are protected in total and not just the perceived valuable individual entities within them.[112]

A second complication here is that arguments for environmental conservation through economic considerations can run into trouble if these environmental considerations (that the economic considerations are based upon) are not borne out. This is a risk as the newly supposed economic value of the environment in many contemporary estimations is remote and nebulous. Consequently, it has been suggested that in certain areas it may become impossible to prove or even detect the connection between conservation and human self-interest which leads to economic valuation.[113]

This presents the problem of the 'radical uncertainties' that surround exactly what the environment can and cannot do.[114] This situation presents itself because many environmental events are not amenable to unequivocal scientific explana-tion and evaluation.[115] Indeed, it is because of this realization that the interna-tional community has moved towards the adoption of the precautionary principle

---

[111] Lockley, D., *New Zealand's Endangered Species* (Auckland University Press, Auckland, 1980), 101.

[112] This realization was first stated by Aristotle who realized that 'Nature never makes anything that is superfluous.' *On the Parts of Animals* (Penguin, Harmondsworth, 1977), 691 B. 4. Or as George Marsh stated in 1874 'We are never justified in assuming a force to be insignificant because its measure is unknown, or even because no physical effect can now be traced to it as its origin.' *The Earth As Modified By Human Action* (Scribner, New York, 1874), 643–4. For modern discussions of this, see Wilson, E. O., 'The Little Things That Run the World', in Pierce, C. (ed.), *People, Penguins and Plastic Trees: Basic Issues in Environmental Ethics* (Wadworth, London, 1995), 139–42. Weizsacker, C., 'Competing Notions of Biodiversity', in Sachs, W. (ed.), *Global Ecology: A New Area of Political Conflict* (Zed, London, 1993), 117, 126–7.

[113] Ehrenfeld, *supra* n. 109, 210.

[114] Shrader, K., 'Environmental Ethics, Uncertainty and Limited Data', in Brown, N. J./UNEP *Ethics and Agenda 21: Moral Implications of a Global Consensus* (United Nations, New York, 1994), 77–81. Norton, B. G., 'Commodity, Amenity and Morality: The Limits of Quantification in Valuing Biodiversity', in Wilson, E. O. (ed.), *Biodiversity* (National Academy Press, Washington, 1988), 200, 202–5. Carpenter, R. A., 'Ecology in Court and Other Disappointments of Environmental Science', *Natural Resources Lawyer*, 15 (1983), 573, 585–93.

[115] Livingston, J., *The Fallacy of Wildlife Conservation* (Toronto University Press, Ontario, 1981), 66. Lemons, J., 'The Scientific and Ethical Implications of Agenda 21', in Brown, ibid. 61, 64–7, 70–1. Randal, P., 'What Mainstream Economists Have to say About the Value of Biodiversity', in Wilson, ibid. 217, 220. Goodland, R., 'Meeting Environmental Concerns Caused By Common-Property Mismanagement', in Berkes, F. (ed.), *Common Property Resources: Ecology and Sustainable Development* (Belhaven, London, 1989), 148, 153.

in environmental management, as scientific uncertainty is, in many areas common.[116] Thus, as chapter 40.2 of *Agenda 21* suggests:

While considerable data already exists, as the various sectoral chapters of Agenda 21 indicate, more and different types of data need to be collected, at the local, provincial, national and international levels, indicating the status and trends of the planet's ecosystem, natural resource, pollution and socio-economic variables.[117]

This restricted nature of the scientific enterprise is often due to the massive complexity of the ecological interactions involved, problems of data gathering, and the impossibility of experimentation for large environmental problems (such as climatic change).[118] For example, as was noted at Prepcom III, with regard to the classification of economic values with forests and biodiversity:

Unfortunately, in most cases there are vast gaps in our understanding of these physical/ biological relationships, e.g., in the case of the forest's role in the carbon cycle and how to specify what contribution a specific area of forest makes as a sink for greenhouse gases. Without such information, the economist cannot proceed to develop value measures . . . in the case of biodiversity . . . the economist faces almost complete uncertainty. It simply cannot be known what the future holds, when another medicinal plant of interest to the chemical industry . . . will emerge and what its value will be in terms of the contribution of the forest. Thus, useful economic values cannot be attached to such potential outputs from the forest.[119]

Due to such problems, some scientists have suggested forecasting becomes so vexatious that 'ecological prediction' is often no more than a contradiction in terms. This leads to the difficulty that if a certain risk cannot be concretely evaluated or if the ecological possibilities cannot be definitely shown, then it becomes impossible to evaluate the situation in economic terms.[120]

There are also methodological problems in trying to assimilate the concepts from the distinctly different disciplines of economics and ecology. Environmental effects are inherently and irreducibly multidimensional. A single numerical index, such as monetary valuation, fails to convey very important contextual information.[121] Finally, there is also the problem that many academic ecologists are becoming less willing to talk about 'maximum sustainable yield' or 'optimum yield,' as to do so is seen by many as a way of authorizing the destruction of the environment.[122]

---

[116] See Principle 11. *Rio Declaration on Environment and Development*. A/CONF 151/5. 1992. 3–14 June.   [117] *Agenda 21*. A/CONF 187/26 (Vol. III). 1992. 14 Aug.

[118] Carley, M. and Christie, I., *Managing Sustainable Development* (Earthscan, London, 1992), 43–4. Carpenter, *supra* n. 114, 591.

[119] Prepcom III. *Third Session, Working Group* 1. A/CONF 151/PC/64. 1991. 10 July. Paras. 84 & 85.

[120] Ehrenfeld, D., 'Why Put a Value on Biodiversity?', in Wilson, *supra* n. 114, 212, 215. Hanemann, P., 'Economics and the Preservation of Biodiversity', also in Wilson, 193, 199. Jacobs, *supra* n. 99, 62. Livingston, *supra* n. 115, 66.

[121] Stirling, A., 'Environmental Valuation: How Much is the Emperor Wearing?', *Ecologist*, 23 (1993), 97, 98. Brouwer, F., 'Integrated Regional Economic-Environmental Modelling', in Hall, *supra* n. 86, 19.

[122] Lohmann, L., 'Dismal Green Science', *Ecologist*, 21 (1991), 194. Ehrenfeld, *supra* n. 109, 198.

The third major difficulty in this area is that economic values are constantly changing. The problem of fluctuating value leading to 'interchangeable natural capital' is also an implicit idea within ecological economics. Such a focus realizes that Nature's 'services' will be at times made redundant or substituted. Thus, the economic value of natural capital is only as secure as the technology, social conditions, and cultural needs which enable that value to be realized, and these can be quite fragile.[123] If, for example, markets (reflecting consumers' preferences) change (i.e. people decide the economic value of a wetland converted into a Disney complex is higher than the economic value of a wetland in its pristine state) then what was once protected soon falls out of the protection bracket.[124] Likewise, previous economic justifications for environmental preservation may become redundant upon swings within the market strictures of supply and demand. This problem is reflected in the notion that tropical forests could be saved because of their economic value as a source of alternative, non-timber products. However, by 1992 the market for wild crops and products from the Amazon had been flooded, thus offering little new economic justification for its preservation.[125] Consequently, a once common justification for the preservation of tropical forests evaporated because the economic value of their preservation changed.

Changing values can also be destructive in other ways. For example, when the whaling moratorium came in the mid 1980s, the price of whale teeth went from almost nothing to over $200 each. Likewise, as the rhinoceros lurches closer to extinction the value of its horn has increased from $1,400 per kilogram in 1988 to over $6,000 per kilogram in 1993.[126] These rapidly inflating prices are driving the extinction process.

2. THE SOCIAL PROBLEMS OF ECONOMIC CONSIDERATIONS

Economic rationales present social problems in three contexts. Firstly they are ethnocentric. Secondly, they fail to understand the dichotomy between an individual as a self-interested individual and an individual as a member of a community. Finally, people are not used to valuing the environment in a social context.

Dealing with the first issue, it can be seen that value is something that is determined differently by each culture. In this sense the economic viewpoint is noto-

---

[123] Serafy, S. E., 'The Environment as Capital', in Costanza, R. (ed.), *Ecological Economics: The Science and Management of Sustainability* (Colombia University Press, New York, 1991), 168, 175. Holland, A., 'Natural Capital', in Attfield, R. (ed.), *Philosophy and the Natural Environment* (Cambridge University Press, Cambridge, 1994).

[124] O'Neill, *supra* n. 73, 76–81.

[125] Monbiot, G., 'Supplying the Demand', *Guardian*, 23 Mar. 1992, 27. Ashford, J., 'Brazil Nuts Crumble', *BBC Wildlife* 11:2 (1993), 59.

[126] Environmental Investigation Agency, *CITES: Enforcement Not Extinction* (London, 1995), 26–7. Day, D., *The Whale War* (London, 1987), 141. Ehrenfeld, *supra* n. 109, 202.

riously colour blind in that it recognizes the cost-benefit relation with extreme clarity, but it is incapable of perceiving other dimensions of cultural and social reality.[127] Thus, resource accounting is highly ethnocentric since many indigenous groups have a relationship with the environment which is not based on economic considerations at all. As was noted in Prepcom III in the run-up to UNCED on the negotiations on forests:

It should be pointed out, however, that decisions concerning the use of forests, are not necessarily made on the basis of a comparison of costs and benefits using traditional economic science approaches. Rather, a great number of political, social, cultural and religious factors enter the picture.[128]

A good example of the other factors at play and the ethnocentric basis of economic valuation can be seen with the statement by the chief of one of the principal bands of the northern Blackfeet who stated upon being asked to sell the tribe's land:

Our land is more valuable than your money. It will last forever. It will not perish by the flames of fire . . . we cannot sell the lives of men and animals, therefore we cannot sell this land. It was put here for us by the Great Spirit and we cannot sell it because it does not belong to us . . .[129]

To ask these people how much they are willing to pay to protect the environment or how much they are willing to accept to destroy it, is a pointless question, as they deal with the environment outside of economic equations.[130] This is because the outlook of these people is incompatible with Western neoclassical economic analysis.

Economic ethnocentricity can also be seen in how economic valuation and CBA is dependent upon the existence of a political consensus within society concerning the requisite values involved.[131] Specifically, it is built around the primacy of the self-interested atomistic individual. However, many communities

---

[127] Norgaard, R., *Development Betrayed* (Routledge, London, 1994), 122–35. Redclift, M., 'Sustainable Development and Popular Participation: A Framework for Analysis', in Ghai, D. and Vivian, J. (eds.), *Grassroots Environmental Action: Peoples Participation in Sustainable Development* (London, Routledge, 1992), 23, 27. Redclift, M., 'Environmental Economics, Policy Consensus and Political Empowerment', in Turner, R. K., *Sustainable Environmental Economics: Management, Principles and Practice* (Belhaven, London, 1993), 106, 110. Redclift, *supra* n. 86, 16. Lohmann, L., 'Resisting Green Globalism', in Sachs, *supra* n. 112, 164. Sachs, W., 'The Economists' Prejudices', in Ekins, *supra* n. 87, 5, 6.

[128] Para. 81, Prepcom III; *supra* n.119.

[129] Chief of Northern Blackfeet, in McLuhan, T. C. (ed.), *Touch the Earth* (Abacus, London, 1971), 129.

[130] As the editors of the *Ecologist* stated, 'For them, the notion that cost-benefit analysis might be an aid to decision making could only be a joke', *Ecologist*; 'Whose Common Future?', *Ecologist*, 22 (1992), 174–8. See also Brazier, C., 'The Economist's Blind Eye', *New Internationalist*, 232 (1992), 15, 16. Sachs, *supra* n. 127, 5–6, 8, 10.

[131] Mishan, E., 'How Valid are Economic Evaluations of Allocative Changes?', *Journal of Economic Issues* 14 (1980), 29–47.

do not deal as a group of individuals. Their decisions are reached by a process of consensus, not through a mass of individual opinions tallied up.[132]

Working in a more contemporary Western context, it can be seen that economic rationales present a problem with the dichotomy of social placement of the modern citizen. This is because people are not accustomed to valuing the environment as they do other commodities in the market-place and public environmental goods are not commodities. Since they are not traded in markets and they are not consumed individually, their value is appreciated collectively. This leads to a fundamental division between the individual as a self-interested consumer, and an individual as a member of a community, whose objectives may differ. The problem is that the idea that social phenomena are based solely on ideas of 'economic man' and 'social rationality' as determined by economic theory is wholly unconvincing. People pursue both economic self-interest and wider social interests and these interests do not always coincide.[133] For example, many individuals will act for environmental protection on a collective basis (i.e. arguing for overall limitations in car numbers) yet act against this objective on a personal basis (i.e. continue to use their own car).[134]

In social situations people are often faced with a choice between the lower and higher considerations, or in other words, between concern for themselves and concern for others. This choice is often present, although it is more acute and critical in some situations. The distinct difficulty that arises from this choice if individuals choose only to follow their own direct self-interest is that many goals which society seeks to achieve need to sometimes transcend the direct self-interests of individuals.

Such a statement does not represent a radically communitarian proposition. Indeed, even the most staunch advocates of the self-interest position recognize that people often do operate beyond the mere recognition of pure individualistic self-interest. This, of course, is in contrast to the alleged driving factors of the rationale for the self-interest position. In fact, Adam Smith missed a fundamental point in his own argument about self-interest (and the invisible hand), as illustrated with his analogy of the butcher, brewer, and baker, all pursuing their own self-interest, which is believed to be beneficial to all. The point that Adam Smith overlooked was that if self-interest was the only motivation, then why should they not cheat each other, as they could probably benefit individually even more?

---

[132] Ecologist, *supra* n. 130, 178. Norgaard, *supra* n. 127, 122–5, 131–2.

[133] Pearce, D. and Turner, K., *The Economics of Natural Resources and the Environment* (Harvester, Hempstead, 1990), 11–12. Svedin, H., 'Economic and Ecological Theory: Differences and Similarities', in Hall, *supra* n. 86, 31, 32. Etzioni, A., 'The I and We Paradigm', in Ekins, *supra* n. 87, 48, 50–3. Norgaard, *supra* n. 127, 131–3. O'Neill, *supra* n. 73, 171–4. Sagoff, M., 'Technological Risk: A Budget of Distinctions', in Cooper, D. and Palmer, J. A. (eds.), *The Environment in Question* (Routledge, London, 1992), 195, 198–201. Sagoff, *supra* n. 73, 283, 304. Peterson, J. J. and T. R., 'A Rhetorical Critique of Non-Market Economic Valuations for Natural Resources', *Environmental Values*, 2 (1993), 47, 58–9.

[134] Hanemann, *supra* n. 120, 193, 194.

The saving grace is supposed to be the invisible hand of competition. Yet often competition does not exist. Smith's other caveat on the operation of the free market—'that they do not violate the laws of justice'[135]—also implies the existence of factors beyond pure, individualized self-interest. These are social objectives that may be at loggerheads with economic self-interest. A prime example of this is found with environmental protection.[136] As Michael Jacobs explained:

In the one case, as consumers, people's behaviour is individualistic and self-interested; in the other, as citizens, it has at least the opportunity to acknowledge wider interests and values.[137]

Therefore, as people make different decisions when working collectively from those they make individually, the decision on how to use the environment is a political one based on consensus, not an individual one based on the mass aggregate of economic wants. In the political process, the matter is discussed in the open, the consequences are made clear, and collective decisions are enforced through collective actions.[138]

A third interrelated difficulty in this area is that value is relative to the starting point of the discussion. If someone is asked what they would be willing to pay: 'I have no idea' is probably the most honest answer possible. This answer is probable because the average person has very little idea of how to value a natural environment.[139] Likewise, people are unaccustomed to the idea of paying to keep developers from exploiting the environment. Rather, the presumption has always been the other way around. This of course raises the issue of why should they have to pay, for example, for clean air.[140]

As respondents may have insufficient knowledge about what the environment may be 'worth', they are liable to give very random results when questioned about the economic value of the environment.[141] To avert this situation it has been suggested that respondents would react more favourably if given an economic figure around which to base their response, so that they could then choose a figure that was a bit higher or a bit lower. Yet as Michael Jacobs noted, 'This figure could be almost anything and one would behave in the same way. The resulting valuation would be practically meaningless.'[142]

This suggests not that the values generated by monetary valuations are inaccurate but that no determinate monetary values exist at all. There may simply be no figure that corresponds to the value that people put on the environment—because people do not and cannot know what it is.[143]

---

[135] Smith, Adam, *An Enquiry Into the Nature and Causes of the Wealth of Nations* (Methuen, Book 1, 1904), 257–8. See also Lux, *supra* n. 70, 80–93.

[136] Hanemann, *supra* n. 120, 193, 194   [137] Jacobs, *supra* n. 99, 215.

[138] Ibid. 214. Sagoff, *supra* n. 87, 1283, 1285–7, 1290. O'Neill, *supra* n. 73, 171–4.

[139] Kelman, *supra* n. 92, 130. Parker, *supra* n. 96, 353, 365.

[140] Jacobs, *supra* n. 99, 34–5.   [141] Stirling, *supra* n. 121, 97, 100.

[142] Jacobs, *supra* n. 99, 210.

[143] Ibid. 210.

3. POLITICAL PROBLEMS

The political problems of the economic approach fall into three areas. These involve the allocation process of the market, the equitable considerations of the market, and the democratic processes that economic rationales can undermine.

First, it is postulated that under the economic approach, in order to prevent exploitation, it must be demonstrated that the unexploited environment has a higher monetary value in its natural state than from any other possible uses. This presents a difficulty, as this use of monetary valuation can legitimize the exploitation of Nature when the use of the environment commands a higher price than that obtained by an alternative economic utility of the area, through some form of conservation minded economic use. In this way, Nature is subordinated to the choices that have a higher economic value in the market. Thus, once in the market, it is at the whim of the highest bidder.[144]

This raises a problem for although the 'new economic values' that are currently being ascertained will sometimes be higher than other competing uses, this will not always be the case. This will become more evident as environmental groups, of which the largest thirteen in the United States have a combined revenue of 400 million dollars per year, are forced to compete economically with the largest multinationals like Exxon and Mobil who make more than that sum every day.[145] Following on from this imbalance, the free market will allocate the environment to the highest economic bidder.[146]

An intertwined part of this problem is that the exploited environment, or aspects of it, can reach very high prices. For example a single rhino horn can fetch up to $100,000 (US) in the Far East.[147] Likewise, whale meat in Tokyo can be sold for up to $80 (US) per pound,[148] or a single gall bladder from an Asiatic Black bear at $55,000; a tiger skin for $2,700; or a pound of ivory at $125.[149] These sums may be larger than all the other economic values that have been created to justify environmental conservation of these creatures. Additionally, the costs of environmental protection, (i.e. $6,200 per year, per rhino) also help to detract from the economic justification for their conservation.[150] These problems

---

[144] Freeman, A. M., 'Economics, Incentives and Environmental Regulation', in Vig, N. J. and Kraft, M. E. (eds.), *Environmental Policy in the 1990s* (Washington, 1990), 145, 146. Beckerman, W., *In Defence of Economic Growth* (Cape, London, 1974), 141.

[145] Funk, 'Free Market Environmentalism: Wonder Drug or Snake Oil?', *Harvard Journal of Law and Public Policy*, 15 (1992), 511, 514. Peterson, *supra* n. 133, 47, 53.

[146] Caldwell, L., *Between Two Worlds: Science, the Environmental Movement and Policy Choice* (Cambridge University Press, Cambridge, 1990), 76. Barbier, E. W., 'Tropical Deforestation', in Pearce, *supra* n. 93, 138. Ehrenfeld, *supra* n. 109, 201. Carpenter, *supra* n. 114, 573, 585.

[147] See Environmental Investigation Agency, *Save the Rhino* (London, 1992), 2. 'Rhino Rescue?', *Environmental Policy and the Law*, 23 (1993), 15. Carew, G., 'Agenda', *Guardian*, 25 June 1993, 19.

[148] Greenpeace, *The Whale Catchers* (London, 1992), 10.

[149] Fitzgerald, S., *International Wildlife Trade: Whose Business Is It?* (World Wildlife Fund, New York, 1989), 33, 39, 65, 188.

[150] Pearce, F., *Green Warriors: The People and Politics Behind the Green Revolution* (Bodley, London, 1991), 91.

are particularly acute when combined with the economic practice of discounting which is discussed below.

This also leads to the fact that when attempting to price everything at its optimum value, then the economic approach is eventually likely to set Nature against Nature in an attempt to work out which area is the 'best' to preserve.[151]

The second problem in the political context of economic instruments concerns the issue of equity. This becomes evident because economic rationales are largely based on a broadly utilitarian outline. This means that 'distributional questions are beyond the scope of cost-benefit analysis'.[152] All the costs and benefits of a project are added up without discrimination as to whom they affect. One pound of benefit is assumed to have the same value to a rich person as to a poor one. This raises a number of issues. Firstly, why should a wealthier person's financial bidding (and subsequent choices) for the environment be given greater weight than a poor person's? There is no clear reason (outside of self-justifying economic theories) why this should be so.[153]

Secondly, this approach takes no account of the differences in the effect of economic outcomes, despite the fact that the costs and benefits of decisions are often borne by different groups. From an equity perspective, this makes CBA socially inadequate. As Barry Commoner explained:

This effort leads to politically regressive results. Because this value is customarily based on a person's earning power, it turns out that a man's life is worth more than a woman's; a Black person's life is worth much less than a White's. In effect the environmental risk is considered small if the people it kills are poor.[154]

This leads to two propositions. First, the level of value is dependent upon which socio-economic group is valuing.[155] Therefore, an environmentally and equitably perverse situation can arise which is caused by standard economic logic. For example, with toxic waste 'the expense of proper waste management in coded sites makes dumping in the Second and Third World an attractive proposition'.[156] As Lawrence Summers, the former chief economist and Vice President of the World Bank argued:

From this point of view a given amount of health-impairing pollution should be done in the country with the lowest cost, which will be the country with the lowest wages. I think that the economic logic behind dumping a load of toxic waste in the lowest-wage country is impeccable and that we should face up to that.[157]

[151] Ragsdale, J. W., 'Ecology, Growth and Law', *Ecology Law Quarterly*, 16 (1980), 214, 245.

[152] Barbour, I., *Technology, Environment and Human Values* (Englewood Cliffs, New Jersey, 1980), 167.

[153] Booth, D. E., 'The Economics of Old-Growth Forests', *Environmental Ethics*, 14 (1992), 43, 60.

[154] Commoner, B., 'Economic Growth and Environmental Quality: How to Have Both', *Social Policy*, 16 (1985), 18, 25; *Making Peace With the Planet* (Gollancz, London, 1990), 46.

[155] Burtraw, D., 'Environmental Policy in the United States', in Helm, *supra* n. 91, 289, 303. Adams, *supra* n. 75, 14, 16.

[156] Summers, L., 'Why the Rich Should Pollute the Poor', *Guardian*, 14 Feb. 1992, 29. Vidal, J., 'Drawing the Poison', *Guardian*, 23 Apr. 1992, 8.   [157] Summers, ibid.

The second proposition is that economic poverty greatly restricts the bidding power of billions of people against those who have large economic reserves. For example, when the 'bids' of the Yanomamai Indians of the Amazon are placed against those of the cattle ranchers and the loggers, the latter will easily override the former.[158] This is simply due to the unequal bargaining power of the rich compared to the poor, which in turn shows that the economic instruments which set out to achieve an objective basis for making decisions, are actually inherently biased towards those with financial capital.[159] The upshot of this is that more of the world's resources, regardless of their geographic origin, will go to richer nations and groups, than to poor ones.[160]

The end result is that people or their environment are exploited because this represents the best economic choice. At the same time, the victims are forced to accept these decisions as they need the small economic benefits that are offered to them.[161] The problem here is that those who accept and use these economic benefits are not challenging the fundamental economic inequities that force people or nations to accept the environmental devastation that will result from such 'economically logical' transactions.[162] Rather they are exploiting their economically inferior position.[163] This is because the free market is predicated upon efficiency, not justice or any other concern.[164] This separation of the economic and social dimensions is what over two hundred years of socialist and anarchist doctrine has fought.[165] Yet the new economic approach fails to reconcile or even acknowledge this.

A final problem in the political context pertains to the use of economic tools as decision-making instruments. The difficulty is that economic instruments can erode democratic considerations in decision-making areas. This is distinctly problematic as environmental decisions should be public decisions. However, economic method, controlled by experts, illegitimately divests both

[158] Goodin, R., 'Ethical Principles for Environmental Protection', and Elliot, R., 'Why Preserve Species?', in Elliot, R. and Gare, A. (eds.), *Environmental Philosophy* (Queensland University Press, Queensland, 1983), 5.

[159] Redclift, 'Sustainable Development', *supra* n. 127, 23, 28. Jacobs, *supra* n. 99, 213.

[160] Jacobs, *supra* n. 99, 32.

[161] Johansson, P., 'Valuing Environmental Damage', in Helm, *supra* n. 91, 132. Porter, G. and Brown, J. W., *Global Environmental Politics* (Westview, Colorado, 1991), 85–8. Leonard, C., 'The International Waste Trade: A Greenpeace Report', in Saunders, P. M. (ed.), *The Legal Challenge of Sustainable Development* (Canadian Institute of Resource Law, Calgary, 1990), 387, 390.

[162] Blumm, M. C., 'The Fallacies of Free Market Environmentalism', *Harvard Journal of Law and Public Policy*, 15 (1992), 371, 376. Gudynas, E., 'The Fallacy of Ecomessianism', in Sachs, *supra* n. 112, 170, 176.

[163] Ransom, D., 'Green Justice', *New Internationalist*, 230 (1992), 5, 6.

[164] See Daly, H. E. and Cobb, J., *For the Common Good: Redirecting the Economy towards the Community, the Environment and a Sustainable Future* (Beacon, Boston, 1989), 58–60.

[165] Lutz, M., 'Humanistic Economics: History and Basic Principles', in Ekins, *supra* n. 87, 90–112. Ekins, *supra* n. 87, 39–54.

the public and decision-making bodies of their responsibilities.[166] The technical basis of CBA also moves the level of discourse one step away from the under-lying assumptions which are often in dispute, while lending an air of legiti-macy to the final result.[167] This problem is compounded by the fact that although economic analysis is often disputed, the courts are primarily reluctant to interfere in economic matters.[168] Thus, the role and work of the economic expert is increasingly hard to challenge. This is not desirable as environmental issues are ethical, social, and political. They are not the sole province of economic experts.

4. MARKET PROBLEMS

There are four issues that are concerned with market and theoretical problems in this area. These issues relate primarily to the limitations of the current climate that contemporary economic orthodoxy exists within. These reflect not so much the ethical and political limitations of economic critique discussed above, rather they focus on some of the existing limitations to the implemen-tation of the new environmental economic rationales. That is, these are compli-cations that are *not* necessarily incompatible with environmental economics, as much as they are problems within the current economic orthodoxy that must first be overcome before the new environmental economic regimes can be implemented.

The first problem concerns economic capital and interest. It has been calcu-lated that quick profits from immediate exploitation are often greater than a sustained, lower use of an intact resource over a long period. This problem will continue despite increased economic values. This is due to the economic phenomenon of discounting and the logic of capital and interest.[169]

The economic term for dealing with the future is discounting. Quite simply, the weight attached to the future gets increasingly smaller, the further into the future the analyser goes. In other words, 'discounting contains a built in bias

[166] Heap, J., 'The Role of Scientific Advice in the Antarctica Treaty System', in Wolfrum, D. (ed.), *The Antarctica Challenge* (Oxford University Press, Oxford, 1988), 21, 23. Adams, *supra* n. 107, 146–7. Norgaard, *supra* n. 127, 150–3. O'Neill, *supra* n. 73, 115–18, 146–8. Underdal, A., 'The Politics of Science in International Resource Management', 'in Andresen, S. and Ostreng, W. (eds.), *International Resource Management: The Role of Science and Politics* (Belhaven, London, 1989), 253, 254–7. Stirling, *supra* n. 121, 97, 102. Shrader, *supra* n. 114, 79–81.

[167] Bern, M., 'Governmental Regulation and the Development of Environmental Ethics Under the Clean Air Act', *Ecology Law Quarterly*, 17 (1990), 539, 568.

[168] Stevenson, C. P., 'A New Perspective on Environmental Rights After the Charter', *Osgoode Hall Law Journal*, 21 (1983), 390, 393.

[169] See Munasinghe, M., *Environmental Economics and Sustainable Development* (World Bank, Washington, 1993), 35–7. Pearce and Turner, *supra* n. 133, 219, 223.

against future generations'.[170] Discount rates arise because people prefer to have their benefits now as opposed to later. Impatience causes what is known as a time preference.[171] Consequently, as we prefer to focus on the present, the future gets discounted, and the further into the future one looks, the less value it is accorded. Hence, the perceived environmental costs of future damages are considerably less than what they would be if they existed in the present.

Also relevant in this area is the concern about interest rates and their effect upon the productivity of capital. The basic observation about capital is that if an investor diverts some economic resources for investment (capital formation) rather than consumption, those resources will be able to yield a higher level of consumption in a later period than if the investor consumed them now.[172] The higher the interest rates are, the greater the value of $100 today compared with the same sum in a decade's time. Consequently, as Frances Cairncross explained:

On this arithmetic, on-term interest rates of 10% a year mean that it is not worth paying more than $73 now to avoid an ecological loss of a million dollars expected to happen in a hundred years time. Even if interest rates fell to 2%, costs incurred 35 years into the future are only half as important as those suffered now. Using such logic, governments argue that it is more important to use up oil today than to keep it in the ground for future generations; and more important to sell teak forests than to leave them standing.[173]

The same logic also argues against the long term sustainability of whaling when the argument proceeds from the basis of maximizing the return of economic capital. This is because whale populations increase at much slower rates than money invested in the bank. It has been estimated that whales reproduce between 1 per cent and 4 per cent of the total population annually, while the income from a dead whale would be likely to reap, say, 10 per cent interest in the bank. Economically speaking, it makes much more sense for the whaling industry to kill as many whales as possible, reinvest the proceeds, and thereby maximize profit. Sustainable harvesting, if it were possible, could not compete.[174] Thus, 'The

---

[170] Pearce, D. W. and Warford, J. J., *World Without End: Economics, Environment and Sustainable Development* (World Bank, Washington, 1993), 65–80. Pearce and Turner, *supra* n. 133, 221–2. Or as W. Ophuls stated, 'Posterity is therefore damned if decisions are made economically'; *Ecology and the Politics of Scarcity* (Freeman, San Francisco, 1977), 180. For additional discussions of discounting in an environmental context, see Splash, C. L., 'Economics, Ethics and Long Term Environmental Damage', *Environmental Ethics*, 15 (1993), 117–33. Gowdy, J. M., 'Further Problems With Neo-Classical Economics', *Environmental Ethics*, 16 (1994), 161, 167. Pearce, *supra* n. 91, 6–10, 132–52. Goodin, *supra* n. 89, 66–72.

[171] Gowdy, ibid. 166–9. Splash, ibid. 118–21. Goodin, ibid. 68–70. O'Neill, *supra* n. 73, 47–51, 59–61.

[172] Pearce and Turner, *supra* n. 133, 213, 218–19.

[173] Cairncross, F., *Costing the Earth* (Economist Books, London, 1991), 32. Pearce, *supra* n. 91, 133.

[174] McGonigle, M., 'The Economising of Ecology: Why Big, Rare Whales Still Die', *Ecology Law Quarterly*, 12 (1980), 120, 122–3. Clark, A., 'The Economics of Over-exploitation', in Hardin, G. (ed.), *Managing the Commons* (Freeman, San Francisco, 1977). Ehrlich, P., 'Will Economists Learn to Respect Mother Nature?', *Business and Society Review*, (1989), 60–3.

economic incentives for conservation of such resources may be quite minimal, as far as the commercial industry is concerned'.[175] The same logic of these examples extends across to all environmental resources that reproduce or take longer to mature than set interest rates.[176] For example, forests that are anything but fast growing make no economic sense at all. This is because young forests add wood at a comparatively high annual rate, up to approximately one hundred years of age. To maximize the amount of woody material for human use, from an economic standpoint, old-growth forests should be harvested and converted to managed, even-aged forests that are harvested every sixty to one hundred years, as opposed to every thousand years.[177]

The second major area of concern with environmental economics and the current prevailing economic logic, concerns those involved in the economic valuations of the environment and those not so involved. This difficulty applies not only to future generations, but also to geographically distant people who will be affected in the present by current decisions. For example, the Scandinavians should be surveyed to find out their opinion about the economic efficiency of the British energy/acid rain policy. Yet this does not, and will not, happen.[178] Political realities and economic theories show that uneven weight is given to different interests. For example, as was noted at Prepcom III in the run-up to UNCED on the issue of forestry:

One major problem in calculating a comprehensive value of forests is that the costs and benefits linked to this resource are not necessarily charged to or received by the same people. For example, firewood, wildlife and medicinal plants may benefit the local dwellers while hardwood logs will have more attractive markets far away from the forest. At the same time the greenhouse gas storage capacity of a forest will play an important role perceived mainly at a global level while it has little importance, if any to the local farmer. Its role as regulator of the water cycle will be of higher interest to the farmer in the lowlands than to the one in the highlands. The value of forests and their products also varies according to the cultural and market values and strongly depends on their relative geographical location.[179]

Economic valuations of the environment are also myopic in their concentration on only current generations.[180] This presents a special problem for long-term environmental problems such as toxic and nuclear waste.[181] The conclusion here

[175] Greenpeace, *supra* n. 148, 2. See the Norwegian economic argument in the same document at 13.

[176] Helliwell, C., 'Discount Rates and Environmental Conservation', *Environmental Conservation*, 2 (1975), 199, 205. Sargent, C. and Bass, S. 'The Future Shape of Forests', in Holmberg, J. (ed.), *Policies for a Small Planet* (Earthscan, London, 1992), 295, 306.

[177] Hardin, G., 'Why Plant A Redwood', in Miller, F. (ed.), *Living In The Environment* (London, 1975), 154. Evernden, *supra* n. 110, 16. Booth, *supra* n. 153, 43, 45.

[178] Jacobs, *supra* n. 99, 65–70.

[179] Prepcom III. *Supra* n. 119, para. 78. See also para. 81.

[180] Pearce and Turner, *supra* n. 133, 20–3.

[181] See pages 112–14 of this book.

for economic rationales is that if interests are sufficiently distant in a geographical or temporal sense, then they will not appear within a CBA, and will consequently be excluded from the decision-making process.[182]

The third problem in this area is that environmental economics are dependent upon two factors. The first assumption is that the free market works perfectly and that alternative uses are not subsidized to the point that they become more attractive options.[183] Such economic subsidies do, as the World Commission on Environment and Development noted, 'dilute the pressure to conserve resources'.[184] The example of tax credits being given in Brazil in the 1980s, which made it economically beneficial to clear rain forest, illustrate the point well.[185] Likewise the 'consistently and drastically undercharged' loggers currently operating within Malaysia represent another example of this.[186] These examples illustrate how the market has been distorted so that uneconomic choices have gained precedence over true economic costs that should lean towards environmental protection.[187] Such distortions often represent distinct political choices, and to attempt to change them to incorporate correct economic pricing would invoke what the Commission on Global Governance classified as 'considerable political difficulties'.[188]

The theory of the free market also works on the assumption that all competitors have perfect information about the goods and services on offer, so that they are able to make fully rational choices. However, this is predominantly not the case. Hence the market is distorted and perfect competition through the provision of relevant information needed to make economically rational choices does not exist.[189]

The second assumption about the new economic values for the environment is that governments will recognize these as legitimate costs and pay them.

---

[182]   Tribe, L., 'Trial By Mathematics: Precision and Ritual In Legal Process', *Harvard Law Review*, 84 (1971), 1361.

[183]   Flevares, *supra* n. 77, 2039, 2055. Barbier, E., 'Economic Policy and Sustainable Natural Resource Management', in Holmberg, *supra* n. 176, 65, 70, 71, 76. Goodland, *supra* n. 115, 148, 152.

[184]   World Commission, *supra* n. 104, 222.

[185]   Mahar, D. J., 'Fiscal Incentives For Regional Development: A Case Study of the Western Amazonian Basin', *Journal of Interamerican Studies and World Affairs*, 18 (1976), 357–8. Fearnside, P. M., 'Practical Targets For Sustainability in Amazonia.', in Polunin, N. and Burnett, J. H. (eds.), *Maintenance of the Biosphere: Proceedings of the Third International Conference on Environment Future* (Edinburgh University Press, Edinburgh, 1990), 167–73. Cairncross, *supra* n. 173, 70. Note, that this practice has been reintroduced to Brazil. See Ghazi, P., 'U.K. Imports Hasten Ruin of Rainforest', *Observer*, 5 June 1994, 15.

[186]   World Bank, *Malaysia: Forestry Subsector Report* (Oxford University Press, Oxford, 1992), 13.

[187]   Pearce, D., 'The Global Commons', in Pearce, *supra* n. 93, 11, 27. Barbier, E., 'Tropical Deforestation', also in *Blueprint Two* 138, 157.

[188]   The Commission on Global Governance, *Our Global Neighbourhood* (Oxford University Press, Oxford, 1995), 212.

[189]   Ekins, P., 'Towards a Progressive Market', in Ekins, *supra* n. 19, 322–6. Gowdy, *supra* n. 170, 169–70.

However, this is not always the case. For example, the United States refused to accept that the rain forests provided a 'carbon absorption service' that was worthy of compensation at the 1992 Earth Summit.[190] Likewise despite the calculated 3.2 billion dollars existence value of the tropical rain forest, actually collecting the $8 for every person in Northern countries and giving it to the Southern countries is hugely problematic.

The fourth problem in this area is that, just as the market is manipulated, so too can be economic rationales. In this sense, the hope that economic rationales are founded upon full and complete objective knowledge is not always the case. They are often manipulated by exploiting certain areas such as scientific uncertainty.[191] The highly political settings that these decisions are made within can also lead to a desire to manipulate supposedly value free decisions. This, of course, is exactly the opposite of what an objective assessment should achieve.[192] The final problem is that environmental economics has been relegated to the margins of the economic community. Indeed, many economists remain unconvinced that the environmental resources present a challenge which neoclassical economics can, or should, address.[193] This rejection of environmental economics is also mirrored in the fact that certain government departments in the United Kingdom have refused outright to recognize the new forms of environmental valuation.[194]

---

[190] Taylor, A., *Choosing Our Future: A Practical Politics of the Environment* (Routledge, London, 1992), 53. Vidal, J., 'Earth Soundings', *Guardian*, 3 Apr. 1992. Watkins, K., 'Trade Route of Almost All Evils', *Guardian*, 6 Mar. 1992, 29.

[191] Young, O., 'Natural Resources Policy: A Modest Plea for Political Analysis', *Ocean Development and International Law Journal*, 8 (1980), 183, 193.

[192] This has happened within such areas as the acid rain controversy. This has been documented in both the US and the UK. See Ruckelshaus, N., 'Risk, Science and Democracy', *Issues in Science and Technology*, 3 (1985), 28. Latin, H., 'Ideal Versus Real Regulatory Efficiency', *Stanford Law Review*, 37 (1985), 1267, 1332. Freeman, *supra* n. 144, 145, 149. Jacobs, *supra* n. 99, 220. Sagoff, *supra* n. 133, 194, 195.

[193] Indeed, some economists reject outright the idea that environmental externalities exist at all, and current prices within the market-place already reflect the correct price for goods. For a useful discussion of this, see Sagoff, M., 'Four Dogmas of Environmental Economics', *Environmental Values*, 3 (1994), 285–91, 294–97. Redclift, M., *Sustainable Development: Exploring the Contradictions* (Routledge, London, 1987), 39–40.

[194] Taylor; *supra* n. 190, 195–6.

IV

Religious Justifications for Environmental Protection

1. INTERNATIONAL LAW AND RELIGION

Historically, there has been a 'deep and abiding interaction between international law and religion'.[1] This was found in part through its close links with the theological elements of natural law.[2] For example, both Jean Bodin[3] and Hugo Grotius[4] relied heavily on theological considerations in their conceptions of international law. Although this continued in various guises it is now accepted that a religious influence in international law largely disappeared with the Peace of Westphalia and the collapse of the Holy Roman Empire.[5] Thus, the works of Vattel, Austin, Oppenheim and Brownlie all attempt to distance themselves from the influence of religion on international law. Consequently, in a modern context the religious interface within international law is seen to be largely historical.[6]

However, religious undertones are still evident within international law. For example, the *Declaration of Human Rights* is believed to have a parentage in modern religion.[7] Likewise, James Nafziger has asserted that:

International environmental law is rooted in basic Judaeo-Christian values, as is the concept of a 'common heritage of mankind' which has at times influenced international environmental law. . .[8]

In a contemporary context, religious influence, although much less significant in modern Western settings, remains a force through the power of both religious institutions and religiously motivated people who continue to influence both

---

[1] Nafziger, J. A. R., 'The Function of Religion in the International Legal System', in Janis, M. W. (ed.), *The Influence of Religion on the Development of International Law* (Nijhoff, Netherlands, 1991), 148, 152.

[2] Noyes, J. E., 'Christianity and Late Nineteenth Century British Theories of International Law', in Janis, ibid. 85.

[3] Bodin, J., *On Sovereignty* (Cambridge University Press, Cambridge, 1988). Nafziger, *supra* n. 1, 155.

[4] Grotius, H., *De Jure Belli Ac* (Cambridge University Press, Cambridge, 1925), 336. Janis, M. W., 'Religion and the Literature of International Law: Some Standard Texts', in Janis, *supra* n. 1, 61. Nafziger, *supra* n. 1, 155. Janis, M. W., 'Religion and International Law', *American Bar Association Journal of International Law*, (1989), 195, 196.

[5] Kennedy, D., 'Images of Religion in International Legal Theory', in Janis, *supra* n. 137, 138.

[6] Janis, *supra* n. 4, 61. Kennedy, ibid. 139, 195, 198, 201.

[7] Arsanjaki, M. H., 'Religion and International Law', *American Bar Association Journal of International Law* (1989), 195, 206–8. Nafziger, *supra* n. 1, 148, 159.

[8] Nafziger, *supra* n. 1, 148, 157.

international politics and international law. For example, the 1994 International Conference on Population and Development was careful to point out that its Action Plan was to be implemented 'with full respect for the various religious values . . .' of the countries at the Conference.[9]

The religious influence upon domestic law is more evident than it is on international law. Indeed, the politicization of theology is not an uncommon phenomenon. In these situations there may be little separation between politics (and subsequently law) and religion.[10] This can be seen with some Islamic societies[11] and even some Western societies such as Israel and the United States.[12] In these settings it can be suggested that religious ideas are still an active part of domestic cultural life, and also continue to exercise an influence, albeit greatly restricted, in international law.[13]

2. ENVIRONMENTAL PROTECTION, LAW, AND RELIGION

Religious and spiritual undercurrents have also now entered international environmental policy and law through three avenues.

First, there is the explicit recognition of religious principles within international environmental documents. For example, the first *World Conference on National Parks* in 1962 stated in its fourth Recommendation that national parks should be created because:

The beauty and character of landscapes and sites are necessary to the life of man, providing a powerful physical, moral and regenerative spiritual influence.[14]

Similar objectives were restated with the 1983 Declaration of the World National Parks Congress.[15] Religious justifications for environmental protection were also notable at the 1992 Earth Summit. For example, Principle 8(f) of the *Global Consensus on the Management, Conservation and Sustainable Development of all Types of Forest*, stated:

---

[9] Preamble. Chapter II. *Report of the International Conference on Population and Development.* A/CONF 171/13. 1994. 18 Oct.

[10] Robertson, R., 'Modern Religion and Globalization', in Robbins, T. (ed.), *Cults, Culture and the Law: Perspectives on New Religious Movements* (Scholars Press, California, 1985), 31, 39. McBride, J., 'There Is No Separation Between God and State: The Christian New Right', also in Robbins, 205, 215. Reisman, M. H. A., 'Islamic Fundamentalism and Its Impact on International Law and Politics', in Janis, *supra* n. 1, 107.

[11] Reisman, ibid. 107.

[12] Roberts, R., 'Law, Morality and Religion in a Christian Society', *Religious Studies*, 20 (1984), 79. McClay, W. M., 'Religion in Politics: Politics in Religion', *Commentary*, 86 (1988), 43. Diamond, S., *Spiritual Warfare: The Politics of the Christian Right* (South End, Boston, 1989), 62–5. Janis, *supra* n. 4, 195.

[13] Kennedy, *supra* n. 5, 137, 142.

[14] Recommendation 4, *First World Conference on National Parks.* 1962. IUCN. Reprinted in Rusta, B. and Simma, B. (eds.), *International Protection of the Environment* (Oceana, New York, 1976), Vol. 5, 2383.

[15] Preamble, *Declaration of the World's National Park Congress. Environmental Policy and the Law*, 10 (1983), 62.

Conservation and sustainable development of forests should include the protection of ecologically viable representatives of spiritual . . . religious and other unique and valued forests of national importance.[16]

Section 11.14 of *Agenda 21* (which also dealt with deforestation) reiterated very similar objectives.[17] It was also suggested with the creation of the *Convention for the Preservation of Biological Diversity*, that, 'Common religious concepts could be used to get a large number of countries united in this effort'.[18]

The second area in which religion is influencing international environmental policy is through a number of international organizations that are indirectly influenced by religious considerations. For example, the United Nations Environmental Programme receives 'periodic input from all major world religions'.[19] Likewise, major environmental lobby groups, such as the World Wildlife Fund also have strong links with religions of most denominations.[20] In a similar vein, in 1990 over one thousand prominent people from over eighty-three countries gathered in Moscow for a conference on the environment. The *Declaration* of the Moscow meeting stated that it was necessary to find 'a new spiritual and ethical basis for human activities on Earth'.[21]

Lastly, religious considerations are indirectly coming to protect the environment through the guarantees of religious freedoms, and attempts to safeguard indigenous peoples and their cultures.[22] The importance here is that when a religion focuses on the natural world, then it may become necessary to protect the environment so as to safeguard that religious practice.[23] For example, in the United States the religious freedom of American Indians has become the subject of a large amount of litigation. This litigation has in places been successful in the

---

[16] *Statement of Principles for a Global Consensus on the Management, Conservation and Sustainable Development of all Types of Forest*. UNCED. 1992. Doc. A/CONF 151/6/Rev. 1. *International Legal Materials* 31 (1992), 881, 885.

[17] *Agenda 21*. UNCED. 1992. Doc. A/CONF 151/4. Also reprinted in Johnson, S. P. (ed.), *The Earth Summit* (Graham and Trotman, London, 1993).

[18] S. Bilderbeck (ed.), *Biodiversity and International Law: The Effectiveness of International Environmental Law* (IOU, Amsterdam, 1992), 134.

[19] Gosling, D., 'Religion and the Environment', in Angell, D. J. R., Comer, J. D., and Wilkinson, M. L. N. (eds.), *Sustaining Earth: Response to the Environmental Threats* (Macmillan, London, 1990), 97. Engel, J. R., 'The Ethics of Sustainable Development', in Engel, J. R. and J. G. (eds.), *The Ethics of Environment and Development: Global Challenge, International Response*. (Belhaven, London, 1990), 1, 12–13.

[20] Daly, H. E. and Cobb, J., *For the Common Good: Redirecting the Economy Towards the Community, the Environment and a Sustainable Future* (Beacon, Boston, 1989), 376. Gosling, *supra* n. 19, 97, 102.

[21] The 1990 *Moscow Conference* included Perez de Cuellaer, Al Gore, and Mikhail Gorbachev. It is recorded in Starke, L. (ed.), *Signs of Hope: Working Towards Our Common Future* (Oxford University Press, Oxford, 1990), 158–9.

[22] *Declaration on the Elimination of Religious Intolerance and Discrimination*. UNGA Res. 1781, 17 UN GAOR Supp. (no. 17), at 33. UN Doc. A/517. (1962). Arts. 2 and 18 of the *Universal Declaration of Human Rights*. UNGA Res. 217A (III) GA Records, 3rd Sess. Part 1, 71.

[23] See *Wilson v. Black* 708 F 2d. 735 (DC Cir. 1983), at 740. See also the case of *Sequoyah* 6220 F 2d. 1165 (1980).

securing of traditional Indian lands for the practice of their religion.[24] The resulting acquisition of these areas often coincides with the need to preserve these sites in their natural condition. This implicitly leads to environmental protection,[25] which when taken within an environmental context, is helping to shape the development of the law.

3. ENVIRONMENTAL PROTECTION AND RELIGION

It is important at the beginning of this section to make the distinction between protecting the environment because of a traditional religious, i.e. theological, type of motivation, as opposed to protecting the environment because of a spiritual value system, which may be derived from philosophical, political, and ecological values.[26] Religious justifications for environmental protection in the first sense can be taken to include forms of supernatural purpose and meaning. This type of approach is a form of pantheism. Pantheism, which is associated with important theorists like Spinoza, works on identifying a religious meaning, i.e. an identification of God in Nature.[27] Despite this overlap, the following discussion concerns a generally more restricted, and therefore traditional, theological approach to environmental questions.

Religiously motivated justifications for environmental protection have deep historical roots. The religious importance of environmental protection is now recognized in most religions.[28] However, owing to limitations of space, it is prudent to illustrate only one—the Christian stewardship ethic. However, before this is demonstrated, it is relevant to display some of the background arguments for a religious environmental ethic.

The creation of an 'environmentalism of the spirit' as a way to protect the

[24] For some useful discussions of this development, see Stambor, H., 'Manifest Destiny and American Indian Religious Freedom', *American Indian Law Review*, 10 (1982), 59. R. S. Michaelsen, 'American Indian Religious Freedom Litigation: Promises and Perils', *Journal of Law and Religion*, 3 (1985), 47, 51. Gordan, S. B., 'Indian Religious Freedom and Governmental Development Of Public Lands', *Yale Law Journal*, 94 (1985), 1451.

[25] Michaelsen, ibid. 47, 51.

[26] For further discussion on this distinction, Macy, J., 'Faith and Ecology', in Button, J. (ed.), *The Green Fuse* (Quartet, London, 1990), 97, 105. Skolimowski, H., *Eco-Philosophy: Designing New Tactics For Living* (Boyars, London, 1981), 34–5.

[27] Spinoza, *Ethics* (Dent and Sons, London, 1959). For some discussion on Spinoza, see Clarke, J. J. (ed.), *Nature in Question: An Anthology of Ideas and Arguments* (Earthscan, London, 1993), 112. Marshall, P., *Nature's Web: An Exploration of Ecological Thinking* (Simon and Schuster, London, 1992), 194–213. For a general discussion of pantheism, see Wood, H. W., 'Modern Pantheism As An Approach To Environmental Ethics', *Environmental Ethics*, 7 (1985), 159. Levine, M. P., 'Pantheism, Ethics and Ecology', *Environmental Values*, 3 (1994), 121, 122–5.

[28] For the Muslim position on Nature, see the 'Muslim Declaration on Nature', *Environmental Policy and the Law*, 17 (1987), 47. 'Islamic Principles for the Conservation of the Natural Environment', *Environmental Policy and the Law*, 11 (1983), 83. Discussion of other religious approaches can be found in Wynne-Tyson, J. (ed.), *The Extended Circle: An Anthology of Humane Thought* (Cardinal, Sussex, 1990), 201–2. LaChance, A. *Greenspirit* (Element, Dorset, 1991), 138–71.

natural world has been suggested by a number of prominent figures in the environmental movement. For example, Al Gore,[29] Fritz Schumacher,[30] Rudolph Bahro,[31] Lynn White,[32] Petra Kelly,[33] and Jonathan Porritt[34] have all argued that a religious infusion into the environmental debate is necessary.

The first rationale used to justify the need for a religious environmental ethic is that a solution to the environmental crisis is not believed to be possible without a theistic basis. As shown in the first section on anthropocentricism, God was originally considered the metaphysical ground of reality. However, once his/her existence could not be proved philosophically, then humanity became the absolute value. The answer to this problem of unrestrained anthropocentricism is believed to lie in rediscovery of God or the infusion of superhuman morals.[35]

Linked to this position is the belief that new non-anthropocentric moral theories to protect the environment do not go 'far enough'.[36] For example, Henryk Skolimowski argues that environmental ethics do not answer 'the supreme questions' such as 'what are we here for?'[37] Consequently, it is asserted that while being in harmony with the biotic community is admirable, it is 'not enough'.[38] Hence, 'a truly ecological worldview would have religious overtones'.[39] This is because a religious basis would help place the planet, and all those upon it in a theologically 'meaningful universe'.[40]

[29] Gore, A., *Earth in Balance: Forging A New Common Purpose* (Earthscan, London, 1992), 238–9, 260–2; 'The Environmental Challenge: What We Must Do To Survive', *Vermont Law Review*, 14 (1990), 550, 556.

[30] Schumacher, F., *Small is Beautiful* (Abacus, London, 1973), 93–4. Spretnak, C., *The Spiritual Dimension of Green Politics* (Bear, New Mexico, 1986), 46.

[31] Bahro, R., *From Red to Green* (Heretic, London, 1984), 221.

[32] White, L., 'The Historical Roots of Our Ecological Crisis', *Science*, 155 (1967), 1203, 1205.

[33] Kelly, P. in Spretnak, C. and Capra, F., *Green Politics* (Bear, New Mexico, 1986), 55.

[34] Porritt, J. and Winner, D., *The Coming of the Greens* (Fontana, London, 1988), 233–53; 'Let the Green Spirit Live', in Button *supra* n. 26, 139.

[35] Nasr, S. H., *Man and Nature: The Spiritual Crisis in Modern Man.* (London, Unwin, 1968), 20. Bryce-Smith, C., 'Ecology, Theology And Humanism', *Zygon*, 12 (1977), 225–30. White, *supra* n. 32, 1205.

[36] Greenawalt, K., 'The Limits of Rationality and the Place of Religious Conviction: Protecting Animals and the Environment', *William and Mary Law Review*, 27 (1986), 1011, 1044–6, 1059. Darling, F., 'Man's Responsibility for the Environment', in Ebling, F. (ed.), *Biology and Ethics* (Institute of Biology, London, 1971), 120.

[37] Skolimowski, H., 'Eco-Philosophy and Deep Ecology', *Ecologist*, 18 (1988), 124–5. Foley, G., 'Deep Ecology and Subjectivity', *Ecologist*, 18 (1988), 119, 120. Note, however, that Skolimowski steers more towards a non-theistic position in his earlier work. See Skolimowski, *supra* n. 26.

[38] Skolimowski, H., *Living Philosophy* (Akrana, London, 1992), 123. Skolimowski, 'Eco-Philosophy and Deep Ecology', ibid. 124–5. Fabel, A. J., 'Environmental Ethics and the Question of Cosmic Purpose', *Environmental Ethics*, 16 (1994), 303, 304–7.

[39] Skolimowski, *Living Philosophy*, ibid. 124. Skolimowski, 'Eco-Philosophy and Deep Ecology', ibid. 124–5.

[40] Haught, J. F., 'The Emergent Environment And The Problem Of Cosmic Purpose', *Environmental Ethics*, 8 (1986), 139. Schwartz, W. and D., *Breaking Through* (Green Books, Devon, 1987). 235, 237–8, 245–6. McCloskey, H. J., 'Ecological Ethics and Its Justification', *Australian National University Department of Philosophy*, 2 (1980), 65, 72. Sessions, G., 'The Deep Ecology Movement: A Review', *Environmental Review*, 11 (1987), 107. Sterling, S., 'Towards An Ecological World View', in Engel and Engel, *supra* n. 19, 77, 83.

The second vindication for a religious environmental ethic is in the strength that is supposedly found with the identification of God or something supernatural in Nature. Thus, to pollute the Earth is to defile God.[41] This idea of God and Nature being defiled in the same act is not new. John Calvin, for example, came close to equating God with Nature, and insults to Nature were, for him, offensive to God, as the Creator and Sustainer of Nature.[42] In a similar sense other eco-theologians propose that God actually calls upon believers to improve the environment.[43] Therefore to protect and look after the Earth, is to work in praising God.

4. THE ENVIRONMENTAL ARGUMENT IN A BIBLICAL CONTEXT

The Old and New Testaments represent the Christian and Hebrew perspectives. From these, two different views can be derived with regard to the protection of the natural world. The first of these is the stewardship ethic.

There can be no disputing that the Bible states that humanity is the centre of God's creation.[44] However, the concept of dominion referred to in the passages of Genesis 1:26 and 1:28 can lead to an approach which is beneficial from an environmental perspective. For example, after creating the Earth, God saw that 'it was very good'.[45] God blessed creation[46] and creation praises or glorifies God.[47] Additionally, God's covenant is made not only with humanity, but also with 'all living creatures'.[48] These statements show that God has a continuing concern for creation and that creating is continually able to respond to God. Thus, it is noted that God saw all of creation as good, not just the human race. Associated with this is the fact that the world belongs to God and not to anyone

---

[41] Reinhart, P., 'The Eleventh Commandment: Access to Christian Environmentalism', *Whole Earth Review*, 50 (1986), 85. Sherrard, P., *The Rape of Man and Nature* (Golgonooza, Suffolk, 1987), 101–3. Jantzen, G., *God's World: God's Body* (Westminster, Philadelphia, 1984), 156–7. Skolimowski, *Living Philosophy*, *supra* n. 38, 119. Levine, *supra* n. 27, 126–7. Montefiore, D., 'Man And Nature: A Theological Assessment', *Zygon*, 12 (1977), 211.

[42] See Golding, A., *The Sermons of John Calvin* (Oxford University Press, Oxford, 1975), 560–2, 774, 776, 877. See also Scharlemann, R. P., 'A Theological Model of Nature', *Bucknell Review*, 20 (1972), 104. Cooper, T., *Green Christianity: Caring For the Whole Creation* (Spire, Suffolk, 1990), 53–7.

[43] Reinhart, P., 'To Be Christian Is To Be Ecologist', *Epiphany*, 6 (1985), 84. Seelman, H., 'Towards Ecological Justice', *Christ and Crisis*, 38 (1978), 250. Caldicott, J. B., 'A Christian Cosmology', in Button, J. (ed.), *The Best of Resurgence* (Devon, 1991), 200, 201. Schilling, H. K., 'The Whole Earth Is The Lords', in Barbour, I. (ed.), *Earth Might Be Fair* (New York, 1972), 105–10. Artson, B., 'On That Day, God's Name Shall Be One: Jewish Ethics and Agenda 21', in UNEP, *Ethics and Agenda 21* (United Nations Publications, New York, 1994), 115–18. Fackre, G., 'Ecology and Theology', in Barbour, I. (ed.), *Western Man and Environmental Ethics* (Addison, London, 1973), 116, 120–4. Haught, *supra* n. 40, 148.   [44] Gen. 1:26, 1:28.

[45] Gen. 1:21, 1:25, and 1:31. For a discussion of this, see Bratton, S., 'Christian Ecotheology and the Old Testament', *Environmental Ethics*, 6 (1984), 200.

[46] See Ps. 148:3–10, Isa. 55:12.   [47] Ibid. Ps. 104:1–3.

[48] See Gen. 1:2–5.

or anything else.[49] In other words, human dominion over Earth is always limited by a higher authority.[50] Also, the blessing given to go forth and multiply was given to all living things and not just people; thus, it could be argued that God's other creatures were meant to exist, whether they were useful to humans or not.[51] Furthermore, although dominion was given over Nature, people are also instructed to behave with compassion and justice.[52]

Additional references such as Matthew 6:28–29, which proclaims 'Consider the lilies of the field, how they grow; they toil not, neither do they spin: And yet I say unto you, That even Solomon in all his glory was not arrayed like one of these' point to the beauty of the natural world. The importance of the natural world can also be seen in other sections such as Luke 12:6 which emphasizes that not a single sparrow is forgotten, and that sparrows are precious to God.[53] The worth of the natural environment can also be grasped from a number of examples where God reveals himself through Nature.[54] Additionally, holistic instructions can be grasped from passages like Job 12:8 which advises, 'Speak to the earth, and it shall teach thee'.

The demonstrated value of Nature poses some unanswered questions, and can challenge the traditionally untouchable position of *Homo sapiens* in the cosmological hierarchy. For example, the Ark story goes beyond caring for simple human needs, whereby the survival of all species was sought.[55]

Recognition of worth can also be shown in how God instructed that the traditional assumption that the Deity wanted innumerable and continuous sacrificial animals was not to be followed.[56]

The recognition of the concept of the sabbath as the day of rest may also be interpreted to have positive environmental implications. This is because with the sabbath the ideal is to rest and enjoy rather than strive and exploit. These instructions indicate that the Earth needs to replenish, and be cared for. The implication is that although the human stay may be brief, preservation of the natural world is still required. This view coincides with Genesis 2:15 where 'The Lord took the man and put him in the garden to keep it and till it'.

Having recognized all of these considerations, a religious ethic of environmental stewardship for the Earth is suggested. This position is encompassed by the warning in Corinthians 4:1 which advises believers to be ready to be held to account as 'stewards of the mysteries of God'.[57] Additionally, in Luke 16:2

---

[49] Ps. 24:1, 19:11. Lev. 25:23, 1 Chr. 29:11.

[50] See Heirs, R., 'Ecology, Theology and Methodology', *Zygon*, 19 (1984), 43. Press, K., 'Kosher Ecology', *Commentary*, 79 (1985), 58.

[51] For a discussion of this question, see Heirs, ibid. 45.

[52] Matt. 12:11, Luke 14:5. Rev. 7:3, Deut. 8:7–9.

[53] Luke 12:6; but see also Luke 12:7 and Matt. 10:31.

[54] Acts 14:17, Rom. 1:20, Ps. 8:1, 42:4, 104:24–5, 147:15–18. Cooper, *supra* n. 42, 145–74.

[55] See e.g. Gen. 6:13–7:24.

[56] Is. 66:1–3, Amos 5:25, Jer. 7:21–3.

[57] Cor. 4:1. See also Dubos, R., 'Conservation, Stewardship and the Human Heart', *Audubon Magazine*, (1972), 21, 24.

God said to the unfaithful steward, 'Give an account of thy stewardship, for thou mayest no longer be steward'.[58] From here the stewardship ethic is created.[59]

The stewardship ethic was implemented by a number of biblical figures. The first post-New Testament Christians to adopt the 'reverential attitude' towards the environment were the early monks who entered into the wilderness and seemed to have had special relationships with the other creatures in their environment.[60] The intentions and actions of Saint Benedict a few centuries later are also believed to have been 'compatible with the maintenance of environmental quality'.[61] The form of environmentally benign stewardship offered by these early examples has been traced to a large enough number of other early Christian theologians to suggest that this was not a 'minority tradition'.[62]

Saint Thomas Aquinas, writing in the thirteenth century, despite some fundamentally anthropocentric statements, also appeared to recognize the stewardship ethic. He suggested that Nature honours God, and that, consequently, studying the world is better than consuming it. Further, it was possible to have a metaphorical friendship with various elements of the natural world. In coming to this point, he rejected an earlier perspective that any creature could be essentially evil.[63] This was actually a development of Saint Augustine's work which proclaimed that all 'created things' reflect the 'goodness of the Creator'.[64] Thomas Aquinas noticed, too, the connections between Nature and used metaphors to speak of harmony and equilibrium.[65] This idea was also explored by Augustine, who recognized the holistic nature of the Earth, in the basic genre of the Gaia thesis.[66] Finally, Thomas Aquinas also recognized the interests of future human beings, which currently forms the basis of a common argument ('the rights of future generations') for environmental conservation.[67]

---

[58] Luke 16:2.   [59] Cooper, *supra* n. 42, 41–69.

[60] See Bratton, S., 'The Original Desert Solitaire', *Environmental Ethics*, 10 (1988), 31, 34. Waddel, H., *Beasts and Saints* (Constable, London, 1949), 17–23. Wynne-Tyson, *supra* n. 28, 9.

[61] Dubos, R., 'Saint Francis Versus Saint Benedict', *Psychology Today*, (1973), 544, 559.

[62] Attfield, R., 'Western Traditions and Environmental Ethics', in Elliot, R. and Gare, A. (eds.), *Environmental Philosophy* (Queensland University Press, Queensland, 1983), 201, 211. Merchant, C., *Radical Ecology: The Search for a Livable World* (Routledge, London, 1992), 124–5. Ponting, C., *A Green History of the World* (Sinclair-Stevenson, London, 1991), 144–8. Wynne-Tyson, *supra* n. 28, 15–16, 76–7, 82.

[63] Aquinas, T., *Summa Theologica* (Burns and Oates, London, 1922), Vol. 1, Q45, Arts. 1, 3. For a useful discussion of this Aquinas, see Halligan, P., 'The Environmental Policy Of Saint Thomas Aquinas', *Environmental Law*, 19 (1984), 789.

[64] Augustine, 'Enchiridion', in Dodds, M. (ed.), *Works of Saint Augustine* (Clark, Edinburgh, 1877), Vol. 9.   [65] Halligan, *supra* n. 63, 799.

[66] Augustine, 'The City of God', in Dodds ibid. 286–7, 289–90.

[67] Halligan, *supra* n. 63, 799.

Preaching five hundred years before he was to be ordained as the patron saint of ecology, Saint Francis of Assisi was more forthright in his vision of steward-ship.[68] He tried to depose the human position of monarchy and saw all of God's creatures as equals. Consequently, he preached of an equality of all living crea-tures and that it was important not to hurt them.[69] His views of Nature and humanity rested on the premise that all things, animate and inanimate, were designed for the glorification of the Creator.[70]

From the seventeenth to the nineteenth century, Christian thought provided a solid basis for the early attempts at protecting the natural world.[71] This trend drew from a number of areas. For example, in 1691 John Ray in his 'The Wisdom of God Manifested in the Works of Creation', preached that all Nature had the primary purpose of exhibiting evidence of God's glory, and all had inherent value. He attacked the prevailing assumption that there was no other end for any creature, other than in some way to be serviceable to humanity.[72] Similar ideas were reiterated between the seventeenth and nineteenth century in Britain.[73] Alexander Pope probably represents the most well-known advocate of Christian stewardship at this time. Many of his works centred around the idea that, the more the world was submitted to human power, 'the more answerable we should seem for our mismanagement of it'.[74]

At the end of the twentieth century many branches of the Christian Church and a number of practising Christians have formally recognized the stewardship ethic. The Archbishop of Canterbury has argued forcefully for the adoption of

---

[68]   Caldicott, J. B., 'The Patron Saint of Ecology', in Button, *supra* n. 43. 316. Hughes, J. D. 'Francis of Assisi and the Diversity of Creation', *Environmental Ethics*, 18 (1996) 311–20.

[69]   Bonaventura, H., *The Life of Saint Francis* (Cambridge University Press, Cambridge, 1973), 148.

[70]   Francis, 'The Canticle of the Sun', in *The Writings of Saint Francis*, (Casa Editrice, Assisi, 1989), 21–5.

[71]   See Thomas, K., *Man and the Natural World: Changing Attitudes in England 1500–1800* (Penguin, Harmondsworth, 1984), 154–8. Glacken, C. J., 'The Origins of Conservation Philosophy', in Burton, I. and Kates, R. W. (eds.), *Readings in Resource Management and Conservation* (University of Chicago Press, Chicago, 1965), 158.

[72]   Ray, J., *The Wisdom God Manifested in the Works of Creation* (Oxford University Press, Oxford, 1958).

[73]   Bruckner, W., *A Philosophical Study Of The Animal In Creation* (London, 1768), in Wynne-Tyson, *supra* n. 28, 157–8. Clarke, *supra* n. 27, 100–5. Wall, D. (ed.), *Green History: A Reader in Environmental Literature, Philosophy and Politics* (Routledge, London, 1994), 198–9. Cooper, *supra* n. 42, 48–9. Thomas, *supra* n. 71, 84, 166–7.

[74]   Pope, A., *An Essay on Man* (Indianapolis, MacMillian, 1965). Pope, A., 'Of Cruelty to Animals', in Vallance, P. (ed.), *A Hundred English Essays* (Macmillan, London, 1950), 159. Or as William Blake said, 'Every thing that lives is Holy.' See Keynes, G. (ed.), *The Complete Writings of William Blake* (London, 1957), 160.

[75]   Shaiko, R. G., 'Religion, Politics and Environmental Concern: A Powerful Mix of Passions', *Social Sciences Quarterly*, 68 (1987), 244, 245, 258. Cooper, *supra* n. 42, 41. For an example of the 'hands on' approach of the Catholic Church, see Lynch, O. J. and Talbott, K., 'Legal Responses to the Philippine Deforestation Crisis', *International Law and Politics*, 20 (1988), 679, 680, 706.

the stewardship ethic and has suggested that, 'nature does not exist simply and solely for the benefit of humankind'.[76] Likewise, Pope John Paul II has stated, 'respect for life and for the dignity of the human person also extends to the rest of creation, which is called to join man in praising God'.[77] Extrapolating from these positions it has been suggested by certain theologians that:

The eleventh commandment is that the Earth is the Lord's and the fullness thereof, thou shall not despoil the Earth, nor the life thereon.[78]

THE PROBLEMS WITH RELIGIOUSLY INSPIRED CONSERVATION AS A SUITABLE SOURCE OF ENVIRONMENTAL PROTECTION

1. DIFFERING, CHANGING, AND FAILING INTERPRETATIONS

The initial objection to religiously derived environmental ethics divides into three areas. The first of these concerns the fact that there are often differing interpretations of environmental questions when taken from a religious basis. This is demonstrated with the contrasting view (as opposed to the stewardship ethic above) that can be derived from the Bible. The second difficulty is that religious ethics are liable to change. This leads to the third problem, that if they do change, the protection they formerly offered is no longer of any value.

Nature can have a different relationship with humankind when guidance is taken from the Old and New Testaments. For example, starting from the Fall, God declares that the Earth and all upon it are corrupt.[79] Elsewhere, plants and animals actually ascend in the Bible's moral landscape and dominate people who misbehave.[80] Additionally, the Bible condemns the worship of anything but a biblical God.[81] Blaise Pascal went on to argue from this point that, 'everything that drives us to become attached to creatures is bad, since it prevents us from serving God'.[82]

Within the Old and New Testaments, God is seen as completely transcendent from the creation. The initial downfall of 'man' was attributed to a woman and

---

[76] Archbishop of Canterbury, in 'Green Crusaders', *Green Magazine*, (1991), 6 June 1991. Archbishop of Canterbury, in Gosling, *supra* n. 19, 97, 103.

[77] Pope John Paul II, 'Peace with God the Creator, Peace With All Of Creation', 1 January 1990. Reprinted in Starke, *supra* n. 21, 158–9. The idea that 'we . . . are only stewards of the common patrimony of the planet' was reiterated at the Earth Summit by the Secretary of the Holy See, Cardinal Angelo Sodano. In *Report of the United Nations Conference on Environment and Development.* A/CONF 151/26/Rev. 1. Vol. 3. 196, 197.

[78] Reinhart; *supra* n. 41, 84. Reinhart, *supra* n. 43.

[79] Gen. 6:7, 6:11–12.

[80] See Jer. 15:14; Hos. 13:8; Joel 1:4; Isa. 10:13–19, 13:17–22; Amos 4:6–9.

[81] See Deut. 4:16–19; Ezek. 8:16.

[82] Pascal, B., *Pensees* (Penguin, Harmondsworth, 1975), 158.

an animal. The idea that Nature could be manipulated by powerful forces re-emerged in the dark and middle ages. A hatred of Nature is also evident in a number of Biblical curses. With such a collection of examples, it has been asserted by some that 'the sanction and injunction is to conquer nature—the enemy of Jehovah'.[84]

This ecologically destructive Judaeo-Christian attitude was manifested in an extreme form with the early Puritans. The natural world was viewed as a test of their faith, and as a step to the promised land.[85] This led to a view of repugnance of the natural world. Thomas Merton has explained how they even went so far as:

to regard the 'hideous and desolate wilderness' of America as though it were filled with conscious malevolence against them. They hated it as a person, as an extension of the Evil One, the enemy opposed to the kingdom of God.[86]

In a contemporary setting, many fundamentalists explicitly reject the new environmental approach that is shown by some of their brethren.[87] They retain a strictly anthropocentric basis.[88] For example, Steven Schwarzschild argues from a traditional Jewish standpoint that he is obliged by the commands in the Bible (Genesis 1:28–30) to actually dislike, despise, and conquer the natural world.[89]

Another important detrimental influence upon a 'positive environmental outlook' is also found in the nomadic lifestyle of the people of the Old Testament, and the belief in the transitory character of the world. This is a common theme throughout both the Old and New Testaments.[90] The central idea here is that the present is to be negated, left behind, or abandoned with all its problems and defects. Such an approach does not necessitate care for the environment because the believers are only here for a short time and these pastures are not to accompany the believers on their departure.

Closely akin to this belief is the view that, 'Nature is nothing more than the scenery or stage setting for the unfolding history of human salvation'.[91] For

---

[83]   Gen. 3:14–15, 2 Sam. 1:21; Matthew 21:19.

[84]   See McHarg, I., *Design With Nature* (Garden City, New York, 1969), 26.

[85]   Carrol, M., *Puritanism And The Wilderness* (Garden City, New York, 1969), 2, 62.

[86]   See Short, J. R., *Imagined Country: Society, Culture, Environment* (Routledge, London, 1991), 13, 92–3. Merton, T., 'The Wild Places', in Disch, R. (ed.), *The Ecological Conscience* (Spectrum, New Jersey, 1970), 37, 38.

[87]   For discussions of some of these positions, see Merchant, C., *Radical Ecology: The Search for a Livable World* (Routledge, London, 1992), 66, 126. Gosling, D., 'Religion and the Environment', in Angell, D. J. R., Comer, J. D., and Wilkinson, M. L. N. (eds.), *Sustaining Earth: Responses to Environmental Threats* (Macmillan, London, 1990), 97, 103, 110. Spretnak, C., *The Spiritual Dimension of Green Politics* (Bear, New Mexico, 1986), 52.

[88]   Daly, H. E. and Cobb, J., *For the Common Good: Redirecting the Economy Towards the Community, the Environment and a Sustainable Future* (Beacon, Boston, 1989), 383, 386.

[89]   Schwartzchild, S., 'The Unnatural Jew', *Environmental Ethics*, 6 (1984), 347.

[90]   See 2 Pet. 3:10, 12–13, Heb. 11:1–6 & 13:14. See also Oelschlaeger, M., *The Idea of Wilderness* (Yale University Press, New York, 1991), 64–7. White, L., 'The Historical Roots of the Environmental Crisis', *Science*, 155 (1967), 1205.

[91]   Brunner, H., *Revelation and Reason* (Switzerland, 1946), 33.

example, Karl Barth argued, the whole of creation was simply, 'a theatre of the covenant [between God and man], radically incapable of serving any other purpose'.[92] Consequently, approval is voiced to use resources, often exploitatively around them.[93] A good modern example of the application of this type of idea is found with the American Interior Secretary in the early 1980s, James Watt. He justified his desire to open up nearly eight hundred million acres of Federally owned land for immediate corporate exploitation because his 'responsibility is to follow the Scriptures which call upon us to occupy the land until Jesus returns'.[94] With such a perspective, Watt represented a very literal interpretation that the Earth was only a temporary way station on the road to eternal life. It is thus an unimportant place except as a testing ground to get into heaven.[95]

Another important influence upon the dominion perspective comes from the close relationship between God and humanity. This is evident from Psalm 8:5–8 which declares,

What is Adam's breed that it should claim care? Thou has placed him a little below the angels, crowning him with glory and honour, and bidding him rule over the works of thy hands. Thou has put them all under his dominion, the sheep and the cattle, and the wild beasts besides; the birds in the sky, and the fish in the sea . . .'

This view specifically implies that the natural world does not enjoy the same privileged position that exists between God and humanity. Thus, as Cornelius Agrippa proclaimed in the sixteenth century: 'Man is the most beautiful and finished work' in 'the image of God'. Consequently, 'He has a supreme destiny beyond the common range of other creatures'.[97] Indeed any species made in God's own image must have more importance than those in less important forms.[98] The importance of this was recognized by Saint Augustine[99] and Indicopleustus who claimed in the sixth century, that 'man is the king of all things on earth and regions along with the Lord Christ in the heavens'.[100] This

[92] Barth, K., *Church Dogmatics* (Clark, Edinburgh, 1961), noted in Clarke, J. J. (ed.), *Nature in Question: An Anthology of Ideas and Arguments* (Earthscan, London, 1993), 180–2.

[93] Gen. 1:26, 1:28–9. See also Crownfield, D., 'The Curse of Abel: An Essay in Biblical Ecology', *North American Review*, 258 (1973), 59. Cooper, T., *Green Christianity: Caring For the Whole of Creation* (Spire, Suffolk, 1990), 65–6.

[94] Brown, D., 'James Watt's Land Rush', *Newsweek*, 29 June 1981. 24.

[95] Brown, ibid. For a detailed discussion, see Bratton, S., 'The Ecotheology of James Watt', *Environmental Ethics*, 5 (1983), 202.

[96] See Sherrard, P., *The Rape of Man and Nature* (Golgonooza, Suffolk, 1987), 15, 18, 20, 24–5, 29–30, 33, 39.

[97] Cornelius Agrippa, 'On the Occult Philosophy', in Hersey, G. (ed.), *Pythagorean Palaces* (Cornell University Press, Ithica, 1976), 90–4.

[98] See Nasr, S. H., *Man and Nature: The Spiritual Crisis in Modern Man* (London, Unwin, 1968), 55–6. Clarke, *supra* n. 92, 60.

[99] Augustine, *Confessions* (Penguin, Harmondsworth, 1961), 13, 30–1, 343–4.

[100] Indicopleustus, *Christian Topography* (London, 1932). Ponting, C., *A Green History of the World* (Sinclair Stevenson, London, 1991), 144. For similar views, see Thomas, K., *Man and the Natural World: Changing Attitudes in England 1500–1800* (Penguin, Harmondsworth, 1984), 138–42.

type of idea presents a fundamental problem and is compounded by the fact that there are few relationships of equals of any kind in the Testaments.[101]

In the fifth century Augustine pursued this position and interpreted the New Testament in such a way as to hold that 'There is no legal or moral tie of any kind between man and animal'.[102] Additionally, on speaking of the somewhat vague commandment 'thou shall not kill', Augustine explicitly rejected its application to anything but humanity.[103] Eventually Augustine came to the conclusion that God was quite unconcerned about the human treatment of Nature, and was only concerned with issues involving people and the Church.[104] Likewise, Thomas Aquinas maintained that, 'it is lawful for [humanity] to take the life from plants . . . and from animals for the use of men'.[105] Aquinas maintained that the only reason for which people should be concerned about cruelty to animals, is that it may lead to cruelty against humans.[106] He believed sins could only be against God, against oneself, or against one's neighbour. Animals could not be our neighbours as they were not rational.[107] Thus the limits of morality were seen to exclude non-humans as there was no category for sinning against them.[108]

The use of the natural environment for human comfort is also in accordance with biblical doctrine. For example, Aquinas suggested 'It matters not how man behaves to animals, because God has subjected all things to man's power . . .'.[109] He demonstrated to his own satisfaction that humanity was meant to have dominion over the Earth. Indeed, it is 'proved by the order of Divine Providence which always governs inferior things by the superior'.[110] John Calvin suggested with his commentary upon Genesis that, 'the end for which all things were created [was] that none of the conveniences and necessities of life might be wanting to men'.[111] This is not a surprising position to reach, given that within the Scriptures there are a number of references which suggest that Nature is to be subservient to human kind.[112] This absolute stamp of dominion over a 'land in which they would lack nothing' came when God blessed Noah.[113] Thus:

And the fear of you and the dread of you shall be upon every beast of the earth, and upon every fowl of the air, upon all that moveth upon the earth, and upon all the fishes of the

[101] Kay, J., 'Concepts of Nature in the Hebrew Bible', *Environmental Ethics*, 10 (1988), 315. Passmore, J., 'Removing the Rubbish: Reflections on the Ecological Craze', *Encounter*, (1974), 21.

[102] Augustine, *The City of God* (Clark, Edinburgh, 1877), 31. Passmore, J., *Man's Responsibility For Nature* (Duckworth, London, 1974), 111, 199.

[103] Augustine, ibid. 30–2.					[104] Passmore, *supra* n. 24, 143.

[105] Aquinas, T., *Summa Theologica*, (Burns and Oates, London, 1922), Vol. 2, 2. Q 64, Art. 1.

[106] 'Through being cruel to animals, one becomes cruel to men.' Aquinas. T., *Summa Contra Gentiles*, in the *English Dominican Fathers* (Burns and Oates, London, 1928), Vol. 2, 222.

[107] Aquinas, *supra* n. 105. Vol. 2, 2. Q 72, Art. 4.

[108] Aquinas, *Summa Contra Gentiles*, *supra* n. 106. Vol. 3, Q 2, Art. 12.

[109] Ibid. Vol. 1, Q 64.1 and 65.3					[110] Ibid. Vol. 1, Q 96 & Vol. 2, Q 77, Art. 3.

[111] Calvin, J., *Commentaries on the first book of Moses* (London, 1847), Book 1, 96. For similar view, see Thomas, *supra* n. 100, 17–22.

[112] See Joel 1:12; Amos 1:2; Jonah 3:7–9; Isa. 14:7–8.					[113] Deut. 8:7–9.

sea; into your hands are they delivered . . . Every moving thing that liveth shall be meat for you; even as the green herb have I given you all things.[114]

Over the centuries these beliefs, and variations thereon, have led to extreme anthropocentricism and the demand for mastery over Nature. These demands have been echoed by many prominent people from Francis Bacon[115] and Rene Descartes[116] to Ronald Reagan, who argued that, 'We want, as men on earth, to use our resources for the reason that God gave them to us—for the betterment of man'.[117] This is a commonly accepted belief within Christian teachings and actions.[118] Having surveyed both of the above, Lynn White's famous thesis 'The Historical Roots of Our Ecological Crisis', concluded:

Christianity is the most anthropocentric religion the world has ever seen . . . Christianity not only established a dualism of man and nature but also insisted that it is God's will that man exploit nature for his proper ends . . . Christianity made it possible to exploit nature in a mood of indifference to the feelings of natural objects.[119]

This argument and variations upon it have been repeated many times.[120] In attempted refutation of this conclusion, it has been argued that this alleged environmentally detrimental attitude did not contribute to general human development (and subsequent actions) until recent centuries, and therefore did not influence the philosophical base for many actions.[121] A second rebuttal is that human made environmental damage was already in existence before the Old Testament, and it has continued in areas where the Old Testament is not read. Hence, environmentally destructive attitudes are not unique to those from a background of the Testaments.[122] Finally, a different interpretation exists of the Bible which was illustrated earlier with the stewardship ethic.

However, whichever way the argument is viewed, the main point taken from the biblical examples is that the student trying to resolve the question of

[114] Gen. 9:1–3.

[115] Bacon, F. 'The New Organon', in Anderson-Fulton, H. (ed.), *The New Organon and Related Writings* (Macmillan, London, 1974). See also Clarke, *supra* n. 92. 85. Thomas, *supra* n. 100. 18–19.

[116] Descartes, R., 'Principles of Philosophy', in the *Philosophical Works of Descartes* (Cambridge University Press, Cambridge, 1955), Vol. 1, 271. 'Discourse on Method', in the same collection, 119.

[117] Reagan, R., 'Presidential Address on Environmental Issues', *Environmental Protection Agency Journal*, 10 (1984), 35.

[118] Baer, R. A., 'Higher Education, the Church and Environmental Values', *Natural Resources Journal*, 17 (1977), 485. Shaiko, R. G., 'Religion, Politics and Environmental Concern: A Powerful Mix of Passions', *Social Sciences Quarterly*, 68 (1987), 244, 245.

[119] White, *supra* n. 90, 1204, 1207. For a further defence of this position, see White, L., 'Continuing the Conversation', in Barbour, I., *Western Man and Environmental Ethics* (Addison, London, 1973), 55–64. For earlier identifications of this position, see Thomas, *supra* n. 100, 22–4.

[120] Huxley, A., *The Perennial Philosophy* (Chatto and Windus, London, 1946), 120–34. McHarg, I., 'Values, Processes and Forms', in Disch, R. (ed.), *The Ecological Conscience* (Spectrum, New Jersey, 1970), 21, 24. Daly and Cobb, *supra* n. 88, 103–5.

[121] Cohen, J., 'The Bible and Nature in Western Thought', *Journal of Religion*, 65 (1985), 55.

[122] Dubos, R., 'Saint Francis Versus Saint Benedict', *Psychology Today*, (1973), 54, 55; 'A Theology of Faith', in Barbour, *supra* n. 119, 43, 46–7. Cobb, J. B., *Is It Too Late: A Theology of Ecology* (Bruce, Beverley Hills, 1972), 4. Gosling, *supra* n. 87, 97. Thomas, *supra* n. 100, 23–4.

environmental relationships from the Testaments in this area is at a disadvantage. The problem with this debate is that, taken as a whole, it is conducted at a high level of abstraction and it is probably very easy to misconstrue passages. The point is that none of these interpretations, be they stewardship or domination, can be proved to be intrinsically correct. The implication of this is that, without any theological touchstone, it is possible to argue against environmental protection, just as it is possible to argue for it with either of the Testaments.[123] This deadlock means that when proceeding from the Scriptures, there can be *no* authoritative interpretation on the relationship with the natural world.

The second objection to religiously motivated environmental ethics is found in the desire to find meaning in what is currently unknown. The problem is that as natural phenomena have been explained scientifically, former explanations vanish and any environmental attitudes which may have been attached to them may do the same. This difficulty is particularly noticeable as fundamentalist religious dogma becomes increasingly arduous to reconcile with scientific fact. For example, to maintain that humanity is unique in evolutionary terms (or even not of Nature) *and* above all other forms of existence on the planet, or to argue that the Earth was created in six days, is to base an argument ultimately on very shaky ground.

In a similar fashion, religious ethics can change and develop over time. This can be evidenced with the early American settlers, with whom the initial religious overtones of Nature that some of them possessed were overlooked as the realization of the prosperity that the natural world could materially provide (i.e. through its exploitation) became apparent. The end result is that environmental protection could no longer be established.[124]

2. RELIGIOUS HOSTILITY, INDIFFERENCE, AND MOTIVATIONAL CONCERNS WITH REGARD TO ENVIRONMENTAL PROTECTION

The ability to act against environmental interests because of religious instruction can be seen through various types of religious practice. For example, the Hebrew religion demands that the animal eaten by the Jewish people be killed by a certain method. In modern times, this type of slaughter has been classified as, 'a grotesque travesty of any humane intentions that may have once lain behind it'.[125] Nevertheless, due to its religious significance, it is exempted from the requirements of the humane treatment of animals.[126]

---

[123]   See Williams, G., *Wilderness and Paradise in Christian Thought* (Harper, New York, 1962), 4–5.

[124]   See Sagoff, M., 'On Preserving The Natural Environment', *Yale Law Journal*, 84 (1974), 234. Myers, N., 'An Introduction To Environmental Thought', *Indiana Law Journal*, 50 (1975), 432.

[125]   Shaddow, T. H., 'Religious Ritual Exemptions: Sacrificing Animal Rights for Ideology', *Loyola of Los Angeles Law Review*, 24 (1991), 1367, 1370.

[126]   See Arts. 13, 17(1) and 19 of the 1979 *European Convention for the Protection of Animals. Official Journal of the European Communities* 21, No. L. 323 (17 Nov.), 12–17. For a useful discussion of this problem in the US, see Shaddow; ibid. 1367–95.

A more pertinent example of religious hostility is illustrated by the debate over rising human populations.

Population and Theology

. . . and God said unto them, Be fruitful, and multiply, and replenish the earth . . .

Genesis 1:26–8

World population is currently estimated at 5.6 billion, and is growing rapidly. While the rate of growth is on the decline, absolute increments have been increasing, currently exceeding 86 million persons per annum. This annual increment is likely to remain constant until the year 2015. By the year 2050 there will be between 7.9 billion people (as a lower estimate) on the Earth or 11.9 billion (as a higher estimate). The middle estimate postulates 9.8 billion people within 55 years time. (*Report of the International Conference on Population and Development*. A/CONF 171/13. 18 October. 1994. Paragraphs 1.3–1.4.) This rapid increase in world population, in terms of both the exacerbation of poverty in Southern countries, and over-consumption in Northern countries (paragraph 3.25) is the foremost environmental problem.

In an attempt to address this crucial issue the *Report of the International Conference on Population and Development* recognizes in Principle 8 that 'All couples and individuals have the basic right to decide freely and responsibly the number and spacing of their children and to have the information, education and means to do so'. Paragraphs 3.7 and 3.27 request governments to establish mechanisms for effective population policies in the context of sustainable development, including reproductive health and family-planning programmes are required at all levels in the policy making processes. Specifically, it is 'the right of men and women to be informed and to have access to safe, effective, affordable and acceptable methods of family planning of their choice, as well as other methods of their choice for regulation of fertility which are not against the law' (paragraphs 7.2 and 7.3). The action plan then goes on to emphasize the importance of contraception as a method of population control (paragraph 7.9) and abortion (paragraph 7.6) where the emphasis is upon the protection of women's health, and not as a method of birth control (paragraph 8.25).

These suggestions may not sound radical, given the severity of the problem of increased population growth. However, this is the first international document that has been able to address this problem in this way.

The international importance of slowing global population growth has been hotly debated since the first international conferences in Bucharest in 1974 and Mexico City in 1984. However, at both of these events, attempts to slow population growth through enhanced family planning were thwarted. Despite the Pearson Commission in 1969, the first Brandt Commission in 1980, the Bruntland Commission in 1987, and the South Commission in 1990 all recommending that definitive measures be taken to address population growth, the problem had been avoided. The most spectacular example of this was at the 1992 Earth Summit, where despite the pleas from numerous Northern and Southern governments and official organizations, the issue of population growth was largely sidelined. Indeed, the only recognition of population comes in Chapter 5 of *Agenda 21* (UNCED. 1992. Doc A/CONF 151/4) in which any suggestion that population growth should be limited was conspicuously absent as was the suggestion that direct and effective methods of family planning be implemented, whereas the importance of 'ethical and cultural considerations' (paragraph 5.50) was enhanced.

This position, between 1974 and 1992, developed—increasingly so—because of religious doctrine, with which the Vatican has been at the forefront. This is due to its theological beliefs. (See the 1968 encyclical *Humanae Vitae* (Of Human Life) which states that 'direct interruption of the generative process . . . [is] absolutely excluded as illicit means of birth control'.) This belief places a near absolute ban on the 'artificial' interference with the reproduction process. This position was justified at the 1992 Earth Summit by Cardinal Angelo Sodano, Secretary of State for the Holy See, who stated that 'The church is aware of the complexity of the problem [of rising population levels . . . but . . .] the urgency of the situation must not lead into error in proposing ways of intervening. To apply methods which are not in accord with the true nature of man actually ends up causing tragic harm'. (*Report of the United Nations Conference on Environment and Development*. A/CONF 151/26/Rev.1. Volume 3, 197.)

In 1993, in the run-up to the 1994 Cairo Conference on population the Vatican reissued the *Veritatis Splendour* and re-emphasized its position against contraception. The encyclical went on to condemn the uses of contraception as 'intrinsically evil' and 'irremediably evil acts, per-se'. However, this entrenchment could not stall the momentum which had built after UNCED of the absolute necessity to address exponential population growth. Nevertheless, the Vatican continually tried to stall the eventual document, classifying it as lacking a clear ethical vision, the social abdication of responsibility, and the encouragement of irresponsible actions of young people. (*Statement of the Holy See*, Prepcom III. 1994. 5 April.)

Although the Vatican's positions and objections did not find their way into the outcomes of the 1994 Cairo Conference, they have, because of their theological considerations been at the forefront of stopping effective measures, i.e. contraception, being implemented to address the foremost international environmental problem.

The problem of indifference to environmental problems, as a derivative of religious views of Nature, can be seen with the influential environmentalist Ralph Waldo Emerson. For despite the influence of transcendental pantheism upon his eco-centric outlook, he was still indifferent towards the vast initial plundering of the American countryside. In his opinion the recoupable powers of Nature were a sufficient guarantee that the destruction of Nature would not lead to any form of final devastation.[127] In a more modern context, the Gaia hypothesis, when taken with a broadly religious perspective, can have a similar result. For example, James Lovelock, when explaining what is ultimately important to Gaia, does not consider problems from pollution to nuclear war as of foremost concern. He argues strongly that Gaia is not fragile and that many of the measures taken to protect Nature are unnecessary from the Gaian perspective. Thus, apart from protecting Gaia's vital organs (the wetlands, the continental shelves, and the rain forests) little else needs to be of concern.[128] This approach may lead people to a state of indifference and subsequent inaction on environmental concerns.[129]

The problem of indifference is also evident with certain schools of 'Green spirituality' such as New Ageism, which often altercates against social and political change. Rather, it tends to focus primarily upon just the individual, without reference to any exterior considerations, (i.e. environmental issues).[130] Consequently, New Ageism often does not require its adherents to significantly change their ecological impacts.[131] This leads to the Marxist argument that the point is not just to interpret the world (as New Ageism attempts to do), but to have a method to change it.[132] Mystical contemplation of the kind highlighted above will not directly protect the environment.

The third and final problem in this area concerns the motivation behind the religious environmental ethic. Here it should be noted that there is a difference in possible religious motivations in this area. For example, a truly pantheistic approach to environmental issues does not practise conservation out of simple spiritual self-interest, but rather as a spiritual motivation, inspired by reverence

[127] Emerson, R. W., *Nature: Addresses And Lectures*, (Boston, 1876), 10. See also Udall, S., The Quiet Crisis (Gibbs Smith, Utah, 1963), 48–55.

[128] Weston, A., 'Forms Of Gaian Ethics', *Environmental Ethics*, 9 (1987), 220. Joseph, L. E., *Gaia: The Growth of an Idea* (Arkana, London, 1990), 153–72, 192, 204, 217. Dryzek, J., 'Green Reason: Communicative Ethics For the Biosphere', in Gruen, L. and Jamieson, D., *Reflecting on Nature: Readings on Environmental Philosophy* (Oxford University Press, Oxford, 1994), 159, 164.

[129] See Commoner, B. in Chrisholm, A., *Philosophers of the Earth: Conservations with Ecologists* (Scientific Book Club, London, 1974), 122, 138–9. Mellor, M., *Breaking the Boundaries* (Virago, London, 1992), 45–9.

[130] See Francis, D., 'How to Survive an Attack of New Age Ideology', *Green Line*, 87 (1991), 12–13. Passmore, *supra* n. 101, 21, 26.

[131] See Bookchin, M., *The Philosophy of Social Ecology: Essays on Dialectical Naturalism* (Black Rose Books, Montreal, 1990), 11. Devall, B., *Simple in Means, Rich in Ends. Practising Deep Ecology* (Green Print, Surrey, 1990), 45. Deeson, H., 'The New Age Rage', *Green Magazine*, (1991), Apr. 1991, 40, 42.

[132] Marx, K. and Engels, F., 'Critique on Hegel', in Marx and Engels, *On Religion* (Foreign Publishing, Moscow, 1955), 11–12, 20.

for the world. This is because the identification of the sacredness of the Earth demands reverent behaviour.[133] However, most religiously justified action does not act like this. Rather, the actions that protect the environment are indirectly linked to what that religious practice can give a follower. Thus, the ethic remains primarily self-interested. For example the Pygmies of the Congo have a relationship with the forest which is based on their belief that the forest is a guardian who can be counted on to sustain and support them.[134] Reverence for the forest is thus ultimately derived from what the forest will give its children.

The overall problem here is that the environment is not respected for what it is. Rather it is respected for what it can give or can do for the worshippers or those who depend upon it.[135] Such an ideal does not attribute inherent value to natural objects, nor need the prohibitions implied by it be justified by non-anthropocentric reasoning. Rather they are justified by independent religious principles which benefit the followers of that particular faith. Views such as this can be justly described as weakly anthropocentric because the locus of concern is human values. The value that is presupposed here is instrumental value for the satisfaction of human objectives.[136] This leads to the problem of the dichotomy between inherent and instrumental value which is discussed in chapter eight. An additional concern in this instance is that instrumental value can change with the valuers, whereas intrinsic value cannot. Hence, as circumstances and outlooks change, so too can the status of the environment that is meant to be protected.[137]

3. THE LIMITED ROLE OF RELIGION IN A SECULAR SOCIETY

The final objection concerns the general applicability of religion in modern societies which are secular and seek a rational basis for decision making. Consequently they recognize that religion is a private matter that 'belongs to the realm of ideals, not to that of interests'. It follows that religious considerations, as they affect morality, should have 'no place in law making'.[138] Even when proof is difficult to obtain, it is hoped, in the words of J. S. Mill, 'to present

---

[133]   Wood, H. W., 'Modern Pantheism as an Approach to Environmental Ethics', *Environmental Ethics*, (1985), 161.

[134]   Turnbull, C., *The Forest People* (Triad Paladin, London, 1962), 92.

[135]   Merchant, C., *The Death of Nature: Women, Ecology and the Scientific Revolution* (Wildwood, London, 1982), 246–52.

[136]   Regan, T., 'The Nature And Possibility Of An Environmental Ethic', *Environmental Ethics*, 3 (1981), 25–6.

[137]   Fox, W., *Towards a Transpersonal Ecology: Developing New Foundations For Environmentalism* (Shambhala, Boston, 1990), 180–1.

[138]   Mitchell, B., *Law, Morality and Religion in a Secular Society* (Oxford University Press, Oxford, 1970), 100. Solomon, R. C., *Introducing Philosophy* (Harcourt, Florida, 1993), 423–8. Morito, B., 'Value, Metaphysics and Anthropocentricism', *Environmental Values*, 4 (1995), 31, 33–5. Watson, R., 'Challenging The Underlying Dogmas Of Environmentalism', *Whole Earth Review*, 45 (1985), 9.

considerations capable of determining the intellect'.[139] However, few, if any religions either achieve or demand this.[140] Consequently, religiously derived ethics are seen as quite inadequate for considerations concerning modern, secular societies.[141]

This archetype has been reflected in some of the new ideas advocated by certain environmental theorists who explicitly reject any imputations of the supernatural.[142] For example, James Lovelock has strongly resisted any religious overtones that have been associated with his Gaia theory. While he acknowledges that Gaia may be worthy of worship, there can be no suggestion that there is some mysterious force making it all work.[143] Likewise, deep ecology and social ecology reveal positions that can demand compliance, *without* the necessity to answer or even approach metaphysical questions. The objectives of these theories are not primarily to find theological answers, but rather to reconcile human activity with other processes within the biosphere and society.[144]

Finally, the importance of a society based upon secular values, when dealing with radical ecology, is necessary to help avert the type of atrocities that have been committed using 'Nature's laws' as justifications when holistic theories and a form of religious interfacing have been combined. This problem ranges from human sacrifices to the Gods of Nature in the Old Testament, through to the sacrifices of the individual and the greater holistic good emphasized by the Nazis.[145]

The idea that environmental concerns and deep ecology may be manipulated for ulterior reasons is becoming increasingly feared. The problems that this may present are discussed in the section on misanthropy.[146] It is because of this fear, that it is important to provide philosophical explanations of, and responses to, the international environmental *problematique* without religious overtones.

---

[139] Mill, J. S., *Utilitarianism, Liberty and Representative Government*. (Dent, London, 1910), 128. Indeed, as Mill emphasized in the introduction to *On Liberty*, the physical or moral good of individuals who choose their own path and do not hurt others, is not a legitimate concern of the State.

[140] Smart, N., *The Philosophy of Religion* (Random House, New York, 1970), 3–39.

[141] Rawls, J., 'Justice as Fairness: Political Not Metaphysical', *Philosophy and Public Affairs*, 14 (1985), 223, 225. Ackerman, B. A., *Social Justice in a Liberal State* (Yale University Press, New Haven, 1980), 103.

[142] See Brennan, A., *Thinking About Nature* (Routledge, London, 1988), 31–5, 192–5, 197. Rodman, J., 'Four Forms of Ecological Consciousness Reconsidered', in Scherer, D., *Ethics and the Environment* (Englewood Cliffs, New Jersey, 1983), 82, 85.

[143] Lovelock, J., in Joseph, *supra* n. 128, 208. Young, J., *Post Environmentalism* (Belhaven, London, 1990), 124.

[144] Caldwell, L., *Between Two Worlds: Science, the Environmental Movement and Policy Choice* (Cambridge University Press, Cambridge, 1990), 108. Bookchin, M., 'Deep Ecology Versus Social Ecology: A Challenge For the Ecology Movement', *The Raven*, 1 (1987), 219. Goodin, R. E., *Green Political Theory* (Policy, Cambridge, 1992), 40. Skolimowski, H., *Eco-Philosophy: Designing New Tactics For Living* (Boyars, London, 1981), 86. Naess, A., 'Deep Ecology and the Ultimate Premises', *Ecologist*, 18 (1988), 128, 129.

[145] See Bramwell, A., *Ecology in the 20th Century: A History* (Yale University Press, New York, 1989), 161–205. Dominick, R., 'The Nazis and the Nature Conservationists', *Historian*, 49 (1987) (US), 522. Dryzek, *supra* n. 128, 164.   [146] See ch. X 5.4 *infra*.

V

Aesthetic, Cultural, and Recreational Justifications

1. AESTHETIC JUSTIFICATIONS FOR ENVIRONMENTAL PROTECTION

A. Aesthetic and International Environmental Law

The aesthetic appreciation of the environment provides a common justification for its preservation. For example, in 1933 the *Convention Relative to the Preservation of Fauna and Flora in their Natural State* suggested in Article 2 that the signatories set up national parks 'for the propagation, protection and preservation of . . . objects of aesthetic importance'.[1] In 1962 the United Nations Educational, Scientific, and Cultural Organization issued a *Recommendation Concerning the Safeguarding of the Beauty and Character of Landscapes and Sites*. This was because:

At all periods men have sometimes subjected the beauty and character of landscapes and sites forming part of their natural environment to damage which has impoverished the cultural, aesthetic and even vital heritage of whole regions in all parts of the world.[2]

Ten years later the *Convention on International Trade in Endangered Species of Flora and Fauna* noted in its preamble that the signatories were 'Conscious of the ever growing value of wild fauna and flora from aesthetic [and other] points of view'.[3] Similar considerations are reflected in the 1972 *Convention for the Protection of the World Cultural and Natural Heritage*, which recognizes that 'aesthetic' factors and 'beauty' are considerations that go towards the definition of cultural and natural heritage.[4]

---

[1] Art. 2, *Convention Relative to the Preservation of Fauna and Flora in Their Natural State.* 1933. 1 LNTS Vol. 172 (No. 3995), 241.

[2] United Nations Educational, Scientific, and Cultural Organization (1962), *Recommendation Concerning the Safeguarding of the Beauty and Character of Landscapes and Sites*, Reprinted in Rusta, B. and Simma, B. (eds.), *International Protection of the Environment* (Oceana, New York, 1976), Vol. 5, 2398.

[3] Preamble, *Convention on International Trade in Endangered Species of Wild Fauna and Flora.* UNTS Vol 973 (No. 1: 14537), 243. 12 ILM 1973. 1088.

[4] See Arts. 1 and 2, of the *World Heritage Convention Concerning the Protection of World Cultural and Natural Heritage.* UNTS Vol. 1037 (No. 1: 15511), 151. See also, IUCN Commission on National Parks and Protected Areas, 'Categories, Objectives and Criteria for Protected Areas', in McNeely, J. A. (ed.), *National Parks, Conservation and Development* (International Union for the Conservation of Nature, Geneva, 1982), 47, 53.

The preamble of the *Convention Concerning the Conservation of Migratory Birds and their Environment* recognizes the importance of birds from a number of considerations, including aesthetic ones.[5] Comparable acknowledgements are reflected in the preambles of the *Convention on the Conservation of Migratory Species of Wild Animals*,[6] the *Convention on the Conservation of European Wildlife and Natural Habitats*,[7] and the *Convention on Conservation in the South Pacific*.[8] Aesthetic considerations are further reflected in Articles I and VII of the *Convention on Nature Protection and Wildlife Preservation in the Western Hemisphere*[9] and Article 4 of the *African Convention on the Conservation of Nature and Natural Resources*.[10]

The *World Charter for Nature* states that in 'The allocation of areas of the Earth to various uses . . . due account shall be taken of . . . the natural beauty of the area concerned'.[11] In 1987, the World Commission on Environment and Development recognized that aesthetic considerations can justify environmental preservation.[12] The 1988 *Antarctic Mineral Resource Convention* also recognized aesthetic considerations as a reason to protect the environment.[13] This principle was repeated in the 1991 *Antarctic Protocol on Environmental Protection*.[14]

The aesthetic approach, in the context of domestic public regulation, is gaining in importance in a number of Western countries.[15] Traditionally, the pursuit of aesthetic concerns within certain domestic jurisdictions was often seen as an unaffordable luxury. However, attitudes and times are changing in favour of preserving the environment from aesthetic points of view.[16]

---

[5] 25 UST 3329; TIAS No. 7990.

[6] Preamble, *Convention on the Conservation of Migratory Species of Wild Animals*. British Command Paper Cmnd. 7888, Misc. 11 (1980) and Cm. 1332 TS 87 (1990).

[7] See the preamble to the *European Convention on the Preservation of Wildlife and Natural Habitats*. UKTS No. 56 (1982) Cmd. 8738. Europ TS No. 104.

[8] *Convention on the Conservation of Nature in the South Pacific*. 1976. Apia. 12 June. In Kiss, A. C. (ed.), *Selected Multilateral Treaties in the Field of the Environment* (UNEP, Kenya, 1982), 463.

[9] *Western Hemisphere Convention*. UNTS Vol. 161 (No. II 485). 193.

[10] *African Convention on the Conservation of Nature and Natural Resources*. 1968. Algiers. 15 Sept. UNTS Vol. 1001 (No. 14689). 3.

[11] *World Charter for Nature*. Reprinted in *Environmental Policy and the Law*, 10 (1983), 30, 35. UN GAOR, Annex 2, 2. UN Doc. A/35/141/1980.

[12] World Commission on Environment and Development, *Our Common Future* (Oxford University Press, Oxford, 1987), 155.

[13] See Art. 4(2)(e) of the *Wellington Convention on the Regulation of Antarctic Mineral Resource Activities*. UN Doc. AMR/SCR/88/78. (1988).

[14] Art. 3. *Protocol on Environmental Protection. International Legal Materials*, 30 (1991), 1462.

[15] Karp, J. P., 'The Evolving Meaning of Aesthetics in Land Use Regulation', *Colombia Journal of Environmental Law*, 15 (1990), 307. Broughton, R., 'Aesthetics and Environmental Law', *Land and Water Law Review*, 7 (1972), 451, 472.

[16] For discussions of this trend, see Hunton, G. 'Aesthetic Regulation and the First Amendment', *Virginia Journal of Natural Resources Law*, 3 (1984), 237. Woodbury, S. E., 'Aesthetic Nuisance: The Time Has Come to Recognise It', *Natural Resources Journal*, 27 (1987), 877, 878, 882.

B. The Arguments for Aesthetic Environmental Considerations

Many modern-day preservation arguments recognize aesthetic considerations as a justification for environmental protection.[17] As Eugene Hargrove stated:

Human interest in wildlife is fundamentally aesthetic. Although wild animals are not straightforwardly regarded as aesthetic objects, they are a key ingredient in various kinds of human experiences that are aesthetic in a broad sense.[18]

The recognition of the experience of beauty in Nature is believed to motivate a relationship with Nature which in turn affirms moral value in non-human existence.[19] Inherent value in Nature, through the consideration of beauty, can be established with George Edward Moore's famous thought experiment where he gets the reader to compare the most ugly world they could imagine (without humans on it) and the most beautiful (again, without humans). On the assumption that the reader will agree that the beautiful world is better than the ugly, then it is asserted that an inherent value in beauty exists.[20] Such values can lead to direct environmental protection arguments. As Holmes Rolston suggested, 'people are learning to respect natural things . . . because we find a beauty we are unwilling to destroy'.[21] Aesthetics are also believed to temper reason in a healthy orientation towards the environment. Thus, for Aldo Leopold, a healthy environment was beautiful and deserved consideration for its beauty, whatever its contribution to human utility.[22]

A second theory for the preservation of Nature based on aesthetic considerations is that individual elements of the natural world are often regarded as attractive and this beauty, like great works of art, is believed to justify their continued existence.[23] It is further argued that the only difference between human and

---

[17] Paehlke, R., *Environmentalism and the Future of Progressive Politics* (Yale University Press, New York, 1989), 145, 172. Passmore, J., *Man's Responsibility For Nature* (Duckworth, London, 1974), 55–6. Austin, R. C., 'Beauty: A Foundation For Environmental Ethics', *Environmental Ethics*, 7 (1985), 197–208. Sadler, B., *Environmental Aesthetics: Essays in Interpretation* (Sadler & Carlson, Toronto, 1982), 1–3.

[18] Hargrove, E., *The Foundations of Environmental Ethics* (Prentice Hall, New Jersey, 1989), 132. See also Hargrove, E., 'An Overview of Conservation and Human Values', in Western, D. and Pearl, M. (eds.), *Conservation for the Twenty-first Century* (Oxford University Press, Oxford, 1989), 227.

[19] See Callicott, J. B., 'The Land Aesthetic', in Callicott, J. B., *Companion to a Sand County Almanac: Interpretative Essays* (University of Wisconsin Press, 1987). Callicott explains aesthetics in a holistic sense, not the 'trivial' conventional meaning of visual appeal; 157, 158, 160–1, 165–6. See also Thompson, J., 'Aesthetics and the Value of Nature', *Environmental Ethics*, 17 (1995), 291, 294–6. Note, this section of this book is concerned with the 'trivial' interpretation.

[20] See, Moore, G. E., *Principia Ethica* (Cambridge University Press, Cambridge, 1903), 83–4.

[21] Rolston, H., 'Is There An Ecological Ethic?', *Ethics*, 85 (1974), 103. Lane, J., 'The Language of the Soul', in Button, J. (ed.), *The Best of Resurgence* (Green Print, Devon, 1991), 145.

[22] Leopold, A., *A Sand County Almanac* (Oxford University Press, Oxford, 1949), 39, 96.

[23] Hargrove, *supra* n. 18, 192. Indeed, as Alfred Etter suggested, 'Animals are the ultimate art of the universe . . . we are destroying the masterpieces of creation.' Reprinted in Wynne-Tyson, J. (ed.), *The Extended Circle: An Anthology of Humane Thought* (Cardinal, Sussex, 1990), 121–2. Goldsworthy, A., 'Art in Nature', in Button, *supra* n. 21, 169. Hargrove, *supra* n. 18, 203.

'natural art' is that human art can be recreated if necessary whereas 'natural art' cannot.[24]

Others have taken aesthetic considerations at a prima facie level as a basis for conservation. Indeed, many people find beauty in the natural world, viewing natural objects, both living and non-living, with a sense of admiration, wonder, and awe. The existence of weekly Nature television programmes and hundreds of 'natural history' books capturing stunning visual images testify to this.[25]

In a similar sense, surveys show that environmental measures are supported more by the public when the species is considered beautiful.[26] From such a perspective, environmental protection is often justified.[27]

Sealing and Aesthetics

Sealing is one of the oldest forms of commercial exploitation of wildlife. Starting in the late eighteenth century, commercial sealing expanded steadily during the course of the nineteenth century, reaching a peak about 1890. By the early 1900s, so many seal populations had been depleted, with some on the verge of extinction, that the need for controls on their exploitation became imperative.

By the 1970s there were four major sealing conventions in force. Two of these were of specific importance to the sealing campaign of the 1970s and 1980s. These were the 1957 *Interim Convention on the Conservation of North Pacific Fur Seals* (314 UNTS 105) and the 1957 *Agreement* (updated in 1971) *on Measures to Regulate Sealing and Protect Seal Stocks of the Northeastern Part of the Atlantic Ocean* (309 UNTS 269).

Both of these Conventions have as their purpose the 'sustainable productivity' or 'optimum productivity' of 'seal resources'. These treaties have been highly successful in terms of the stabilization of the seal populations and the ability to achieve a sustainable take of these seals. For example, in 1982 alone, under the Interim Convention, it was estimated that 210,000 harp seals and 21,000 hooded seals could be sustainably harvested by Canada and Norway. However, in 1983 the European Economic Community introduced its first directive banning the importation of harp and hooded seal skins into the European Community. (*Council Directive* 83/129/EEC.) This move followed an extremely successful campaign to protect the seals.

The 'Save the Seals' campaign originated in the late 1950s, but was concerned primarily with sustainable harvests and the humaneness of the

---

[24] Sears, P. B., 'Ethics, Aesthetics and the Balance of Nature', in Burton, I. and Kates, R. W. (eds.), *Readings in Resource Management and Conservation* (University of Chicago Press, Chicago, 1965), 272, 273. [25] See pages 35–6.

[26] See Gunn, A., 'Preserving Rare Species', in Regan, T. (ed.), *Earthbound: New Introductory Essays in Environmental Ethics* (Random House, New York, 1982), 298.

[27] See Pearce, F., *Green Warriors: The People and Politics Behind the Environmental Revolution* (London, Bodley Head, 1991), 37.

killing procedures. However, by the mid-1960s the campaign changed focus, with an emphasis upon questions of 'morality', 'compassion', 'cruelty', 'baby seals', 'innocence', and 'luxury fur'. (See Canadian Royal Commission (1986), *Seals and Sealing in Canada*. Volume 2. Chapter 9.) Central to this very media and image orientated campaign was the fact that 'the seals were very young and very attractive; the killing took place in the open on the ice; and the killing was bloody and looked brutal'. (Royal Commission. Volume 2, 67.) The question of the sustainability of the take, despite being noted in the preamble of the European Directive could not be justified as the populations of these seals are actually increasing, and have been doing so since the early 1970s. (Royal Commission. Volume 1, 25–8.) Thus, the campaign was fought and won largely on the grounds of considerations that had little to do with sustainability in a strict sense. Rather, it had everything to do with aesthetic appeal and response. As Brian Davies, the man credited with largely stopping the seal hunts in the 1980s, said, 'The seals are beautiful, so they struck a special chord. If they had been ugly little monsters, they'd probably still be out there killing them'. (T. Sykes, 'Interview: Brian Davies', *Green Magazine*, March 1992, 31, 32.)

The aesthetic appreciation of Nature has been recorded by great thinkers from Nietzsche,[28] and Kant,[29] through to important philosophers at the beginnings of Western civilization like Plotinus with his famous quote, 'Without beauty, what would become of being'.[30] Other important thinkers like Montaigne were more vocal, suggesting that human art could never improve on Nature, who 'makes our vain and frivolous enterprises wonderfully ashamed'.[31] Likewise, as Antony Cooper, the Earl of Shaftesbury, proclaimed in the eighteenth century:

I sing of Nature's order in created beings, and celebrate the beauties which resolve in thee, the source and principle of all beauty and perfection.[32]

This genus of aesthetic appreciation of Nature reached its peak with the Romantics. This school included famous writers and artists like Coleridge, Johnson, Wordsworth, Keats, Byron, Shelley, and Ruskin who all advocated the values that could be derived from (wild) aesthetic Nature.[33]

---

[28] Nietzsche. F., *A Nietzsche Reader* (Penguin, Harmondsworth, 1977), 125–48.

[29] See Arendt, L., *Lectures on Kant's Political Philosophy* (University of Chicago Press, Chicago, 1982).   [30] Plotinus, *Enneads* (Penguin, London, 1981), 5.8.9.

[31] See Florio, A. (ed.), *Montaigne's Essays*, (Cambridge, 1892), Book 1, 219.

[32] Antony Cooper, Earl of Shaftesbury, 'The Moralists', in Stanley, G. (ed.) *Characteristics* (Bobbs-Merril, New York, 1964), 64–7, 97–9.

[33] For discussions of these people, see Clayre, A. *Nature and Industrialisation* (Oxford University Press, Oxford, 1977), 30–45, 59–63, 205–21, 313–21. Clarke, J. J. (ed.), *Nature in Question: An Anthology of Ideas and Arguments* (Earthscan, London, 1993), 142–4. Marshall, P., *Nature's Web: An Exploration of Ecological Thinking* (Simon and Schuster, London, 1992), 267–80. Short, J. R., *Imagined Country: Society, Culture and Environment* (Routledge, London, 1991), 15–18. Thomas, K., *Man and the Natural World: Changing Attitudes in England 1500–1800* (Penguin, Harmondsworth, 1984), 68–9, 257–8.

These ideals have made their way into environmental thought. For example, the *Statute of the International Union for the Conservation of Nature and Natural Resources* states:

Natural beauty is one of the sources of inspiration of spiritual life, and the necessary framework for the needs of recreation, intensified now by man's increasingly mechanised existence.[34]

In a similar spirit, the United Nations Educational, Scientific and Cultural Organization issued a *Recommendation Concerning the Safeguarding of the Beauty and Character of Landscapes and Sites* in 1962. It stated that it was important to protect natural environments as:

It is necessary to the life of men for whom it represents a powerful physical, moral and spiritual regenerating influence, while at the same time contributing to the artistic and cultural life of peoples, as innumerable and universally known examples.[35]

C. The Problems with Aesthetics as a Basis for Environmental Concern

(i) Subjectivity

Alexander Gottlieb Baumgarten introduced the term aesthetics to name his 'science of perception' in 1735.[36] However, aesthetics is not a science, as the interpretation of aesthetics is relative. Recent efforts to identify formal visual qualities such as line, colour or proportion that correlate systematically with either positive or negative aesthetic responses have been unsuccessful. Therefore, the conclusion that a particular place is beautiful or not has little to do with the tenets of any school of aesthetic formalism. Consequently, beauty is in the eyes of the beholder, not within inherent visual properties.[37] Thus as Protagoras said, 'Beauty is relative and subjective'.[38] Hume,[39] Kant,[40] Locke,[41]

---

[34] *Statute of the International Union for the Conservation of Nature and Natural Resources.* 1948. In *International Protection, supra* n. 2; Vol. 1, 8.

[35] United Nations Educational, Scientific, and Cultural Organization, *Recommendation Concerning the Safeguarding of the Beauty and Character of Landscapes and Sites, supra* n. 2.

[36] See Collinson, D., 'Aesthetic Experience', in Hanfling, O. (ed.), *Philosophical Aesthetics: An Introduction* (Blackwell, Oxford, 1992), 110, 111.

[37] See Solomon, R. C., *Introducing Philosophy* (Harcourt, London, 1993), 876–914. Costonis, J. L., 'Law and Aesthetics', *Michigan Law Review*, 80 (1982), 355, 367–8. Linder, D. O., 'New Directions for Preservation Law: Creating an Environment Worth Experiencing', *Environmental Law*, 20 (1990), 49, 57.

[38] Protagoras, in Sullivan, M., *The Four Seasons of Greek Philosophy* (Efstathiadis, Cyprus, 1982), 84.

[39] Hume, D., 'The Sceptic', in Lenz, J. W. (ed.), *Hume's Essays* (Bobbs-Merril, Cambridge, 1965), 124–5. Hume, D., 'On the Standard of Taste', also in Lenz, 6.

[40] Kant, I., *Critique of Judgement* (Oxford University Press, Oxford, 1952), 51. See also Hargrove, *supra* n. 18, 27–9.

[41] Locke, J., *An Essay Concerning Human Understanding* (Thomas Tegg, London, 1972), Vol. III, 3, 6, 11.

and Santayana[42] have also all recognized this position and consequently argued against the possibility of objective aesthetics.

The subjectivity of aesthetics in an environmental context has also been reflected in a number of domestic jurisdictions. For example, in the American case of *Metromedia* v. *City of San Diego* it was stated, 'Aesthetic judgments are necessarily subjective, defying objective judgment'.[43] Accordingly, in another American case of *Ness* v. *Albert* in 1983, it was suggested that:

Aesthetic considerations are fraught with subjectivity. One man's pleasure may be another man's perturbation . . . Judicial forage into such a nebulous area would be chaotic.[44]

The related problem to this is that not all the natural world is aesthetically pleasing. For example, Plato believed mud-flats and wetlands were, 'not . . . in the least worthy to be judged beautiful by our standards'.[45] Working with a similar idea, Aristotle defined the chief form of beauty as 'relating to order and symmetry and definiteness which the mathematical sciences could demonstrate'.[46] Augustine believed that 'beautiful things please by proportion . . . with pairs of equivalent members responding to each other'.[47] Edmund Burke listed seven conditions with which beauty must correspond, such as smallness, smoothness, colour, etc. He maintained that large objects could not be considered beautiful, and in support of his argument about delicacy, he claimed that, 'It is not the oak, the ash, or the elm or any of the robust trees of the forest, which we consider as beautiful'.[48] Others took an actual dislike to the natural world and argued that no beauty could reside within it. For example, English poet Andrew Marvell wrote in the seventeenth century that mountains were 'ill-defined excrescences that deform the Earth and frighten heaven'. In a similar sense, Thomas Burnett argued in 1681 that mountains were not part of God's creating but a product of human sinfulness.[49]

The realization of the problems associated with relative aesthetics is beginning to permeate contemporary environmental thinking and has been commented

[42]   Santayana, G., *The Sense of Beauty* (Dover, 1955), 28–9.
[43]   *Metromedia* v. *City of San Diego* 453 US 490 (1980). For discussions of this, see Williams, D., 'Subjectivity, Expression and Privacy: The Problems of Aesthetic Regulation', *Minnesota Law Review*, 62 (1977), 1–57. Sibley, F., 'Aesthetic Concepts', in Kennick, W. E. (ed.), *Art and Philosophy* (London, 1964), 351. Karp, *supra* n. 15, 307, 322.
[44]   *Ness* v. *Albert* 665 SW 2d. 1. (1983). Williams, ibid. 1, 6.
[45]   Plato, *Phaedo* (Penguin, Harmondsworth, 1969), 184 d.
[46]   Aristotle, 'Metaphysics', in the *Basic Works of Aristotle* (Random House, London, 1976), 1078 b.
[47]   Augustine, 'De Musica', in Hanfling, *supra* n. 36, 41.
[48]   Burke, E., *A Philosophical Inquiry into the Origin of Our Ideas of the Sublime and the Beautiful* (Routledge, London, 1956), 94. For examples of this idea in other settings, see Thomas, *supra* n. 33, 256–7.
[49]   Noted in Short, *supra* n. 33, 15. See also Tuan, Y., *A Study of Environmental Perception, Attitudes and Values* (Prentice Hall, New Jersey, 1974), 72–3. Similarly, Thomas, *supra* n. 33, quotes the Earl of Carnarvon who regarded trees as 'an excrescence of the earth', at 200.

on by theorists such as Jonathan Porritt[50] and John Cobb.[51] When such limitations are realized, it becomes obvious that aesthetic considerations lose something of their importance as a basis for environmental protection. This is in part because 'This argument could allow the extermination of species and ecosystems which most people do not find appealing'.[52] As Mostafa Tolba pointed out when speaking of the Northern hemisphere's obsession with African elephants, while ignoring less aesthetically pleasing species:

Someone once coined the phrase 'megafauna' to describe the hold on the imagination exercised by a few large, noble animals . . . I am entirely in favour of conserving those species by whatever means necessary. But we must not be mesmerised by megafauna alone. We must learn to look at a more representative range of species.[53]

Indeed, Tolba's statement can be justified by a brief glance at the species which are listed as protected under the *Convention on the International Trade in Endangered Species*. As a recognition of this type of problem there has been a reaction within environmental circles against the 'bambification' of Nature and a movement to base environmental considerations on other than aesthetic elements.[54] Likewise, just as the aesthetic approach cannot protect parts of the environment which are not beautiful, nor can it give guidance on the larger environmental issues which have little to do with ideals of aesthetics, such as overpopulation.

The increasing rejection of aesthetics is also moving from theory to environmental practice.[55] For example, with the American National Park service, the former pursuit of aesthetic objectives led to what was known as 'façade management' in an attempt to create 'take your breath away scenes'. This had to change, for as biological factors became increasingly ignored, a wilderness was being propagated that was artificial and not strictly natural.[56] Consequently, this position has now been rejected.

---

[50] Porritt, J., 'Comment', *Green Magazine*, 11 May 1992. Porritt was commenting upon the current debate about wind farms. For the continuation of this issue, see Smith, L., 'A Hurricane Whipped Up By Windmills', *Independent*, 25 Jan. 1992, 15; 'Tilting at Eyesores', *Guardian*, 21 Aug. 1993, 19. Engel, M., 'Gone With the Wind', *Guardian*, 11 Mar. 1994, 2–3. For a better analysis of this issue, see Fairlie, S., 'White Satanic Mills?', *Ecologist*, 224 (1994), 85–6.

[51] Cobb, J., 'Beyond Anthropocentricism In Ethics And Religion', in Morris, R. (ed.), *On The Fifth Day: Animal Rights and Human Ethics* (Acropolis, Washington, 1978), 139–40.

[52] Doremus, H., 'Patching the Ark: Improving Legal Protection of Biological Diversity', *Ecology Law Quarterly*, 18 (1991), 265, 279. Eckersley, R., *Environmentalism and Political Theory: Towards an Ecocentric Approach* (UCL Press, London, 1992), 40.

[53] Tolba, M., in Moore, J., 'The Future Looks Bad For Ugly Species Too', *Daily Telegraph*, 23 Mar. 1992, 8.

[54] Pearce, F., *Green Warriors: The People and Politics Behind the Environmental Revolution* (Bodley Head, London, 1991), 6, 42–3.

[55] Foresta, E., *America's National Parks and Their Keepers* (New York, 1984), 33, 34.

[56] Callicott, J. B., *The Wilderness Idea Revisited* (Beacon, Boston, 1991), 69. Sellers, W., 'Science or Scenery? A Conflict in Values in National Parks', *Wilderness*, 52 (1989), 29, 30, 35–8. Rowntree, R. A., 'The United States National Parks System', in Nelson, J. G. (ed.), *International Experience With National Parks and Related Reserves* (University of Waterloo Press, 1978), 91, 100–1. Doremus, *supra* n. 52, 265, 278.

(ii) Collective Aesthetics

In an attempt to avert arguments about the subjectivity of aesthetics, Emile Durkheim argued that there existed a common collective conscience, i.e. beliefs and sentiments 'common to the average citizens of the same society'.[57] Specifically, G. E. Moore came to believe in the 'common sense' of terms like beauty in the sense that all people have a common understanding of the concept in question.[58] Therefore, it can be suggested that the subjective and the objective are actually different ends of the spectrum, in that a general agreement about the aesthetic quality of most works can be reached somewhere in the middle.

However, to argue for a general collective view of aesthetics is to ignore the Marxist theory of aesthetics, which argues that aesthetic experience is socially and culturally determined.[59] This cultural recognition of the aesthetic value of Nature may lead to its protection. However, the converse may also eventuate as what one culture (or one section of a particular culture) may think is worth preserving because it is aesthetically pleasing, may well be rejected by another.[60] For example, as Waitari said of the beauty of elephants:

Meat! It was the oldest, the most true and sincere and the most universal aspiration of humanity . . . to the black man, the elephant always merely meant meat . . . the idea of 'beauty' of the elephant, of the 'nobility' of the elephant was the idea of a man who had enough to eat, a man of restaurants and two meals a day and of museums and abstract art—an ideal typical of a decadent society.[61]

---

[57] Durkheim, E., *The Division of Labour Within Society* (Allen and Unwin, London, 1933), 79–80.

[58] Moore, G. E., *The Philosophy of G. E. Moore* (Routledge, London, 1942), 83–93.

[59] See McLean, D. (ed.), *Karl Marx: Selected Writings* (Oxford University Press, Oxford, 1978), (the economics), 358–60. See also Sim, S., 'Marxism and Aesthetics', in Hanfling, *supra* n. 36, 411. Mitchell, W. J. T., *Landscape and Power* (University of Chicago Press, Chicago, 1994), 6–12, 14–15, 20–1, 118, 128–9, 132. Sobevilla, D., 'Aesthetics and Ethnocentricism', in Dascal, M. (ed.), *Cultural Relativism and Philosophy* (Brill, New York, 1991), 215–21. For discussions of the cultural aspect of environmental aesthetics, see Livingston, J., *The Fallacy of Wildlife Conservation* (Toronto University Press, Ontario, 1981), 38. Rowe, J. S., 'In Praise of Beauty', in Hanson, S. (ed.), *Environmental Ethics: Philosophical and Political Perspectives* (Simon Fraser University Press, Toronto, 1986), 45, 46–7, 177. Haldane, J., 'Admiring the High Mountains: The Aesthetics of Environment', *Environmental Values*, 3 (1994), 97, 99, 101–2. Binder, R., 'Ngugi Wa Thiong'o and the Search for a Populist Landscape Aesthetic', *Environmental Values*, 3 (1994), 47, 49–50, 57–8. Yuan, *supra* n. 49, 59–74.

[60] See Morito, B., 'Value, Metaphysics and Anthropocentricism', *Environmental Values*, 4 (1995), 31, 33. Sagoff, M., 'On Preserving the Natural Environment: A Non-utilitarian Rationale For Preserving the Natural Environment', *Yale Law Journal*, 84 (1974), 245, 248–51. Binder, ibid. 49–50.

[61] Waitari, G., *The Roots of Heaven* (London, 1958), 60. Gordon Orians also notes that 'aesthetic manipulations only appear when basic survival needs are fully satisfied', in 'An Ecological and Evolutionary Approach to Landscape Aesthetics', in Penning-Rowsell, E. C., (ed.), *Landscape Meanings and Values* (Allen & Unwin, London, 1986), 1, 10. Orians goes on to postulate that aesthetics is also related more to the function of the object which, also, is often culturally determined, 17–20. However, Morito rejects this kind of evolutionary approach to aesthetics due to the fact that 'operators of large earth-moving equipment often describe the feeling associated with levelling a grove of trees as an aesthetic experience to be valued in itself quite apart from the financial values associated with it. These sorts of values cannot be categorically ruled out as non-aesthetic values.' Morito, ibid. 35.

In addition, it has been recognized that these communal concepts of beauty will change along with social attitudes and knowledge.[62] This can be seen by simply comparing the differences in the aesthetic interpretations of Nature between the artists of the Renaissance period and those of the school of the Romantics. This introduces an additional factor, namely, that what is viewed as beautiful runs the risk of being the victim of changes in fashion. So, the aesthetic appeal of the environment may well be a passing fad.[63]

(iii) Residual Problems with Aesthetics

The aesthetic justification also runs into difficulty through risks and problems with comparisons of other aesthetic objects. Consider, if everything is beautiful, and all things should be preserved because they are such, then there is no basis for discrimination and a ranking of natural objects—from overgrown rubbish dumps, to manicured gardens to extreme wilderness.[64] Accordingly, without an objective ranking system (already an impossibility because of the subjective nature of the area) then risks of decision-making grid-lock may eventuate.

The aesthetic approach is also problematic in that saying something is beautiful does not say anything about an object as such, rather it is saying something about the interpretations of the person appraising the object in question. The problem here is that nothing can be said to be inherently beautiful as the question of beauty is determined by human perception and preference. Consequently, the concept lacks an overall basis outside humanity.[65]

Akin to this is the suggestion that the prospects of continued existence of humans or non-human Nature should not be based simply on their beauty. This is because to do so would not only be a weak criterion for general preservation, it could also be repugnant, as it could be seen as trivializing the object. Finally, as regards the argument involving the analogy between art and Nature, it should be noted that this analogy may be going too far. No one argues that all art must be preserved. The obligation can only ever go so far as to protect exceptional pieces of art.

[62] Broughton, *supra* n. 15, 451, 467. Yuan, *supra* n. 50, 70–5.

[63] Passmore, J., *Man's Responsibility For Nature* (Duckworth, London, 1974), 109–10.

[64] Oelschlaeger, M., *The Idea of Wilderness: From Prehistory to the Age of Ecology* (Yale University Press, London, 1991), 298. Hargrove, *supra* n. 18, 179. Thompson goes even further, in suggesting that if we value the beauty of Nature, we must value also overgrown rubbish dumps and other less pleasing aspects of Nature. These cannot be traded away against more pristine aesthetics as, if all Nature is beautiful, then all Nature must be protected. Thus, we will end up without a clear reason or criterion for the protection of Nature. Thompson, *supra* n. 19, 296–8, 304–5.

[65] O'Neill, J., *Ecology, Policy and Politics* (Routledge, 1993), 166–7. Hargrove, *supra* n. 18, 180. Additionally, as Tuan explained, aesthetic appreciation of Nature is often fleeting and 'clearly falls short of the authentic' as it does 'not enjoin man and Nature'. *Supra* n. 49, 93–5.

2. THE CULTURAL JUSTIFICATION FOR ENVIRONMENTAL PROTECTION

A. Culture and International Environmental Protection

'Culture' represents unique ways of acquiring, storing, and transmitting knowledge about the world. Often, these views necessitate the protection of the environment. This idea, of protecting the environment because it is culturally important to do so, is found in a number of international environmental documents.[66] For example, the preamble of the *Convention on International Trade in Endangered Species of Fauna and Flora* recognized, 'The ever growing value of wild fauna and flora from . . . cultural points of view'.[67] This kind of concept is also reflected in the *Convention on Wetlands of International Importance*,[68] the *Convention on the Conservation of Migratory Species of Wild Animals*,[69] the *Convention on Nature Protection and Wildlife Preservation in the Western Hemisphere*,[70] the 1975 *South Pacific Conference on National Parks and Reserves*,[71] and the 1982 *Declaration of the World's National Parks Congress*.[72] It was noted in the preamble of the *World Heritage Convention*, that:

The deterioration or disappearance of any item of cultural or natural heritage constitutes a harmful impoverishment to all nations of the world.[73]

Consequently, the signatories recognized the importance of preserving 'exceptional combinations of natural and cultural elements'.[74] The importance of

[66] For the importance of the protection of culture, see the *Convention Concerning the Protection of Indigenous and Other Tribal Populations in Independent Countries of the International Labour Organisation*. 1957. ILO 107. Art. 1.2 of the *International Covenant on Economic, Social and Cultural Rights*. United Nations Resolutions on the Importance of Cultural Values. UNGA Res. 31/39. 1976, and the *Preservation and Further Development of Cultural Values*. UNGA Res. 3148 xxviii.

[67] *Convention on International Trade in Endangered Species of Fauna and Flora*. UNTS Vol. 973 (No 1: 14537) 243.

[68] Preamble, *Convention on Wetlands of International Importance*. UKTS 34 (1976) Cmnd. 6465.

[69] Preamble, *Convention on the Conservation of Migratory Species*. British Command Paper Cmnd. Misc. 11 (1980) and Cm. 1332 TS 87 (1990). 15.

[70] The preamble recognizes the 'historic' value of natural objects. *Convention on Nature Protection and Wildlife Preservation in the Western Hemisphere*. UNTS Vol. 161 (No. 11: 485) 193.

[71] See the preamble of the *Convention for the Protection of the Marine Environment and Coastal Area of the South East Pacific*. 1981. In Rummel-Bulska, I. (ed.), *Selected Multilateral Treaties in the Field of the Environment* (Grotius, Cambridge, 1991), 130. Also, see the preamble of the *Convention for the Protection of Natural Resources and the Environment of the South Pacific Region*. 1986, in the same volume, at 386. See also Recommendation 4, *South Pacific Conference on National Parks and Reserves*. 1975. In Rusta, B. and Simma, B. (eds.), *International Protection of the Environment* (New York, 1976), Vol. 5, 22538.

[72] Preamble, *Declaration of the World's National Park Congress. Environmental Policy and the Law*, 10 (1983), 62. See also McNeely, J., 'Protected Areas are Adapting to New Realities', in McNeely, J. A. (ed.), *National Parks, Conservation and Development* (IUCN, Geneva, 1982), 1, 4.

[73] Preamble, *The Convention for the Protection of World Cultural and Natural Heritage*. 1972. UNTS Vol. 1037 (No. 1 15111) 151. See also Slater, R., 'The World Heritage Convention: Introductory Comments', in McNeely, ibid. 734, 735, 746.

[74] See Listing Criteria and Art. 4, of the *Convention for the Protection of World Cultural and Natural Heritage*. Ibid.

different cultural traditions and their role in the preservation of biodiversity has also been emphasized.[75]

In 1972 the *Declaration of the United Nations Conference on the Human Environment* recognized that the preservation of the environment through cultural considerations was important.[76] This view was echoed in the 1976 *European Ministerial Conference on the Environment* which recommended the conservation of natural and cultural values of the countryside as they 'satisfy the essential needs of mankind'.[77] In 1987 the World Commission on Environment and Development also recognized that cultural justifications were important to environmental preservation.[78] This idea was repeated and expanded upon in the 1994 *Program of Action for the Sustainable Development of Small Island States.*[79]

The most prominent area where cultural values, environmental protection, and law have overlapped has been with indigenous peoples. Here, a growing plethora of legislation, both domestic and international, has developed. For example, Principle 22 of the *Rio Declaration on Environment and Development* suggests:

Indigenous people and their communities, and other local communities have a vital role in environmental management and development because of their knowledge and traditional practices. States should recognise and duly support their identity, culture and interest and enable their effective participation in the achievement of sustainable development'.[80]

Another prominent example of this type of realization is encapsulated in paragraph 9 of the preamble of the *Draft Declaration on the Rights of Indigenous Peoples* which recognizes:

---

[75] Bilderbeck, S., *Biodiversity and International Law: The Effectiveness of International Environmental Law* (IOS, Amsterdam, 1992), 142.

[76] See Recommendation 95 of the *Declaration of the United Nations Conference on the Human Environment.* 1972. UN Doc. A/CONF 48/14/Rev. 1. Also in *International Protection, supra* n. 71, Vol. 1, 125.

[77] Resolution 1. *European Ministerial Conference on the Environment.* 1976. In *International Protection, supra* n. 71, 1174.

[78] World Commission on Environment and Development, *Our Common Future* (Oxford University Press, Oxford, 1987), 155.

[79] *Draft Programme of Action for the Sustainable Development of Small Island States.* A/CONF 167/9. 1994. 18 Mar. Paras. 1, 10, 40, & 43.

[80] The *Rio Declaration on Environment and Development.* UNCED. Doc. A/CONF 151/5/Rev. 1. Similar pronouncements can be found with Ch. 26 of Agenda 21 from the 1992 Earth Summit which recognized, 'Indigenous people and their communities have an historical relationship with their lands and are generally descendants of the original inhabitants of such lands . . . Indigenous people and their communities represent a significant percentage of the global population. They have developed over many generations a holistic traditional scientific knowledge of their lands, natural resources and environment . . . Their ability to participate fully in sustainable development practices on their lands has tended to be limited as a result of factors of an economic, social and historical nature. In view of the interrelationship between the natural environment and its sustainable development and the cultural, social, economic and physical well-being of indigenous people, national and international efforts to implement environmentally sound and sustainable development should recognise, accommodate, promote and strengthen the role of indigenous people and their communities.' A/CONF 151/26 (Vol. III). 14 Aug. 1992.

that respect for indigenous knowledge, cultures and traditional practices contributes to sustainable and equitable development and proper management of the environment.[81]

This form of recognition, that indigenous peoples have an important role to play in the protection of the environment, has been replicated in a number of domestic settings. One of the better examples of this is found in New Zealand/ Aotearoa.

Maori, Culture, and Environmental Protection

Traditional resource legislation in New Zealand excluded Maori concerns. This began to be remedied in 1977 with the Planning Act which stipulated that 'The relationship of the Maori people and their culture and traditions with their ancestral lands' was to be considered a matter of national importance (along with a number of other matters). (Section 3 *Town and Country Planning Act*. 1977. Public Act. 121.) This provision provided an entry point by which the courts began to slowly take a proactive, and positive interest in Maori environmental concerns. (*Huakina Development* v. *Waikato Valley Authority* [1987]12 NZTPA 129.) This drive was furthered greatly in 1991 when the New Zealand legislature passed the Resource Management Act. This Act, which completely revamped the domestic environmental arena, set out as an objective the incorporation of 'Maori interests and values and the Treaty of Waitangi'. (Ministry of the Environment, *People, Environment and Decision Making: The Government's Proposals For Resource Management Law Reform*. 1988. Wellington. 23–4.) The enhanced consideration of Maori considerations originates through four sections.

The first is Section 5 which deals with the central objective of the Act—the sustainable management of physical and natural resources. It defines sustainable management as including the development or protection of natural resources in a way which will 'enable people and communities to provide for their social, economic and *cultural* well-being'. (My italics.) Secondly, Section 6 (e) requires decision makers to recognize, 'The relationship of Maori and their culture and traditions with their ancestral lands, water, sites, waahi tapu [areas or objects of cultural importance] and other taonga. [treasures]. The third provision is found in Section 8 of the Act which requires decision makers to 'take into account the principles of the Treaty of Waitangi'. (The founding document of New Zealand, specifying the agreement between the Crown and Maori.) Finally, Section 7 requires decision makers to have particular regard to, amongst other considerations, 'kaitiakitanga'. *Kaitiakitanga* is defined in the Act to mean, 'The exercise of guardianship; and, in relation to a resource, includes the ethic

---

[81] *Draft Declaration on the Rights of Indigenous Peoples*. UN Doc. E/CN 4/Sub.2/1994/2 (5 Apr. 1994).

of stewardship based on the nature of the resource itself'. For a full discussion of this area, see Gillespie, A., 'Environmental Politics in New Zealand/Aotearoa: Clashes and Commonality Between Maori and Conservationists', *New Zealand Geographer* (forthcoming).

B. The Cultural Argument

From ancient times to modern day, cultural attitudes that concern human interaction with the natural environment have been important.[82] Consequently, it is suggested that in certain instances to preserve the environment is to preserve the natural expressions of the values of culture and history.[83] This argument that Nature should be preserved because of its importance to culture is well illustrated with the example of the American Frontier. The 'wild west' traditions, from Daniel Boone and Davey Crockett to Huckleberry Finn, all help in the assemblage of a 'lasting legacy' in contemporary American culture. Indeed, the environment has been preserved in parts to reflect the former 'Great American Frontier'.[84] In a similar sense, the British also have 'a very close cultural relationship with nature and the land'.[85] A strong national identity is forged from the idealized view of the British national environment.[86] This has developed from traditional composers like Elgar, Delius, and Holst, a strong tradition of landscape paintings from artists like Constable and Turner, and from great writers associated with the Romantic movement like William Blake who coined the line 'England's green and pleasant land', with his epic poem 'Jerusalem'.[87]

[82] See Short, J. R., *Imagined Country: Society, Culture and Environment* (Routledge, London, 1991), 28–34. Wilson, A., *The Culture of Nature* (Blackwell, London, 1992), 11–14. Mitchell, W. J. T., 'Imperial Landscape', in Mitchell, W. J. T. (ed.), *Landscape and Power* (University of Chicago Press, Chicago, 1994), 5, 6–9, 12, 14, 17, 20–3. Bunn, D., 'African Landscapes', also in Mitchell, 127–9, 136, 138.

[83] See the *National Environmental Policy of the United States*. 42 USC § 4331 (b) (4). 1989. Tuan, Y., *A Study of Environmental Perception, Attitudes and Values* (Prentice Hall, New Jersey, 1974), 100–2. Norton, B. G., 'The Cultural Approach to Conservation Biology', in Western, D. and Pearl, M. (eds.), *Conservation for the Twenty-first Century* (Oxford University Press, Oxford, 1989), 241–6. McNeely, J. A., 'Protected Areas and Human Ecology', also in Western and Pearl, 150, 152–3. Binder, R., 'Ngugi Wa Thiong'o and the Search for a Populist Landscape Aesthetic', *Environmental Values*, 3 (1994), 47, 50, 57–8. Lucas, P. H., 'How Protected Areas Can Help Meet Society's Evolving Needs', in McNeely, *supra* n. 72, 72, 74–5.

[84] Udall, S., *The Quiet Crisis and the Next Generation* (Gibbs Smith, Utah, 1988), 25–38. Leopold, A., *A Sand County Almanac* (Oxford University Press, Oxford, 1949), 177–87. Short, *supra* n. 82, 179–96. Norton, *supra* n. 83, 244–6.

[85] See Porritt, J. and Winner, D., *The Coming of the Greens* (Fontana, London, 1988), 81, 112. Sullivan, A., *Greening the Tories* (Centre For Policy Studies, London, 1985).

[86] See Clayre, A. (ed.), *Nature and Industrialisation* (Oxford University Press, Oxford, 1977), 30–45, 59–63, 205–21, 313–21. Clarke, J. J. (ed.), *Nature in Question: An Anthology of Ideas and Arguments* (Earthscan, London, 1993), 142–4. Short, *supra* n. 82–4, 57–90.

[87] See Marshall, P., *Nature's Web: An Exploration of Ecological Thinking* (Simon and Schuster, London, 1992), 274–7. Helsinger, E., 'Turner and the Representation of England', in Mitchell, *supra* n. 82, 103–19. Short, *supra* n. 82, 30–5. The importance of the Romantic movement to the cultural importance of Nature cannot be understated. See Oelschlaeger, M., *The Idea of Wilderness: From Prehistory to the Age of Ecology* (Yale University Press, New York, 1991), 110–21.

Cultural symbolization values can also act as a method for the protection of parts of the environment because they can represent 'powerful symbols of human freedom'. In Mark Sagoff's words:

The obligation to preserve nature. . . is an obligation to our cultural tradition, to the values which we have cherished and in terms of which nature and this nation are still to be described . . . Our rivers, forests, and wildlife . . . serve our society as paradigms of concepts we cherish, for example—power, freedom and integrity . . . as a nation we value these qualities: the obligation towards Nature is an obligation towards them.[88]

Cultural value of the environment may also represent national identities. For example, the kiwi represents New Zealand, the kangaroo represents Australia, and the bald eagle symbolizes the United States. These parts of Nature are protected because they express the cherished cultural values.[89]

Finally, there is the often overt alleged connection of indigenous peoples and their culture with environmental protection. In such situations, the connection is not of the piecemeal approaches noted above, as much as it is seen as all-encompassing within their holistic outlooks.

This recognition began with the Enlightenment and the development of interest in non-Western, indigenous cultures and the idealization of the 'noble savage'.[90] In recent decades this interest has been revived and the focus has shifted to examine traditional management systems used by indigenous peoples as it has become apparent that these disappearing societies often have a knowledge that is very valuable to modern society in the search for viable models of sustainable development.[91] These views are frequently sought because indigenous populations often adopt strategies that work towards long term horizons and consequently adopt some of the most 'sustainable and most efficient uses

[88] Sagoff, M., 'On Preserving the Natural Environment', *Yale Law Journal,* 84 (1974), 245, 264–7.

[89] Tribe, L., 'From Environmental Foundations To Constitutional Structures: Learning From Nature's Future', *Yale Law Journal,* 84 (1974), 548. For historical examples of this line of thinking, see Thomas, K., *Man and the Natural World: Changing Attitudes in England 1500–1800* (Penguin, Harmondsworth, 1984), 64–8.

[90] See Marshall, *supra* n. 87, 235–44. For a specific example, see Rousseau, J., *Discourse on the Origins of Inequality Among Men* (Everyman, London, 1961), 222–4.

[91] For the classic advocacy of ecologically and socially balanced indigenous societies, i.e. North American Indians, see Heizer, R. and Elsasser, A. and their 'true ecological man', *The Natural World of the Californian Indians* (Los Angeles, University of California Press, 1980), 209–20. See also Callicott, J. B., 'Traditional American Indian and Western European Attitudes Toward Nature: An Overview', *Environmental Ethics,* 4 (1982), 293, 312–18. Booth, A. L., 'Ties That Bind: Native American Beliefs As A Foundation For Environmental Consciousness', *Environmental Ethics,* 12 (1990), 27. For some more general views on the environmental values of indigenous cultures see Berkes, F. (ed.), *Common Property Resources: Ecology and Community Based Sustainable Development* (Belhaven, London, 1989), 2, 6, 14–15, 19. Barsh, R. L., 'Indigenous Peoples' Role In Achieving Sustainable Development', in Fridtjof Nansen Institute, *Green Globe Yearbook: 1992* (Oxford University Press, Oxford, 1992), 25–34. Weiming, T., 'Towards the Possibility of A Global Community', in Hamilton, L. S. (ed.), *Ethics, Religion and Biodiversity* (White Horse Press, Birmingham, 1993), 65, 72–4. Ecologist, 'Whose Common Future', *Ecologist,* 22 (1992), 179–81.

possible'[92] of the environment. Thus, as a generalization, indigenous communities may offer good examples of harmony with the ecological world.

C. Initial Difficulties with the Cultural Exception

The main problem with the cultural argument is that just as cultural considerations can be used to protect the environment, they can also be used to justify its exploitation. For example, for cultural culinary delicacies both Asiatic and North American black bears, a number of types of whales, and sea turtles have been taken to such an extent that they are now endangered. For fashion, tigers, ocelots, sea and giant otters, black bears, crocodiles, alligators and caimans, lizards and snakes have all been taken for their skins. Vicunas for their highly prized wool. Elephants, for ivory to be made into jewellery. Parrots and raptors as pets. Tigers, musk deer, and the black bears for their use in Asiatic folk medicine.[93] All of these have been taken to endangered status in the name of culture. Perhaps the best example of this is with the rhino.

Rhinoceros and Culture

The rhinoceros may be the most endangered of all the large mammals. The Sumatran, Javan, Indian, black, and white rhinoceroses are all critically endangered. There are only between 500–900 Sumatran rhinos left alive. There are under 90 Javan rhinos and only 1,900 Indian rhinos left on the planet. The black rhino has suffered a 96 per cent decline in its population from over 70,000 in the 1960s down to around 2,500 in 1992. All five species of rhino were placed on Appendix 1 (meaning it is threatened with actual extinction, re: Article 2) of the *Convention on International Trade in Endangered Species of Fauna and Flora* (UNTS Vol. 973) in 1975. The parties to CITES have been absolutely direct on the position of rhinos, issuing direct recommendations in 1981 (CITES Doc.COP Conf.3.11) and 1987 (CITES Doc.COP Conf.6.10) in which they stipulated the necessity of the complete prohibition of all sales and trade in rhinoceros parts and the destruction of all stocks of rhinoceros parts. In 1993 the Standing Committee of CITES stated that 'the existence of illegal stockpiles of rhinoceros horn [was] . . . totally unacceptable to and incompatible with the implementation of the Convention, and accordingly calls for direct action to obtain and destroy rhinoceros horn'. (CITES Doc.SC.28.15.) In 1994 the Standing Committee expressed 'Concern that the actions agreed by the authorities in Taiwan . . . towards meeting the minimum requirements have not yet been

---

[92] Burger, J., *The Gaia Atlas of First Peoples* (Gaia Books, London, 1990), 36–50.
[93] See Fitzgerald, S., *International Wildlife Trade: Whose Business Is It?* (WWF, Washington, 1989), 32–3, 38, 51, 70–2, 115, 122–3, 149–51, 157, 170–1, 187–9, 203, 227.

implemented'. This inaction by Taiwan is not surprising given a continual reluctance to fully confront this problem which dates back to 1985. Currently, evidence adduced by the Environmental Investigation Agency suggests that in 1994 at least one third of all pharmacies surveyed in Taiwan can supply rhino horn on the premises. This is believed to reflect a possible supply of up to 10 tonnes of rhino horn on the island. (Environmental Investigation Agency. (1995), *CITES : Enforcement Not Extinction*, 26–7.)

The current primary use of this horn is found in Asiatic pharmaceutical products. Ground into powder or manufactured into tablet form, its principal purpose is to treat fever. In addition, it is supposed to expel fear, cure devil possession, keep away evil spirits, ease melancholia and remove toxic materials. It is also believed that it can act as an aphrodisiac. (See TRAFFIC (1994), *Endangered Species and Patented Oriental Medicines in Trade.*) The rhino horn does none of these things. These are simply cultural superstitions. Nevertheless, the beliefs are so powerful that people are willing to pay exorbitant prices to obtain the product. For example, in 1990 a kilogram of Sumatran horn was selling wholesale for $54,000 (US).

The former driving factor in the decline of the rhino, especially the black rhino, was the demand for rhino horn dagger handles, which are worn as status symbols in Yemen. This issue was directly addressed in the 1981 and 1987 meetings noted above. Thankfully, the 1987 collapse in oil prices and changing cultural priorities amongst young Yemenis has stemmed the demand for dagger handles.

Despite this fall in demand in Yemen, the demand has continued to grow in Asia, with a particularly strong market in Taiwan. In all cases the rhino has been taken to the absolute brink of extinction, for overtly cultural reasons.

Aside from the driving of species to extinction, culture also justifies irreducible cruelty to a number of other species. From bullfighting in Spain, to bear-baiting in Turkey and the infamous Faroe whale hunt. All of these activities have been justified behind the pretext of culture.[94]

Just as the idea that all cultures are environmentally benign has been exposed, as above, so too has the idea that there is a 'special factor' in indigenous cultures. This has been directly challenged as many historical records and contemporary practices have combined to show specific indigenous cultures as being the antithesis of environmental sustainability. This has become increasingly apparent as certain indigenous cultures have apparently exchanged their supposed belief systems for financial rewards. Indeed, on this issue many environmentalists and indigenous peoples are at odds, as the necessity for

---

[94] Re BBC 2, *Close Encounters of the European Kind: Blood Relations*, 24 Apr. 1992. Environmental Investigation Agency, *Don't Buy The Faroe Pilot Whale Slaughter* (London, 1993).

economic survival has been ranked higher for these people than the sustainable management of the environment. This problem has occurred in numerous countries.[95] Certain commentators have taken this even further than questions of political economy, and have challenged the idea that indigenous communities are suitable examples of sustainable livelihoods overall.[96] Specific case studies of New Zealand and Maori environmentalism have reached similar conclusions.[97]

This is *not* to suggest that no indigenous communities are exemplars of environmental sustainability. Rather, the point is that no generic claims can be based suggesting that all indigenous cultures are environmentally benign. In terms of comparing cultures, perhaps the only generic comment pertaining to culture and Nature that might be able to be made is that *all* of modern Western culture that has assimilated the liberal, positivist, economic industrial values and the anthropocentric biases are the very antithesis of environmental concern.[98]

D. The Defence of Environmentally Destructive Cultures

The preservation of culture is recognized as a legitimate and worthy pursuit by the international community.[99] Indeed, in recent years the international commu-

[95] Rowe, H., 'Kakadu Man's Concession', *Green Magazine*, Apr. 1991, 61–4. Pearce, F., *Green Warriors: The People and the Politics Behind the Environmental Revolution* (London, Bodley Head, 1991), 135–6. Regan, T., 'Environmental Ethics and the Ambiguity of the Native American Relationship with Nature', in Regan, T. (ed.), *All That Dwells Therein: Essays on Animal Rights and Environmental Ethics* (University of Berkley Press, California, 1982), 231–8.

[96] For the challengers of this type of view, see Martin, C., *Keepers of the Game: Indian Animal Relations* (University of California Press, Los Angeles, 1978), 71, 77, 116, 186–7. Diamond, J., *The Rise and Fall of the Third Chimpanzee* (Radius, London, 1991), 287–98. Ross, A., *The Chicago Gangster Theory of Life: Nature's Debt To Society* (Verso, London, 1994), 9–10, 26–7, 29–41, 52, 56–9, 65–7, 69–72. Lewis, M. W., *Green Delusions: An Environmentalist's Critique of Radical Environmentalism* (Duke University Press, London, 1992), 43–73. Buege, D. J., 'The Ecologically Noble Savage Revisited', *Environmental Ethics,* 18 (1996), 71–88. Kessell, J. L., 'Spaniards, Environment and the Pepsi Generation: An Historian's View', *Historian*, 36 (1973), 82–9.

[97] See Gillespie, A., 'Indigenous Environmentalism: Commonality, Clashes and Commitments Within Canada, Australia and New Zealand', in Haverman, P. (ed.), *New Frontiers: First Nations' Rights in Settler Dominions* (Oxford University Press, Sydney, 1997 (forthcoming)); 'Are Maori Environmental Guardians?', *Wilderness Magazine*, Oct. 1995, 42; 'Environmental Politics In New Zealand/Aotearoa: Clashes and Commonality Between Maori and Conservationists', *New Zealand Geographer* (forthcoming).

[98] See Moncrief, L. W. 'The Cultural Basis of Our Environmental Crisis', in Barbour, I. (ed.), *Western Man and Environmental Ethics* (Addison, London, 1973), 31, 33–4, 39–40. Devall, B. and Sessions, G., *Deep Ecology: Living As If Nature Mattered* (Gibbs Smith, Utah, 1985), 2. Devall, B., 'Deep Ecology and Radical Environmentalism', *Society and Natural Resources*, 4 (1991), 247, 256–7. Atkinson, A., *The Principles of Political Ecology* (Belhaven, London, 1991), 77–90. Sterling, S., 'Culture, Ethics, and the Environment: Towards a new Synthesis', *The Environmentalist*, 5 (1985), 197, 199, 204. [99] See n. 66.

nity has gone further, with demands for the enhancement of cultural diversity and the respect for cultural diversity and pluralism.[100]

Taking this position one step further, some commentators and governments have forcefully argued that as a result of cultural considerations, special exemptions should be made from environmental objectives. For example, this has been argued for the Inuit, Japanese, and Norwegians in the area of whaling.[101] From the Japanese position it has been suggested that to object to the whaling of minke whales is to violate cultural traditions.[102] This argument was adopted by the Japanese delegation at the 1993 meeting of the International Whaling Commission which warned the anti-whaling governments that they may be forced to leave the IWC. This was because they found the anti-whaling nations views objectionable because they were ethnocentric and did not respect other countries culture and traditions.[103] In the same year Norway also adopted this basic form of argument to counter criticisms for its decision when threatening to leave the IWC. Norway stated that Western governments were 'In fact practicing cultural imperialism by dictating how Norway should behave'.[104] Finally, Indigenous Survival International have suggested that any attempts to stop whale hunting is akin to 'cultural imperialism'.[105] This is despite the

---

[100] See Commitment 4 (a) & (c); *Report of the World Summit For Social Development.* A/CONF 166/9. 1995. 19 Apr. Report of the International Commission on Peace and Food, *Uncommon Opportunities: An Agenda for Peace and Equitable Development* (Zed, London, 1994), re: 'cultural values are the foundation for all lasting social achievements', 178–81. Commission on Global Governance, *Our Global Neighbourhood* (Oxford University Press, Oxford, 1995), 52–3.

[101] This exemption is provided for in Para. 2 of the Schedule to the International Convention on Whaling which prohibits any whaling of certain types of whales, 'Except where the meat and products of such whales are to be used exclusively for local consumption by the aborigines'. This exception has been catered for because of the cultural importance of whaling. Indeed, the IWC Cultural Anthropology Panel found that the 'complex of whaling and associated activities is perhaps the single most important element in the Eskimos' culture and society'. Para. 2 of the Schedule to the *International Convention for the Regulation of Whaling.* 161 UNTS 72. TIAS No. 1849. See also International Whaling Commission, *33rd Meeting.* 1982. Rep.IWC 33 (1983). App. 3, *Resolution Concerning Aboriginal Subsistence Whaling,* from the 33rd Meeting, which adopted the *Report of the Committee concerning the Principles for the Subsistence Catches of Cetaceans by Indigenous Peoples.* IWC/34/15. Para. 14. S. 13 of the IWC Schedule, as amended by the Commission at the 35th Annual meeting, 1983. Reproduced in Birnie, P., *The International Regulation of Whaling* (Oceana, New York, 1985), 707–24, esp, 717. For discussion of this, see 485–6, 500–10, 604–5, 611, 619, 629, 707–24.

[102] 'A uniculture is not an ultimate goal of mankind. On the contrary, each nation should maintain its cultural identify. A culture is in essence diversified.' Re: Sumi, K., 'The Whale War Between Japan and the United States: Problems and Prospects', *Denver Journal of International Law and Policy,* 17 (1989), 317, 338–41, 350.

[103] See Brown, P., 'Whalers Steered Towards Tourism', *Guardian,* 14 May 1993, 8.

[104] See Vidal, J., 'Weeping and Whaling', *Guardian,* 7 May 1993, 18. See also Royal Norwegian Ministry of Foreign Affairs, *Information on Whaling* (Norway, 1993). Skare, M., 'Whaling: A Sustainable Use of Natural Resources or a Violation of Animal Rights?', *Environment,* 36 (1994), 12, 14–15, 19, 30–1.

[105] Indigenous Survival International, *Resolution on Norwegian Whaling.* ISI. 7th GA/Res.8.1993. 18 Aug. For the specific importance of whaling and sealing to the Inuit culture, see Wenzel, J., *Animal Rights, Human Rights: Ecology, Economy and Ideology in the Canadian Arctic* (Belhaven, London, 1991), 35–6, 177–84. Lynge, F., *Arctic Wars: Animal Rights and Endangered Peoples* (Dartmouth, Hanover, 1992), 37, 40, 42–3, 45–65. Report of the Royal Commission, *Seals and Sealing in Canada.* (Government Printer, Ottawa, 1986), Vol. II, 56–9.

fact that the Inuit are allowed to kill whales, including the bowhead whale, which is the only whale threatened with actual, rather than commercial, extinction.[106]

E. The Final Refutations

It is necessary to make three points with regard to the above arguments. First, at the moment there is often a choice between interfering with a way of life of an important and distinct culture, or allowing the extinction of a species. If a species is on the verge of extinction and the choice is between killing it off completely in the present because it is important for a culture to do so, or allowing it to survive and perhaps recover in the distant future, then surely the culture will also be saved for the future. To kill off a species now in the name of cultural tradition is to kill off the culture. The tradition either dies completely now, or continues in a different form. The choice for the culture should not be hard. The choice for the ecosystem or specific animal is simple as there are more than cultural inter-ests at stake.[107] The survival of entire species and ecosystems should override cultural considerations.

Secondly, the fact that earlier, often colonial, cultures ruthlessly exploited Nature does not give cultures with a traditional interest in the exploitation of Nature the right to finish off the job. Even if cultures do 'respect' the environ-ment that does not matter to the specific aspect of Nature which they are destroy-ing.[108]

Finally, just because something is derived from, or common within, culture does not make it ethically defensible. Indeed, cultural relativism cannot be seen as an absolute excuse for any actions that cultures may wish to condone. Culture should never be seen as something which is homogeneous, bounded, and fixed, and therefore free from criticism. For without the ability to criticize cultural prac-

---

[106] See Hawkins, S. M., 'The United States Abuse of the Aboriginal Whaling Exception: A Contradiction in US Whaling Policy and a Dangerous Precedent', *University of California Davis Law Review*, 24 (1990), 489, 521. Doubleday, N. C., 'Aboriginal Subsistence Whaling: The Right of the Inuit to Hunt Whales and its Implications', *Denver Journal of International Law and Policy*, 17 (1989), 373, 392. Note, this situation has changed somewhat since when these comments were made in 1989. For a fuller discussion of this entire area, see Gillespie, A., 'The Ethical Question in the Whaling Debate', 9 *Gergetown International Environmental Law Review*, 9 (1996).

[107] D'Amato, A. and Chopra, S., 'Whales: Their Emerging Right to Life', *American Journal of International Law*, 85 (1991), 25, 58–60.

[108] Ibid. Likewise, it is suggested that 'the cultural card' is overplayed, with catalogued abuses of the provisions. See 'Aboriginal Subsistence Whaling: A Category in Decay', *International Harpoon*, 4 (1995), 1–2. There is also a collection of arguments that suggests that the indigenous lifestyle 'rights' that are claimed do not coincide with the twentieth-century benefits that they bring to their position. This involves the distinctly unindigenous methods of utilizing their traditional claims and the financial benefits that they extract (as opposed to using them for local-indigenous con-sumption) from their traditional 'rights'. See Pearce, *supra* n. 95, 35, 43, 45–6. The evidence sug-gests that the Inuit exploited their 'cultural exception' as their culture has become increasingly divorced from their traditional ways. Thus, many more whales than were historically taken each sea-son were being claimed as an important part of their culture, with the assistance of 'grenade lances'.

tices genocide, slavery, cannibalism, infanticide, female circumcision, racism, and sexism would all have to be tolerated. These can be deemed ethically repugnant because it is believed that certain ethical norms are higher than cultural relativism.[109] The same argument exists for certain anthropocentric actions (irrespective of culture) which disrupt or destroy parts of non-human Nature.[110] Thus, culture should not be seen as a panacea for environmental destruction.

3. RECREATIONAL VALUES AND THE IMPORTANCE OF WILDERNESS AS JUSTIFICATIONS FOR ENVIRONMENTAL PROTECTION

Recreational values have been at the forefront of environmental preservation since modern conservation began. For example, the creation of the first national park in the United States in 1864, was done largely in response to the importance of the recreational benefits of the environment.[111]

This recreational ideal has become incorporated into international environmental law. For example, reference to the importance of recreational and educational values of the environment is found in the *Declaration of the World's National Parks Congress*,[112] the *Convention on Trade in Endangered Species of Flora and Fauna*,[113] the 1971 *Convention on Wetlands of International Importance, Especially as Waterfowl Habitat*,[114] the 1979 *Convention on the Conservation of European Wildlife and Natural Habitat*,[115] the *Convention Concerning the Conservation of Migratory Birds and their Environment*,[116] the 1979 *Convention on the Conservation of Species of Migratory Wild Animals*,[117]

[109]   See Hartung, F., 'Cultural Relativism and Moral Judgements', *Philosophy of Science*, 21 (1954), 118–26. Kluckholn, C., 'Ethical Relativity', *Journal of Philosophy*, 52 (1955), 663–7. Solomon, R. C., *Introducing Philosophy* (Harcourt, London, 1993), 656–61. For a discussion that this problem has produced in the area of human rights, see Renteln, A. D., *International Human Rights: Universalism vs Relativism* (Sage, California, 1990).

[110]   See Pierce, C. and Van De Veer, D., 'Cultural Diversity and Moral Relativism', in Pierce and Van De Veer (eds.), *People, Penguins and Plastic Trees: Basic Issues in Environmental Ethics* (Wadsworth, London, 1995), 112–15.

[111]   See Lyster, S., *International Wildlife Law* (Grotius, Cambridge, 1985), 62–4.

[112]   Preamble, *Declaration of the World's National Parks Congress. Environmental Policy and the Law*, 10 (1983), 62. Note, the international importance of parks dates back to 1959 when the United Nations Economic and Social Council charged the IUCN with the task of creating a list of the world's parks and reserves. This was followed with the first World Conference on National Parks in 1962. For a discussion of this, see also McNeely, J. A., 'Protected Areas are Adapting to New Realities', in McNeely, J. A. (ed.), *National Parks, Conservation and Development: The Role of Protected Areas in Sustaining Society* (IUCN, Geneva, 1982), 1–5.

[113]   Preamble, *Convention on International Trade in Endangered Species of Fauna and Flora*. UNTS Vol. 973 (No. 1: 14537) 243. 12 ILM. 1973. 1088.

[114]   Preamble, 1971 *Convention on Wetlands of International Importance*. UNTS Vol. 996. 244. 11 ILM 1972. 963.

[115]   Preamble of 1979 *Berne Convention on the Conservation of European Wildlife*. Europ TS No. 104. UKTS No. 56 (1982) Cmd. 8738.

[116]   See the 1972 Convention. 25 UST 3329; TIAS No. 7990. For a discussion of this treaty, and similar treaties to do with birds, see Lyster; *supra* n. 111. 75–6.

[117]   Preamble of the 1979 *Convention on the Conservation of Species of Migratory Animals*. British Command Paper Cmnd. 7888. Misc. 11 (1980) and Cm. 1332 TS 87 (1990) 19 ILM. 1980. 15.

and the *Convention on the Conservation of Nature in the South Pacific*.[118] Recreational and educational interests in the environment are also being increasingly cited as reasons for preservation in domestic contexts.[119]

Within this approach to environmental protection, it is important to note the relevance of the central precept of 'wilderness'. Wilderness, in this setting is seen predominantly as something without human inhabitants. This idea is captured by the 1964 *Wilderness Act* of the United States which provided the following definition:

A Wilderness, in contrast to those areas where man and his own works dominate the landscape, is hereby recognised as an area where the earth and its community are untrammelled by man, where man himself is a visitor who does not remain.[120]

This view also reflects a traditional conservation argument that people, no matter where, are detrimental to the natural environment and that in certain instances the environment should be left free from all forms of human exploitation.[121] This form of idea is captured in the African Convention on the Conservation of Nature and Natural Resources, which allows the designation of certain areas as 'strict nature reserves' where:

any form of hunting or fishing, any undertaking connected with forestry, agriculture or mining . . . and generally, any act likely to disturb the fauna or flora . . . are strictly forbidden.[122]

There are a number of reasons for the justifications of large areas of wilderness for recreational and related pursuits.

---

[118] Art. 1, of the *Convention on Conservation of Nature in the South Pacific*. 1976. In Kiss, A. C., (ed.), *Selected Multilateral Treaties in the Field of the Environment* (UNEP, Kenya, 1982), 463.

[119] Linder, D. O., 'New Directions for Preservation Law: Creating an Environment Worth Experiencing', *Environmental Law*, 20 (1990), 49, 68–70. Boman, D. L., 'Recent Developments in Efforts to Enhance the Protection of Animals', *Washburn Law Journal*, 30 (1991), 271, 277–80.

[120] *Wilderness Act*. 1964. 16 USC 1131–6. For a useful discussion of this, see Nash, R., 'The American Invention of National Parks', *American Quarterly*, 22 (1970), 726–35.

[121] The World Park Congress categorizes reserves into ten types, of which only one type—that of scientific research/strict Nature reserve—has no or absolutely minimal human contact. All of the other nine categories have varying degrees of human involvement. See IUCN Commission on Natural Parks, 'Categories, Objectives and Criteria', in McNeely, *supra* n. 112, 47, 49–53. See also Nelson, J. G., 'International Experience With National Parks and Related Reserves', in Nelson, J. G. (ed.), *International Experience With National Parks and Related Reserves* (University of Waterloo, 1978), 1, 5–6, 9, 12. Note however, many environmental philosophers would prefer much stricter definitions in which humanity is restricted all the more. For example, John Muir suggested that 'The Wild Parks' should be protected to such an extent that 'men' cannot change or mark them any more than 'butterflies', *Our National Parks* (Houghton Mifflin, Boston, 1901), 4–7, 37, 56–8. In a modern context, see Devall, B., *Simple in Means, Rich in Ends: Practising Deep Ecology* (Green Print, London, 1990), 17, 161–5. Foreman, D., 'Wilderness Preserve System', *Whole Earth Review*, 53 (1989), 42–5.

[122] See Art. III, 4 (a) (ii). *African Convention on the Conservation of Nature and Natural Resources*. 1001, UNTS 3. The idea of Nature reserves originated in an international setting in the 1900 *Convention for the Preservation of Wild Animals, Birds and Fish in Africa*. 94 BSFP 715. See Art. II (5) This Convention not only established the idea of 'Strict Natural Reserves' (Art. III (1)), but also prohibited the killing, hunting, capture, collection or destruction of flora or fauna in specific areas. (Art. II(1) & (2).) For a discussion of this see Lyster, *supra* n. 111, 112–15. Note that there is a division that is evident in the 1940 *Convention on Nature Protection and Wildlife Preservation*

Firstly, although there is no single definitive definition of the value of wilderness[123] there are some common themes of why wilderness should be protected. These are often justified on the grounds of what wilderness can do for the individual, in terms of philosophical, physical, and social growth. For example, it is often believed in a generic sense that 'nature [is] the source of human existence'.[124] For the individual, it is believed that wilderness provides a niche that meets deep-seated psychosomatic needs.[125] Abstracting from this, it is suggested that wilderness is essential, and to protect the wilderness that they need is to protect the values that are important to society. This approach mirrors Henry Thoreau's oft quoted dictum 'in wilderness is the preservation of the world'.[126] More specifically, John Muir, one of the giants of wilderness philosophy, wrote in the first paragraph of his book *Our National Parks*:

Going to the mountains is going home; that wilderness is a necessity; and the mountain parks and reservations are useful not only as fountains of timber and irrigating rivers, but as fountains of life.[127]

Finally, parts of the environment are believed to play a unique role in providing leisure settings where social bonds are created and enhanced.[128] For example, on the larger view, wilderness has inspired many activities, from the logging camps in the 1930s Depression to modern day summer camps and Outward Bound courses. What is valued here is the challenge of physical and mental endurance, in teamwork or alone, with reflection on skills acquired and values learnt.[129] Involvement with the natural world has also been credited as the place where the 'seedbeds of social change' are created.

A. The Problems of Wilderness and Recreation

The first problem with the recreation argument is that the wilderness is only valued until an alternative method or place is located. Indeed, it should be realized

---

in the Western Hemisphere, between Nature Reserves that are classified as National Parks where Nature can be 'utilised' and 'strict wilderness reserves' where the idea is to keep the Reserves where there is 'no provision for the passage of motorised transportation and all commercial developments are excluded'. See Art. 1, (1), (2), (4). *Western Hemisphere Convention*. 1940. UNTS Vol. 161 (No. II 485) 193–216. *The African Convention* makes similar distinctions in Art. III (4).

[123]　Oelschlaeger, M., *The Idea of Wilderness* (Yale University Press, New York, 1991), 281–2.

[124]　Contemporary environmental philosophy often justifies wilderness due to its ability to 'connect people back to Nature'. See Oelschlaeger, ibid. 164–8, 317, 320–1, 352–3.

[125]　See Lucas, P. H. C., 'How Protected Areas Can Help Meet Society's Evolving Needs', in McNeely, *supra* n. 112, 72, 75–6.

[126]　Thoreau, H. D., *Excursions and Poems* (Houghton, Boston, 1906), 224.

[127]　Muir, J. *Our National Parks* (Houghton, Boston, 1901), 1.

[128]　Burch, B., 'The Social Meaning of Forests', *Humanist*, 39 (1979), 39–44. See also Naess, A. *Ecology, Community and Lifestyle* (Cambridge University Press, Cambridge), 177–81. Lucas, ibid.

[129]　Leopold, A., *A Sand County Almanac* (Oxford University Press, Oxford, 1949), 165–8, 171–4. Hill, T. E., 'Ideals of Human Excellence and the Preservation of the Natural Environment', in Gruen, L. and Jamieson, D., *Reflecting On Nature: Readings In Environmental Philosophy* (Oxford University Press, Oxford, 1994), 98, 106–9.

that the idea of wilderness and the benefits thereof is only a relatively recent idea, dating back to the late eighteenth century, which was (and remains) heavily influenced by Romanticism.[130] Therefore, it can be postulated that the idea of wilderness is fundamentally cultural, and may change.[131]

The differing cultural views of wilderness and the problems that this may present are well illustrated with the imposition of Western wilderness values upon Southern countries. Here, it has been argued that the idea of 'wilderness' or 'nature reserves for recreation' are a manifestation of Western 'imperial power'.[132] This is because the application of such a concept in Southern countries has led in a number of cases to the uprooting of human populations. This has resulted in disastrous consequences in terms of political, social, economic, and religious considerations, as local communities have been separated from their environment. Additionally, once such peoples are displaced they are driven to poaching and other such practices in the parks to survive.[133]

Nevertheless, a number of 'human free wilderness areas' have been developed in Southern countries as they respond to Northern demands such as debt for Nature swaps, or markets for 'Green tourism'. The problems with excluding indigenous peoples from the environment they inhabit have been documented in numerous financially poor countries from Northern Africa to South East Asia.[134]

However, such 'human free areas' are *not* believed to be well-suited to countries with large populations, or countries whose population is closely intertwined

---

[130] Wilson, A., *The Culture of Nature: North American Landscape from Disney to the Exxon Valdez* (Blackwell, London, 1992), 23–7. Oelschlaeger, *supra* n. 123, 93.

[131] For an examination of the wilderness idea, Tuan, Y., *A Study of Environmental Perception, Attitudes and Values* (Prentice Hall, New Jersey, 1974), 109–12. Grumbine, R. E., 'Wilderness, Wise Use and Sustainable Development', *Environmental Ethics*, 16 (1994), 227, 230–1. Hales, D., 'Changing Concepts of National Parks', in Western, D. and Pearl, M. (eds.), *Conservation For the Twenty-first Century* (Oxford University Press, Oxford, 1989), 139, 142.

[132] Birch, T. H., 'The Incarceration of Wilderness: Wilderness Areas As Prisons', *Environmental Ethics*, 12 (1990), 3, 23. Johns, D. M., 'The Relevance of Deep Ecology to the Third World; Some Preliminary Observations', *Environmental Ethics*, 12 (1990), 235. Burnett, G. W., 'Wilderness and the Bantu Mind', *Environmental Ethics*, 16 (1994), 145, 146. Pearce, F., *Green Warriors: The People and Politics Behind the Environmental Revolution* (Bodley, London, 1991), 77–88.

[133] Guha, R. 'Radical American Environmentalism and Wilderness Preservation: A Third World Critique', *Environmental Ethics*, 11 (1989), 71, 75–9. Marglin, F. A. and Mishla, P. C., 'Sacred Groves; Regenerating the Body, the Land, and the Community', in Sachs, W. (ed.), *Global Ecology* (Zed, London, 1993), 197, 198. Isaccson, R., 'Big Game Parks: What Future?', *Green Magazine*, June 1991, 40. Pearce, ibid. 78, 85–8. Note, the IUCN—the body behind the international policy on parks—is emphatic that indigenous populations should not be ejected from protected areas. See para. 10, *Recommendations of the World National Park Congress*, in McNeely, *supra* n. 112, 765, 770.

[134] See Lynch, O. J. and Talbott, K., 'Legal Responses to the Philippine Deforestation Crisis', *International Law and Politics*, 20 (1988), 679. Mahony, R., 'Debt for Nature Swaps: Who Really Benefits?', *Ecologist*, 22 (1992), 97. Wiggins, A., 'Indian Rights and the Environment', *Yale Journal of International Law*, 18 (1993), 345, 349–51. Pearce, *supra* n. 132, 88, 247. Isaccson, ibid. 40. BBC 2, 'Fair Game', 15 Oct. 1991. Niang, C. I., 'From Ecological Crisis in the West to Energy Problems in Africa', *International Social Sciences Journal*, 42 (1990), 226.

with the surrounding environment.[135] Consequently, in some parts of the Southern world, a modified, non-Western definition of Nature is required. This must be one where Nature is seen not as a human free wilderness, but rather one where people may coexist in their surrounding environment. Thus, it can be suggested that isolated wildernesses are often unsuitable in meeting more integrative ideas of sustainable development.[136] This problem is also relevant to Northern countries with large Western populations which are alienated from Nature.[137]

A second overall problem with the recreation justification is that there is only a need to preserve as much environment as is required for recreational purposes. Additionally, recreational pursuits frequently destroy both environments and individual animals.[138] A good example of this is the problems presented by tourism, which can be devastating to both local communities and the environment.[139]

This point leads to the larger problem that to focus strictly on the idea of recreation and wilderness, as a justification for environmental protection, is to omit the myriad of other environmental conditions that cannot be addressed by this static approach, such as over-consumption and social justice as a prerequisite for environmental protection.[140]

Finally, not all people benefit from the 'wilderness experience'—and there is little evidence to suggest that such persons are lesser people for their lack of response.[141] This failure to benefit connects to the larger problem that wilderness is being preserved only for instrumental, anthropocentric reasons.[142] As this definition is defined by humans, it can also be altered by humans if the justifications for which it was enacted fail to come to fruition.

[135] Mellor, M., *Breaking the Boundaries: Towards A Feminist Green Socialism* (Virago, London, 1992), 91–3. Spindle, G. S., 'A Response to Elliot Richardson', *John Marshall Law Review*, 25 (1991), 33–5. Birch, *supra* n. 122.

[136] Callicott, J. B., 'The Wilderness Idea Revisited: The Sustainable Development Alternative', *The Environmental Professional*, 13 (1991), 236–42, 245. Birch, *supra* n. 132, 23, 24. Grumbine, *supra* n. 131, 243–4. Isaccson, *supra* n. 133, 40. IUCN, WWF, WRI, *Conserving the World's Biological Diversity* (IUCN, Gland, 1990), 50. Malik, A., 'Protected Areas and Political Realities', in McNeely, *supra* n. 112, 10–11. Burnett, *supra* n. 132, 150, 157, 159. Eidsvik, H. K., 'The Status of Wilderness: An International Overview', *Natural Resources Journal*, 29 (1989), 47, 58. Cf. Rolston, H., 'The Wilderness Idea Reaffirmed', in *The Environmental Professional*, 13 (1992), 370–7.   [137] Callicott, ibid. 240–2.

[138] Routley, R., 'Critical Notice of Passmore's Man's Responsibility for Nature', *Australasian Journal of Philosophy*, 53 (1975), 177, 183. Leopold, *supra* n. 129, 169–71, 176.

[139] See Pleumaron, A., 'The Political Economy of Tourism', *Ecologist*, 24 (1994), 142–9. Prosser, R. F., 'The Ethics of Tourism', in Cooper, D. E. (ed.), *The Environment in Question: Ethics and Global Issues* (Routledge, London, 1992), 37–50. Wilson, *supra* n. 130, 19–24, 41–4, 49–51.

[140] Guha, *supra* n. 133, 81. Kothari, S. and Parajuli, P., 'No Nature Without Social Justice', in Sachs, *supra* n. 133, 234, 238. Gudynas, E., 'The Search For An Ethic of Sustainable Development in Latin America', in Engels, J. R and J. G., *The Ethics of Environment and Sustainable Development: Global Challenge, International Response* (Belhaven, London, 1990), 145. Callicott, *supra* n. 136, 240–1.

[141] Hill, T. E., 'Ideals of Human Excellence and the Preservation of the Natural Environment', in Gruen and Jamieson, *supra* n. 129, 98, 101–5. Rowntree, R. A., 'The United States National Park System', in Nelson, *supra* n. 121, 91, 114–17.

[142] See O'Neill, J., *Ecology, Policy and Politics: Human Well-Being and the Natural World* (Routledge, London, 1993), 15.

VI

The Rights of Future Generations as a Justification for Environmental Protection

1. INTERNATIONAL LAW AND THE RIGHTS OF FUTURE GENERATIONS

Since the Second World War, States have been expressing concern in international documents for the welfare of future generations. A growing number of international agreements, declarations, charters, and United Nations General Assembly resolutions recognize this justification for many forms of human action. For example, the opening paragraph of the United Nations charter states, 'We, the peoples of the United Nations, determined to save succeeding generations from the scourge of war . . .'.[1]

In an environmental context, the idea of conservation for the benefit of future generations has been evident for a number of decades. For example, the United States Congress in 1916 passed an act for the protection and creation of national parks. The act stated that it was necessary to:

conserve the scenery . . . and the wildlife . . . in such a manner and by such means as will leave them unimpaired for the enjoyment of future generations.[2]

Within international environmental law, the idea of the protection of Nature for future generations begins in a contemporary setting with the 1946 *International Convention for the Regulation of Whaling*. This document recognizes 'the interests of the Nations of the world in safeguarding for future generations the great natural resources represented by whales'.[3] Despite such early recognition, this idea did not become common within international environmental documents until the late 1960s and 1970s. One of the most notable documents of this period is the 1972 *Stockholm Declaration of the United Nations Conference of the Human Environment*, which recognized in Principle 1 that 'Man, . . . bears a solemn responsibility to protect and improve the environment for present and future generations'.[4]

Similarly, the 1972 *Convention Concerning the Protection of the World*

---

[1] *UN Charter,* adopted San Francisco, 26 June 1945. 59 Stat. 1031, T.S. No. 993.
[2] Recorded in Udall, S., *The Quiet Crisis and the Next Generation* (Gibbs Smith, Utah, 1988), 124.
[3] Para. 2, preamble, *International Convention for the Regulation of Whaling.* 161 UNTS 72. TIAS No. 1849.
[4] Principle 1, *Stockholm Declaration of the United Nations Conference on the Human Environment.* UN Doc. A/CONF 48/14 (1972). 11 ILM. 1972. 1416.

Cultural and Natural Heritage,[5] the 1973 *Convention on International Trade in Endangered Species of Wild Fauna and Flora*,[6] and *the Convention on the Conservation of Migratory Species of Wild Animals*[7] all acknowledged concerns for future generations. Even the United Nations 1974 *Charter on the Economic Rights and Duties of States* recognized that 'The protection, preservation and the enhancement of the environment for the present and future generations is the responsibility of all states'.[8]

In 1980 'the historical responsibility of states for the preservation of Nature for Present and Future Generations' was declared by the United Nations General Assembly at its 49th Plenary meeting.[9] In the same year the first Brandt Commission recognized that 'the rights of future generations' must be considered as a reason to protect the environment.[10] The 1982 *World Charter for Nature*[11] and the 1982 *Nairobi Declaration* also emphasized the importance of environmental protection for future generations.[12] In 1987 the World Commission for Environment and Development defined the concept of sustainable development to mean that the present generation meets its own needs without compromising the ability of future generations to meet theirs.[13] The leader of this Commission, Gro Bruntland, went on to argue that consideration of future generations should form a 'new global ethic,' that is needed to find an answer to the current international environmental problematique.[14]

In 1989 the United Nations General Assembly placed on its agenda, 'The protection of global climate change for present and future generations of mankind'.[15] In 1990 the *Interparliamentary Conference on the Global*

---

[5] Art. 4, *Convention Concerning the Protection of the World Cultural and Natural Heritage.* 1921. 27 UST, 37, TIAS. No. 8226.

[6] Preamble, *Convention on International Trade in Endangered Species of Wild Fauna and Flora.* 1973. 27 UST. 1087, TIAS No. 8249.

[7] Preamble, *Convention on the Conservation of Migratory Species of Wild Animals.* British Command Paper Cmnd. 7888, Misc. 11 (1980) and Cm. 1332 TS 87 (1990).

[8] See Art. 30 of the *Charter of Economic Rights and Duties of States.* UNGA Res. 3281 (XXIX). 1974.

[9] Principles 1 and 3, *Historical Responsibility of States for the Preservation of Nature for Present and Future Generations.* UN Doc. A./RES/35/8 (1980). 30 Oct.

[10] The Brandt Commission, *North-South: A Programme For Survival* (Pan, London, 1980), 115.

[11] Preamble, *World Charter for Nature.* Adopted by UN 9 Nov. 1982, UNGA Res. 37/7, 37 UN GAOR Supp. (no. 51), 17. UN Doc. A/37/51 (1982).

[12] *Nairobi Declaration,* 18 May, 1982, UNEP report. 37 UN GAOR Annex 2, Supp. (no. 25) at 49, UN Doc. A/37/25 (1982).

[13] World Commission on Environment and Development, *Our Common Future* (Oxford University Press, Oxford, 1987), 8, 40.

[14] Gro Bruntland, 1988. Recorded in Starke, L. (ed.), *Signs of Hope: Working Towards Our Common Future* (Oxford University Press, Oxford, 1990), 28. See also Bruntland, G. H., 'Our Common Future: A Call for Action', in Polunin, N. and Burnett, J. H. (eds.), *Maintenance of the Biosphere. Proceedings of the Third International Conference on Environmental Future* (Edinburgh University Press, Edinburgh, 1990), 186, 192.

[15] *Protection of the Global Climate for Present and Future Generations of Mankind.* UNGA/Res./43/53.A/44/862. 1989. For a useful discussion of inter-generational equity in this area, see Redgwell, C., 'Intergenerational Equity and Global Warming', in Churchill, R. and Freestone, P. (eds.), *International Law and Global Climate Change* (Graham and Trotman, London, 1991), 41–56.

Environment recognized the justification of future generations as a reason for environmental action.[16] In the same year the South Commission's report on *The Challenge of the South*, recognized that considerations of future generations are important.[17] The *Bergen Ministerial Declaration on Sustainable Development* echoed similar sentiments.[18] The importance of future generations was uppermost at the 1992 Earth Summit.[19] It was also important within the 1994 Report of the International Commission on Peace and Food,[20] the *Conference on the Sustainable Development of Small Island States*,[21] and the 1994 *International Conference on Population and Development*.[22] Finally, it was also recognized at the *World Summit for Social Development*,[23] and the 1995 Report of the Commission on Global Governance suggested that 'People and governments alike need to pay greater heed to the interests of future generations, for whom this generation acts as a trustee'.[24]

Individual Charters for Europe, Africa, the League of Arab States and also constitutional provisions encompassing dozens of countries recognize duties to posterity.[25] This is also evident in a number of domestic

---

[16] Para. 5, *Decision of the Interparliamentary Conference on the Global Environment. Environmental Policy and the Law.* 20 (1990), 112.

[17] The South Commission, *The Challenge to the South* (Oxford University Press, Oxford, 1990), 23, 280.

[18] Preamble, *Bergen Ministerial Declaration on Sustainable Development in the EEC Region.* Reprinted in *Environmental Policy and the Law,* 20 (1990), 104.

[19] See Principle 3 of the *Rio Declaration on Environment and Development.* 'The right to development must be fulfilled so as to equitably meet development and environmental needs of present and future generations.' A/CONF 151/5. (1992). 3–14 June. Note, that most of the major participants at UNCED recognized this position. See the individual speeches in the *Report of the United Nations Conference on Environment and Development.* A/CONF 151/26. Vol. 3. 1992.

[20] Report of the International Commission on Peace and Food; *Uncommon Opportunities: An Agenda For Peace and Equitable Development* (Zed, London, 1994), 6–9. Note, the reference to future generations in this document is implicit within its emphasis upon the possibilities of the future.

[21] Para. 1. Preamble. *Draft Programme of Action for the Sustainable Development of Small Island Developing States.* A/CONF 167/9. 1994. 18 Mar.

[22] Principle 3. *Report of the International Conference on Population and Development.* A/CONF 171/13. 1994. 18 Oct.

[23] Para. 26 (b); *Declaration and Programme of Action of the World Summit for Social Development.* A/CONF 166/L 3/Add.1. 1995. 10 Mar.

[24] Commission on Global Governance, *Our Global Neighbourhood* (Oxford University Press, Oxford, 1995), 47.

[25] See the preamble of the 1981 *Convention for the Co-operation in the Protection and Development of the Marine and Coastal Environment of the West and Central African Region.* In Rummel-Bulska, I. (ed.), *Selected Multilateral Treaties in the Field of the Environment* (Grotius, Cambridge, 1991), Vol. 2. 118. *The Kampala Declaration on Sustainable Development in Africa.* Declared at the First African Regional Conference on the Environment and Development. 1989. Kampala, Uganda. 12–16 June. Reprinted in Starke, L. (ed.), *supra* n. 14, 28. *The Statute For The Council Of Europe.* 5 May 1949, 87 UNTS, 104 . *Charter for African Unity.* 25 May, 1963, 479 UNTS, 39. *Pact of Arab States.* 70 UNTS, 237, 248. For a number of individual state constitutions concerning the consideration of future generations, see Weiss, E. B., *In Fairness To Future Generations* (United Nations University, Japan, 1989), App. B.

areas.[26] Certain countries have gone so far as to create an ombudsman to represent future generations.[27]

The idea of environmental protection based upon the consideration of the interests of future generations is also common rhetoric within contemporary politics. For example, John Major,[28] George Bush,[29] Al Gore,[30] and Shridath Ramphal[31] have all raised and supported this common conservationist position.[32] Finally, as mentioned above, the consideration of future generations is also important with regard to the concept of sustainable development.[33] In this context, approval of the consideration of future generations has been argued from theoretical,[34] economic,[35] and legal perspectives.[36]

2. THE MORAL CONSIDERABILITY OF FUTURE GENERATIONS: PAST AND PRESENT

Although the theory of consideration of future generations has only been in popular usage in international environmental law for a relatively short period, its

---

[26] *National Environmental Policy Act.* 42 USC, § 4331 (b) (1) (1982). See for example, *United States* v. *Vogler* 859 F 2d. 638, 641 (1988). For a discussion of this approach in the US, see Brady, T. P., 'But Most of it Belongs to Those Yet to be Born', *Environmental Affairs,* 17 (1990), 621. For a recent case in the Philippines, which recognized that the plaintiffs had standing to represent future generations, see *Minors Opesa* v. *Secretary of the Department of Environment and Natural Resources.* This is recorded in *International Legal Materials,* 33 (1994). 173–206. For other individual approaches of other States, see Weiss, ibid.

[27] Art. 4. *Nordic Convention.* 1974. *International Legal Materials* 13 (1974), 591. See also the *GOA Guidelines. Environmental Policy and Law,* 18 (1988), 190–1. For discussions of how these may be put into practice, see Kavka, G. S. and Warren, V., 'Political Representation for Future Generations', in Elliott, R. and Gare, A (eds.), *Environmental Philosophy* (Queensland University Press, Queensland, 1983), 1. See also Weiss, E. B., 'The Planetary Trust: Consequences and Intergenerational Equity', *Ecology Law Quarterly,* 11 (1984), 453, 564–72. Susskind, L. E., *Environmental Diplomacy: Negotiating More Effective Environmental Agreements* (Oxford University Press, Oxford, 1994), 53–8.

[28] Major, J. in *Report of the UNCED, supra* n. 19, 25, 28.

[29] Bush, G. in *Report of the UNCED, supra* n. 19, 79.

[30] Gore, A., *Earth in Balance: Forging a New Common Purpose* (Earthscan, London, 1992), 170.

[31] Ramphal, S., *Our Country the Planet* (Lime Tree, London, 1992), 206.

[32] For the support of this position in general environmental theory, see Passmore, J., *Man's Responsibility For Nature* (Duckworth, London, 1974), 73–100. Attfield, R., *The Ethics of Environmental Concern* (Blackwell, Oxford, 1983), 92–108. See also Pinchot, G., *The Fight For Conservation* (Harcourt Brace, New York, 1910), 79–81.

[33] See Chowdhury, S. R., 'Intergenerational Equity: Substratum of the Right to Sustainable Development', in Chowdhury, S. R. (ed.), *The Right to Development in International Law* (Graham and Trotman, London, 1992), 233, 244–6.

[34] Gundling, L., 'Our Responsibility for Future Generations', *American Journal of International Law,* 84 (1990), 207, 208.

[35] Pearce, D., Markandya, A. and Barbier, E. B., *Blueprint for a Green Economy* (Earthscan, London, 1989), 48, 34–6, 173–85.

[36] *Legal Principles by the Experts' Group on Environmental Law of the World Commission on Environment and Development.* World Commission, *supra* n. 13, 248.

historical origins go back much further. It appears within Islamic doctrine[37] and within the Judaeo-Christian tradition.[38] Traditional indigenous perspectives also often have a strong recognition of the importance of future generations.[39]

The links between continuous generations have also influenced many of the most important philosophical and political theorists. For example, Cicero,[40] Kant,[41] Bentham,[42] Locke,[43] and Marx[44] all recognized the idea of future generations as a legitimate concern. Once all of these views are surveyed it can be seen that the idea of owing something to the future is not a view peculiar to any one philosophy or religion. However, these different schools of thought have advocated differing (political) methods to recognize this obligation. Nevertheless, despite these differences, the basic concern for future generations continues. Consequently, as Edith Weiss stated, it can be claimed that the concept of a planetary trust is founded on the:

nearly universal recognition and acceptance among peoples of an obligation to protect the natural and cultural heritage for future generations.[45]

In a contemporary setting the main basis of the argument supporting the rights of future generations is found in an awareness of the fact that humanity has hitherto unknown powers of a vast and potentially devastating nature which could have a ruinous effect on the environment and future generations. Consequently, it is argued that, along with a change in the situation, a change in ethics is required. Traditional ethics, derived from historic and less threatening situations, are seen as inadequate to face the new problematique for the end of the twentieth century.

Additionally, there is the ethical argument that the future is barely represented in most contemporary decision making. Yet, by the time future generations are living with the environmental problems that this generation has left them, this

---

[37] See IUCN, *Islamic Principles For The Conservation Of The Natural Environment* (Saudi Arabia, 1983), 13–14. Khadduri, A., *The Islamic Conception of Justice* (Cambridge, 1984), 137–9, 219–20, 233–9.

[38] See for example, Gen. 1: 1–31; 17: 7–8. Pope John Paul II, 'Peace With God the Creator', reprinted in Starke, *supra* n. 15, 28. Seiger Derr, H. 'The Obligation To The Future', in Partridge, E. (ed.), *The Rights Of Future Generations* (Prometheus, New York, 1981), 43.

[39] Burger, J., *The Gaia Atlas of First Peoples* (Gaia Books, London, 1990), 11–13, 20–1, 88–9, 112–23, 140–3, 162–3, 172–7.

[40] Cicero, *De Finibus* (Penguin, Harmondsworth, 1971), 3, 64.

[41] Kant, I., 'Idea For A Universal History With A Cosmopolitan Purpose', in Nisbet, F., *Kant's Political Writings* (Cambridge University Press, Cambridge, 1970), 50.

[42] Bentham, J. noted in Narveson, J., 'Utilitarianism and Future Generations', *Mind*, 76 (1967), 64. Cf. Carr, I. M., 'Saving the Environment: Does Utilitarianism Provide a Justification', *Legal Studies*, 12 (1992), 92, 98–9.

[43] Locke, J., *An Essay Concerning The True Original, Extent And End Of Civil Government* (London, 1970), paras. 25, 31, 33, 37.

[44] Marx, K., *Capital* (Wishart, London, 1972), Vol. III, 776. See also Marx, K. and Engels, F., *8 Selected Works* (Foreign Publishing, Moscow, 1954), 76–7.

[45] Weiss, *supra* n. 27, 495, 500.

generation will have gone, having taken the benefits of such decisions, but leaving the costs behind.[46] The classic example of this is found with nuclear waste.[47]

Nuclear Waste and Future Generations

In 1994, the world's 431 commercial nuclear reactors created more than 10,000 tons of irradiated fuel, bringing the total accumulation of used fuel (or nuclear waste) to 130,000 tons. (*Vital Signs: 1995–1996*, 88). This figure is expected to increase rapidly in forthcoming years. Of the waste that is produced, there are three types. These are low-level, intermediate, and high-level. It is the high-level waste (typically, spent nuclear fuel) to which the above figures refer. High-level waste contains at least 95 per cent of all the radioactivity in radioactive waste, yet is no more than 3 per cent of its total volume. Nevertheless, this should not be seen to detract from the estimated 200,000 cubic metres of low-level and intermediate waste produced annually.

There are three options for the disposal of radioactive waste. The first is through the reprocessing of nuclear wastes. This is currently considered unattractive due to the economic costs involved. The second is through disposal, via either discharge into the sea or trade with a third party.

The disposal of high-level radioactive waste into the sea was first rejected by the international community with the *Convention on the Prevention of Marine Pollution By Dumping of Wastes*. (26 UST. 2403. Annex. 1 in 1972). In 1993 this ban was extended to cover all types (i.e. also low-level and intermediate level) of radioactive waste. Likewise, the possibility of trading nuclear waste with other countries has been largely curtailed. (See *Convention on the Control of Transboundary Movements of Hazardous wastes and their Disposal*. Article 1 (3). 1989. 28 ILM 657.)

Due to the fact that the recycling, sea dumping, and trade options have become largely unavailable as methods to control nuclear waste, countries have been forced to examine a third alternative. This final way of disposal is through long-term geological storage. This appears set to become the primary way of dealing with at least intermediate and high-level nuclear waste in forthcoming years.

Current methods of disposal through geological storage envision

---

[46]   Gower, B., 'What Do We Owe Future Generations?', in Cooper, D. and Palmer, J. (eds.), *The Environment in Question: Ethics and Global Issues* (Routledge, London, 1992), 1.

[47]   Routley, R. and V., 'Nuclear Energy and Obligations to the Future', *Inquiry*, 21 (1978), 128. Gunn, A., *Ethics and Hazardous Waste Management: Why Should We Care About Future Generations* (Waikato University, Occasional Paper, 1987). Shrader-Frechette, K., 'Equity, Consent and Hazardous Wastes', in UNEP (ed.), *Ethics and Agenda 21: Moral Implications of a Global Consensus* (United Nations, New York, 1994), 83–7. Logan, B. L., 'An Assessment of the Environmental and Economic Implications of Toxic-Waste Disposal in Sub-Saharan Africa', *Journal of World Trade*, 25 (1991), 61, 67–72

the waste to be encapsulated in a metal canister (iron, copper or titanium). It is then surrounded by a clay back-fill/buffer material. Finally, it is surrounded by bedrock, at a depth of between 500–1000 metres deep.

Such extreme measures are deemed necessary as the final residues of high-level nuclear waste will be radioactive for up to hundreds of thousands of years. Despite rapid cooling of the spent waste over the first 40 years, and a further reduction of radioactivity down to 1 per cent of its original level over a further 1000 years, the remaining percentage will remain active for multiple millennia into the future. This will thus create a legacy for future generations.

In response to this charge it has been argued that the proper geological disposal of radioactive waste does not place 'an unacceptable burden on later generations'. (The Uranium Institute (1991). *The Management of Radioactive Waste,* 17.) Indeed, the Nuclear Energy Agency (NEA) of the OECD has stipulated that such waste disposal 'takes intergenerational equity into account, notably by applying the same standards of risk in the future as it does to the present, and by limiting the liabilities bequeathed to future generations'. (NEA (1995). *The Environmental and Ethical Basis of Geological Disposal,* 8.) The NEA goes on to justify this position due to the fact that all generations leave behind a mixture of burdens and benefits for the future, and the issue, therefore, is to make a choice whereby the impacts caused for future generations is not disproportionate to the benefit that this generation obtains by the usage of nuclear power (12–13, 16–17). The conclusion of this position can be found in the International Atomic Energy Agency's *Principles of Radioactive Waste Management.* Principle 4 recognizes 'Radioactive waste shall be managed in such a way that predicted impacts on the health of future generations will not be greater than relevant levels of impact that are acceptable today'. Principle 6 suggests that 'Radioactive waste shall be managed in such a way that will not impose undue burdens on future generations'. (IAEA, *Safety Fundamentals: The Principles of Radioactive Waste Management. Safety Series.* No. III.F.)

This above position is highly arguable and charges of unethical conduct may be levelled against it. This is because a highly dangerous product will be left to forthcoming generations. However, despite the fact that the future generations may be the only ones who are detrimentally affected by the decisions made today pertaining to nuclear waste, these are the very people who are *not* represented in the decision-making process. The question of ethics is furthered by their lack of consent to be possibly harmed, the lack of justification (i.e. self-defence/lack of alternatives) to harm them, and the failure to provide compensation for them.

When such arguments are raised, it is suggested that this generation should take the interests of those not yet born into consideration when making decisions that could affect them. The desired result of this foresight is the recognition of a principle that has been broadly stated by Edith Weiss who suggested that:

We as a species, hold the natural and cultural environment of our planet in common, both with other members of the present generation and with other generations, past and future. At any given time, each generation is both a custodian or trustee of the planet for future generations and a beneficiary of its fruits.[48]

3. THEORIES OF THE RIGHTS OF FUTURE GENERATIONS

A. John Rawls and the Ideal Observer

One of the most commonly argued philosophical justifications for future generations is derived from the 'ideal observer' theory that was offered by John Rawls. Briefly, Rawls endeavoured to locate the principles of justice on the basis of an elaborate thought experiment.[49]

This idea entails a volunteer to be asked what principles would be adopted by subjects who are rational and self-interested and situated behind a 'veil of ignorance'.[50] Behind such a veil, the subjects would be ignorant of their own social, sexual, and ethnic life and not informed of any talents they may possess. Therefore, the ideal observer theory should check all emotional sympathies and self favouritism that the person behind the veil of ignorance may have had before being so situated. Consequently, strict impartiality will be guaranteed. The ideal observer will be acquainted with all the non-moral facts. Additionally, they will be able to identify with all the parties involved and their respective positions (this does not mean adopt all the viewpoints concerned, but simply to be able to understand all the differing perspectives). They will also be disinterested, dispassionate, and consistent in their approach. Therefore, it would be irrational in Rawls's view to endorse principles which could possibly disadvantage the person behind the veil. The ideal observer would tend to adopt policies that would cover the least advantaged in society as there is a possibility that it could be them.[51] The end result is that the rightness or wrongness of some act can then be finally seen as it is, judged by an objective bystander.

In the context of future generations, Rawls proposed that the ideal observer, 'must choose principles the consequences of which they are prepared to live with whatever generation they turn out to belong to'.[52] Here, Rawls extended the veil of ignorance to cover the aspect of time. This means that the individual behind the

---

[48] Weiss, *supra* n. 25, 17.

[49] Rawls, J., *A Theory of Justice* (Oxford University Press, Oxford, 1972).

[50] Ibid. 136–42.   [51] Ibid. 137.

[52] Ibid. 137. See also Singer, B., 'An Extension of Rawls' Theory of Justice to Environmental Ethics', *Environmental Ethics*, 10 (1988), 219.

veil would not know where they would fit in on a time-scale, i.e. whether it was the first, middle or last generation. Rawls believed that the compromise, which a rational person behind the veil would choose, would be one whereby they could inherit the world in the same condition as the generation before had enjoyed. Each generation could then be read as a trustee for the planet with an obligation to care for it, and as a beneficiary with rights to use it to a limited degree.[53]

Rawls classified this realization as the 'just savings' principle. This can be regarded as an understanding between generations that each generation would carry its fair share of the burden of realizing a just society. In this instance, the 'just savings' principle is intended to improve the welfare of the least advantaged group extending over future generations.[54]

B. The Cross-Temporal Argument

A second theory for supporting the consideration of the needs of future generations comes from the 'cross-temporal approach'. This idea necessitates a view of human society as an ongoing current of which all generations form part of a larger whole. This perspective suggests that past generations have made sacrifices for both the present and future generations.[55]

The object of such former sacrifices by past individuals or groups is often to promote a greater community and make possible a higher quality of life in the future. As Immanuel Kant noted, people live in societies that are far from ideal but still strive for a better society in the future, of which they may well *not* be part.[56] On a more reductionist level, individuals may develop identities that clearly go beyond themselves or just their small group. Here, ideas of cultural and social identity and placement, as opposed to merely individual perception, are pertinent. The central theme is that to have such cross-temporal identities it is necessary for individuals of any existing generation to have a concern for future generations. As Edmund Burke wrote:

People will not look forward to posterity who never look back towards their ancestors . . . as the ends of such a partnership cannot be obtained in many generations, it becomes a partnership not only between those who are living, but between those who are living, those who are dead, and those who are yet to be born.[57]

---

[53] Ibid. 284–93. For an application of this approach, see Routley, *supra* n. 47.

[54] Ibid. 287, 289.

[55] O'Neill, J., *Ecology, Policy and Politics: Human Well-Being and the Natural World* (Routledge, London, 1993), 32–4. Weiss, *supra* n. 27. 495. Kavka and Warren, *supra* n. 27, 1, 31. Baier, A., 'The Rights of Past And Future Persons', in Partridge, *supra* n. 38, 177–81. Callahan, D., 'What Obligations Do We Have To Future Generations', also in Partridge, 77. Hardin, G., 'Who Cares For Posterity?', in Partridge, 226.

[56] Kant, *supra* n. 41 at 182. See also Rolston, H., 'The River Of Life: Past, Present, and Future', in Partridge, *supra* n. 38. 127. O'Neill, ibid. 34–6, 39.

[57] Burke, E., *Reflections On The Revolution In France* (Penguin, Harmondsworth, 1961), 45.

The idea of a cross-temporal perspective is also recognized as the 'concept of self transcendence', the basis of which can be found in the area of transpersonal psychology which seeks to achieve 'self-actualisation and personal growth'.[58] The central forces behind this school of thought are Abraham Maslow's and Antony Sutich's work.[59] This school of thought grew out of ideas like Freud's id, ego, and superego, and Marx's wider sense of alienation.[60] Consequently, as Warwick Fox claimed:

the larger welfare of the individual depends upon the extent that he can identify himself with others, and . . . the most satisfactory individual identity is that which identifies not only with a community in space, but also with a community extending over time from the past into the future.[61]

Thus, well-functioning human beings are believed to identify with, and actually seek, the well-being of communities and everything associated with them from their institutions to their people. Additionally, such people are believed to hope that both individuals and institutions that they are involved in, will flourish beyond their own life times. The upshot of this is that the individual, by her/his very origin and nature, transcends her/his atomistic physical locus. This in turn leads to their happiness and 'secure placement'.[62] Such a placement can lead to the sacrifices and attitudes that are required to recognize their place in the 'greater stream of life'.[63] This type of perspective visualizes each generation of humanity as a small cross-section in the temporal continuity of the moral community. Thus 'life' is inherited from past generations, flows through the present generation and then on to future generations. Consequently, each individual should be concerned with the past, present, and the future, as they are connected with the entire process.

This view of cross-temporal life shows a distinct evolution of the conscience. In doing so, human empathy is believed to go beyond immediate kinship, and subsequently to be concerned for all (human) life without chronological boundaries, as the individual subjects are part of the greater 'stream of humanity'.[64]

---

[58] Fox, W., *Towards A Transpersonal Ecology: Developing New Foundations for Environmentalism* (London, Shambhala, 1990), 289–99.

[59] For an examination of the relevant work of these authors, see Fox, ibid. 289–99.

[60] Marx, K., *Early Writings*, 77–87 and the *Economics*, 515–17. Both in McLean, D. (ed.), *Karl Marx: Selected Writings* (Oxford University Press, Oxford, 1978). See also Tolman, C. 'Karl Marx, Alienation and the Mastery of Nature', *Environmental Ethics*, 3 (1981), 63, 64–9.

[61] Fox, *supra* n. 58, 198–215. See also Polak, F. L., *The Image of the Future* (Oceana, New York, 1961).

[62] Fox, *supra* n. 58. 295–9. Goodin, R. E., *Green Political Theory* (Polity, Cambridge, 1992), 39–40.

[63] Westra, A., 'Let It Be: Heideggger And Future Generations', *Environmental Ethics*, 7 (1985), 348, 349. Dooley, K., 'The Ambiguity Of Environmental Ethics: Duty Or Heroism', *Philosophy Today*, 30 (1986), 54. Rolston, *supra* n. 56, 127.

[64] Cercera, H., 'A Response To Professor De George', in Dias, J. (ed.), *Law And The Ecological Challenge* (Random House, New York, 1971), 43. Hartmann, T., *Ethics: Moral Values* (Doubleday, New York, 1972), 305–8.

THE PROBLEMS WITH THE FUTURE GENERATIONS ARGUMENTS

1. MOTIVATIONAL AND PRACTICAL PROBLEMS

It would be fair to propose that many people can recognize, or could be brought to recognize, that certain actions should be taken to safeguard the needs of future generations. However, the hope that people will move from a purely self-interested position to one directed by ethical concern to consider the interests of the next generations is *not* always realized. This is because it is commonly believed that future generations are too vaguely connected with the present generations and that future generations can offer little to contemporary generations that would necessitate any required sacrifices by them.[65] Or as John Trumbull, writing around the turn of the nineteenth century, said, 'What has posterity ever done for us?'[66] This type of lack of affiliation with future generations indicates that many people have not seen sufficient justification to make the sacrifices that are required of them.[67] As Robert Heilbroner stated:

after all, why should we make sacrifices now to ease the lot of generations whom we will never live to see . . . one possible answer lies in our capacity to form a collective bond with future generations . . . indeed it is the absence of just such a bond with the future that casts doubt on the ability of nation states or socio-economic orders to take now the measures needed to mitigate the problems of the future.[68]

The basic premise here is that people may have little interest in what cannot touch them. For example, although millions of people can see through the media that thousands of people are starving, only a small number of those who witness these tragedies will actually do anything to help alleviate the starvation. If people cannot be moved to act to help current generations in jeopardy, there is little hope that they will take action to protect the interests of future generations.[69]

The lack of concern about future generations is further entrenched with the

---

[65] Golding, M. P., 'Obligations To Future Generations', *Monist,* 56 (1972), 97. Hardin, G., 'Who Cares For Posterity?', in Partridge, E. (ed.) *The Rights of Future Generations* (Prometheus, New York, 1981), 222–6. Sieger Derr, H., 'The Obligation To The Future', also in Partridge, 39. Heilbroner, R. L., *An Inquiry Into The Human Prospect* (Norton, New York, 1974), 135. For a practical example of the effect of not considering the future, see the section on economics and the effect of 'discounting' at Ch. III s. 4 *infra.*

[66] Bowden, D. (ed.), *The Satiric Poems Of John Trumbull* (Texas, 1962), 129.

[67] Care, N. S., 'Future Generations, Public Policy, And The Motivation Problem', *Environmental Ethics,* 4 (1982), 207, 210. Heilbroner, R. L., 'What Has Posterity Ever Done For Me?', in Partridge, *supra* n. 65, 192. Gower, B., 'What Do We Owe Future Generations?', in Cooper, D. and Palmer, J. (eds.), *The Environment in Questions: Ethics and Global Issues* (Routledge, London, 1992), 1, 3.

[68] Heilbroner, *supra* n. 65, 114–15, 131, 132, 135–6.

[69] See Stretton, H., *Capitalism, Socialism and the Environment* (Cambridge University Press, Cambridge, 1978), 7.

existence of societal alienation.[70] According to Erich Fromm, an alienated person is one who:

Does not experience himself as the active bearer of his own powers and richness, but as an impoverished 'thing', dependent on powers outside of himself, unto whom he has projected living substance.[71]

It is within this alienation that the individual retreats into herself/himself. Indifference, apathy, and intense narcissism flow from this position or, according to Fromm, 'a failure of relatedness'.[72] The result is the complete antithesis of any form of self transcendence that may establish an empathy with future generations.[73]

Another point to note here concerns the 'river of life' argument and the alleged duty to perpetuate the human race by which no means can be taken as absolute. For example, if an examination of the other side of human biological nature is taken, an alternative view develops. This is because for as long as humanity has been on the planet, people have murdered, cheated, pillaged, and gone to war. 'Iron curtains', East-West barriers, North-South divides, racism, nationalism, and a multitude of other political and social creations show that humanity does *not* regard itself as anything near a unified whole searching for a continued existence.

The argument of immediate self-interest is also well illustrated with what is known as 'the tyranny of the immediate'.[74] The argument here is that extreme current realities are generally rated as being more important by those 'on the ground' than future possibilities. As the *World Conservation Strategy* observed, malnourished and destitute people, 'are compelled to destroy the resources necessary to free them from starvation and poverty'.[75] Or as Garrett Hardin said, 'People will sacrifice every promise of tomorrow for the merest scrap of food today (if they are hungry enough)'.[76] Consequently, it is commonly suggested that it is more pertinent to spend time and energy working on problems of the present, rather than those of the future.[77]

---

[70] Partridge, E., 'Why Care About The Future?', in Partridge, *supra* n. 65, 215. O'Neill, J. (1993), *Ecology, Policy and Politics: Human Well-Being and the Natural World* (Routledge, London, 1993), 38–43.

[71] Fromm, E., *The Sane Society* (Routledge, New York, 1955), 111. See also Lasch, C., *The Culture Of Narcissism: American Life In An Age Of Discriminatory Expectation* (Abacus, London, 1978), 39–40.

[72] Fromm, ibid., 114. See also Keniston, K., *The Uncommitted* (Brace and World, New York, 1965), 441. Lasch, ibid.   [73] Keniston, ibid.

[74] The phrase, 'the tyranny of the immediate' is discussed in Starke, L. (ed.), *Signs of Hope: Working Towards Our Common Future* (Oxford University Press, Oxford, 1990), 28.

[75] See point 2 (b). IUCN, *World Conservation Strategy* (Switzerland, 1980), reprinted in Rusta, B. and Simma, B. (eds.), *International Protection of the Environment* (Oceana, New York, 1982), Vol. 13, 427.   [76] Hardin, *supra* n. 65, 227.

[77] Stretton, *supra* n. 69, 7–8. Lee, J. A., 'Conservation in a World in Search of a Future', in Western, D. and Pearl, M. (eds.), *Conservation for the Twenty-first Century* (Oxford University Press, Oxford, 1989), 284, 285. Baier, A., 'The Rights Of Past And Future Persons', in Partridge, *supra* n. 65, 172–4. Callahan, D., 'What Obligations Do We Have To Future Generations?', in Partridge, *supra* n. 65, 81.

Therefore, any theory of future generations must be limited by the requirement that the important needs of present generations are considered. As Gifford Pinchot suggested at the turn of the century, 'the welfare of this generation first, and afterward the welfare of future generations to follow'.[78] Thus, inter-generational equity cannot exist without *intra*-generational equity.[79] This is not suggesting that the consideration of future generations should not be contemplated, rather, that these considerations should not be accorded excessive weight.

A second problem here is that environmental realities and the theory of future generations may point in opposite directions and many contemporary theories of future generations fail to fully recognize this issue. All too often theories of future generations are apolitical. This is not to suggest that the cross-temporal argument has no validity. Rather, it is likely to be overborne by other considerations. If societies were changed in accordance with other ecological and social goals then it might be possible to bypass this part of the objection to the possibility of the moral consideration of future generations.

2. THEORETICAL PROBLEMS

A. Knowledge, Distance, and Cost

Early in the twentieth century, Henry Sidgwick foresaw a problem with the argument for the consideration of the interests of future generations. He noted that there must be limits on how far considerations of the future can be taken owing to a limited knowledge of the certainties with which it is currently possible to obtain and how it may affect the future generations.[80]

Basically, the considerations that need to be taken into account in determining how the present generation should act must be reasonably predictable and have a weight according to the degree of probability of the needs of future generations.[81] However, when it comes to assuming anything more than basic physical needs of future generations, any propositions are nothing more than speculation.[82] As Martin Golding contended:

---

[78] Pinchot, G., *The Fight For Conservation* (Harcourt Brace, New York, 1910), 10, 35.

[79] Weiss, E., *In Fairness To Future Generations* (United Nations University, Japan, 1988), 55. Attfield, R., *The Ethics of Environmental Concern* (Blackwell, Oxford, 1983), 92. Note that this is an important point as some theorists appear willing to sacrifice current generations to protect future ones. See Hardin, G., who asserted 'Every life saved this year in a poor country diminishes the quality of life for subsequent generations.' *Stalking the Wild Taboo* (Kaufman, California, 1978), 234, 256–9.

[80] Sidgwick, H., *The Methods of Ethics* (Routledge, London, 1962), Book 3, 81.

[81] Sprigge, K., 'A Utilitarian Reply To McCloskey', in Bayles, M. D. (ed.), *Contemporary Utilitarianism* (Doubleday, New York, 1968), 263.

[82] Jamieson, D. 'The City Around Us', in Regan, T. (ed.), *Earthbound: New Introductory Essays in Environmental Ethics* (Random House, New York, 1982), 56.

It is only possible to know what the wants of future generations are, when they are closer to the present generation in time. Therefore, the present generation essentially ought to confine its attention to only helping immediate posterity.[83]

One reply to this argument is that it is unlikely that future generations will have changed sufficiently in a biological sense not to have the same basic needs as the current generation. An analogy can be made with current individual lives. Individuals do not know what their goals and desires in forty years will be, let alone what their concept of a good life would contain. However, it is possible to postulate that they would include the basics of good health, food, shelter, security, and so on.[84]

Therefore, ignorance of the degree to which future generations will share current conceptions of the good life, does not seem to be a valid reason for considering the interests and needs of *only* the next few generations. Notwithstanding this concession, there is still merit in this objection and it must still be recognized as a limitation in any possible actions to assist distant future generations. This is because beyond the area of physical necessities, current generations know nothing of the other needs of their counterparts in the future. For example, one hundred years ago it would have been impossible to predict that petroleum or plutonium would be so important to this generation. Accordingly, this generation has no idea of what the 'essentials' of the future will be. Consequently, the open question remains, how is it possible to save for future generations anything above the biologically obvious?[85]

Such specific questions as those highlighted above have led to only general formulations of what should be saved for future generations. For example, it is suggested that the current generation ought to leave the Earth for future generations in a condition which is no worse than that in which they received it. Consequently, Gifford Pinchot proclaimed that:

No generation can be allowed needlessly to damage or reduce the future general wealth and welfare by the way it uses or misuses any natural resource.[86]

Edith Weiss, the prominent advocate for the theory of the consideration of future generations, has also adopted this view. She believes that to protect the welfare of future generations there are three things that this generation is required to preserve, namely:

---

[83]   Golding, *supra* n. 65, 97–8.

[84]   Kavka, G. and Warren, V., 'Political Representation for Future Generations', in Elliot, R. and Gare, A. (eds.), *Environmental Philosophy* (Queensland University Press, Queensland, 1983), 1, 24. Kavka, G., 'The Paradox Of Future Individuals', *Philosophy and Public Affairs,* 11 (1982), 103, 105. Barry, M., 'Justice Between Generations', in Hacker, P. M. S. (ed.), *Law, Morality and Society: Essays in Honour or H. L. A. Hart* (Clarendon Press, Oxford, 1977), 274–5. Attfield, *supra* n. 79, 93.

[85]   Passmore, J., *Man's Responsibility For Nature* (Duckworth, London, 1974), 75–8.

[86]   Pinchot, G., 'What it all Means', in Burton, I. and Kates, R. W. (eds.), *Readings in Resource Management and Conservation* (University of Chicago Press, Chicago, 1965), 255.

To sustain the life support systems of the planet; to sustain the ecological processes and environmental conditions necessary for the survival of the human species; and to sustain a healthy and decent environment.[87]

The end result of this approach is that existing generations may be required to sacrifice some of their non-basic needs for the interests of posterity. This approach does not dictate that it is illegitimate to exhaust certain resources, because the environment may have to be changed and certain trade-offs may be inevitable. However, for the current generation to 'change' the environment, it is necessary for them to pass on a sufficiently increased level of income, capital and knowledge to enable future generations to find alternatives for what the previous generation depleted and methods for abating the pollution they may have caused.[88]

Additionally, there are some actions that are required to be taken by the present generation. These involve a two-stage process. First, it is necessary to redress current environmental problems such as climatic change, the loss of genetic diversity, and the ozone hole; and secondly, a limitation in consumption for most Northern countries.[89] The problem is how these necessities are going to be achieved, as often the political will to protect the environment is *currently* not present (the motivational problem again).

Even if the motivational problem could be sidestepped, the absolute obligation to the most distant future generation could easily result in a near seizure of modern society due to the possibly limitless numbers of future generations and their needs. As John Passmore observed:

Anything we can do would, over millions of years, be infinitesimal in its effects; not even by reducing our consumption of petrol to a thimbleful apiece could we ensure the availability of a similar quantity to our remotest descendants.[90]

Thus, it becomes obvious that where *all* possible time-scales of future generations are considered, then the degree of consideration required may make the obligation almost nonsensical.[91] Accordingly, realism may suggest that any one generation cannot attempt to share the resources that the present generation possesses with the whole of posterity. The best that could be hoped for in this situation is to make, 'some savings for its sake'.[92] Or as John Rawls suggested, each generation should attempt at least to, 'hand on to our immediate posterity a rather better situation than we ourselves have inherited'.[93]

---

[87] Weiss, E. 'The Planetary Trust: Conservation And Intergenerational Equity', *Ecology Law Quarterly,* 11 (1984), 511.

[88] Sterba, J. P. 'The Welfare Rights Of Distant People And Future Generations: Moral Side-Constraints On Social Policy', *Social Theory and Practice,* 7 (1981), 110. Weiss., 'The Planetary Trust', ibid. 523.   [89] Sterba, ibid. 113, 114.

[90] Passmore, *supra* n. 85, 78–9.

[91] Carr, I. M., 'Saving the Environment: Does Utilitarianism Provide a Justification', *Legal Studies,* 12 (1992), 92, 99. Cf. Attfield: such obligations 'are not unrealistically exacting'. *Supra* n. 79, 102, 105.   [92] Gower, *supra* n. 67, 1, 9, 10–11.

[93] Rawls, J., *A Theory of Justice* (Oxford University Press, 1972), 289–90.

This point is reinforced by the suggestion that the demands of the present more often than not cloud over any intentions of the long-term future. This is especially so as the distance of concern for the future increases. Because of such a limitation, once an ethical consideration beyond grandchildren is speculated problems are encountered. This is because future persons become increasingly indeterminate and remote. As Herman Daly and John Cobb said:

Your great-great grandchild will also be the great-great grandchild of 15 other people in the current generation, many of their identities now unknown. Presumably, your great-great grandchild's well being will be as much an inheritance from each of these 15 others as from yourself. Therefore, it does not make sense for you to worry too much about your particular descendant, or take any action on his or her behalf.[94]

Consequently, it is argued that only the claims of those closely located to the valuer are of importance.[95] It is suggested that the capacity for care diminishes with distance. This position has caused many to speculate that any obligation to future generations can go no further than the next generation. This is known as the 'potential principle'. Here, the most distant obligations which are owed to future peoples will be found in the parent of yet unborn children. After that the obligation radically decreases.[96]

However, there are two problems with this reformulation of placing the priority of one (the nearest) future generation over another. The first is that of arbitrariness: the time when an individual exists should be morally irrelevant to any decision about how that individual should be treated. Secondly, an ethic based primarily on the interests of generations that are quite close to the present generation will not generate long-term obligations to protect the environment. For example, the casual dumping of long-term toxic waste would be quite acceptable under the potential principle as its results would not be felt by this, or probably the next, generation. The fact that they are of relevance only in the future is of no concern as the emphasis is only upon protecting generations closely related in time.

B. Interests and Existence

A further problem with regard to the moral considerability of future generations concerns the interests they may have at stake. The basic argument for future generations maintains that it is highly probable that humanity will have future

---

[94] Daly, H. E. and Cobb, J., *For the Common Good: Redirecting the Economy Towards the Community, the Environment and a Sustainable Future* (Beacon, Boston, 1989), 39.

[95] Thompson, G., 'Are We Obliged to Future Others?', in Partridge, *supra* n. 65, 201. Bateson, M. C., 'Caring For Children, Caring For Earth', *Christ and Crisis*, 40 (1980), 68.

[96] De George, R. T., 'The Rights of Future Generations?', in Dias, J. (ed.), *Law and the Ecological Challenge* (Random House, New York, 1971). See also Burrill, D. B., 'Obligation Language and Future Generations', also in Dias. Passmore, *supra* n. 85, 78–80. Cf, Attfield, *supra* n. 79, 97–8.

descendants, and that those descendants will have approximately the same basic needs and wants that the present generation has today. In this sense, future generations do have *interests* that can be affected by the policies of existing generations. This leads on to a moral concern and the necessity for practical action.[97]

The problem is that this idea of having interests as a prerequisite to moral considerability is also applicable in other areas, such as with the arguments for the moral value of animals. However, the latter view has been challenged on the basis that the recipients of the moral concern do not possess the rudimentary cognitive equipment required for the existence of interests.[98] The outcome of the same logic with the future generations approach, and the idea of interests is obvious. For, as they do not exist, they cannot have cognitive equipment and therefore cannot have interests.

The advocates who argue for the moral considerability of animals have responded by proving that many animals do have the requisite cognitive equipment or, alternatively, that the moral consideration should be given for the possession of sentience or an existing 'good' which may be harmed or benefited. Beyond these areas, the issue moves into an area of unidentifiable holders of moral considerability, with interests that cannot be qualified. Drawing the line for moral considerability here has distinct implications for future generations, because if future generations and their non-sentient interests cannot be identified, then they are not currently in possession of anything that can be the subject of any moral consideration. Therefore, as Virginia Warren said, 'What does not exist, cannot be harmed or wronged or have its rights violated'.[99] Existence in the present is seen as the minimum prerequisite for moral concern.[100]

A final argument in this area is Derek Parfit's vexing paradox of future generations. Simply, Parfit has argued that if any future people exist at all, then they cannot bemoan the fact that an earlier generation wronged them. For if an earlier generation acted differently, then via multipliers such as the Chaos effect, the specific persons of the generation that was complaining would not exist at all. Thus, given that any (in the vast majority of cases) existence is better than no existence, then they have no right to complain. For if things had been different,

---

[97] Feinberg, J., 'The Rights of Animals and Unborn Generations', in Blackstone, W. T. (ed.), *Philosophy and the Environmental Crisis* (University of Georgia Press, Athens, 1974), 65. Norton, B. G., 'Environmental Ethics And The Rights Of Future Generations', *Environmental Ethics,* 4 (1982), 322.

[98] Feinberg, ibid. 159–84.

[99] Macklin, R., 'Can Future Generations Correctly Be Said to Have Rights?', in Partridge, *supra* n. 65, 152. Warren, K. J., 'Do Potential Persons Have Rights?', in Partridge, *supra* n. 65, 261. De George, R. T., 'The Environment, Rights and Future Generations', in Regan, T. (ed.), *Ethics And Problems Of The Twenty-first Century* (Random House, New York, 1976), 52, 95.

[100] Narveson, J., 'On the Survival of Humankind', in Elliot and Gare, *supra* n. 84, 41, 48. For the discussion on the animal rights part of this, see Ch. VIII of this book.

they would not exist. This problem presents a fundamental dilemma, because this consideration suggests that short of creating no future at all, we, in effect, cannot harm future generations.[101]

C. The Anthropocentric Assumptions within the Theories for the Moral Consideration of Future Generations

The theories about the moral considerability of future generations are distinctly anthropocentric. The consideration of anything non-human is currently outside the sphere of the debate.[102] This raises the questions of whether such an anthropocentric approach is justifiable. This specific issue is addressed in chapters eight, nine, and ten.

A significant contribution to the anthropocentric perspective comes from Rawls's *Theory of Justice* for the moral considerability of future generations. However, this is artificially restricted by the assumption that only human considerations could be contemplated behind the veil of ignorance. For if the original position behind the veil were to be truly neutral, then its participants would not only be ignorant of race, sex, and social position but also of species membership. This idea of not being embodied in any particular form when behind the veil is also consistent even with the full range of human possibilities. That is, observers behind the veil of ignorance must face the possibility of being cast into any number of human incapacities.

Once reasoners behind the veil take into account the possible interests of such people, who Brent Singer classifies as 'abnormal beings with interests', then the scope of possibilities for the consideration of non-human entities is widened considerably.[103] This is because, like severely retarded humans, many animals have interests in how they are treated. If the reasoners behind the veil face the possibility that they may turn out to be a retarded infant, then they must realize they could also turn out to be a healthy animal with very similar interests. Therefore, a true ideal observer would be one which was not only non-egotistical but also not necessarily human.[104]

As it stands, Rawls took it for granted that the veil of ignorance was to be

[101] Parfit, D., *Reasons and Persons* (Oxford University Press, Oxford, 1984), 351, 355–65, 372, 378, 382, 387–8, 434–5, 451.

[102] Gundling, L., 'Our Responsibility to Future Generations', *American Journal of International Law*, 84 (1990), 207, 208–9. Hooker, C., 'Responsibility, Ethics and Nature', in Cooper and Palmer, *supra* n. 67, 147, 152. Narveson, ibid. 41, 45. Weiss, *supra* n. 79, 17. Attfield, *supra* n. 79, 106.

[103] Singer, B., 'An Extension of Rawls' Theory of Justice to Environmental Ethics', *Environmental Ethics*, 10 (1988), 219, 226–7. Regan, T., *The Case for Animal Rights* (Routledge, London, 1988), 179–82.

[104] Elliot, R., 'Rawlsian Justice and Non-Human Animals', *Journal of Applied Philosophy*, 1 (1984), 95, 99–103. Manning, S., 'Environmental Ethics and Rawls' Theory of Justice', *Environmental Ethics*, 3 (1981), 155. Van De Veer, D., 'Of Beasts, Persons and the Original Position', *Monist*, 62 (1979), 371.

restricted only to humans as only humans have a capacity for justice. Rawls suggested that a sense of justice develops within humanity through family institutions, social arrangement, and social reciprocity. The end result is that Rawls excluded any moral duties to anything but humans.[105]

Nevertheless, there is a problem in these assertions. The first part of the problem is that many humans do not have this capacity for justice. Secondly, Rawls's definition of a being's good consists of the successful execution of a rational plan of life.[106] However, he restricted this conception by properties within it relating to the acquisition of income and wealth. Thus, he unjustifiably restricted the ambit of the discussion through anthropocentric goals before it fully develops. Therefore, it can be suggested that the veil should be constructed to also be impartial to species membership.

The first asserted problem to this reconstruction of the veil of ignorance is that to adopt a non-anthropocentric position behind the veil of ignorance could lead to decisions which might cause problems for humanity if taken to their ultimate conclusion (such as the individual 'right' of life for other animals leading to the necessity for most humans to become vegetarians).[107] The difficulty with this argument is that those who fear this possible outcome understand the situation perfectly but cannot accept it.

The second alleged problem is that it is impossible for an ideal observer to interpret the world from anything but a rational homocentric viewpoint.[108] However, as noted above, if an ideal observer is expected to be able to identify with severely retarded people, there is no fundamental difference in kind why they should not be able to identity with the interests of at least the higher animals. Rational observers should be able to identify non-rational interests or basic needs that are applicable to both well-functioning and severely disabled people, *and* to non-human animals.

The last difficulty with the argument that the participants behind the veil must have a capacity for justice, i.e. rationality, is that if an ideal observer maintains a rationality prerequisite before being placed behind the veil of ignorance, then they could well choose principles that would benefit only the rational members of society over the non-rational. Therefore, the rationality capacity, as a theoretical prerequisite to being placed behind the veil, cannot be retained, and the possibility must be realized that the participants may become non-rational.[109]

The final justification for the future generations argument that is myopic is the

---

[105] Rawls, J., *A Theory of Justice* (Harvard University Press, Cambridge, 1971), 164, 177–8, 511, 517. Rawls, J., 'The Sense of Justice', *Philosophical Review*, 72 (1963), 284. Taliaferro, C., 'The Environmental Ethics of an Ideal Observer', *Environmental Ethics*, 10 (1988), 233.
[106] Rawls, ibid. 92.
[107] Robinson, W. L., 'Rawls and Other Beings', in Dias, *supra* n. 96, 87.
[108] Spitler, G., 'Justifying a Respect for Nature', *Environmental Ethics*, 4 (1982), 256. Elliot, *supra* n. 104, 95, 103.
[109] Van De Veer, *supra* n. 104, 369–70.

cross-temporal approach. In this area the 'extended self' which is used to identify with future generations has also been artificially restricted by anthropocentric assumptions.[110] To reorientate this view to take into consideration non-anthropocentric concerns would correspond with a central theme found in the writings of deep ecology which focuses upon the identification of the self within larger biospheric considerations. Here it is argued that, 'trans-human identification is centred in the cosmos'.[111] Such a realization would lead to moral concern for the future continuation of *not* only the human species, but *also* of other natural entities as well.

[110] See Fox, W., *Towards a Transpersonal Ecology: Developing New Foundations for Environmentalism* (Shambhala, London, 1990), 202–3.

[111] Fox, ibid. 296. Naess, A., *Ecology, Community and Lifestyle* (Cambridge University Press, Cambridge, 1989), 165–6. See also pages 21–2 of this book.

VII

The Growth of New, Non-Anthropocentric Ideals within International Environmental Law

1. THE CHANGE OF VALUES

Slowly, the ethical basis within international environmental law and policy appears to be changing. For example, over twenty years ago the 1972 *Stockholm Declaration on the Human Environment* recognized that, 'Man has a special responsibility to safeguard and wisely manage the heritage of wildlife and its habitat . . .'.[1] The reasons for conservation were strictly in terms of human interest. Yet as time has progressed the reasons have been slowly developing.[2] For example, the 1973 *European Ministerial Conference on the Environment* noted that 'the environment must be taken care of because of its own value, as a part of the world's heritage'.[3] In the same year the *Convention on International Trade in Endangered Species of Wild Fauna and Flora*[4] was created which sets out to preserve species that are endangered as 'they are an irreplaceable part of the natural systems of the earth which must be protected for this and the generations to come'.[5] Thus, steps must be taken to prevent the endangerment of the survival prospects of overall species[6] (as opposed to individual animals). Six years later the 1979 *Convention on the Conservation of European Wildlife and Natural Habitats* recognized in its preamble that wild fauna and flora has intrinsic value.[7] In 1980 the *World Conservation Strategy* in its preface to Chapter 18 pronounced that:

Ultimately the behaviour of entire societies towards the biosphere must be transformed if the achievement of conservation objectives is to be assured. A new ethic, embracing

---

[1] Principle 4, (Ch. II) *Stockholm Declaration*. UN Doc A/CONF 48/14 (1972). 11 ILM. 1972. 1416.

[2] See Birnie, P. W. and Boyle, A. E., *International Law and the Environment* (Clarendon Press, Oxford, 1992), 213, 323–424.

[3] Preamble to Resolution number 1 of the *European Ministerial Conference on the Environment*. 1973. Press release of the *European Ministerial Conference on the Environment*. 1973. 31 Mar. Reprinted in Rusta, B. and Simma, B. (eds.), *International Protection of the Environment* (Oceana, New York, 1975), Vol. 1, 172.

[4] *Convention on International Trade in Endangered Species of Wild Fauna and Flora*. TIAS. No 8249; 12 ILM. 1085.

[5] Preamble. Ibid.   [6] See Art. 2. Ibid.

[7] *Convention on the Conservation of European Wildlife and Natural Habitats*. UKTS. No. 56 (1982). Europ TS No. 104.

plants and animals as well as people, is required from human societies to live in harmony with the natural world on which they depend for survival and well-being. The long term task of environmental education is to foster or reinforce attitudes compatible with this new ethic.[8]

In 1982 the *World Charter for Nature* stated:

Every form of life is unique, warranting respect regardless of its worth to man, and to accord other organisms such recognition, man must be guided by a moral code of action.[9]

General Principle 1 of the Charter proclaims, 'Nature shall be respected and its essential processes shall not be impaired'.[10]

In 1986 The *Declaration of Fontainebleau*, adopted at the fortieth anniversary of the IUCN, stated:

If humanity is to find a way forward, it must base its advance on a code of values that is less aggressive and more caring for the earth. A code that reflects a deep sensitivity to the ecological interdependence of our planet, and a respect for life in all its forms.[11]

In 1987 the World Commission on Environment and Development concluded its Report with the warning that 'Human survival and well-being could depend on the success of elevating sustainable development to a global ethic'.[12] The Report went so far as to specify that 'The case for the conservation of nature should rest not only with development goals. It is part of our moral obligation to other living beings and future generations.'[13] Also in 1987 the *European Convention for the Protection of Pet Animals* recognized 'that man has a moral obligation to respect all living creatures' and also took note that pet animals have 'a special relationship to man'.[14]

In 1990 over one thousand people (including prominent politicians such as Al Gore and Mikhail Gorbachev[15] from eighty-three countries came together in Moscow for an international conference on the environment that concluded:

---

[8]   Para. 1, Ch. 18 of the *World Conservation Strategy*. In *International Protection. Supra* n. 3, Vol. 13, 424.

[9]   *World Charter for Nature*. GA Res. 7, 36. UN GAOR Supp. (No. 51) at 17, UN Doc. A/51 (1982).

[10]   Preamble, General Principle 1, *World Charter for Nature*. Ibid. Note however, that the Charter was never intended to be anything more than a philosophical and political framework to 'guide and judge' worldwide efforts at conservation. See Wood, H. W., 'The United Nations Charter for Nature', *Ecology Law Quarterly*, 12 (1985), 977, 990. Norman, A., 'Interpreting the Signals', in Angell, D. J. R., Comer, J. D., and Wilkinson, M. L. N. (eds.), *Sustaining the Earth: Responses to Environmental Threats* (Macmillan, London, 1990), 181, 183.

[11]   *Declaration of Fontainebleau*. IUCN Bulletin. 20. 7.

[12]   World Commission on the Environment and Development, *Our Common Future* (Oxford University Press, Oxford, 1987), 308.

[13]   Ibid. 13, 57.

[14]   Preamble, *European Convention for the Protection of Pet Animals*. 1987. ETS 125. Also in Rummel-Bulska, I. (ed.), *Selected Multilateral Treaties in the Field of the Environment*, (Grotius, Cambridge, 1991), Vol. 2, 404.

[15]   For Gorbachev's own calls for an 'ecology of the should' see Lean, G., 'Gorbachev Plots a Green Revolution to Save World', *Observer,* Apr. 1993, 12.

We must find a new spiritual and ethical basis for human activities on Earth: Humankind must enter into a new communion with Nature, and regain respect for the wonders of the natural world.[16]

In 1991 the Dorbis Conference (on the environment in Europe) involving representatives from thirty-six countries, concluded that:

Environmental protection involves . . . changes of human values and behaviour . . . the on going discussion of human values and environmental ethics is of the utmost relevance . . . public education and wide spread philosophical, cultural and ethical endeavours in search of harmony between Human kind and Nature are the substantial means of environmental improvement.[17]

Also in 1991, Maurice Strong emphasized that 'new moral values' were essential to find a workable basis for humanity in the face of the international environmental *problematique*.[18] Willy Brandt,[19] Shridath Ramphal,[20] Fidel Castro[21] and Al Gore[22] came to make similar pleas in 1992. Also in 1992 at the Earth Summit, *Agenda 21* noted that:

Increased ethical awareness in environmental and developmental decision-making should help to place appropriate priorities for the maintenance and enhancement of life-support systems for their own sake.[23]

The *Rio Declaration on Environment and Development* noted in its preamble, 'The integral and interdependent nature of Earth, our home', and Principle 7 recognized the necessity to 'conserve, protect and restore the integrity of the Earth's ecosystem'.[24] This idea is similar to the preamble of the 1991 *Protocol on Mining in Antarctica*, which recognized the intrinsic value of the whole Antarctic ecosystem.[25] Likewise, in 1992 the preamble of the *United Nations Convention on Biological Diversity* recognized the 'intrinsic value of biological diversity'.[26]

---

[16] The important parts of this conference are reprinted in Starke, L. (ed.), *Signs of Hope: Working Towards our Common Future* (Oxford University Press, Oxford, 1990), 158–9.

[17] See para. E, of the conclusions of the *Dorbis Conference*. These are reprinted in Prins, G. (ed.), *Threats Without Enemies: Facing Environmental Insecurity* (Earthscan, London, 1993), 109, 110.

[18] Strong, M. in Ramphal, S., *Our Country the Planet* (Lime Tree, London, 1992), 206.

[19] Brandt, W. in his foreword to Ramphal, ibid. xiv.

[20] Ramphal, S., *supra* n. 18, 196–9, 204.

[21] Castro, F., *Tomorrow is Too Late: Development and the Environmental Crisis in the Third World* (Ocean Press, Melbourne, 1993), 14.

[22] Al Gore is an outspoken advocate of the necessity for new environmental values. He has suggested that humanity requires 'higher values in the conduct of human affairs' and that humanity must display a 'new reverence for their place in the natural world'. See Gore, A., *Earth in Balance: Forging a New Common Purpose* (Earthscan, London, 1993), 167–82. Gore, A., 'The Call for a SEI', *New York Times*, 3 Apr. 1990, A. 23.

[23] S. 31.8. *Agenda 21*. UNCED Doc. A/CONF 151/4. Also reprinted in Johnson, S. P. (ed), *The Earth Summit* (Graham and Trotman, London, 1993).

[24] *Rio Declaration*. UNCED. UN Doc. A/CONF 151/5. 1992. 7 May.

[25] Art. 2, *Protocol on Environmental Protection to the Antarctic Treaty*. 30 ILM. 1991. 1462. For other approaches to the ethical content of this area, see Deihl, C., 'Antarctica: An International Laboratory', *Boston College of Environmental Affairs Law Reporter*, 18 (1991), 423, 432.

[26] Para. 1, preamble, *United Nations Convention on Biodiversity*. UNCED. 1992. UNEP. Bio. Div./CONF L2. 1992.

In 1994 the United Nations Environmental Program attempted to raise the profile of the ethical dimensions of the human relationship with Nature with their publication *Ethics and Agenda 21*.[27] This was taken one step further in the 1995 *World Summit for Social Development* where Elizabeth Dowdeswell, the executive director of UNEP suggested:

The consideration of the fundamental questions facing humanity is a moral and an ethical one. So far ethics and morality have been sideshows in the drama of restless change. Now they have to step to the centre stage. Morality . . . encompasses the entire planet. We are all part of nature . . .[28]

The necessity for increased ethical awareness was also raised by the 1994 International Commission on Peace and Food, which realized the importance of being 'in harmony with the environment'.[29] The 1995 Commission on Global Governance also acknowledged 'the integrity of the planet and its life support systems'[30] amidst calls for revitalized 'neighbourhood' and 'global' ethics.[31]

These trends, towards the non-anthropocentric value of Nature can also be seen within domestic contexts. For example, in New Zealand, the *Resource Management Act* of 1991 attempted to give recognition to certain parts of the objectives of the *World Charter for Nature* by recognizing that resource management should have regard, amidst other factors, to the intrinsic value of ecosystems.[32] As the former New Zealand Prime Minister Geoffrey Palmer said:

The concept of intrinsic value has been added to the list of considerations relevant to the interpretation of sustainable management.[33]

The *New Zealand Environment Act* of 1986 states in its preamble that the purpose of the Act is to:

ensure that, in the management of natural and physical resources, full and balanced account is taken of,

(i)   The intrinsic values of ecosystems; and,

(ii) All values that are placed by individuals and groups on the quality of the environment; . . .[34]

---

[27]   UNEP/Brown, N. J., *Ethics and Agenda 21: Moral Implications of a Global Consensus* (United Nations, New York, 1994). See especially 2, 11, & 62–3.

[28]   Dowdeswell, E. *Speech at World Summit on Social Development*. 1995. 7 Mar. UNEP Speech 1995/3. See also her speech at the *Symposium on Values for a Sustainable Future*. 1994. 2 June. UNEP Speech 1994/10, where she stated 'I believe and hope that we are at the beginning of a paradigm shift in values.'

[29]   International Commission on Peace and Food, *Uncommon Opportunities: An Agenda For Peace and Equitable Development* (Zed, London, 1994), 177, 180.

[30]   The Commission on Global Governance, *Our Global Neighbourhood* (Oxford University Press, Oxford, 1995), 47.

[31]   Ibid. 46–8, 335.

[32]   *Resource Management Act* 1991. Number 69. See also Palmer, G., *Environmental Politics: A Greenprint for New Zealand* (McIndoe, Dunedin, 1990), 100.

[33]   Palmer, ibid.   [34]   *New Zealand Environment Act* 1986. Number 127.

Likewise, the 1987 *New Zealand Conservation Act* defines conservation as, 'The preservation and protection of natural and historic resources for the purpose of maintaining their intrinsic values . . .'.[35]

With such trends evident in both a domestic and the international setting, it has been suggested that certain non-human entities possess (or should possess) a very high-ranking moral considerability. For example, Anthony D'Amato and Sudhir Chopra have argued that whales have almost achieved 'a right to life'. This represents 'a most radical philosophical shift in accordance with an increase in the breadth of consciousness'.[36] This, i.e. a right to life, they have argued, would have been achieved if a permanent moratorium upon whaling was achieved. This in effect would have been the seventh and final step taken by the international community through the IWC, with each step being greater than the last, to achieve the protection of the whale.[37]

However, such views which run a close parallel to what is commonly recognized as 'animals rights' must be regarded as premature. For despite a growing body of domestic, regional, and international legislation which attempts to limit the pain that may be inflicted on individual animals,[38] there are currently no international legal documents which contain provisions consistent with the proposed *Universal Declaration of the Rights of Animals*.[39]

The Philosophical Problems of Protecting Endangered Species

Within international environmental law and policy it is commonly suggested that the foremost area dealing with the protection of the

---

[35] *New Zealand Conservation Act* 1987. Number 65.

[36] D'Amato, A. and Chopra, S., 'Whales: Their Emerging Right to Life', *American Journal of International Law*, 85 (1991), 25, 48.　　　　　　　　　　　[37] D' Amato and Chopra, ibid. 25.

[38] See for example, the preamble and Art. 2 of the *European Convention for the Protection of Animals During International Transport*. 1979. ETS 103. 22 IPE 387. Art. 3 of the *Additional Protocol of the European Convention for the Protection of Pet Animals*. ETS 125; and Art. 2 of the *European Convention for the Protection of Animals Kept for Farm Purposes*. 1976. 9 ETS 87. 20 IPE 10353. See also the *European Council Directives on the Protection of Animals Used for Experimental Purpose. Official Journal of the European Communities* 29, No. L 358 (18 Dec.) 1–13; and the *Directive on the Protection of Laying Hens in Battery Cages. Official Journal of the European Communities*. 29, No. L 95 (10 Apr.), 45–8. *International Trade in Endangered Species of Flora and Fauna*. UNTS Vol. 973 (No. I 14537), 243–438. Also Art. 7 (a) of the 1972 *Convention for the Conservation of Antarctic Seals*. British Command Paper Cmnd. 5302, Misc. II (1973); Cmnd. 7209 Treaty Series 45 (1978).

[39] The *Universal Declaration of the Rights of Animals* begins with the principle that 'All animals are born with an equal claim on life and the same rights to existence.' The Declaration was adopted by the International League of the Rights of Animals in 1977, 21 Sept., London. It is reprinted in Magel, C. R., *Animal Rights* (Mansell, London, 1989), App. B. For the failure of this approach in international law, see Bowman, M., 'The Protection of Animals Under International Law', *Connecticut Journal of International Law*, 2 (1989), 487–98. Animal Welfare Institute, *Animals and Their Legal Rights* (AWI, Washington, 1978). Considering the 'right to life' of whales, it should be realized that the International Whaling Commission is now moving towards 'sustainable whaling' rather than no whaling at all, which would have created such a right. See pages 45–7.

environment (or parts therein) in terms of an ethical commitment, is found with the protection of endangered species. However, the actual protection of endangered species, *per se*, is not directly apparent within any of the documents pertaining to international environmental law. Rather, there is only a general obligation upon signatories to the *United Nations Convention on Biological Diversity* (31 ILM (1992), 818) 'to conserve' the biological diversity—of which endangered species are obviously a part—within their jurisdictions (preamble and Article 1). The most prominent other international environmental law in this area is the 1973 *Convention on International Trade in Endangered Species of Wild Fauna and Flora* (TIAS. No. 8249; 12 ILM. 1085). This Convention recognizes (but only in its preamble) that 'Wild fauna and flora in their many beautiful and varied forms are an irreplaceable part of the natural systems of the earth which must be protected for this and the generations to come'. The only other Conventions which come close to this are the 1979 (Berne) *Convention on the Conservation of European Wildlife and Natural Habitats* (UKTS 56 (1982)) and the 1979 (Bonn) *Convention on the Conservation of Migratory Species of Wild Animals* (19 ILM (1980), 15). The Berne Convention not only obliges its signatories 'to conserve wild flora and fauna' but also 'particular emphasis is given to endangered and vulnerable species' (re Articles 1 and 3). In a similar sense, the Bonn Convention while 'acknowledg[ing] the importance of migratory species being conserved . . . pay[s] special attention to migratory species the conservation status of which is unfavourable,' and obliges its signatories to 'take the necessary steps to conserve such species and their habitats' (Article II). Outside of these areas, the directives to protect endangered species typically fall within national jurisdictions. For example, the 1973 *Endangered Species Act* of the United States suggests 'The purposes of this Act are to . . . 'provide a program for the conservation of endangered species and threatened species' (Section 2:5.(b)).

All of the above documents point to a perhaps axiomatic assumption that it is necessary to protect endangered species. However, this assumption should not be taken lightly, as the justification—to protect what is endangered species—may well be problematic.

The first difficulty with protecting endangered species is that it is the species, not the individuals within it, which are of concern. However, a species, as a taxonomic group has no interests outside of its individual members. That is, the species cannot feel pain, or suffer any loss in itself. It either exists, or it does not exist. Accordingly, the focus, since it is not upon the individual interests within the genus, is upon the existence of the group. Thus, it can be taken as given, that existing, or the preservation of what is in existence, should be furthered. Hence, the aim is to protect endangered species, as a whole. The individuals, at the end of the day, matter little. This assumption has been directly reproached by those who argue for the moral considerability of (individual) animals (chapter nine). Conversely, only to focus upon individual species may draw attention away from the need to protect whole ecosystems (chapter eleven).

As will be discussed in chapter ten, another approach to environmental ethics is to protect what is 'alive', and in this regard, the protection of endangered species may be seen to fall within this rubric. However, this introduces the second problem, namely, if the objective is to protect what is alive and take it back from its rare status, where is the line to be drawn over what is valuable and therefore protected? That is, should all things in existence, which are threatened—such as the Orthopox virus (smallpox)—also be protected? Indeed, what is it *above* being in existence that may justify protection for some living entities, but not for others? The logical answer would be, that what is in existence may be of some benefit to humanity, such as from economic, aesthetic, cultural, religious or self-interest justifications. However, as seen in all the preceding chapters, such anthropocentric justifications are all flawed and cannot offer a suitable basis for the justification to protect many parts of Nature.

A third problem is found with the actual category of 'endangered'. The difficulty is that as human concern only kicks in when a species becomes so rare that it is endangered, the focus of how humans should relate to other non-endangered species does not appear. Indeed, an overt focus upon endangered species may imply that ethical issues arise only in connection with rare and threatened species, and not non-threatened species. The overflow of this point leads to the earlier problem pertaining to the greater issue of sustainability—that is, if something can be sustainably harvested (i.e. taken—but not to a point of endangerment), is that ethically acceptable? For many, the answer to this is 'no'.[39a]

2. THE CHANGE OF OBJECTIVES

The second area of international environmental law where there is a movement towards a broader, holistic approach is with the focus upon ecosystems—as opposed to individuals.[40] This is because it is destruction of ecosystems which is

[39a] For a full discussion of this area, see Gillespie, A., 'Endangered Species: What they are and the Vexing Question of why to save them', in *Journal of Wildlife Management Law and Policy* (forthcoming).

[40] Birnie and Boyle, *supra* n. 2, 423–4. Doremus, H., 'Patching the Ark: Improving Protection of Biological Diversity', *Ecology Law Quarterly*, 18 (1991), 265, 268, 285, 303–9. Lyster, S., *International Wildlife Law* (Grotius, Cambridge, 1985), 299–303. Chopra, S., 'Towards a Developing Right of Survival as Part of an Ecosystem', *Denver Journal of International Law and Politics*, 17 (1989), 255, 269. Freestone, D., *The Road From Rio: International Environmental Law After the Earth Summit* (Hull University Press, Hull, 1992), 17–22.

the biggest threat to individual species.[41] For example, in relation to the preservation of biodiversity, it has been documented that biodiversity can best be preserved through the protection of complete ecosystems as opposed to the preservation of individual examples of unique biodiversity.[42]

Similar examples of holistic objectives are found in the 1972 *Declaration of the United Nations Conference on the Human Environment*,[43] the *World Conservation Strategy*,[44] the 1992 *Rio Declaration on Environment and Development*,[45] and a number of specific international treaties. For example, the convention concerning the *Conservation of Antarctic Marine Living Resources*,[46] the *Convention on Wetlands of International Importance*,[47] the *Convention for the Protection, Management and Development of the Marine and Coastal Environment of the East African Region*,[48] the 1985 *ASEAN Agreement on the Conservation of Nature and Natural Processes*,[49] the *Convention of the Conservation of European Wildlife and Natural Habitats*,[50] and the *Agreement on the Conservation of Polar Bears*[51] all place a greater focus upon the whole, as opposed to the individual entities within the whole. Similar objectives are reflected in regional agreements for the protection and development of the

---

[41] Batchelor, A., 'The Preservation of Wildlife Habitat in Ecosystems: Towards a New Direction Under International Law to Prevent Species Extinction', *Florida International Law Journal*, 3 (1988), 307, 318. Walker, B., 'Diversity and Stability in Ecosystem Conservation', in Western, D. and Searle, M. (eds.), *Conservation for the Twenty-first Century* (Oxford University Press, Oxford, 1989), 121–30.

[42] As the preamble of the *Biodiversity Convention* notes, 'The fundamental requirement for the conservation of biological diversity is the in-situ conservation of ecosystems and natural habitats and the maintenance and recovery of viable populations of species in their natural surroundings.' 'In-situ conservation' is defined as 'the conservation of ecosystems and natural habitats', *re* Art. 2. See also S. 14.54 and 55 of *Agenda 21*, *supra* n. 23. Fowler, C. and Mooney, P., *The Threatened Gene: Food, Politics and the Loss of Genetic Diversity* (Lutterworth, Cambridge, 1990), 163–71, 218–19.

[43] Recommendation 38. *Declaration of the United Nations Conference on the Human Environment. Supra* n. 1.

[44] The *World Conservation Strategy* works around the central precept of the maintenance of 'essential ecological processes and life support systems'. WCS, *supra* n. 8.

[45] Principle 7 recognizes, 'States shall co-operate in a spirit of global partnership to conserve, protect and restore the health and integrity of the earth's ecosystem.' *Rio Declaration*, *supra* n. 24.

[46] Art. 2 (b) *Convention on the Conservation of Antarctic Marine Living Resources*. TIAS No. 10240. Lyster, *supra* n. 40, 159, 301.

[47] See the preamble of the *Convention on Wetlands of International Importance*. UKTS No. 34 (1976). Cmnd. 6465.

[48] Para. 4, preamble. *Convention for the Protection, Management and Development of the Marine and Coastal Environment of the East African Region*. 1985. (French) Journal Official 1989, 7729.

[49] *ASEAN Agreement on the Conservation of Nature and Natural Resources*. 1985. Text in Burhenne No. 985: 47. Also reprinted in *Selected Multilateral Treaties*, *supra* n. 14, 343.

[50] Art. 1, *Convention on the Conservation of European Wildlife and Natural Habitats*. UKTS No. 56. 1982. Cmnd. 8738. Europ TS No.104. See also the *Convention on the Conservation of Nature in the South Pacific*. 1976, in Kiss, A. C. (ed.), *Selected Multilateral Treaties in the Field of the Environment* (UNEP, Kenya, 1982), Vol. 1, 463.

[51] *Agreement on the Conservation of Polar Bears*. TIAS. No 8409.

marine and coastal environments of the West and Central African Regions, as well as the South East Pacific,[52] and the 1995 *Agreement on Straddling and Highly Migratory Fish*.[53]

3. THE POSSIBILITIES OF THE NON-ANTHROPOCENTRIC APPROACHES

It would appear that new ethical bases of international environmental law and policy are developing. However, they are still in only the most rudimentary of stages. At the present time, only the recognition of the need for a new approach is evolving. Consequently, the question of the content and implications of these new approaches is gravely lacking. This is a problem as there are three major philosophical positions which a non-anthropocentric approach could adopt in attempting to extend the basis of human ethical concerns to the non-human world.[54] The first of these concerns the moral considerability of animals. The second is concerned with all entities that are alive. The third, known broadly as deep ecology or the land ethic, places its ethical focus upon the welfare of the whole, at both an ecosystem and biospheric level.

Each of these three approaches stands for different objectives. They are not, prima facie, complementary and cannot easily be joined together in a form of moral pluralism. Rather, they are based upon different conceptions of moral monism. This entails that moral consideration is built upon a single salient moral theory by which to filter all ethical problems. The problem is that to attempt to unify all ethics with regard to the environment under a single framework capable of answering all questions, may be overly optimistic and, consequently, an alternative possibility of moral pluralism has been mooted. Such an approach avoids some formidable problems, such as inflexibility and the continuing elusiveness of a single philosophical touchstone.[55] This approach is especially attractive in situations where there need be no conflict between the relevant ethical theories, i.e. with the moral considerability of

---

[52] Para. 3, preamble. *Convention for the Co-operation in the Protection and Development of the Marine and Coastal Environment of the West and Central African Region*. 1981. ILM, 20 (1988), 746–61. *Agreement on Regional Co-operation in Combating Pollution of the South East Pacific*, in *Selected Multilateral Treaties, supra* n. 14, Vol. 2, 134.

[53] See Arts. 5 & 6 of the *Conference on Straddling and Highly Migratory Fish*. A/CONF, 164/22. 1994. 23 Aug.

[54] Eckersley, R., *Environmentalism and Political Theory: Towards an Ecocentric Approach* (UCL Press, London, 1992), 58.

[55] See Callicott, J. B., 'The Case Against Moral Pluralism', *Environmental Ethics*, 12 (1990), 99. Stone, C., 'Moral Pluralism and the Course of Environmental Ethics', *Environmental Ethics*, 10 (1988), 147, 149. Wenz, P. S., 'Minimal, Moderate and Extreme Pluralism', *Environmental Ethics*, 15 (1993), 61, 66–8, 70, 72, 74. Johnson, L. E., *A Morally Deep World: An Essay on Moral Significance and Environmental Ethics* (Cambridge University Press, Cambridge, 1991), 236–8. Ball, M. S., 'Moral Pluralism, The Tardis, and Rattlesnakes', *Tennessee Law Review*, 56 (1988), at 21.

animals in domestic settings, and environmental ethics in a larger holistic ambit.

However, in other settings moral pluralism is more problematic because it may involve fundamentally incompatible objectives, for example the moral considerability of animals in the wild and the good of the ecosystem as a whole.[56] A second obstacle with moral pluralism is, who exactly will draw the moral maps that can be used interchangeably, and more importantly, how will the one which governs each particular situation be decided? This is a major problem as the call for moral pluralism does not usually offer any answers when there is a direct conflict in objectives.[57] This leads to the final problem, which is that without such a guideline, in effect, no moral theory will have any substance. Ethical bases require concrete foundations.

As moral monism is the preferred approach, it becomes essential to understand the differences between the various ethical theories relating to non-human Nature, and effectively, to attempt to ascertain which is the most appropriate theory.

---

[56] Wenz, P., *Environmental Justice* (State of New York University Press, Albany, 1988), 313. Cf. Sterba, J. P., 'From Biocentric Individualism to Biocentric Pluralism', *Environmental Ethics*, 17 (1995), 191, 204–5.

[57] See Hargrove, E., 'The Role of Rules in Ethical Decision Making', *Inquiry*, 28 (1985), 30.

VIII

The Moral Considerability of Animals

1. THE UTILITARIAN APPROACH

Peter Singer is often credited with laying the intellectual foundations for the contemporary basis for the moral respect for animals. Singer's commitment is to the utilitarian doctrine, according to which moral agents are expected to do those acts which, directly or indirectly, can reasonably be expected to yield the best consequences or lead to the greatest happiness. Conversely, moral agents should seek to minimize the occurrence of badness in the world.[1] These considerations are determined by the extent to which satisfaction of preferences is maximized and dissatisfaction minimized for the moral individuals whose interests are to be taken into account. The ultimate goal is to achieve the best balance of good over bad. To achieve this, all interests, no matter which entity they relate to, are meant to be taken into account. This is because every interest is just what it is, and counts for its own weight. Accordingly, as Jeremy Bentham said, 'The question is not can they reason? Nor can they talk? The question is can they suffer?'[2]

The central point that can be extracted from Bentham's and Singer's argument is that animal interests should be (prima facie) considered in the course of moral deliberations as animal interests in avoiding pain are very similar to those of humans.[3] Drawing the line at interests (in pain and pleasure) is seen as the only possible line of demarcation as all other supposedly unique human qualities, such as rationality etc., are not in fact shared by all humanity, i.e. infants or the mentally disabled.[4] Nevertheless, despite all humanity not sharing the 'higher' capacities like intelligence (which animals are traditionally supposed not to have) all humans from infants and imbeciles to 'normal' functioning people have an interest in the avoidance of physical suffering. However, this is a characteristic of all sentient creatures, and not just humans. Therefore, membership of the human species cannot justify a difference in moral treatment, as the relevant

---

[1] Singer, P., *Animal Liberation: Towards an End to Man's Inhumanity to Animals* (Cape, London, 1976), 21–44. Singer, P., *Practical Ethics* (Cambridge University Press, Cambridge, 1993), 1–15, 110–35. Singer, P., 'All Animals are Equal', *Philosophic Exchange*, 1 (1974), 103–16.

[2] Bentham, J., *An Introduction to the Principles of Morals and Legislation* (Russell, London, 1962), Book 1, 328.

[3] Singer, P., 'Unsanctifying Human Life', in Ladd, J. (ed.), *Ethical Issues Relating to Life and Death* (Oxford University Press, Oxford, 1979), 41.

[4] See Mill, J. S. *Collected Works* (University of Toronto Press, Toronto, 1986), Book 3, 952; Book 10, 167–89, 209–14, 398–9; Book 24, 925, 952–4; Book 25, 1172–3. Singer, *Ethics, supra* n. 1, 60, 74–6.

consideration, the avoidance of pain, is also applicable to non-human beings which are sentient.[5] Throughout the ages, this has been noted by Montaigne,[6] Primatt,[7] Rousseau,[8] Hume,[9] and J. S. Mill.[10] However, it was Henry Salt at the turn of the twentieth century who turned this into strong ethical argument. He argued:

> If rights exist at all, they cannot be consistently awarded to men and denied to animals, since the same sense of justice and compassion apply in both cases. Pain is pain, whether it be inflicted on man or on beast; and the creature that suffers it, whether man or beast, being sensitive of the misery of it while it lasts, suffers evil . . . if man, as a sentient and intelligent being, should be exempt from all avoidable suffering, it follows that other beings who are also sentient and intelligent, though in a lower degree, should have, in lower degree, the same exemption.[11]

This benchmark has subsequently become established with the arguments for the moral considerability of animals. Sentience, consciousness or awareness are seen as necessary for having a good of one's own. Anything which cannot suffer, cannot therefore be an object of moral concern.[12]

Thus, in so far as animals can suffer equally with humans, they have an equal claim to relief, as pain is pain. It is the suffering of pain and not the type of

---

[5] See Anstotz, C., 'Profoundly Intellectually Disabled Humans and the Great Apes: A Comparison', in Cavalieri, P. (ed.), *The Great Ape Project: Equality Beyond Humanity* (Fourth Estate, 1993), 158, 168–70.

[6] Montaigne, M. E., 'Apology for Raymond Sebond', in Trechman, E. J., *Essays of Montaigne* (Oxford University Press, Oxford, 1927), 451–2, 460.

[7] Primatt, H., *A Dissertation on the Duty of Mercy and the Sin of Cruelty to Animals* (Constable, Edinburgh, 1834), 21.

[8] Rousseau, J. J., *The Social Contract* (Dent, 1973), 41–2, 178–80, 184–6.

[9] Hume, D., *An Enquiry Concerning the Principles of Morals* (Open Court, La Salle, 1946), S.3, Part 1; *Status of Animals in the Christian Religion* (Universities Federation For Animal Welfare, London, 1957), 73.

[10] Mill, J. S., 'Three Essays on Religion', in Robinson, J. M. (ed.), *John Stuart Mill: Essays on Ethics, Religions and Society* (Routledge, London, 1969), 184–7. Note, however, that Mill, Hume and Bentham all considered the idea that it may be possible to accept animal pain if they (the animals) receive less pain in domestic settings (and are subsequently killed for human consumption), than they would have endured in the wild. Alternatively, it was suggested that the pain an animal suffered, in being killed and eaten, could be less than the pleasure that a human obtained by eating them. See Whewell, W., *Lectures on the History of Moral Philosophy of England* (Parker, London, 1852), 225–33. Mill, J. S., 'Whewell on Moral Philosophy', in Priestly, T. (ed.), *Collected Works of J. S. Mill* (Oxford University Press, Oxford, 1954), 128. Hume, ibid. S. 3, Part 1. The problem with these approaches is that they both ignore the essence of the consideration, that pain, and not utility, is the foremost consideration.

[11] Salt, H., *Animal Rights Connected in Relation to Social Progress* (George Bell, London, 1987), 50–1, 77. For the historical development of this argument in England, see Thomas, K., *Man and the Natural World: Changing Attitudes in England 1500–1800* (Penguin, Harmondsworth, 1984), 159, 176–81.

[12] Singer drew the final line of moral considerability for sentience at 'somewhere between a shrimp and an oyster'. See *Animal Liberation, supra* n. 1, 8–9. Singer, *Ethics, supra* n. 1, 57–9. See also Hare, R. M., 'Moral Reasoning About the Environment', *Journal of Applied Philosophy*, 4 (1987), 3, 10. Kaufman, F., 'Machines, Sentience and the Scope of Morality', *Environmental Ethics*, 16 (1994), 57, 66–8.

sufferer of pain that is normally significant. The claim here is not that sentience leads to equal consideration in all matters, such as an animal's right to vote. Rather, such a capacity leads to the necessity of weighing like interests equally.[13] Animals, unlike humans, clearly have no interest in voting but they do have an interest in avoiding pain, as humans do.

A. Problems with the Utilitarian Approach

The utilitarian goal intends to maximize benefit over loss. Thus, an optimal policy for a utilitarian could be one which allows some suffering or pain to animals, provided that the best overall result is achieved with the least possible suffering. Therefore, painless commercial animal farming could be acceptable.[14] This problem is known as the 'no-pain' argument. Simply, if no pain is involved in the utilization of animals, then utilitarianism may have nothing to object to. This is especially so if the animal that is killed painlessly is replaced straight away with another. Therefore, the amount of pleasure in the world stays constant, if not increased, by those using the animal's carcass.[15]

Singer responded to this argument by pointing out a number of facts. Firstly, current farming methods do not create benefits for animals and, if anything, for most of them life is a burden. Secondly, if it is good to create life because of the utilitarian calculus, then it would be better to have more human life which could be accommodated by stopping most animal farming and using land-intensive methods to feed expanding populations. Additionally, Singer points out, this is clearly a calculation question and if the aim is to provide the maximum of pleasure over pain, then moral agents are approaching it the wrong way. This is because if all humanity adopted a vegetarian diet, then little would be given up on the part of the meat eaters, which is in stark contrast to the massive increase in benefit to the animals. Thirdly, even if an animal is brought up and killed for food and then replaced, it does not follow that it is the correct thing to do. For example, human infants would be just as replaceable, yet valuers do their best to avoid reaching such a conclusion.[16] Finally, as Robert Nozick pointed out, to argue that it is better for something to have existed than never to have existed at

---

[13] Singer, P., 'Not for Humans Only: The Place of Nonhumans in Environmental Issues', in Regan, T. (ed.), *Ethics and the Twenty-first Century* (Random House, New York, 1976), 194. Singer, *Ethics, supra* n. 1. 58–9. See also Hanula, R. W. and Waverly Hill, P., 'Using Metaright Theory to Ascribe Kantian Rights to Animals Within Nozick's Minimum State', *Arizona Law Review*, 19 (1977), 255.

[14] See Johnson, L. E., *A Morally Deep World: An Essay on Moral Significance and Environmental Ethics* (Cambridge University Press, Cambridge, 1991), 47–9, 53.

[15] Cave, G. P., 'Animals, Heidegger and the Right to Life', *Environmental Ethics*, 4 (1982), 249.

[16] Singer, P., 'Utilitarianism and Vegetarianism', *Philosophy and Public Affairs*, 9 (1979–80), 327. Singer, P., 'Killing Humans and Killing Animals', *Inquiry*, 22 (1979), 152. Despite these retorts, Singer concedes the basic 'steady level of pleasure' is problematic, where the animals are not self-conscious, i.e. of birds and creatures 'below them'. See *Ethics, supra* n. 1, 132–3.

all, is tantamount to arguing that any kind of treatment should be tolerated (provided the overall level of pain/pleasure is not lowered) for a living creature as it is better to be alive for a period, than never to have had that life.[17]

A second difficulty with the utilitarian pain-over-suffering calculus is that it may be a better outcome if a smaller number of beings suffer if such suffering might provide a greater overall good for an even greater number of beings.[18] This leads to the problem of how the conclusion of the greatest good for the greatest number is reached and how and when should 'one's' interests in not suffering be overridden so as to create a greater benefit for another.[19] This is an important problem for utilitarianism generally, for by seeking to achieve maximum good over bad, a few individuals could be made to suffer greatly, if the gain obtained by the many *more* than compensates the loss suffered by the few. Accordingly, with regard to moral problems like animal testing, if the consequences of the tests would produce the best aggregate balance of good over bad, then harmful experimentation is obligatory.[20]

The third objection to the utilitarian approach is that it is problematic to try to calculate the total distribution of happiness in any given situation.[21] While this may be possible within small communities, the further the range of interests that are considered spreads, the more difficult this task becomes, until it may well become impossible.[22]

A fourth issue with utilitarian calculus is that pain and pleasure are largely autonomous concepts and little consideration is given to where the pain or pleasure is located. This presents a distinct problem in relation to endangered species. For example, suppose that a utilitarian moral agent has to choose between saving the last member of an endangered species, or another sentient individual belonging to a species that is plentiful, and that the death of the latter would cause *greater* pain to that individual than the death of the endangered sentient creature. The utilitarian view requires that the valuer save the animal that is at risk of greater pain. This conclusion is in spite of the fact that the endangered species would probably become extinct.[23] Likewise, under Singer's approach, to kill the last of an endangered species painlessly, would be less wrong than to kill a common animal by slow torture.[24] This is because at the end of the day, it is the

[17]   Nozick, R., *Anarchy, State and Utopia* (Oxford University Press, Oxford, 1974), 35–42.

[18]   See Zak, S., 'The Case for Animal Rights', *Loyola of Los Angeles Law Review*, 20 (1987), 1236.

[19]   Hoch, D., 'Environmental Ethics and Nonhuman Interests. A Challenge to Anthropocentric License', *Gonzaga Law Review*, 23 (1989), 335.

[20]   See Regan, T., *The Case for Animal Rights* (Routledge, London, 1988), 210, 229, 392–3. Indeed, Singer accepts animal (and human) experimentation in this setting. See *Ethics, supra* n. 1, 66–8.   [21]   Johnson, *supra* n. 14, 186.

[22]   See Marshall, P., *Nature's Web: An Exploration of Ecological Thinking* (Simon and Schuster, London, 1992), 436–7. Singer himself barely acknowledges this problem. See *Ethics, supra* n. 1, 276.

[23]   Regan, *supra* n. 20, at 202.

[24]   Gunn, A., 'Preserving Rare Species', in Regan, T. (ed.), *Earthbound: New Introductory Essays in Environmental Ethics* (Random, New York, 1984), 312.

individual and its capacity for harm and benefit that decides how decisions are made. The interests of a sentient individual member of an endangered species in avoiding pain are no greater than that of a member of a non-threatened species.

A fifth problem is this area is presented by Tom Regan, who believes that utilitarian models cannot go 'deep enough' in ethical decisions. This is because utilitarians have no choice but to determine the wrongfulness of something by its consequences.[25] For example, Cora Diamond pointed out that humans decline to kill people for food not because it would cause suffering, but because it is morally repugnant. This is backed up by the fact that 'we' decline to eat people who are already dead, even though to eat them would cause no pain to them.[26] This decision is reached without recourse to the pain/pleasure calculus. It is reached out of a concern for 'deeper ethics'. Regan suggested that in the context of animal issues, such an approach should revolve around the 'inherent value of the individual'. George Edward Moore defined inherent value in 1922 in such a way that the value a thing possesses, and the degree to which it possesses it, depend solely on the inherent nature of the thing in question. This means that a moral entity is not 'good as a means' but rather is 'good as an end' in itself and valuable for its own sake.[27]

The implications of this are that every entity which is recognized as possessing inherent value is an end in itself, and should not be used in utilitarian calculations. Therefore, net gains in utility that may be created under the utilitarian calculus do *not* justify the injustices that may be done to individuals in the search for the greatest maximization of pleasure for the greatest number.[28]

2. INHERENT VALUE

It is believed in most modern (Western) societies that all humans have an equal inherent dignity.[29] This is despite the fact that certain humans are more intelligent than others, certain lives are more fulfilling than others, and that certain lives are more valuable to society. Nevertheless, modern legal systems emphasize that people must be treated equally. People's respect and protection at law do not

---

[25] Regan, T., *All That Dwell Within: Essays on Animal Rights and Environmental Ethics* (University of California Press, Berkeley, 1982), 56. Regan, *supra* n. 20, 230. For the problems this has caused for Singer, see *Ethics*, ch. 7 and the Appendix, on the problem of euthanasia, *supra* n. 1.

[26] Diamond, C., 'Eating Meat and Eating People', *Philosophy*, 53 (1978), 474. For Singer's rejection of this see Singer, *Ethics*, *supra* n. 1.

[27] Moore, G. E., 'The Concept of Intrinsic Value', in Moore, G. E., *Philosophical Studies* (Routledge, London, 1922), 260. This type of definition is also attributed to Kant. See, *The Groundwork of the Metaphysics of Morals* (Bobbs-Merril, London, 1965), 96.

[28] Regan, *supra* n. 20, 328. But see Regan's 'Miniride principle' with a suspicious resemblance to utilitarianism, 300–2.

[29] Dworkin, R., *Taking Rights Seriously* (Oxford University Press, Oxford, 1977), ch. 4. Lukes, T., *Individualism* (Harper and Row, New York, 1973), 49. MacPherson, C. B., *The Political Theory of Possessive Individualism* (Oxford University Press, Oxford, 1962), 220.

depend upon their individual qualities and/or abilities. Indeed, although grading merit makes sense, grading inherent worth does not. Thus, people who are mentally retarded gain their respect and protection because of their possession of inherent value. They have this inherent value because of what they are, i.e. humans, and *not* what they possess, i.e. capabilities.

However, inherent value is generally taken to reside exclusively, or at least pre-eminently, in humans. This distinction allows for humans to be classified above all other forms of Nature as they, allegedly, are the only species to possess inherent value.[30] Once it is established that only humans have inherent value, then it follows that everything else has only instrumental value[31] or, as Kant argued, Nature cannot be a final purpose in itself.[32] This, however, is an arbitrary anthropocentric judgement. It is based upon unquestioning value assumptions concerning human lives in contrast to those of non-human entities.

The follow on from this point is that it is wholly unclear why one class of entities (i.e. humanity) should be recognized as having inherent worth, whereas other classes (i.e. animals) are not. To argue that human capacities create inherent value overlooks what it is that gives all living things inherent worth. It is not their capacities taken by themselves. Rather, it is these capacities that go to the creation of a 'good of their own' that should give rise to inherent value.[33] Non-human individuals, despite their limited range of capacities, can still realize their own good at an optimum level by the use of those capacities in the right environment. They do not need the additional capacities that humanity may (or may not) have to operate effectively. This leads to the question of why non-human capacities should be downgraded in comparison to human ones. The fact that *Homo sapiens'* capacities may be different to other natural entities should *not* give them alone inherent worth, any more than inherent worth should be given just to sharks for having the capacity to be superb underwater predators.

Inherent value is not some kind of objective property that can be discovered by scientific or empirical investigation. The reason for recognizing inherent value in an entity is derived from the way the world is seen. However, when seen solely from an anthropocentric position an arbitrary distinction for inherent value develops. To correct this, it is suggested inherent value should be located where entities are the 'subject of a life'. Regan came to stipulate that the conditions for being the subject of a life are:

[30] Goodpaster, K. E., 'On Being Morally Considerable', *Journal of Philosophy,* 75 (1978), 317. Taylor, P., 'Frankena On Environmental Ethics', *Monist,* 64 (1981), 375. Lombardi, L. G., 'Inherent Worth, Respect and Animals Rights', *Environmental Ethics,* 5 (1983), 260. Eckersley, R., *Environmentalism and Political Theory: Towards an Ecocentric Approach* (UCL Press, London, 1992), 2.

[31] Whitehead, A. N., *Science and the Modern World* (Macmillan, London, 1925), 129. Marcuse, H., *One Dimensional Man* (Routledge, London, 1964), 146–8.

[32] Kant, I., *Critique of Judgement* (Macmillan, London, 1914).

[33] Taylor, P., 'Are Humans Superior to Animals and Plants?', *Environmental Ethics* (1984), 157.

Having beliefs and desires, perception, memory, a sense of future and self, an emotional life including feelings of pleasure and pain, the ability to initiate action, a psychophysical identity over time, interests and welfare.[34]

As such entities have a life of their own, it is suggested that they have an inherent value of their own, aside from any instrumental value they may also possess in the eyes of others.[35] In the context of environmental theory, Paul Taylor defines what it means for a being to have inherent worth as:

to say that it possesses inherent worth, is to say that its good is deserving of the concern and consideration of all moral agents, and that the realisation of that good has intrinsic value, to be pursued as an end in itself and for the sake of the entity whose good it is.[36]

In one of the theories of environmental ethics, the implications of this definition have been interpreted as stipulating that there is a duty not to harm entities possessing inherent value. Secondly, there is the duty not to interfere with them. Finally, there is duty to provide restitution where an entity with inherent value has been wronged.[37] Note, however, that Regan himself only went so far as to suggest that entities with inherent value must receive equal moral treatment.[38]

The traditional argument against inherent value is that it is a human act that defines inherent value. Thus, objective values cannot exist without a valuer. For the value to exist, it must be perceived, therefore, 'non-sensed value is nonsense'.[39] This argument is unconvincing. Non-human Nature, in both a holistic and an individual sense, uses a combination of instrumental and inherent values. That is, non-human Nature pursues its own inherent value, while also using other Nature for instrumental purposes. Thus, it can be suggested that living non-human Nature has *a good of its own* (this will be discussed in the following chapter). Consequently, non-human living entities possess their own inherent value. These values exist to the entities concerned *before* a human valuer recognizes them and are therefore independent.[40]

---

[34] Regan, T., 'The Moral Basis of Vegetarianism', *Canadian Journal of Philosophy*, 5 (1975), 181. Regan, *supra* n. 20, at 178, 243. See also Naess, A., *Ecology, Community and Lifestyle* (Cambridge University Press, Cambridge, 1989), 11.

[35] Ibid. 236.

[36] Taylor, P., 'The Ethics of a Respect for Nature', *Environmental Ethics*, 3 (1981), 201.

[37] Taylor, P., *Respect for Life: A Theory of Environmental Ethics* (Princeton University Press, Princeton, 1986), 172–3, 273, 283, 292.

[38] Regan, *supra* n. 20, 112, 264. Taylor, *supra* n. 33, 149. For Singer's position of equality, see *supra* n. 16, 145. Singer, *Ethics, supra* n. 1, 55–82, but note 105–9.

[39] See Rolston, H., 'Values and Duties to the Natural World', in Bormann, F. H. and Keller, S. R. (eds.), *Ecology, Economics, Ethics: The Broken Circle* (Yale University Press, New York, 1991), 73, 93. See also Windelband, W., *An Introduction to Philosophy* (Fisher Unwin, London, 1921), 215.

[40] See Rolston, H., 'Value in Nature and the Nature of Value', in Attfield, R., *Philosophy and the Natural Environment* (Cambridge University Press, Cambridge, 1994). Naess, A., *Ecology, Community and Lifestyle* (Cambridge University Press, Cambridge, 1989), 11. Rolston, ibid. 73, 94–7. Sylvan, R., 'On the Value Core of Deep Green Theory', in Oddie, G. and Perrett, R. (eds), *Justice, Ethics and New Zealand Society* (Oxford University Press, Oxford, 1992), 222, 223.

3. FURTHER PHILOSOPHICAL CHALLENGES

The above positions of both Singer and Regan have been attacked by what is broadly known as contractualism.[41] The basic precept here is that entities must be able to enter into 'contracts' in order to be recipients of moral consideration. Although those who deny the moral considerability of animals accept that animals can benefit from actions and that they have 'a good or a welfare', it is suggested that they can still not be the objects of moral consideration because they lack interests that would allow them to enter moral contracts. For the purposes of this argument, interests are considered in two contexts, first, taking an interest, i.e. intellectually, and secondly, having an interest. Animals have an interest in things but they cannot take an interest in them. This is because taking an interest requires an 'epistemic relationship' to one's world, which requires an understanding of what one's interests are, and what may stand in the way of one's interests.[42] This position claims that *only* beings capable of taking an interest can meaningfully be attributed moral considerability. Thus, the interest principle requires that interests are 'compounded out of desires and aims, . . . both of which require at least rudimentary cognitive equipment'.[43] As animals allegedly lack this ability they cannot be given equal moral weight.

The first objection to the interests requirement of cognitive equipment has to do with the requirement of rationality, which is tested by the ability to act logically, to draw conclusions, etc. The difficulty is that when objective assessors examine this ability, it becomes apparent that there are many members of the human genus who would fail such a test—such as the very young, the senile, and the mentally infirm.[44] However, societies do not usually disenfranchise these people from moral considerability because of their lack of ability in holding their interests.[45] Even the search for rationality within 'normal people' is proving elusive as psychology has shown how the human mind comprises the conscious and the unconscious.[46] Additionally, even when an objective is performed unconsciously, it is not said that the person acting has no interest in what they are seeking to obtain.

The second difficulty with the interests requirement is that, in contrast to

[41] Narveson, J., 'Animal Rights', *Canadian Journal of Philosophy*, 7 (1977), 177.

[42] See Sapontzis, S. F., 'The Moral Significance of Interests', *Environmental Ethics*, 4 (1982), 347. For a discussion of this argument, see Johnson, *supra* n. 14, 75–7.

[43] McCloskey, H. J., 'Rights', *Philosophical Quarterly*, 15 (1965), 115. Feinberg, J., 'The Rights of Animals and Unborn Generations', in Blackstone, W. T., *Philosophy and the Environmental Crisis* (University of Georgia Press, Athens, 1974), 52. See also, Frey, R. G., *Interests and Rights: The Case Against Animals* (Clarendon Press, Oxford, 1980), 87–8.

[44] Naess, A., 'Self Realisation in Mixed Communities', *Inquiry*, 22 (1979), 201. Singer, *supra* n. 16, 238. Goodpaster, *supra* n. 30, at 319.

[45] Russell, B., *The Principles of Human Experimental Technique* (Allen and Unwin, London, 1959), 14. Singer, *Ethics, supra* n. 1, 78–82.

[46] Gelb, F., 'Man and Land: The Psychological Theory of Jung', *Zygon*, 9 (1974), 288. Goodpaster, *supra* n. 30, 316.

historical belief, it now appears that the type of intelligence possessed by many species is quite similar to that present in humans and differs only in degree.[47] Further, the traditionally believed human uniqueness due to communication, moral behaviour, the use of tools, and the creation of art have all been proven not to be exclusively human traits.[48] All of these facts have proven that certain animals have cognitive equipment at least comparable to much of humanity.

The final problem with the requirement that objects of moral considerability must be able to take an interest in something, concerns the lack of need to distinguish between having and taking an interest in certain moral calculations. For example, the egalitarianism of both the utilitarian and the subject of a life perspective requires only that the interests of each individual be taken into account and given equal consideration in computing the costs and benefits of the moral calculus. Consequently, from these points of view, the distinction between having an interest and taking an interest does *not* demonstrate a morally significant inequality between relevant entities.[49] Thus, the having/taking an interest argument does not address the relevant criteria that intrinsic value theorists (or sentience theorists) offer for moral considerability.

4. THE MORAL CONSIDERABILITY OF ANIMALS
AND ENVIRONMENTAL ETHICS

Singer and Regan stipulate that a being has to be the 'subject of a life' or sentient to count morally.[50] Seen in this light, the ethical valuing of individual animals rules out any radical forms of holistic environmental ethics. This is because if an

---

[47] As Darwin said, 'There is no fundamental difference between man and the higher mammals in their mental faculties.' Darwin, C. *The Descent of Man and Selection in Relation to Sex* (Collier, New York, 1871), 94–171. See also Rachels, J., 'Darwin, Species and Morality', *Monist,* 70 (1987), 102. Rachels, J., 'Created From Animals', in Pierce, C. and Van De Veer, D. (eds.), *People, Penguins and Plastic Trees: Basic Readings in Environmental Ethics* (Wadsworth, London, 1995), 59, 63–4, 70–1. Johnson, *supra* n. 14. 27–34. Singer, *Ethics, supra* n. 1, 72–8.

[48] Diamond, J., *The Rise and the Fall of the Third Chimpanzee* (Radius, London, 1991), 125–73. Midgley, M., *The Beast and Man: The Roots of Human Nature* (Harvester, London, 1980), 25–6, 205. See also chs. 4 & 5 of *The Great Ape Project, supra* n. 5. Singer, *supra* n. 1, 22. Routley, R. and V., 'Against the Inevitability of Human Chauvinism', in Goodpaster, K. E. and Sayre, K. M. (eds.), *Ethics and Problems of the 21st Century* (University of Notre Dame Press, Notre Dame, 1976), 41, 43.

[49] Varner, G. E., 'Do Species Have Standing', *Environmental Ethics,* 9 (1987), 71. Fox, W., *Towards a Transpersonal Ecology: Developing New Foundations for Environmentalism* (Shambhala, London, 1990), 184. Sapontzis, *supra* n. 42, 353.

[50] Regan, *supra* n. 20, 361–3. Singer, *supra* n. 12. Eckersley, *supra* n. 30, 42–4. Singer, *Ethics, supra* n. 1, 274–6, 284. For discussions of this, see Rodman, J., 'Four Forms of Ecological Consciousness Reconsidered', in Scherer, D. (ed.), *Ethics and the Environment* (Random House, New York, 1983), 82, 85. Attfield, R., *The Ethics of Environmental Concern* (Blackwell, Oxford, 1983), 146–7.

entity is not sentient nor the 'subject of a life', then it cannot be the subject of direct moral consideration. Therefore, the destruction of non-sentient/non-subject of a life entities, cannot, prima facie, be condemned. Only creatures that are sentient or the 'subject of a life' have inherent value, everything else possesses only instrumental value. Therefore, to exterminate a plant species would not be wrong, unless that loss had some detrimental effect on some sentient or 'subject of a life' creature. Conversely, to replace a non-sentient or non-subject of a life entity such as an indigenous forest with an exotic one, capable of supporting the same level of or a greater number of sentient or 'subject of a life' creatures is quite an acceptable swap, even if several types of indigenous plants became extinct in the process.

A second problem for both Regan and Singer is that, when pressed to its logical conclusion, their position would condemn indigenous cultures which use hunting as a form of existence. Additionally, it would require the conversion of all non-human animal carnivores to vegetarianism or at the very least would require a replacement of the food chain with methods that would minimize the suffering of a sentient prey. Finally, it may also go so far as to suggest alleviating the suffering of sentient beings in the wild.[51]

Note, however, that Regan, while agreeing with intervention within society to advance the moral considerability of animals, disagrees when it is an issue between non-human animals in the wild. He asserts this position because he believes that the best policy is to let animals in the wild be left alone, and to allow them to carve out their own destiny. He backs up this claim with assertions that humans do not necessarily know what they are doing when they interfere in natural workings and may consequently cause more harm than good. Additionally, he justifies non-interference on the grounds that animals are not moral agents and so can have none of the duties that moral agents have, including the duty to morally respect other animals.[52]

There are two problems with this. Firstly, Regan's concern is supposed to be with protecting life, not who is and who is not a moral agent. Secondly, if animals are equally subjects of a life with people and have the same basic moral considerability as people, then they belong to the same basic moral community of inherently valuable beings. Thus, there can be no real division between the treatment of wild Nature, and domestic Nature within human control. Therefore, it can be seen on this point, that Regan ultimately represents a very similar position to

---

[51] Callicott, J. B., 'Animal Liberation: A Triangular Affair', *Environmental Ethics,* 2 (1980), 311, 326–8. Sagoff, M., 'Animal Liberation and Environmental Ethics: Bad Marriage, Quick Divorce', *Osgoode Hall Law Journal,* 22 (1984), 304. McCloskey, H. J., *Ecological Ethics and Politics* (Englewood Cliffs, New Jersey, 1983), 122. Fox, *supra* n. 49, 195. Note, that Singer accepts where survival and necessity are at stake, then it may be permissible to kill animals. If they are not, then it is impermissible. See *Ethics, supra* n. 1, 62.

[52] Regan, *supra* n. 20, 357–61. See also Wenz, P., *Environmental Justice* (State of New York University Press, Albany, 1988), 82–9.

Singer, whereby the suffering of animals anywhere creates a human obligation to mitigate it because of that individual's distress.[53]

Having seen that both Regan and Singer represent the same position, the argument can be raised that this position stands in contrast to the theory of environmental ethics which holds that Nature must be left to its own devices, as this is the natural way. As Holmes Rolston pointed out:

Animal rights are not natural in the sense that they exist in spontaneous nature. Rights go with legitimate claims and entitlements, but there are no titles and no laws that can be transgressed in the wilderness.[54]

Ethics concerning the natural world should be consistent with the values within it. Compassion, justice, and fairness are inter-human ethics, not ones found in Nature. To look for them there, may be to make a category mistake.

A further problem in this area can be seen in how the ecological order of Nature is premised on the fundamental principle that all life ultimately depends upon death. To the extent that animal liberationists condemn the taking of life, or the infliction of pain, they are irreconcilably at odds with the ecological facts of existence and any subsequent environmental ethics.[55] For example, the preservation and reintroduction of predators is among the highest priorities on the agenda of a number of current environmental goals. Predatory fish, reptiles, birds, and mammals, however, cause a lot of suffering to other animals. This intention to reintroduce these predatory species is at odds with the positions offered by Singer and Regan to minimize pain to sentient creatures or to give moral considerability to the subjects of lives.

Another large difficulty for the moral considerability of animals is the dichotomy between individuals and ecosystems. This develops as the theory of the moral considerability of animals and, like most of the liberal ethical movements throughout history, is based upon the precept of the individual. Consequently, such a philosophy has difficulty with the concept that entities above the level of individual entities that are sentient or the 'subject of a life' can be the focus of moral worth.[56]

[53] Singer, *supra* n. 16, 201. See also Magel, C. R., *Animal Rights* (Mansell, London, 1989), 17–18, who concludes Regan and Singer 'are in close agreement on their practical conclusions'.

[54] Rolston, H., *Environmental Ethics: Duties and Values in the Natural World* (Temple University Press, Philadelphia, 1988), 48, 225.

[55] Sober, E., 'Philosophical Problems For Environmentalism', in Gruen, L. and Jamieson, D., *Reflecting on Nature: Readings in Environmental Philosophy* (Oxford University Press, Oxford, 1994), 345, 352–4. Conniff, T., 'Fuzzy-Wuzzy Thinking About Animal Rights', *Audubon Magazine,* (1990), 120, 132. Callicot, *supra* n. 51, 333–4.

[56] Sagoff, M., 'Can Environmentalists Be Liberals?', in Sagoff, M., *The Economy of the Earth* (Cambridge University Press, Cambridge, 1988), 157, 162–7. Freyfogle, E. T., 'The Land Ethic and the Pilgrim Leopold', *University of Colorado Law Review,* 61 (1990), 217, 242–3. Feinberg, *supra* n. 43, 55–6. Norton, B. G., 'Environmental Ethics and Nonhuman Rights', *Environmental Ethics,* 4 (1982), 36. Singer, *supra* n. 16, 203. Warren, K. J., 'Feminism and Ecology: Making Connections', *Environmental Ethics,* 9 (1987), 3, 9.

This individualistic approach of the moral considerability of animals is at fundamental odds with the broader holistic view of environmental ethics. This is because an environmental ethic supports the holistic function of an ongoing system, *not* the concerns of individual entities. Consequently, holistic environmental ethics seeks to find inherent value in complete communities or ecosystems.[57] The implication of finding the greater value in the whole, as opposed to the individual, is that in times of ultimate conflict the individual may be sacrificed to preserve the integrity of the whole. This view thinks in terms of collections, systems, and communities. This implies *no* direct duties to individual animals except in the rare instance in which the individual is important to the functioning of a larger community.

In contrast to this, those advocating the moral considerability of animals could sacrifice the ecosystem (assuming that there were no other sentient or 'subject of a life' creatures in the ecosystem) for the good of the individual animal, as the individual animal, not the larger system, is the focus of value. This extreme individualism (of the ethical value of animals) approach conflicts with the emphasis of holistic environmental ethics which places the ethical emphasis upon such objectives as ecosystem integrity, unity, diversity, and stability.[58] With such objectives, the basic ethical precept has been suggested by Aldo Leopold as being:

Our every act must foster the integrity, stability and beauty of the biotic community . . . the good of the biotic community is the ultimate measure of moral value, the rightness or wrongness of actions . . . the effect on ecological systems is the decisive factor in the determination of the ethical quality of actions.[59]

A final objection here, that is relevant for this section and the following ones, is that the capacity of humankind to confer 'rights' upon the non-human world requires all existence to be moved under human control. This is argued to be the case because the concept of rights arises in human social environments which are built on dominance hierarchies, are property based, and individualistic. Consequently, certain theorists have argued that 'rights' (which are often associated with the moral considerability of animals) are not conducive to

[57]   Goodin, R. E., *Green Political Theory* (Polity, Cambridge, 1992), 89–90. Callicott, J. B., 'An Eco-holistic Critique of Animal Liberation/Animal Rights', in Regan, T. and Singer, P. (1989) (eds.), *Animal Rights and Human Obligations* (Englewood Cliffs, New Jersey, 1989). Norton, ibid. 36. Callicott, J. B., 'What's Wrong With Moral Pluralism', *Environmental Ethics,* 12 (1990), 32. Rodman, *supra* n. 50, 82, 87. Callicott, *supra* n. 51, 317–20.

[58]   Rolston, H., 'Challenges in Environmental Ethics', in Cooper, D. and Palmer, J. (eds.), *The Environment in Question: Ethics and Global Issues* (Routledge, London, 1992), 134, 140. Warren, *supra* n. 56, 3, 10. Callicott, *supra* n. 51, 317–20, 336–8. Cf. Hettinger, N., 'Valuing Predation in Rolston's Environmental Ethics: Bambi Lovers Versus the Tree Huggers', *Environmental Ethics*, 16 (1994), 2, 6–9.

[59]   Leopold, A., *A Sand County Almanac* (Oxford University Press, Oxford, 1949), 224–5.

environmental theory.[60] Alternatively, it is suggested that what is required is a different world view that focuses upon holistic qualities as opposed to hierarchical ones. Thus, an escape from the orthodoxies of existing thinking and technique is sought—an escape which the approach based upon the moral consideration of animals does not provide.

[60] See Livingston, J., 'Rightness or Rights?', *Osgoode Hall Law Journal,* 22 (1984), 321. Gragnocauo, C. and Goldstein, H., 'Law Reform or World Reform: The Problem of Environmental Rights', *McGill Law Journal,* 35 (1990), 346, 362, 371. Rodman, J., 'The Liberation of Nature?', *Inquiry,* 22 (1977), 83, 96. Norton, *supra* n. 56, 17. Rolston, H., 'Rights and Responsibilities on the Home Planet', *Yale Journal of International Law,* 18 (1993), 251, 253–9. For the advocacy of the rights approach in the environmental context, see Nash, J. A., 'The Case for Biotic Rights', in the same journal, 235, 237–8.

IX

Respect for Life

1. THE PROPOSAL

The idea behind the respect for life theories is that something about the essence of living organisms requires concern and respect. The basic proposal is that non-sentient beings with life, who possess an inherited biological propensity towards natural growth and existence, are *not* mere 'things', but rather, have independent value.[1] As Holmes Rolston suggested:

So the oak grows, reproduces, repairs its wounds and resists death. The physical state that the organism seeks, idealised in its programmatic form, is a valued state. Value is present in this achievement. A life is defended for what it is in itself . . . [thus] a really vital ethic respects all life, not just animal pains and pleasures, much less just human preferences.[2]

Such recognitions have lead to the rejection of the ability to feel pleasure and pain, or Regan's 'subject of a life' criterion, as the philosophical outer boundary. Additionally, it has been argued that the whole debate about what can and cannot feel is limited, owing to the restrictive nature of current scientific knowledge. Indeed, a substantial amount of empirical evidence indicates that all life forms exhibit aversive behaviour. Aversive behaviour may indicate a capacity for sentience and may demonstrate an interest in the avoidance of suffering. Nevertheless, our knowledge of this is still very limited.[3]

A second reason which has helped instigate a search for a new position can be found in the charge that both Singer's and Regan's positions are basically anthropocentric. This is because their considerations remain set in a comparison between what a human can feel and the existence of similar feelings in non-human Nature. This is implicitly anthropocentric, not only because it supposes that humans are in a position to extend moral considerability to other beings, but also because it offers ethical value only to beings which are the subject of a life, which is more or less the same as humans possess. Everything

---

[1] Rolston, H., 'Values Gone Wild', *Inquiry,* 26 (1983), 191. Johnson, L. E., *A Morally Deep World: An Essay on Moral Significance* (Cambridge University Press, Cambridge, 1991), 138. Attfield, R., *The Ethics of Environmental Concern* (Blackwell, Oxford, 1983), 142, 145.

[2] Rolston, H., 'Challenges in Environmental Ethics', in Cooper, D. and Palmer, J. (eds.), *The Environment in Questions: Ethics and Global Issues* (Routledge, London, 1992), 135, 137–8.

[3] Scherer, D., 'A Disenthropic Ethic', *Monist,* 71 (1988), 6. Sergeant, E., *The Spectrum of Pain* (London, 1969), 72. Losick, R., 'Why and How Bacteria Communicate', *Scientific American*, Feb. 1997, 52–8.

else is classified as only possessing instrumental value and consequently has no moral standing.[4]

A third justification to seek value in non-sentient entities, or Nature which is not the 'subject of a life', is derived from the 'last person' example. This philosophical problem which, like George Edward Moore's thought experiment before it, seeks to search for value by viewing the entity in question in absolute isolation.[5] A modern analogy of this problem envisaged that a single person who is about to die is left on a planet.[6] Before she/he dies, she/he has the option of destroying the last tree on the planet whose existence would continue if they do not take this act. The question they are faced with is, would their last act harm anything of independent intrinsic value? For if they conclude that the tree has no value, then there is no reason for her/him not to destroy the last tree. Alternatively, if it is concluded that, even though the human must die, the tree should still be allowed to live, then the individual conducting the thought experiment must concede that non-human entities have value outside that for which humanity values them.

A common consensus of this thought experiment is that it would be inappropriate for the last person to destroy the last tree unnecessarily, and that if they choose to do so, then the world would be a poorer place. Such a conclusion leads to the premise that the tree is definitely worth some independent value of its own accord. This outcome, that it is usual to value living entities above non-living things, has caused some to question how far our ethical precepts should reach.[7]

Having surveyed all of the above arguments, a number of theorists have advocated a new ethical position. Specifically, this entails a respect for the value of life as the criterion of a valuer's moral concerns. Life, and what is living, have been described as a 'disenthropic enterprise'. Donald Scherer defines a living being as something:

that has structures for maintaining a disenthropic equilibrium for availing itself of forms of energy, which it is capable of using for resisting change incompatible with its continuing functioning.[8]

---

[4] Devall, B. and Sessions, G., *Deep Ecology: Living as if Nature Mattered* (Gibbs Smith, Utah, 1985), 54–5. Fox, W., *Towards a Transpersonal Ecology: Developing New Foundations for Environmentalism* (Shambhala, London, 1990), 164–5. Zimmerman, M. E., 'Towards a Heideggerean Ethos for Radical Environmentalism', *Environmental Ethics,* 5 (1983), 107. Rodman, J., 'The Liberation of Nature', *Inquiry,* 20 (1977), 94.

[5] Moore, G. E., *Philosophical Studies* (Routledge, London, 1922), 260.

[6] Attfield, R., 'The Good of Trees', *Journal of Value Inquiry,* 15 (1981), 45. See also O'Neill, J., *Ecology, Policy and Politics: Human Well-Being and the Natural World* (Routledge, London, 1993), 8–13.

[7] McGinn, T., 'Ecology and Ethics', *International Philosophical Quarterly,* 14 (1974), 155. Attfield, ibid. 51–2. Cf. Hill, T. E., 'Ideals of Human Excellence and Preserving the Natural Environment', in Gruen, L. and Jamieson, D. (eds.), *Reflecting on Nature: Readings in Environmental Philosophy* (Oxford University Press, Oxford, 1994), 98, 100–2.

[8] Scherer, *supra* n. 3, at 10.

2. REVERENCE FOR LIFE

Albert Schweitzer is usually credited with the advocacy of the life-oriented approach, at the beginning of the twentieth century. His basic rule was that, 'It is good to maintain and promote life; it is bad to destroy life or obstruct it.'[9] He stipulated:

A man is truly ethical only when he obeys the compulsion to help all life, which he is able to assist, and shrinks from injuring anything that lives. He does not ask how far this or that life deserves one's sympathy as being valuable, nor beyond that, whether and to what degree it is capable of feeling. Life as such is sacred to him.[10]

From this position, moral agents are to tear 'no leaf, pluck no flower and crush no insect.'[11] The criterion here for inherent worth is the property it possesses— namely, life itself. This property is objective and, on recognition of this, the only fitting attitude is one of respect.[12]

3. THE DIFFICULTIES OF THE LIFE APPROACH

This ethical approach to why Nature should be protected has two difficulties. The first problem here is that the above position is often drawn from religious motivation. This position is especially common with Eastern religions.[13] The overall difficulties involved with the religious approach are discussed in chapter four.

A second more crucial question in this area is that if a tree does not care whether its purposes are frustrated or not, does it matter whether its interests are well or ill served? Indeed, as Joel Feinberg asserted, trees do not have wants or goals, are not conscious, and hence cannot know satisfaction or frustration, pain or pleasure. Consequently, as they cannot suffer, it is *not* possible to be cruel to them. As they lack desire and cognition, they have no interests and hence should *not* be preserved for their own sakes or be considered as moral objects.[14]

---

[9]   Schweitzer, A., *Civilisation and Ethics* (Black, London, 1929), 246.
[10] Schweitzer, ibid. 247.
[11] Schweitzer, A., *Out of My Life and Thought* (Henry Holt, New York, 1961), 225, 230.
[12] Chananie, S., 'Reverence for Life, and Rights for Nature', *Pace Law Review*, 3 (1983), 702–4. Linzey, R., 'Moral Education and Reverence for Life', in Patterson, C. H. (ed.), *Humanistic Education: A Symposium* (Sussex, 1981), 177.
[13] See Cheng, C. Y., 'On the Environmental Ethics of the Tao and the Ch'i', *Environmental Ethics*, 8 (1986), 353. Ip, P. K., 'Taoism and the Foundations of Environmental Ethics', *Environmental Ethics*, 5 (1983), 338. Marshall, P., *An Exploration of Ecological Thinking* (Simon and Schuster, London, 1992), 9–54. Wynne-Tyson, J. (ed.), *The Extended Circle: An Anthology of Human Thought* (Cardinal, Sussex, 1990), 56, 86, 98, 140, 178.
[14] Feinberg, J., 'The Rights of Animals and Unborn Generations', in Blackstone, W. T. (ed.), *Philosophy and the Environmental Crisis* (University of Georgia Press, Athens, 1974), 51–5. For additional discussions of this critical point, see Frankena, W. K., 'Ethics and Environment', in Goodpaster, K. E. (ed.), *Ethics and Problems of the 21st Century* (Notre Dame University Press, Notre Dame, 1976), 17. Lehmann, S., 'Do Wildernesses Have Rights?', *Environmental Ethics*, 3

These views have been countered by the more modern advocates (i.e. post-Schweitzer) of the life approach. They have argued that the sanctity of life arises from the life as it is, in itself, independent of human conceptions that try to limit and define it. It is not valued because it glorifies God, is useful to humanity or has an important role in an ecosystem. It is valued because of the simple fact that *it exists and is alive* with its own goals and can be furthered or damaged by moral actors.

Accordingly, it is argued that something can have a good of its own without having the capacity for sentience or the ability to feel pain.[15] As Paul Taylor asserted, sentience is not an end in itself. Rather, sentience has evolved as a means to the further goal of survival. Therefore, since sentience is ancillary to life, then the capacity to live, rather than the capacity to experience pleasure and pain, should be the criterion of moral considerability.[16] As Kenneth Goodpaster suggested:

Neither rationality nor the capacity to experience pleasure and pain seem to me necessary (even though they may be sufficient) conditions on moral considerability . . . Nothing short of the condition of being alive seems to me to be a plausible and non-arbitrary criterion.[17]

However, this criterion for moral considerability requires that something must still be animate. Accordingly, trees and flowers are in, while rocks and rainbows are out. Something having a good of its own, moves it from being valueless in human eyes (except perhaps previously for interest satisfaction) to a position of moral consideration. It is *not* the ability to feel pain or pleasure, or the capacity to care about this that is at stake. Rather, the emphasis is upon the goal-seeking or teleological character which is manifested in the way animals and plants seek certain elements in their environment, and turn away from other elements, in their desire to stay alive. The fact that living organisms are 'concerned' with the regeneration of their own organizational structure means that they may be thought of as having an interest in avoiding anything that blocks this process of regeneration or threatens their life process.[18]

(1981), 137. Cahen, H., 'Against the Moral Considerability of Ecosystems', *Environmental Ethics,* 10 (1988), 208. Johnson, L. E., 'Animal Liberation Versus the Land Ethic', *Environmental Ethics,* 3 (1981), 265–73. Norton, B. G. 'Environmental Ethics and Non-human Rights', *Environmental Ethics,* 4 (1982), 35–8. Singer, P., *Animal Liberation: A New Ethic for Our Treatment of Animals* (Paladin, Sydney, 1977), 8. Singer, P., 'Not for Humans Only: The Place of Non-humans in Environmental Issues', in Regan, T. (ed.), *Ethics And Problems of The Twenty-first Century* (Random House, New York, 1976), 199–200. Regan, T., 'The Nature and Possibility of an Environmental Ethic', *Environmental Ethics,* 3 (1981), 22. Singer, P., *Practical Ethics* (Cambridge University Press, Cambridge, 1993), 57–9, 274–6, 283–4.

[15] Taylor, P., 'Frankena on Environmental Ethics', *Monist,* 64 (1981), 314.

[16] Taylor, P., *Respect for Nature: A Theory of Environmental Ethics* (Princeton University Press, Oxford, 1986), 100, 119–22; 'The Ethics of a Respect for Nature', *Environmental Ethics,* 3 (1981), 197, 206. Rodman, *supra* n. 4, 126.

[17] Goodpaster, K. E., 'On Being Morally Considerable', *Journal of Philosophy,* 75 (1978), 310.

[18] Rolston, H., 'Values and Duties to the Natural World', in Bormann, F. H. and Keller, S. R.

Each living entity's interest in its own existence, manifested by its goal-oriented activities directed towards its own preservation and well-being, is taken as both necessary and sufficient for moral considerability. This view does not deny the moral relevance of sentience or Regan's criterion of 'subject of a life'; it simply denies that they are the only necessary criteria for moral consideration.[19] Here, the philosophical argument for value places the attitude of respect at the feet of whatever is living and each living thing which is pursuing its own goals. Any entities which fulfil these criteria are therefore eligible for inherent value.

One substantial problem in this area is the 'slippery slope argument'. This argument suggests that many things may have a good of their own, in the sense that various kinds of treatment can be good or bad for them, but moral agents would still not consider that they deserve moral consideration. The case of machinery provides a suitable example of this, as acts can be good or bad for it, but it could not properly be regarded as deserving of moral consideration.[20] The specific issue concerns the possibility of distinguishing between a machine, and trees, plants, and other non-sentient members of the biotic community. For once the door is opened to admit non-sentient beings into the moral considerability club, how is it possible to shut the door and stop ordinary inanimate objects entering?

A common way to counter this argument is to point out that a tree is natural whereas a machine is not. Consequently, the tree strives to produce and sustain its own organizational activity and structure. In other words, the primary product of the living system is itself, not something external to it, as it is with machines.[21] Associated with this answer is the realization that the goals of the machine are really for human objectives. Therefore the machines do not strictly have a good of their own. Thus, a machine has no interest in running properly, rather it is the user or creator of the machine who has an interest in it running properly. A plant, by contrast, has an autonomous interest in staying alive, which is quite independent of any exterior interests in the plant's survival.

The focus upon entropy is another way of showing that there is a goal

---

(eds.), *Ecology, Economics, Ethics: The Broken Circle* (Yale University Press, New York, 1991), 73, 78–80; 'Rights and Responsibilities on the Home Planet', *Yale Journal of International Law*, 18 (1993), 251, 263–5. Mathews, F., 'Conservation and Self Realisation: A Deep Ecology Perspective', *Environmental Ethics*, 10 (1988), 351. Rodman, J., 'Four Forms of Ecological Consciousness Reconsidered', in Scherer, D. (ed.), *Ethics and the Environment* (Prentice Hall, New Jersey, 1983), 82, 88–90. Goodpaster, *supra* n. 17, 317–19. Taylor, *supra* n. 16, 210–11. Attfield, *supra* n. 6, 39.

[19] Fox, *supra* n. 4, 106.

[20] See Kaufman, F., 'Machines, Sentience, and the Scope of Morality', *Environmental Ethics*, 16 (1994), 57, 60–2. Johnson, E., 'Treading the Dirt: Environmental Ethics and Moral Theory', in Regan, T. (ed.), *Earthbound: New Introductory Essays in Environmental Ethics* (Random House, New York, 1984), 350. Spitler, G., 'Justifying a Respect For Nature', *Environmental Ethics*, 4 (1982), 255. Lehman, *supra* n. 14, 135.

[21] Fox, *supra* n. 4, 169–71. Kaufman, ibid. 61–2. Of course, as Kaufman points out, why is the originality of the interests or goods in question an issue, when the focus is upon the frustration, not the origin of these. At 63, 65.

directedness in certain natural objects that is not found in machines. Consider, a plant has a direction of growth and seeks natural fulfilment through the utilization of entropy. A rock or a machine does not, and cannot do this. From here an ethic is attributed to entities that display the property of autopoiesis, which means 'self-production' or 'self-renewal'. Such entities focus upon the regeneration of their own organizational activity and structure.[22] It is this process of self-renewal and self-production that distinguishes living entities from self-correcting machines that appear to operate in a purposeful way.

However, it needs to be noted that the fact that a tree may strive to maintain itself does not make it unique, as machines may eventually (if not already) be programmed to do this and hence eventually also seek to maintain themselves. Thus, the distinguishing factor of autopoietic traits becomes vulnerable. However, when the criteria of goal directedness is combined with that of natural objects, then the position regains plausibility. This is because the machine analogy breaks down when it comes to understanding the growth and development of organisms. Oak trees grow tiny embryos in acorns; elephants develop from small fertilized eggs within the elephant, whereas no machines grow and spontaneously develop from machine-eggs, rather, they have to be assembled from pre-existing parts in factories. They do not reproduce or give rise to new machines from small parts in themselves, nor do they regenerate after damage.[23] Thus, as Samual Coleridge realized in the beginning of the nineteenth century, mechanical forces cannot make life itself.[24] Additionally, if machines are ever able to make life, it must still be realized that such a goal was initially put there by their inventors, and was not originally autonomous.

A second surpassable difficulty arises out of the suggestion that it is not possible to know or perceive the world other than from an anthropocentric perspective, because those making the decisions are, after all, human. This is unconvincing as non-anthropocentric theorists are not claiming that it is possible to know exactly what it is to be a non-human piece of Nature, but only that it is still possible to make certain broad assumptions about the general interests of living entities. Without this ability, a male could not be non-sexist, or a Caucasian, non-racist.

A third problem for the life argument is that to state that all life is sacred, which is implicit in the life claim, is too general a statement. This is because sometimes lives can cease to be worth living. For example, lives can be so ridden with pain that the entity suffering may conclude their life is not worth living.[25]

A fourth complication in this area is that although advocates of the life

---

[22] Eckersley, R., *Environmentalism and Political Theory: Towards an Ecocentric Approach* (UCL Press, London, 1992), 60. Cahen, *supra* n. 14, 205. Goodpaster, *supra* n. 17, at 323.

[23] Sheldrake, R., *The Rebirth of Nature* (Rider, London, 1990), 82. Johnson, *supra* n. 1, 145–7. Taylor, *A Theory, supra* n. 16, 124–5

[24] Coleridge, S., *Philosophical Lectures* (Pilot Press, London, 1949), 18.

[25] Attfield, *supra* n. 6, 47. Singer, *supra* n. 14, 214–15.

position have accused others of being humanistic in bias, and drawing the moral circle too tightly, their own approach is open to the same criticism. Thus, the claim of 'being alive' as the criterion for moral considerability can also be seen as being trapped by humanistic overflows, and that 'being in existence' may be at least as plausible and non-arbitrary a criterion for moral consideration as is being alive.[26]

Connected to this problem is the fact that there may be a limit on the ambit of environmental protection if the criterion of being alive is the ethical yardstick. As Eric Katz explained, 'Many natural entities worth preserving are not clearly the possessors of interests, because they are not alive.'[27] A good example of this type of problem can be seen with endangered species. The problem is that the life theory cannot provide preferred moral standing to a specimen of endangered species, the focus of considerability—the individual being alive—is not distinguishable between endangered or plentiful species.[28] Likewise, it cannot discriminate morally between what is domestic and what is wild. A similar argument is that if crushing one stone raises no moral question, why, when assuming from a moral monist position that the only value is life, would destroying the Grand Canyon (supposing that all living things were removed from it) raise a moral dilemma?

This type of position has been countered in part by the holistic Gaia thesis. For if the Earth is itself a self-sustaining, regenerating organizational activity, as are many ecosystems and species, then the treatment of these entities would in many instances fall under the notion of respect for life.[29] However, this is problematic, as many smaller species are not important to the functioning of Gaia. This realization conflicts with the principles of the life argument in that everything alive is assumed valuable. Additionally, it should be realized that those at the forefront of this position, such as Paul Taylor, have rejected the view that supra- or quasi-organisms can possess a good of their own and hence merit moral consideration. This he reserves for individual organisms.[30]

This claim that only individual living entities are of value is supported by the complication that one of the bases of the life claim (that it is necessary to value entities with goal directedness), rules out larger-than-individual living entities,

[26] Hunt, W. M., 'Are Mere Things Morally Considerable?', *Environmental Ethics*, 2 (1980), 61. Rodman, *supra* n. 4, 94.

[27] Katz, E., 'Organism, Community, and the Substitution Problem', *Environmental Ethics*, 7 (1985), 243. See also Nelson, M. P., 'A Defence of Environmental Ethics', *Environmental Ethics*, 15 (1993), 245, 256–7.

[28] Scherer, *supra* n. 3, 15.

[29] Fox, *supra* n. 4, 172–5. Marshal, *supra* n. 13, 445. Skolimowski, H., *Living Philosophy: Eco Philosophy as a Tree of Life* (Arkana, London, 1992), 208. Skolimowski, H., *Eco-Philosophy: Designing New Tactics for Living* (Boyars, London, 1981), 28–33, 66, 83, 107–8.

[30] Taylor, *A Theory*, *supra* n. 16, 68–71, 119, 124–5. Attfield adopts the same position, *supra* n. 1, 156. Consequently, all non-living, non-individual life can only be preserved for instrumental purposes; 153, 193. Cf. Sterba, J. P., 'From Biocentric Individualism to Biocentric Pluralism', *Environmental Ethics*, 17 (1995), 191–207.

i.e. ecosystems, for moral consideration. This is because the indirect direction of a number of objectives of certain larger entities is often a series of behavioural by-products, which look deceptively like goals. For example, something like ecosystem stability may come about because of an individual species pursuing its own self-interest, that in turn has the incidental result of affecting the stability of the overall ecosystem within which it exists. If this is correct, then moral valuers are not dealing with a systematic goal, but with behavioural by-products. Therefore, ecosystems are not truly goal directed in the same sense that plants and other non-sentient organisms are. Consequently, in this sense, the reverence for life argument cannot be applied.[31]

As a follow on from the above position, it can be pointed out that the individualism of the life approach, like that advocating the moral considerability of animals, is at odds with holistic ecocentric ideals. This is because the life approach places its focus of moral considerability upon individual organisms, whereas holistic environmental ethics place their emphasis upon the complete biotic community and these two objectives may not always coincide.[32]

The final difficulty that encounters the moral considerability of life position is the sheer impracticality of this proposal. However, before proceeding, it is important to note that such 'practical' questions, strictly, have little to do with the philosophical correctness of this (or any other) position. Nevertheless, they do have distinct implications in the considerations of the feasibility of the possible adoption of this, or any other proffered approach. The life principle, like the principle concerning the utilitarian approach to the moral considerability of animals, is both individualistic and reductive. Therefore an equitable system for resolving the conflicts between individuals is the desirable goal. The problem is, that as more and more individuals (i.e. from cancer cells to individual blades of grass) are admitted into the field of moral entitlement the moral space becomes increasingly crowded, more conflicts of interest inevitably arise, and their management becomes increasingly hopeless.[33]

A feasible management of disputes is necessary, for it is essential to have an impartial method for choosing between the interests in conflict.[34] However, the life perspective distinctly rejects conflict resolution through the weighting of the qualities of some living creatures, i.e. sentience, as the standard for decision making. Rather, everything has to be valued on the equal basis of being alive. This presents a vast problem as many of the advocates of this position may find that shooting their neighbour was no more morally reprehensible than swatting a fly, or stepping on a wild flower.[35] However, it should be noted that this view

[31] Cahen, *supra* n. 14, 195. Sterba, ibid. 204, 207.   [32] Fox, *supra* n. 4, 179.

[33] See Regan, T., *The Case for Animal Rights* (Routledge, London, 1988), 243.

[34] Lehmann, *supra* n. 14.

[35] Scherer, *supra* n. 3, 15. Singer, 'Not for Humans Only', *supra* n. 14, 195. Attfield, R., 'Sylvan, Fox and Deep Ecology: A View from the Continental Shelf', *Environmental Values*, 2 (1993), 21, 24–5. Attfield earlier attempted to avoid the conclusion of the life approach by suggesting that 'moral

may be too harsh a reading of the life position. For example, Schweitzer suggested that non-human life could be taken 'under the pressure of necessity' (although he did draw the boundary of necessity quite largely from anthropocentric considerations).[36] Alternatively, Taylor suggested that humanity has the right to protect itself from 'dangerous organisms' and the 'basic interests' of humanity are also allowed to be fulfilled. However, he maintained that the fulfilment of 'non-basic interests' are intrinsically incompatible with respect for Nature.[37]

The problem is that the possible implications of this kind of approach may be implausible. The idea that five billion humans should be obliged to restrain from ever hurting living organisms as the early Pythagorean disciples were, by waiting for fruit to fall from a tree[38] before eating (thus both life is respected and basic needs are met) may be impractical. Absolute equal value of life and the principle of basic needs may quickly lead to a point where overload is reached and the whole idea of an alternative environmental ethic threatens to collapse into absurdity.

However, even if all life is valuable, but not of equal value (a problematic assumption in itself given the basis of this position), as the above paragraph hypothesized, it is still essential to have some way of measuring how much worth should be given to living entities. For example, how valuable is a single insect and how is this value to be reconciled with other living entities?[39] Certain theorists such as Lawrence Johnson have attempted to counter this point with his proposal that, 'we ought to value lives in proportion to the interests that are inherent with them'.[40] However, this principle, as Johnson himself notes, 'does not tell us how to determine what consideration is due to particular interests under particular circumstances'.[41] This is a specific problem in times of conflict where choices of which living entities must be given precedence have to be taken. Additionally, it still falls foul of the same problem as the utilitarian argument for the moral considerability of animals, namely the sheer impracticality of trying to calculate the trillions of interests that this principle would encompass.

---

standing [i.e, the life principle] is not the same as moral significance', *supra* n. 1, 157, 193. However, this effectively revokes any hope of any substantial value of the life position, as what it represents may be very little and could not challenge the anthropocentric licence.

[36] Schweitzer, *supra* n. 9, 256–8. This is ironic as Schweitzer himself noted that it is not possible to really know the value of non-human life. Hence to make a judgement that one is worth more than another is a subjective judgement. See Birch, C. and Cobb, J., *The Liberation of Life* (Cambridge University Press, Cambridge, 1985), 149.

[37] Taylor, *A Theory, supra* n. 16, 264–5. Note, there can be little derogation from this principle (as Taylor suggests at 280–96) if he sticks to his central precept that 'Humans are not inherently superior to other living things' (at 100) and it is individual life that is the moral consideration. See also pages 168–73 of this book.

[38] See Hughes, J. D., 'The Environmental Ethics of the Pythagoreans', *Environmental Ethics*, 2 (1980), 195, 202.   [39] Johnson, *supra* n. 1, 136–7.

[40] Ibid. 140.   [41] Ibid. 185, 186–99, 288.

X

The Land Ethic

1. THE BASIS AND OBJECTIVE

Holistic environmental ethics, deep ecology or the land ethic, start from a rejection of 'the human-in-environment image, in favour of the relational, total-field image'.[1] This basic precept is derived in part from the new sciences that, over the decades, have discredited the traditional paradigms that anthropocentricism has been built upon through challenging old foundations of scientific thought.[2] Although these sciences are all greatly different, many of the new revelations converge on some similar metaphysical notions, such as holistic overviews via dynamic interrelationships and interconnections.[3]

The challenge to the traditional paradigm has come from five main sources. Firstly, quantum theory can now show that the world is not matter alone. Rather, it can be shown that it is alive with energy and vitality. The atoms of old-style materialism—hard, permanent particles of matter moving in a void—are nowhere to be found. Additionally, quantum theory has shown that there is a deep interrelationship between the observed and the observer. Consequently it is not possible for an observer to remain isolated from what is being observed.[4] Secondly, the Chaos theory is also important as it denies static equilibrium. It shows that small perturbations can lead to large changes in system functioning and that there is more than one direction that a system can take depending on its contextual and contingent variables.[5] Both the Chaos theory and the quantum theory stand in stark contrast to the metaphor of the mechanical universe.

A third defiance to the traditional paradigm has come from the fact that the

---

[1] Fox, W., 'Deep Ecology: A New Philosophy of Our Time?', *Ecologist,* 14 (1984), 194.

[2] Whitehead, A. N., *Science and the Modern World* (Macmillan, London, 1925), 29, 167, 175.

[3] Callicott, J. B., 'The Metaphysical Implications of Ecology', *Environmental Ethics,* 8 (1986), 301. Sterling, S., 'Towards an Ecological World View', in Engell, J. R. and J. B. (eds.), *The Ethics of Environment and Development: Global Challenge, International Response* (Belhaven, London, 1990), 77, 81. Pepper, D., *The Roots of Modern Environmentalism* (Routledge, London, 1984), 122. Capra, F., *The Turning Point: Science, Society and the Rising Culture* (Flamingo, New York, 1982), 80, 81. Eckersley, R., *Environmentalism and Political Theory: Towards an Ecocentric Approach* (UCL Press, London, 1992), 49. Oelschlaeger, M., *The Idea of Wilderness: From Prehistory to the Age of Ecology* (Yale University Press, New York, 1991), 301–9.

[4] Sheldrake, R., *The Rebirth of Nature: The Greening of Science and God* (Rider, London, 1990), 68. Capra, F., *The Tao of Physics* (Shambhala, London, 1975), 68–87. Heisenberg, W., *The Physicist's Conception of Nature* (Penguin, Harmondsworth, 1958), 29. Callicott, J. B., 'Intrinsic Value, Quantum Theory and Environmental Ethics', *Environmental Ethics,* 7 (1985), 270–4.

[5] Gleik, J., *Chaos: Making of a New Science* (Viking, Boston, 1987), 273. Sheldrake, ibid. 70–1.

historical belief in the uniqueness of humanity has been consistently eroded with the study of evolution. Here, Charles Darwin's thesis not only presented a dynamic, changing, and interdependent view of the natural world (i.e. that species existed primarily for themselves and not for others), it also began to hint at the strong evolutionary links between humanity and all other natural entities.[6] The fourth element that has led to a need to reconsider the traditional paradigm has come from the science of ecology, which has come to prove that the idea of the insular individual is false and that the individual is not, and never has been, autonomous from the ecological base. Additionally, it has been suggested that no thing and no activity should be regarded in isolation because of the circularity and holistic basis of ecosystems.[7] The idea of an interconnected whole has been further propagated by the Gaia thesis, which is predicated on the idea that the Earth itself is alive, and which shows that 'everything is nicely interconnected'.[8]

In giving such alternative pictures of reality, modern science has, 'been the single most decisive non-anthropocentric intellectual force in the Western world'.[9] Indeed, once the totality of the natural world is viewed in all its aspects, cycles, and interrelationships, then the human position should be carefully re-examined as humanity can make no firm ontological divides in the field of existence. The field of existence is the surrounding natural world. Consequently, it is

---

[6]   Darwin, C., *On the Origin of Species* (Murray, London, 1859), 51–3, 196. Rachels, J., 'Darwin, Species and Morality', *Monist*, 70 (1987), 98. Rachels, J., 'Created From Animals', in Pierce, C. and Van de Veer, D. (eds.), *People, Penguins and Plastic Trees: Basic Issues in Environmental Ethics* (Wadsworth, London, 1995), 59–72. Diamond, J., *The Rise and the Fall of the Third Chimpanzee* (Rider, London, 1991), 15–21. Sheldrake, *supra* n. 4, 54–7. Capra, *supra* n. 3, 105–15. Thomas, K., *Man and the Natural World: Changing Attitudes in England 1500–1800* (Penguin, Harmondsworth, 1984), 133, 168–72. Goldsmith, E., *The Way: Towards an Ecological World View* (Rider, London, 1992), 122–3.

[7]   Caldwell, L., *Between Two Worlds: Science, the Environmental Movement and Policy Choice* (Cambridge University Press, Cambridge, 1990), 46. Udall, S., *The Quiet Crisis and the Next Generation* (Gibbs Smith, Utah, 1988), 78. Commoner, B., 'The Ecological Facts of Life', in Disch, R. (ed.), *The Ecological Conscience* (Spectrum, New Jersey, 1970), 2. Shepard, P., 'Ecology and Man', also in Disch, 56. Goldsmith, ibid. 225–30. Wall, D. (ed.), *Green History: A Reader in Environmental Literature, Philosophy and Politics* (Routledge, London, 1994), 98–9, 133–5. Clarke, J. J. (ed.), *Nature in Question: An Anthology of Ideas and Arguments* (Earthscan, London, 1993), 147, 149–50, 178–80.

[8]   Lovelock, J., *Gaia: A New Look at Life on Earth* (Oxford University Press, Oxford, 1979), 9–11, 92, 148–9, 152; 'The Quest for Gaia', *New Scientist*, 65 (1975), 304. Joseph, L. E., *Gaia: The Growth of an Idea* (Arkana, London, 1990), 207; 'Gaia and the Balance of Nature', in Bourdeau, P. (ed.), *Environmental Ethics: Man's Relationship with Nature* (Official Publication of the European Community, Brussels, 1989), 241. Abram, D., 'The Perceptual Implications of GAIA', *Ecologist*, 15 (1985), 96. Bunyard, P., 'The Gaia Hypothesis and Man's Responsibility to the Earth', *Ecologist*, 13 (1983), 158. Abram, D., 'The Mechanical and the Organic: Epistemological Consequences of the Gaia Hypothesis', in Bunyard, P. and Goldsmith, E. (eds.), *GAIA. The Thesis, the Mechanisms and the Implications* (Wadebridge, Cornwall, 1988), 119, 125, 126. Ravetz, J., 'Gaia and the Philosophy of Science', also in Bunyard and Goldsmith, 133, 135. Goldsmith, *supra* n. 6, 8. Weston, A., 'Forms of Gaian Ethics', *Environmental Ethics*, 9 (1987), 218, 221.

[9]   Sessions, G., 'Anthropocentricism and the Environmental Crisis', *Humboldt Journal of Social Relations*, 2 (1974), 73. Devall, B., *Simple in Means, Rich in Ends: Practising Deep Ecology* (Green Print, Devon, 1990), 21.

asserted that new ethical rules should be extracted from the new holistic paradigm as it is now recognized.[10]

It is from building upon the above foundations, the problems with anthropocentric justifications for environmental protection, and the additional problems
displayed with the moral consideration of animals and the life perspective, that
Aldo Leopold's famous account of right and wrong for the land ethic can be
derived. He stipulated:

A thing is right when it tends to preserve the integrity, stability and beauty of the biotic
community. It is wrong when it tends otherwise.[11]

Baird Callicott has interpreted such an approach as meaning that:

The good of the community of the whole serves as a standard for the assessment of the
relative value and relative ordering of its constitutive parts and therefore provides a means
of adjudicating the often mutually contradictory demands of the parts considered sepa-
rately for equal consideration . . . the idea of the good of the biotic community is the ultimate measure of moral value . . . in every case the effect upon the ecological systems is
the decisive factor in the determination of the ethical quality of actions . . . [12]

Consequently, humanity must dwell within the world, not as its master, but as its
servant endowed with the approach of allowing other entities to fulfil their own
evolutionary destinies. Biocentric equality is the prima facie rule. Thus, 'all ways
and forms of life . . . have an equal right to live and blossom'[13] to the extent that
they do not damage the autopoietic functioning of their ecosystem or the whole
ecosphere.[14]

Associated with this view is the position that everything involved in a natural
process has an inherent value, whether it be found in the individual or in the
whole. However, it should be noted that the emphasis remains upon the whole.
In the broader holistic picture individuals of all species, including humans, are

[10] Naess, A., 'Identification as a Source of Deep Ecological Attitudes', in Tobias, D., *Deep Ecology* (San Diego, 1985), 48. Callicott, *supra* n. 4, 74. Norton, B. G., 'Environmental Ethics and Weak Anthropocentricism', *Environmental Ethics*, 6 (1984), 141. O'Neill, J., *Ecology, Policy and Politics: Human Well-Being and The Natural World* (Routledge, London, 1993), 149–152. Cf. Sherrard, P., who asserts the basic reductionist and positivist values remain the same; *The Rape of Man and Nature* (Golgonooza, Suffolk, 1987), 76–89.

[11] Leopold, A., *A Sand County Almanac* (Oxford University Press, Oxford, 1949), 224–5.

[12] Callicott, J. B., 'Animal Liberation: A Triangular Affair', *Environmental Ethics*, 2 (1980), 311, 324–5. Rodman, J., 'The Liberation of Nature', *Inquiry*, 20 (1977), 94. Thus, as Donald Scherer stated, 'such holism not only includes non-individualistic values—it excludes individualistic values'; 'Anthropocentricism, Atomism and Environmental Ethics', *Environmental Ethics*, 4 (1982), 115, 116.

[13] Naess, A., 'The Shallow and the Deep, Long Range Ecology Movement: A Summary', *Inquiry*, 16 (1973), 90, 95. Eckersley, *supra* n. 3, 20, 28.

[14] Devall, B. and Sessions, G., *Deep Ecology: Living as if Nature Mattered* (Gibbs Smith, Utah, 1985), 15, 21, 67–9, 79. Nash, J. A., 'The Case for Biotic Rights', *Yale Journal of International Law*, 18 (1993), 235, 245–6. Zimmerman, M. E., 'Towards a Heideggerean Ethics for Radical Environmentalism', *Environmental Ethics*, 5 (1983), 123–7. Fox, *supra* n. 1, 194.

no more than small dots on a huge matrix.[15] The ultimate goal of the holistic land ethic is to achieve the values of ecological diversity, stability, complexity, and harmony of individual ecosystems and the overall ecosphere.

This kind of approach leads to the principle of biospherical equality. This principle subscribes to a holistic view which recognizes no 'king of beasts'. Accordingly, humans, too, belong to the whole, but only as part of the whole. In short, 'a land ethic changes the role of Homo-sapiens from conqueror of the land community to plain member and citizen of it'.[16] Therefore, humanity must attempt to let individuals and species function unhindered according to their own evolutionary patterns. This means that when there is no conflict between human interests and the interests of Nature, humanity should not meddle, interfere or destroy the natural world, and must seek minimum impacts upon Nature. Additionally, humans should act to enhance and preserve non-human life.

2. PHILOSOPHICAL PROBLEMS

The is/ought problem is recognized as a central problem of moral philosophy. In this context, science and ethics are recognized as separate disciplines, hence a paradox between facts and values may eventuate. To step from fact to value is to create a 'naturalistic fallacy'.

The fallacy is to state a value conclusion (the ought) that is derived from premises of fact (the is). David Hume (who first realized the dichotomy) regarded finding values in facts as a very important mistake. For example, the fact is that smoking may cause death. It may therefore be suggested to a smoker that she/he should not smoke, as she/he may die. The fallacy has been committed, as a value (that the smoker does not want to die) has been added to the fact that smoking causes death.

In the environmental context, the question, given the fact of the holistic view of Nature and humanity, is how is value or respect for the environment to be

---

[15] Thus, as J. B. Callicott stated, 'The Land Ethic . . . is holistic with a vengeance.' In 'The Conceptual Implications of the Land Ethic', in Callicott, J. B. (ed.), *Companion to a Sand County Almanac: Interpretative Essays* (University of Wisconsin Press, 1987), 186, 196, 205. Merchant, C., *Radical Ecology: The Search for a Livable World* (Routledge, London, 1992), 76–8. Watson, R. A., 'A Critique of Anti Anthropocentric Biocentrism', *Environmental Ethics,* 5 (1983), 253. Devall, *supra* n. 9, 154–7, 168. Atkinson, A., *Principles of Political Ecology* (Belhaven, London, 1991), 182–3. Naess, A., 'Deep Ecology and the Ultimate Premises', in *Ecologist*, 18 (1988), 128, 130. Naess, A., 'The Basics of Deep Ecology', in Button, J. (ed.), *The Green Fuse* (Quartet Books, London, 1990), 130, 135. Eckersley, *supra* n. 3, 54–5.

[16] Leopold, *supra* n. 11, 204. See also Devall, B., 'The Deep Ecology Movement', *Natural Resources Journal,* 20 (1980), 311. Callicott, J. B., 'The Search for an Environmental Ethic', in Regan, T. (ed.), *An Introduction to Modern Moral Philosophy* (Random House, New York, 1984), 76. Skolimowski, H., *Living Philosophy: Eco-Philosophy as a Tree of Life* (Arkana, London, 1992), 102. Johnson, L. E., *A Morally Deep World: An Essay on Moral Significance* (Cambridge University Press, Cambridge, 1991), 224–7. Devall and Sessions *supra* n. 14, 68. Nash, *supra* n. 14, 235, 245–6.

derived? The problem arises because science describes natural history and natural 'laws', whereas ethics prescribe human conduct and moral 'laws'. To join the two involves a category mistake and commits the naturalistic fallacy. This is because Nature's 'laws' are without objective ethical value. It is humanity that allegedly creates ethical values (the oughts) from natural laws (the is). Here, the environmental ethic which argues that it is morally wrong to damage the Earth (the ought) is derived from the ecological fact—i.e. that humans exist within an interdependent biotic community (the is). The obvious question to explore in this context is, why ought the biotic community be cared for?[17]

The first answer to this problem is that humans generally have a positive attitude to the society or community within which they exist, and ecological science has now shown that the natural environment is also a community to which humans belong. Additionally, it can generally be claimed that most humans wish to survive and would preserve the ecosphere to achieve it.[18] Therefore, the human response (the ought) is founded in both physical realizations (the is) and moral views. Here, the leap from fact to value is relatively simple. This is because the psychological fact (that humans live in an ecological community, and that humans want to survive) is derived of itself and not of the ecological fact leading to the problem.

In a similar sense Edward Goldsmith has objected to the is/ought dichotomy on the grounds that the 'is' is drawn substantially from the positivistic paradigm with the insistence upon 'objective', non-intrinsic facts. Consequently, the argument is restricted by the terms within which it occurs. For example, if existence is not taken to be representative of classical physics, but as deriving from a larger environmental paradigm, then the move from is to ought shifts to an entirely different answer. Indeed, the is/ought problem, appears altogether less significant when the valuer moves outside the paradigm within which the 'is' is located, i.e. when the self is located in the larger biosphere—as to protect the biosphere is to protect the self.[19] For just as the new sciences force valuers to abandon the sharp dichotomy between the singular individual and the surrounding world, so too must David Hume's sharp distinction between valuing subjects and value-free objects be abandoned. Or put another way—the division between the is and the ought may need also to be abandoned in the light of the merging of the moral valuer with the object that is valued.[20]

A third way of countering the is/ought dichotomy is by recognizing that by

[17] Fox, W., *Towards A Transpersonal Ecology: Developing New Foundations For Environmentalism* (Shambhala, London, 1990), 188–93. Rolston, H., 'Challenges in Environmental Ethics', in Cooper, D. and Palmer, J. (eds.), *The Environment in Question: Ethics and Global Issues* (Routledge, London, 1992), 135. Blackstone, W. T., 'Ethics and Ecology', in Blackstone, W. T. (ed.), *Philosophy and the Environmental Crisis* (University of Georgia Press, Athens, 1974), 23.

[18] Callicott, J. B., 'Hume's Is/Ought Dichotomy and the Relation to the Land Ethic', *Environmental Ethics*, 4 (1982), 163.

[19] Goldsmith, *supra* n. 6, 403. Fox, *supra* n. 17, 246–7. O'Neill, *supra* n. 10, 22–5.

[20] Merchant, *supra* n. 15, 80.

extinguishing ecosystems and individual non-human species, the wrong that is being committed is that human actions are interrupting the 'historic vitality of life, the flow of natural kinds'.[21] This fact of extinction translates what 'is' to what 'ought' to be. This is because ecosystems exist, they regulate life, and they seek their own good. By trying to help them fulfil these functions, the human action (the ought) is consistent with environmental goals (the is). From this point, it is difficult to say where ethics and science merge. It is ecologically purposeful for ecosystems to survive (fact), which then leads us to postulate how humanity should behave (value). Thus, the way the world is determined is the way it ought to be.[22]

A final way to work around the naturalistic fallacy is to recognize that Nature has inherent value outside of human concern. This inherent value means that the traditional anthropocentric paradigms and the associated previous values are replaced by the inherent value of Nature. Consequently, independent value (the ought) is found in the physical existence (the is) of the natural object which is trying to seek a good of its own. Of course, it remains difficult to say where the natural facts leave off and where the natural values appear, but the general hurdle has been cleared. Accordingly, the precept that it is right to protect the environment because of its independent inherent value, commits no fallacy as no value (inherent value is not a value *per se*, as much as it is axiomatic) is derived from an ecological fact.[23]

3. PROBLEMS WITH ECOLOGICAL THEORY

The environmental ethic perspective has derived several rules from the new sciences. Specifically, theoretical ecology often has a special place and therefore goes to support certain proposals put forward for the land ethic. However, as enquiries into the debate have become deeper, it appears that ecology often raises as many questions as it provides answers.[24] Consequently, it has been argued that it is not possible to derive philosophical foundations from these ideas. This problem has been carried so far as to suggest that ecological 'laws' do not even posit

---

[21] Rolston, *supra* n. 17, 135, 140.

[22] Rolston, *supra* n. 17, 135, 144–5. Merchant, *supra* n. 15, 79–80.

[23] Rolston, H., 'Is There an Ecological Ethic?', *Ethics*, 85 (1974), 93–103. Regan, T. (ed.), *All That Dwell Within: Essays on Animal Rights and Environmental Ethics* (University of California Press, Berkeley, 1982), 203. Fox, *supra* n. 17, 193.

[24] Sagoff, M., 'Fact and Value in Ecological Science', *Environmental Ethics,* 7 (1985), 99, 105. Caldwell, *supra* n. 7, 11–12. Sagoff, M., 'Integrating Science and Law', *Tennessee Law Review,* 56 (1988), 159. Rolston, *supra* n. 17, 93–103. Note, however, that other environmental theorists have pointed out that the norms and tendencies that environmental ethics are based upon are not derived strictly from the science of ecology. Rather, the science of ecology, has acted more as an afterburner, in that it helps inspire and fortify the perspectives of environmental ethics. Naess, A., *Ecology, Community, Lifestyle* (Cambridge University Press, Cambridge, 1989), 35, 39–40. Fox, *supra* n. 1, 194, 196. Goldsmith, *supra* n. 6, 403. Devall, *supra* n. 9, 11, 22–3.

basic environmental protection. For example, it is commonly asserted that the biotic community regularly eliminates species as part of the natural process. Extinction is seen as a fact of ecological life. From here it is argued that as humanity is part of Nature, then human destruction of the environment is just another natural process. Akin to this, it is emphasized that biology reveals both predatory and symbiotic species. Hence ideals about leaving Nature alone and not using it because of any alleged intrinsic value do not sit comfortably. This is because it is the norm for all species to use others as a means to an end and compete for scarce resources.[25] The follow on from these two positions is the allegation that:

There is no categorical imperative that all species must be preserved . . . nor are we under any obligation to preserve every species without discrimination.[26]

The answer to the above accusation is that humanity has already stepped outside the bounds of what may be considered as a natural process. This can be seen in two ways. First, the 'natural freedom for humanity to exploit' is implausible because current human actions bear no resemblance to what non-human Nature can do and has done. Non-human Nature has never even been close to possessing the capacity to destroy with the same speed or intensity that humanity is currently doing.[27]

This problem has been greatly increased in the twentieth century as extinction rates are of a much greater scale and impact than at any previous time in the Earth's history.[28] For example, the rate of extinction that humanity is responsible for (approximately thousands of species per year) is at present two hundred times the previous rate of extinctions within non-human Nature. As Jared Diamond said:

Dismissing the extinction crisis on the grounds that extinction is natural would be just like dismissing genocide on the grounds that death is the natural fate of all humans.[29]

---

[25] Sober, E., 'Philosophical Problems For Environmentalism', in Norton, B. G. (ed.), *The Preservation of Species* (Princeton University Press, New York, 1986), 173, 179–84. Pierce, C. and Van De Veer, D., 'Do What's Natural You Say?', in Pierce and Van De Veer, *supra* n. 6, 103–105. Watson, *supra* n. 15, 255. Johnson, L. E., 'Treating The Dirt: Environmental Ethics In Moral Theory', in Regan, *supra* n. 23, 357. McCloskey, H. J., 'Ecological Ethics and its Justification: A Critical Appraisal', in *Australian National University Department of Philosophy*, 2 (1980), 65, 71. Goodin, R. E., *Green Political Theory* (Polity, Cambridge, 1992), 47–8. Dooley, P. K., 'The Ambiguity Of Environmental Ethics: Duty Or Heroism?', *Philosophy Today*, 30 (1986), 53. Rolston, H., 'Values Gone Wild', *Inquiry*, 26 (1983), 193. Callicott, J. B., *In Defence of the Land Ethic: Essays in Environmental Philosophy* (Random House, New York, 1989), 57.

[26] Moment, J., 'Bears: The Need For A New Sanity In Wildlife Conservation', *Bioscience*, 18, 1105.

[27] As George Perkins Marsh pointed out towards the end of the nineteenth century, 'the action of brutes upon the material world is slow and gradual, and usually limited whereas humanity, with the assistance of technology and culture has managed to surpass the former natural limits'. From Marsh, G. P., 'The Earth As Modified By Human Action', in Burton, I. and Kates, R. W., *Readings in Resource Management and Conservation* (Chicago University Press, Chicago, 1965), 164, 173, 174.

[28] See IUCN, WWF, WRI, *Conserving the World's Biodiversity* (IUCN, Gland, 1990), 39, 41.

[29] Diamond, *supra* n. 6, 324. Diamond, J., 'Overview of Recent Extinctions', in Western, D. and Pearl, M. (eds.), *Conservation For The Twenty-first Century* (Oxford University Press, Oxford, 1989), 37–41. Myers, N., 'A Major Extinction Spasm: Predictable or Inevitable?', also in Western and Pearl, 42–9.

Thus, in this sense, humanity *is* unique as it has managed to step completely outside the ecological pattern. It is out of balance with the biosphere and acts in ways that do not enhance the quality of the ecosystem.[30] Consequently, what humanity is doing cannot be justified because it is 'natural'.

Secondly, humans, as a generalization, possess a unique moral capacity which allows for moral actions. This is a unique capacity in Nature, which allows humanity to choose alternative options. Other entities within Nature do not, as a rule, possess this capacity. When this consideration is added to the fact that humanity is largely aware of its own destructive tendencies, then arguably this consideration also takes humanity out of the general patterns of the natural world.[31]

A second fallacy that is derived from 'natural facts' is the common assertion that humanity is the pinnacle of evolution, and that therefore, under the theory of the survival of the fittest, humanity is entitled to use the rest of Nature as it sees fit.[32]

The first problem for this argument is that humanity is choosing the criteria of progress, namely its own specialities, as representing the pinnacle of evolution. This lacks objectivity. In fact, all species which have managed to survive should be regarded as biologically successful; humanity is no more successful than any other. Secondly, there are certainty problems with the idea that humanity is the highest peak of natural creation as the reconstructed history of fossil development is highly tentative, owing to the fact that the evidence upon which it is based, the fossil record, is incomplete.[33] A third consideration is that there is no way of knowing what the perfect existence is, or what is most evolved. For example, dominant life forms have returned to the marine habitat. Evolution is

---

[30] Note, I have critically re-examined this position in Gillespie, A., 'Endangered Species: What they are and the Vexing Question of Why to Save them? *Journal of Wildlife Management, Law and Policy*, (forthcoming).

[31] Travis, J. L., 'Progressivism and the Human Supremacy Argument', *Philosophical Forum*, 3 (1972), 208–21. Watson, R. A., *supra* n. 15, 253, 256. Baird Callicott also objects to this problem because such actions 'result in biological impoverishment instead of enrichment'. See 'The Conceptual Foundations of the Land Ethic', in Callicott, J. B. (ed.), *Companion to a Sand County Almanac: Interpretative Essays* (University of Wisconsin Press, 1987), 186, 204. Singer, P., *Practical Ethics* (Cambridge University Press, Cambridge, 1993), 70–2. Moroni, A., Mamiani, M., and Zurlini, G., 'From Domination Over Nature to Environmental Ethics: Scientific and Philosophical Foundations', in Bourdeau, *supra* n. 8, 141, 152. Attfield, R., *The Ethics of Environmental Concern* (Blackwell, Oxford, 1983), 157. Rolston, H., 'Biology Without Conservation: An Environmental Misfit and Contradiction in Terms', in Western and Pearl, *supra* n. 29, 232, 239–40. Callicott, J. B., 'The Wilderness Idea Revisited: The Sustainable Development Alternative', *The Environmental Professional*, 13 (1991), 236, 244–5. Note also, just because something is 'natural', i.e. dying, does not mean that it is wrong to attempt to stop the process.

[32] 'Man is on the crest of the evolutionary wave.' de Chardin, T., *The Future of Man* (Harper and Row, New York, 1964), 237. See also O'Neill, J., 'To Kill the Future?', in Hanson, J. (ed.), *Environmental Ethics: Political and Philosophical Perspectives* (Simon Fraser University Press, Toronto, 1986), 163. Travis, *supra* n. 31, 209.

[33] Gardiner, G., 'Between Two Worlds: Humans in Nature and Culture', *Environmental Ethics*, 12 (1990), 339, 347. Diamond, *supra* n. 6, 250, 261. Travis, *supra* n. 31, 210–14. Routley, R. and V., 'Against the Inevitability of Human Chauvinism', in Goodpaster, K. E. (ed.), *Ethics and Problems of the Twenty-first Century* (Notre Dame University Press, Notre Dame, 1976), 41.

an ongoing process. To say that the current make-up of humanity is the conclusion of evolution is, assuming time goes on for a considerable period to come, a radically premature assertion. Finally, even if *Homo sapiens* is an improvement over 'old and inferior' kinds, that in itself does not prove the right to absolute domination. Arguments for the moral considerability of animals, the life approach or the land ethic exist on independent considerations that should not be affected by what the pinnacle of evolution may or may not be.

A third area where ecological theories are problematic is with postulations about the stability or equilibrium of ecosystems. This is a common theme for many holistic environmental theorists.[34] However, there is a body of evidence that challenges many of the assumptions in this area. Change, rather than continual, harmonious equilibrium, is generally recognized as a common biospheric (non-human) quality. Consequently, it has been asserted that the balance of nature 'does not exist' and that such ideas are 'outmoded biological concepts as everything changes over time'.[35]

From such realizations it is postulated that change is both inevitable and often desirable and that what appears to be an ecological disaster is in fact a completely normal ecological event. Without change, the evolutionary process would cease. The overall problem here, is that with such precepts for ecological change, interference within Nature becomes legitimized.

However, the absoluteness of this view, namely that change is constant, has been challenged for over one hundred years.[36] In a modern context it has been argued that stability with slow change, rather than uncontrolled rapid change, is the basic feature of the living world. The natural world is seen as primarily constant and conservative with regard to change, and tends towards stability. Change occurs not because it is desirable *per se*, but because in certain conditions it is necessary as a means of preventing larger and more disruptive change. Indeed, 'quite clearly, natural systems are not geared towards change but towards the avoidance of change'.[37] Therefore, homoeostasis is the objective of living things.

---

[34] Foley, G., 'Lewis Mumford: Philosopher of the Earth', *Ecologist,* 17 (1987), 108, 114. Fox, *supra* n. 1, 194. Goldsmith, *supra* n. 6, 364. Goldsmith, E., *The Stable Society* (Green Print, Devon, 1978), 94. Odum, E. P., *Fundamentals of Ecology* (Saunders, Philadelphia, 1978), 140.

[35] Botkin, D. B., *Discordant Harmonies: A New Ecology For the Twenty-first Century* (Oxford University Press, Oxford, 1990), 6, 10, 62. Walker, B., 'Diversity and Stability in Ecosystem Conservation', in Western and Pearl, *supra* n. 29, 121–30. Worster, D., 'The Shaky Grounds of Sustainability', in Sachs, W. (ed.), *Global Ecology: A New Area of Political Conflict* (Zed, London, 1993), 132, 136–44. Clements, B., 'Stasis—The Unnatural Value', *Ethics,* 86 (1975–76), 130–44. Timmerman, P., 'Mythology and Surprise in the Sustainable Development of the Biosphere', in Clark, W. C. and Mum, R. E. (eds.), *The Sustainable Development of the Environment* (Cambridge University Press, Cambridge, 1986), 435. McElroy, M. B., 'Change in the Natural Environment of the Earth: A Historical Record', also in Clarke and Mum, 199.

[36] Marsh, *supra* n. 27, 164, 169, 172.

[37] Margalef, E., 'Is There a "Balance of Nature"?', in Bourdeau, *supra* n. 8, 225, 227–30. Patten, B. C. and Odum, E. P., 'The Cybernetic Nature of Ecosystems', *American Naturalist,* 118 (1981), 886, 888, 890. Goldsmith, *supra* n. 6, 113–17, 124, 128, 132, 144, 260.

This is not suggesting that homoeostasis is stagnant and immobile. Rather, it is still a dynamic process but with the underlying objective of stability or overall limitation of dramatic change. The incredible stability of world climate over millions of years, as explained by the Gaia hypothesis, exemplifies this point. Indeed, there exist many kinds of probability within ecosystems. Examples like the heights that tides rise to and the way the communities along seashores utilize this demonstrate this point well. However, this is not to assert that ecosystems or the biosphere as a whole show any trend of falling into a 'steady state' with stable structure and function that could be called 'an absolute balance of nature'.[38] Biological systems are often unpredictable within limits, but 'in practice there is an undeniable regularity, in that more energetic disturbances are less frequent'.[39]

Although the idea of a perfect state of equilibrium can be challenged, an underlying basic regularity still exists. Even events such as the ice ages have been explained away, not as attempts at destabilizing the balance of Nature, but as actually in accordance with the greater good of the entire biosphere. Examples like locust plagues and other natural disasters are evidence not of imbalance but of disruption of an earlier balance, through taking something out of, or adding something into, a previously homoeostatic ecosystem.[40]

This is not to deny that competition and evolutionary changes exist as a basic biological consideration; rather, it is to suggest that they may be secondary inter-relationships within ecosystems. Generally, most species appear to coexist without competition, and try to avoid it where possible. For example, of the millions of species on the Earth, all occupy predominantly different niches. Competition is important as a regulator of ecological stability, not as a method to disrupt it.[41]

4. MISANTHROPIC TENDENCIES

Since the beginnings of Western civilization it has been largely realized that there would be limits on how far an individual can act in a democracy and how

---

[38]   Margalef, ibid. 225, 229.

[39]   Ibid. 225, 230.

[40]   See Lovelock, J., 'Discussion on Margalef', in Bourdeau, *supra* n. 8, 233, 235. Margalef, E., 'On Certain Unifying Principles in Ecology', *American Naturalist,* 97 (1963), 363. Marshall, P., *Nature's Web: An Exploration of Ecological Thinking* (Simon and Schuster, London, 1992), 343. Goldsmith, *supra* n. 6, 187–211.

[41]   Goldsmith, *supra* n. 6, 211–15. A final area where the supposed rules of ecological theory have been developing has been with the argument that ecological diversity is necessary for ecosystem stability. However, it would appear that ecological diversity, *per se*, is not the objective of ecosystems, as much as it is the objective of specific settings where Nature attempts to be in a position to adapt to moderate change. However, this may not necessarily entail a drive for increased diversity. See Goodman, D., 'The Theory of Diversity-Stability Relationships', *Quarterly Review Biology,* 50 (1975), 237, 239. Carpenter, R. A., 'Ecology in Court, and Other Disappointments of Environmental Science', *Natural Resources Lawyer,* 15 (1983), 573, 589–92. Ehrenfeld, D., *The Arrogance of Humanism* (Oxford University Press, Oxford, 1978), 191, 194–5. Goldsmith, *supra* n. 6, 221, 269. Commoner, B., *The Closing Circle* (Cape, London, 1971), 33–9.

individual liberty may have to be restricted to protect the greater good of society.[42]

This basic argument, namely that the individual's liberties may have to be subsumed beneath the greater good of society, has become incorporated into some green political rhetoric. In this setting the individual is often seen as excessive, irresponsible, chaotic and defiant rather than obedient to the 'laws of Nature'.[43] Additionally, existing democratic institutions are seen as insufficient to meet the challenge of the greater environmental *problematique*. Consequently, in spite of an overt emphasis upon individualism within contemporary liberal culture, the achievement of collective goods, such as protection of the environment, is seen as a legitimate goal to *impose* upon individuals, by a more centralized and ecologically concerned body.[44] As Robert Heilbroner suggested:

Given these mighty pressures and constraints we must think of alternatives to the present order in terms of social systems that offer a necessary degree of regimentation as well as a different set of motives and objectives . . . There is no escape from the necessity of a centralised administration for our industrial world . . . the centralisation of power is the only means by which our threatened and dangerous civilisation can make way for its successor.[45]

In short, the 'golden age of individualism, liberty and democracy' is all but over, as a public authority will stand above individuals in order to keep them within ecological boundaries.[46] The Club of Rome reiterated this basic position in 1991, suggesting that democracy as it currently operates has distinct limits in its usefulness. Consequently, 'it is no longer well suited to the tasks ahead'.[47]

[42]   Russell, B., *A History of Western Philosophy* (Unwin, London, 1946), 671, 712–13. Sabine, G. H. and Thorson, T. L., *A History of Political Theory* (Dryden, Illinois, 1987), 592–5.

[43]   See Ophuls, W., *Ecology and the Politics of Scarcity* (Freeman, San Francisco, 1977), 226–7. Mellos, K., *Perspectives on Ecology* (Macmillan, London, 1988), 26. O'Riordan, T., *Environmentalism* (Pion, London, 1981), 54–6. Gore, A., *Earth in Balance: Forging a New Common Purpose* (Earthscan, London, 1992), 277. Paehlke, R. C., 'Development, Bureaucracy and Environmentalism', *Environmental Ethics*, 10 (1988), 291, 293. The unfortunate phrase 'laws of Nature' is directly attributable to Malthus, with his advocation of the abolition of the Poor Laws, as he believed that they were ultimately 'imped[ing] the operations of Nature'. *Essay*, 1803, Book IV, Ch. 5.

[44]   Orr, D. W., 'Leviathan, the Open Society, and the Crisis of Ecology', in Orr, D. W. (ed.), *The Global Predicament* (Duke University Press, North Carolina, 1979), 308, 310. Barnet, R. J., *The Lean Years: Politics in the Age of Scarcity* (Abacus, London, 1980), 297–8, 302, 313, 392. Atkinson, A., *Principles of Political Ecology* (Belhaven, London, 1991), 163, 182. Keekok-Lee, *Social Philosophy and Ecological Scarcity* (New York, 1989), 127, 143. Eckersley, *supra* n. 3, 14–16.

[45]   Heilbroner, R. L., *An Inquiry Into the Human Prospect* (Norton, New York, 1974), 136, 161. See also Cripp, S., 'Environmentalism and Utopia', *Sociological Review*, 24 (1976), 25. Ophuls, *supra* n. 43, 26–7.

[46]   Ophuls, W., 'Scarcity Society', *Harpers*, 248 (1974), 25, 42, 51. Ophuls, W., 'The Politics of the Sustainable Society', in Pirages, D. C. (ed.), *The Sustainable Society* (Praeger, New York, 1977), 161, 219. Ophuls, *supra* n. 43, 145, 227. Hoffert, R. W., 'The Scarcity of Politics: Ophuls and Western Political Thought', *Environmental Ethics*, 8 (1986), 5. Mellos, *supra* n. 43, 29–33. Barnet, *supra* n. 44, 296–7, 302–3, 313–14.

[47]   Club of Rome/King, A. and Schneider, B., *The First Global Revolution* (Simon and Schuster, London, 1991), 81.

   In essence these various strands of radical green theory are suggesting that the
liberal principle of individual freedom is inconsistent with the greater environmental good. However, the full extent of this policy can go much further than
minimal impacts upon individual liberties when taken from the view of deep
ecology or the land ethic.

   With the deep ecology perspective, what is known as 'Lifeboat ethics' (i.e. in
times of urgency, sacrifices for the greater good may be required) may eventuate.[48] This idea comes from the central premise that humans are no more than one
more knot in the holistic web, as there are no more 'hierarchies of species with
humans at the top'.[49] Consequently, humanity has no greater value than anything
else and all life has 'the equal right . . . to live and blossom'.[50] Within such a
setting, it is suggested that when faced with a conflict between values (i.e. human
needs as opposed to Nature's needs), then it is appropriate to choose the course
that will minimize harm and maximize the opportunities of the widest range of
organisms and communities to flourish.[51]

   Such a perspective can lead to misanthropy.[52] For example, the principle of
biospheric balance has been extracted from holistic views like that provided by
the Gaia thesis, and in the words of James Lovelock (the person responsible for
the modern Gaia thesis) 'humans have become a plague' or 'planetary disease'.[53]

   Extrapolating from this, certain environmental theorists have argued that the
human population has become so disproportionate, from a biological point of
view, that humanity has to be controlled, at least in problem situations such as
starvation and ecological destruction. Accordingly, Nature should be allowed 'to
take its course'.[54] As Garrett Hardin suggested:

When we send food to a starving population that has already grown beyond the environment's carrying capacity we become a partner in the devastation of their land. Food from

---

   [48] Hardin, G., 'Lifeboat Ethics: The Case Against Not Helping the Poor', *Psychology Today*,
(1974), 382. As Hardin went on to emphasize in 'Living in a Lifeboat', 'Every life saved this year in
a poor country diminishes the quality of life for subsequent generations'. *Bioscience,* 24 (1974), 561,
565. See also Hardin. G., 'Carrying Capacity As An Ethical Concept', *Soundings,* 59 (1976), 120,
124, 127.
   [49] Devall and Sessions, *supra* n. 14, 67–8.
   [50] Scherer, *supra* n. 12, 115, 121–3. Sober, *supra* n. 25, 173, 189–92. Naess, *supra* n. 13, 95–6.
   [51] Eckersley, *supra* n. 3, 194, 199.
   [52] Callicott, *supra* n. 12, 326. Bookchin, M., 'Ecology as a Dismal Science', *Green Line,* 96
(1992), 11–12. Marshall, *supra* n. 40, 357. Pepper, *supra* n. 3, 208–13.
   [53] Lovelock, J., *Gaia: The Practical Management of Planetary Medicine* (Gaia Books, London,
1991), 153, 155, 156, 199.
   [54] Miss Ann Thropy, 'Population and Aids', *Earth First!,* 1 May 1987. Hefferman, J. D., 'The
Land Ethic: A Critical Appraisal', *Environmental Ethics,* 4 (1982), 243, 246. McCloskey, H. J.,
Ecological Ethics and Politics (New Jersey, 1983), 150–5. Tokar, B., 'Social Ecology, Deep Ecology
and the Future of Green Political Thought', *Ecologist,* 18 (1988), 132, 133, 135. Pepper, *supra* n. 3,
208, 211. Chase, S., 'Whither the Radical Ecology Movement?', in Chase, S. (ed.), *Murray Bookchin
and Dave Foreman: Defending the Earth: A Dialogue* (South End, Boston, 1991), 1, 20. Foreman,
D., 'Second Thoughts of an Eco-Warrior', also in Chase, 107, 108. Note, throughout this volume,
Foreman has moved to distance himself from these remarks, which he now recognizes as myopic.

outside keeps more natives alive . . . and transgression results in lowering the carrying capacity in the future. The deficit grows exponentially . . .[55]

Thus, as Arne Naess explained, a central tenet of (his version of) the deep ecology perspective is that:

The flourishing of human life and cultures is compatible with substantial decrease of the human population. The flourishing of non-human life requires such a decrease.[56]

Consequently, the source of the problem (i.e. humans) could be sacrificed for the greater good of the biosphere. This form of collective value holism, with its instrumental view of individuals, may overlook and even dictate against individuals if those individuals are impeding the larger environmental good.[57] Such an approach could allegedly reassert the balance between humanity and the rest of the ecosystem. This approach has been used to justify the condemnation of food aid, the wresting of control of important ecosystems away from people who currently exist within them, and most commonly in the debates around the overt growth in population which is at odds with ecological capacity.[58] Consequently, notable commentators like Paul Ehrlich have suggested 'compulsory Government controls of births is a virtual certainty'.[59]

Such perspectives can (and sometimes do) justify terrifyingly repressive actions on social issues in attempts to balance ecological concerns. These could easily devolve into 'a totalitarian fanaticism, highly reductionist, single-minded, . . . which provides ideological justification for running roughshod over human freedom'.[60] This drive could place democracy in a strait-jacket, as the fundamental conflict between global enviromental concerns and universal humanism is decided in favour of the former. This could come to represent a totalitarian regime, more terrifying than any in history, which manipulated the precepts of centralization and hierarchical models, with a strong emphasis upon duty for survival and the submersion of the individual for the greater

---

[55] Hardin, G., 'Feeding Hungry Countries', *Newsday*, 27 July 1989, 8. Hardin, 'Lifeboat Ethics', *supra* n. 48, 384. Fletcher, J., 'Chronic Famine and the Immorality of Food Aid', *Focus*, 3 (1993), 44, 45.

[56] Naess, *supra* n. 24, 29. Cf. Bookchin, M., 'Thinking Ecologically', *Our Generation*, 2 (1987), 3, 30.

[57] Attfield, *supra* n. 31, 158–60. Singer, *supra* n. 31, 282–3. Attfield, R., 'Development and Environmentalism', in Attfield, R. and Wilkins, B. (eds.), *International Justice and the Third World* (Routledge, London, 1992), 151, 161.

[58] Hardin, G., 'The Tragedy of the Commons', *Science*, 162 (1968), 1245, 1246. Ehrlich, P. R., 'Paying the Piper', *New Scientist*, 36 (1967), 652, 655. Jansen, M., 'The Future of Tropical Ecology', *Annual Review of Ecological Systems*, 17 (1986), 305. Potter, R. B., 'The Simple Structure of the Population Debate: The Logic of the Ecology Movement', in Scherer, *supra* n. 12, 177, 186–90.

[59] Ehrlich, P., 'Playboy Interview', *Playboy Magazine*, Aug. 1970, 53, 55.

[60] See Ross, A., *The Chicago Gangster Theory of Life: Nature's Debt to Society* (Verso, London, 1994), 5, 14–15, 247, 261–2, 264–7. Goulet, D., 'Biological Diversity and Ethical Development', in Hamilton, L. S. (ed.), *Ethics, Religion and Biodiversity: Relations Between Conservation and Cultural Values* (White Horse, Birmingham, 1993), 17, 30.

good.[61] From this position, misanthropic tendencies may easily come into play.

In an attempt to answer the above charges, defenders of the land ethic have tried to create distinct lines of demarcation for making ethical choices between species and, in doing so, heading off both fears of misanthropic possibilities and ethical gridlock in decision making due to the prima facie rule of equal intrinsic value.[62]

To circumvent this problem it has been suggested that the land ethic does *not* hold everything as possessing unbreachable equality. Thus, absolute ecological egalitarianism is not subscribed to within the holistic framework offered by deep ecology.[63] Rather, the emphasis is upon *appropriate* treatment, and not necessarily *equal* treatment. Indeed, as Baird Callicott pointed out, the land ethic implies respect for individual non-human members of the biotic community, but does not accord them inalienable rights.[64] Warwick Fox suggested that in times of genuine conflicts of value:

Then organisms are entitled to moral consideration commensurate with their degree of central organisation (or capacity for richness of experience) for the duration of their existence.[65]

Thus, sentience, self-consciousness, and capacity for richness of experience are relevant factors in any ethical choices to be made. However, choices are also determined by unique patterns of symbiotic relationships with other members, capacity to perform biotic tasks, jobs, and functions, and how much the ecosystem depends upon set individual entities within it. The ultimate criterion for value is the contribution to the well-being of the whole, taking into account such principles as diversity, richness, stability, and scarcity.[66] Therefore, inherent

[61] Beney, G., 'Gaia: The Globalitarian Temptation', in Sachs, *supra* n. 35, 179, 180, 185. Bookchin, M., *The Philosophy of Social Ecology: Essays on Dialectical Naturalism* (Black Rose, Montreal, 1990), 159. This problem has been documented with the idea of survival of the fittest, see Benton, T., 'The Malthusian Challenge: Ecology, Natural Limits and Human Emancipation', in Osborne, P. (ed.), *Socialism and the Limits of Liberalism* (Verso, London, 1991), 241, 249. Bookchin, *The Philosophy of Social Ecology*, ibid. 142–3. Perhaps one of the most interesting examples is with German Fascism, which also had distinct links with ecological holism. See Dominick, R. H., 'The Nazis and the Nature Conservationists', *Historian*, 49 (US) (1987), 516. Bramwell, A., *Ecology in the 20th Century: A History* (Yale University Press, New York, 1989), 161–208. Marshall, *supra* n. 40, 335, 408–9.

[62] Norton, B. G., 'Environmental Ethics and Non-human Rights', *Environmental Ethics*, 4 (1982), 36. Fox, *supra* n. 1, 194, 198.

[63] Naess, *supra* n. 24, 167–8. Naess, *supra* n. 13, 95. Sylvan, R., 'A Critique of Deep Ecology', *Radical Philosophy*, 40. 2, 7. Col. 2.

[64] Nash, *supra* n. 14, 235, 240.

[65] Fox, *supra* n. 1, 194, 199. Attfield, *supra* n. 31, 192–7. Skolimowski, *supra* n. 16, 107. Naess, *Lifestyle*, *supra* n. 24, 169.

[66] Moline, J. N., 'Aldo Leopold and the Moral Community', *Environmental Ethics*, 6 (1986), 113. Gunn, A., 'Preserving Rare Species', in Regan (ed.), *Earthbound: New Introductory Essays to Environmental Ethics* (Random House, New York, 1984), 327. Eckersley, *supra* n. 3, 57. Johnson, *supra* n. 16, 200. Marshall, *supra* n. 40, 438–9.

value is *not* spread evenly across members of the biotic community in situations of genuine value conflict.

An obvious question arising at this point is, how does humanity fit within such an ethical world view? It is suggested that the land ethic does not imply the 'passive surrender' of humanity, as humans, like other species, are recognized as special in their own unique ways and are entitled to modify ecosystems in which they live in order to survive and blossom. Humanity would be allowed to keep life-threatening organisms in check, 'where there is no alternative' and it is necessary to satisfy vital human needs, provided any such actions are carried out with minimum harm. Under such a prescription the activities of humans who wantonly or needlessly interfere with, or threaten, the existence or integrity of other life forms are morally wrong.[67] However, overall, the survival (or 'vital') interests of human beings ought to outweigh those of the rest of the biotic community and the survival interests of the rest of the biotic community ought to outweigh the non-survival interests of human beings.[68] Consequently, the human licence to interfere detrimentally with the natural world would be greatly restricted from what it is now.

However, it must be realized that such an approach is *not* credible. For to advocate biospheric equality and the holistic good as the ethical marker on the one hand, while allowing a species ranking on the other entwined with considerations of basic and non-basic needs does nothing more than allow anthropocentric considerations and justifications to 'sneak around into the house from the back'.[69] Indeed, it is not consistent to claim that we are all equal, but we (i.e. humanity) still have precedence in times of conflict. We are either all equal, or we are not, and deep ecology is premised upon biospheric equality, within which humanity must accept its place as a plain member in the holistic picture. To do so, and then suggest that our basic needs out-trump those of other species is an overt contradiction. Yet to do so and not make that suggestion, is to invite misanthropic overtones into the equation.

[67] Sylvan, R., 'On the Value Core of Deep Green Theory', in Oddie, G. and Perrett, R. (eds.), *Justice, Ethics and New Zealand Society* (Oxford University Press, Oxford, 1992), 222, 228. Fox, *supra* n. 17, 114–18. Naess, A., 'A Defence of the Deep Ecology Movement', *Environmental Ethics*, 6 (1984), 265, 267. Eckersley, *supra* n. 3, 12–13, 29–30, 170–1. Sterba, J. P., 'Reconciling Anthropocentric and Non-Anthropocentric Ethics', *Environmental Values*, 3 (1994), 229, 230–5, 237, 240. Marshall, *supra* n. 40, 442–3. Nash, *supra* n. 14, 235, 247–9. Naess, 'Deep Ecology and the Ultimate Premises', *supra* n. 15, 128, 130. These postulates are very similar to Taylor's five points, which are also often used as the guidelines for this kind of holistic environmental ethic.

[68] Naess, A., 'The Deep Ecology Movement: Some Aspects', *Philosophical Inquiry*, 8 (1986), 14, 20, 22. Heffernan, J. D., 'The Land Ethic: A Critical Appraisal', *Environmental Ethics*, 4 (1982), 243. Naess, *Lifestyle*, *supra* n. 24, 29–30.

[69] French, W. C., 'Against Biospherical Egalitarianism', *Environmental Ethics*, 17 (1995), 38, 40, 45, 49, 53. Sterba, J. P., 'From Biocentric Individualism to Biocentric Pluralism', *Environmental Ethics*, 17 (1995), 191, 199.

5. STRATEGIES FOR PROGRESS

Deep ecology, taken alone, is open to the convincing criticism that it lacks a comprehensive strategy for effective change and implementation of its ideals.[70] This is because the focus of the land ethic pertains to an ecological objective. Consequently, it does not provide the social edicts upon how to get there. Therefore, additional theories are required to address these issues and thereby provide a structured analysis and direction for movement. For example, a very common root cause of environmental destruction is poverty.[71]

The Problem of Poverty

The World Health Organisation estimated in 1995 that one-fifth of the 5.6 billion people in the world live in extreme poverty (this means a condition of exposure to the elements, malnutrition, lack of medical care, and illiteracy that is below any reasonable standard of human decency). Almost one-third of the world's children are undernourished; and half the global population lacks access to essential drugs. (WHO, *Bridging The Gaps*, 1995.) The United Nations Development Programme has estimated that the number of people living in acute poverty was 1.3 billion with another billion living close to desperation. This figure was up half a billion from 1980. (UNDP, *Human Development Report*, 1993, and The Commission on Global Governance, *Our Global Neighbourhood* (1995), 21–2, 139–40.) Due to the increasing nature of this figure and the extreme implications of what it implies for these people the international community committed itself to the eradication of poverty at the 1995 *World Summit for Social Development* (see Paragraph 16 and Commitments 1 and 2).

The eradication of poverty is essential for any kind of development. (Pearson Commission, *Partners in Development* (1969), 1.) It is equally important to eliminate poverty to achieve sustainable development. This was initially recognized in 1971 with the Founex report which saw that the environmental problems of developing countries are 'predominantly problems that reflect poverty and the very lack of development of their societies'. (Founex Report, *Development and Environment*. Reprinted as Annex I to UN Doc.A/CONF 48/10. 1971.) This imperative, to relieve acute poverty—as a prerequisite to environmental protection—was initially raised in the context of underdevelopment.

---

[70] Pepper, D., *Eco-Socialism: From Deep Ecology to Social Justice* (Routledge, London, 1993), 149. Morris, B., 'Reflections on Deep Ecology', in *Deep Ecology and Anarchism* (Freedom Press, London, 1993), 37, 40, 46. Bookchin, M., *Towards An Ecological Society* (Black Rose, Montreal, 1980), 31. Beney, *supra* n. 61, 179, 192. Merchant, *supra* n. 15, 230–3. Ross, *supra* n. 60, 262–3.

[71] UNEP, *Poverty and the Environment: Reconciling Short-Term Needs and Long-Term Sustainable Goals* (Nairobi, 1995). UNCED, *Poverty and Environmental Degradation*. A/CONF 151/PC/45. Geneva. 1991. 8. Davidson, J., *No Time To Waste: Poverty and the Global Environment* (Oxfam, Wiltshire, 1992), 5–17. 'Poverty and the Environment: Breaking the Vicious Circle', *Our Planet*, 5 (1993), 4–11.

(see Paragraph 4 of Chapter 1 of the Stockholm *Declaration on the Human Environment*. UN Doc. A/CONF 48/14/ Rev. 1.)

Here, the emphasis was upon poverty as an environmental problem in itself. It was not necessarily directly recognized as a problem leading to environmental devastation. Consequently, international environmental concerns gave little consideration to poverty as a root cause of environmental destruction *per se*. This did not change until the early 1980s when the issue of poverty (as opposed to underdevelopment) and environmental destruction received recognition in the World Conservation Strategy which recognized that 'Hundreds of millions of rural people in developing countries are compelled to destroy the resources necessary to free them from starvation and poverty'. (IUCN, *World Conservation Strategy* (1980).) From this point on, the reduction of poverty and environmental protection were directly linked. This link increased in strength as specific international environmental concerns, such as tropical deforestation where the link with poverty is paramount, have become highlighted. (See UNCED. Prepcom III.151/PC/64.)

The overt link between poverty and environmental destruction was finally brought to the forefront with the 1987 World Commission on Environment and Development which recognized that poverty is not only a problem in itself, but also that 'A world in which poverty and inequity are endemic will always be prone to ecological and other crises'. Consequently, 'a reduction in poverty itself is a precondition for environmentally sound development'. (World Commission on Environment and Development, *Our Common Future* (1987), 3,8,28,44,49,69.) The recognition of the 'critical issue' of the eradication of poverty as a prerequisite for sustainable development was reiterated continually in the lead up to the 1992 United Nations Conference on Environment and Development and at Earth Summit itself in the *Rio Declaration on Environment and Development* (Principle 5. UNCED Doc. A/CONF 151/5/ Rev.1) and *Agenda 21* (Chapter 3; 3.2. *Agenda 21* 1992. Doc.A/CONF 151/4). At the 1994 *Cairo Conference on Population and Development* the eradication of poverty was recognized as 'an indispensable requirement for sustainable development'. (Principle 7. Report of the International Conference on Population and Development. Doc.A/CONF 171/13.)

Thus it can be asserted that it is essential to address acute poverty before environmental protection can be truly achieved. However, deep ecology takes very little notice of this (and other) important social considerations.[72] Indeed, as noted in the misanthropic objection, its very basis may be working either in ignorance of, or *against* the alleviation of such social objectives.

---

[72] e.g., as Devall states, 'The deep ecology movement is only partly political.' *Supra* n. 9, 22, 160.

XI

Conclusion

The central basis of international environmental law and policy is anthropocentricism. This pillar manifests itself along both direct and indirect avenues which form the paradigms of this area. This is deeply problematic, as all the justifications for environmental protection that spring from this mind-set are either contradictory, limited in scope or plainly indefensible.

The principal justification in this arena is that of self-interest. However, as demonstrated, such considerations are not always conducive to environmental protection. There are two central objections here. First, it only requires that the Nature which is important to humanity is protected (for at least as long as it remains so). Secondly, as the example of climatic change and the differing positions of the parties indicated, self-interests on issues of environmental protection do not always coincide. Indeed, in some instances it is in the self-interest of States to continue to destroy the environment, rather than preserve it.

The second vindication for environmental protection is through economics. This position has received a greatly enhanced status in light of new economic methods, which vastly inflate the economic value of the environment. This has much potential for certain natural resources such as the rain forests. However, this position is limited by considerations of the fact that not all values can be captured by economic instruments. The implications of this, overlapping with the example of the dilemma of sustainable whaling, indicate the difficulties in this area. Secondly, economic instruments do not question the underlying political and social implications behind them, such as overt individualism and the vicissitudes of the free market. Finally, the new economic approaches are curtailed by the limitations imposed through the current economic structure, its in-built biases, and myopic circumferences.

Religious justifications were the third anthropocentric position examined in this volume. These demonstrated a distinct strength, due to the fundamental motivational considerations, and the example of the stewardship ethic demonstrated an established and popular approach. However, this position was found wanting due to the indeterminate nature of biblical positions on the relationship with the Natural world. Indeed, the example of theology and population policy indicated quite clearly that environmental and theological interests may be travelling in opposite directions. The limitations of the religious approach were furthered by the objections to religious considerations within modern secular societies.

The fourth area examined was aesthetics. The strength of this justification was demonstrated through the highly successful campaigns to protect seal-pups and similar 'attractive' species. This position was dismissed due to the subjective nature and cultural lenses through which aesthetic considerations are made.

The cultural exoneration was also found lacking due to its fundamentally subjective positioning, for what one culture may want to protect, another may want to destroy. The example of the rhinoceros was produced to demonstrate the lengths of this difficulty. The attempted rejoinder, of cultural pluralism (and subsequent acceptance of environmentally destructive cultures), was also found to be wanting due to the difficulties of moral relativism.

Recreational considerations were also dismissed due to their distinct limit of applicability, outside of countries with a small population and large spaces which could be exclusively enclosed. The attraction of ingredients which may be harmful to both natural and social communities, such as uncontrolled tourism, also helped to demonstrate the limitations of this position.

The first position which adopted a slightly more enhanced view of environmental protection was the rights of future generations. The example of the storage of nuclear waste provided an entry point into the classic Rawlsian arguments and the ideal of the 'stream of humanity'. Here, despite the attraction of such a position, it was found wanting due to existing social and temporal alienation. This was furthered by current limitations to only really consider and help generations which are closely connected to the present. However, even this approach must be called into question due to considerations of what interests future generations actually possess. Finally, the theoretical justifications for considering the rights of future generations were found to be unnecessarily restricted with their narrow anthropocentric viewpoints.

Following on from all of the above objections, the new non-anthropocentric developments within international environmental law and policy were examined. In this section, multiple instances were brought to light which recognized the growing recognition of intrinsic values, ecological interdependence, and the necessity for having holistic outlooks within the international environmental arena. However, it was also noted that no recognition of such positions as 'animal rights' exists within the current body of international laws, although *de facto* rights may be considered through instruments which seek to prevent the extinction of species. However, the justification pertaining to the protection of endangered species alone may prove problematic.

At this point, the common retort is that even though all of the above justifications may be problematic in part, surely by putting them together, then a suitable body of protection for Nature could be created. Of course, there is merit in this approach, in that whatever justifications can be used to protect Nature should be. However, the limitations and downfalls of each of these approaches should be realized. But overall, the mistake that Augustine made, when proposing the five arguments he deduced for God's existence should be borne in mind. Augustine himself realized that each of his five arguments had difficulties. However, he suggested that when the five arguments were all taken conclusively, then the proof for God's existence was overwhelming. The problem is obvious. Five wrong arguments viewed cumulatively did not (and do not) create one good one.

Overall, it may be stated that anthropocentric justifications for environmental protection are distinctly limited and fail to capture the essence of value of Nature. Due to the increasing interest in non-anthropocentric approaches, and the distinct limitations of the existing human-centred justifications, three prominent alternative models were examined.

The first of these was for the moral considerability of animals. In this area the utilitarian position, with its emphasis upon sentience and the idea of inherent value within humans and animals, was found to be strongly convincing. However, both perspectives failed to provide suitable positions for the inclusion of wider environmental considerations for entities or ecosystems that were not sentient or recipients of intrinsic value.

This limitation lead to the examination of the 'life proposal' which recognizes moral worth in all living entities. However, this was troubled by a similar problem—namely non-living entities, of which anything beyond a living individual (such as ecosystems) was cast outside the rubric of moral considerability. This position was also held back by the failure to provide distinct, workable goals to pursue in an infinitely complex and crowded world.

Finally, the land ethic or deep ecology was examined. This also proved to be a highly attractive doctrine, with its emphasis upon the ecological and ecosystemeric wholes. However, its overt fixation with holism and the negation of the value of individuals had led to distinct flirtations with misanthropy. This pointer is indicative of its other failing—that it provides no social vehicle for which to implement its ecological goals. Indeed, it is this failure which allows the misanthropic considerations to arise.

However, the currently proffered non-anthropocentric justifications, of which deep ecology appears the most appealing, are also distinctly limited by their failure to provide a social path to safely reach their ecological dictates. It is this failure, and its reflection in international environmental law and policy, which is the subject of my follow-up book—*Questions of Politics in International Environmental Law and Policy.*

Bibliography

Abram, D., 'The Perceptual Implication of Gaia', *Ecologist* (1985), 103–9.

Ackerman, B. A., *Social Justice in a Liberal State* (Yale University Press, New Haven, 1980).

Acton, H. B., 'Animal Pleasures', *Massachusetts Review*, 2 (1961), 541–8.

Adams, J. G. U., 'Unsustainable Economics', *International Environmental Affairs*, 2 (1990) 14–21.

Adams, W. A., *Green Development: Environment and Sustainability in the Third World* (Routledge, London, 1990).

Alder, D., 'The Sensing of Chemicals by Bacteria', *Scientific American*, April 1976, 40.

Allen, R., *How To Save the World: The Strategy for World Conservation* (Kegan Paul, Lancashire, 1980).

Anderson-Fulton, H. (ed.), *The New Organon and Related Writings* (Macmillan, London, 1974).

Andreason, C. T., 'Indian Worship v Government Development: A New Breed of Religion Cases', *Utah Law Review*, 22 (1984). 311–19.

Andresen, S. and Ostreng, W. (eds.), *International Resource Management: The Role of Science and Politics* (Belhaven, London, 1989).

Andrews, T., 'Making Headway', *Green Line*, 87 (1991), 4–5.

Angell, D. J. R., Comer, J. D., and Wilkinson, M. L. N. (eds.), *Sustaining the Earth: Responses to Environmental Threats* (Macmillan, London, 1990).

Animal Welfare Institute, *Animals and Their Legal Rights* (AWI, Washington, 1978).

Aquinas, T., *Summa Theologica* (Burns and Oates, London, 1922).

Aquinas, T., *Basic Writings* (New York, 1945).

Aquinas, T., 'Summa Contra Gentiles', in *The English Dominion Fathers*, (Burns and Oates, London, 1928).

Archbishop of Canterbury, in 'Green Crusaders', *Green Magazine*, 6 June 1991, 27.

Arendt, L., *Lectures on Kant's Political Philosophy* (University of Chicago Press, Chicago, 1982).

Argyle, B., *The Philosophy of Happiness* (UCL Press, London, 1987).

Aristotle, *Ethics* (Harmondsworth, Penguin, 1963), 83.

Aristotle, *Politics* (Everyman, New York, 1972).

Aristotle, *Nicomachean Ethics* (Penguin, Harmondsworth, 1977).

Aristotle, 'Metaphysics', in the *Basic Works of Aristotle* (Random House, London, 1976).

Arsanjaki, M. H., 'Religion and International Law', *American Bar Association Journal of International Law* (1989), 195–208.

Ash, M., *The Fabric of the World: Towards A Philosophy of Environment* (Green Books, Devon, 1992).

Ashford, J., 'Brazil Nuts Crumble', *BBC Wildlife* 11:2 (1993), 59.

Atkinson, A., *The Principles of Political Ecology* (Belhaven, London, 1991).
Attfield, R., *The Ethics of Environmental Concern* (Blackwell, Oxford, 1983).
Attfield, R. (ed.), *Philosophy and the Natural Environment* (Cambridge University Press, Cambridge, 1994).
Attfield, R., 'The Good of Trees', *Journal of Value Inquiry*, 15 (1981), 45–53.
Attfield, R., 'Development and Environmentalism', in Attfield, R. and Wilkins, B. (eds.), *International Justice and the Third World* (Routledge, London, 1992), 151, 161.
Attfield, R., 'Sylvan, Fox and Deep Ecology: A View from the Continental Shelf', *Environmental Values*, 2 (1993), 18–27.
Augustine, *The City of God* (Clark, Edinburgh, 1877).
Austin, R. C., 'Beauty: A Foundation For Environmental Ethics', *Environmental Ethics*, 7 (1985), 197–208.
Bacon, F., *Novum Organum* (1620).
Bacon, F., *Essays; The Wisdom of the Ancients and the New Atlantis* (Oldham Press, London, 1977).
Bacon, F., 'The New Atlantis', in Spedding, J. (ed.), *The Works of Francis Bacon* (London, 1857).
Bacon, F., 'The Great Instauration', in Spedding, J. (ed.), *The Works of Francis Bacon* (London, 1857).
Baer, R. A., 'Higher Education, the Church and Environmental Values', *Natural Resources Journal*, 17 (1977), 482–8.
Bahro, R., *From Red to Green* (Heretic, London, 1984).
Baker, C. E., 'The Ideology of the Economic Analysis of Law', *Philosophy and Public Affairs*, 5 (1975) 3–17.
Ball, M. S., 'Moral Pluralism, The Tardis, and Rattlesnakes', *Tennessee Law Review*, 56 (1988), 17–26.
Baram, M. S., 'Cost-benefit Analysis: An Inadequate Basis for Health, Safety and Environmental Regulatory Decision-making', *Ecology Law Quarterly*, 8 (1980) 465–76.
Barber, W. J., *A History of Economic Thought* (Penguin, Harmondsworth, 1967).
Barbier, E., Burgess, J., Swanson, T., and Pearce, D., *Elephants, Economics and Ivory* (Earthscan, London, 1990).
Barbour, I. (ed.), *Earth Might Be Fair* (New York, 1972).
Barbour, I. (ed.), *Western Man and Environmental Ethics* (Addison, London, 1973).
Barbour, I. *Western Man and Environmental Ethics* (Addison, London, 1973).
Barbour, I., *Technology, Environment and Human Values* (Englewood Cliffs, New Jersey, 1980).
Barnet, R. J., *The Lean Years: Politics in the Age of Scarcity* (Abacus, London, 1980).
Barry, N. P., *On Classical Liberalism and Libertarianism* (Macmillan, Basingstoke, 1986).
Barry, N. P., *The New Right* (Croom Helm, New York, 1987).
Barth, K., *Church Dogmatics* (Clark, Edinburgh, 1961).
Batchelor, A., 'The Preservation of Wildlife Habitat in Ecosystems: Towards a New Direction Under International Law to Prevent Species Extinction', *Florida International Law Journal*, 3 (1988), 305–18.

Bate, R. and Morris, J., *Global Warming: Apocalypse of Hot Air?* (Institute of Economic Affairs, London, 1994).

Bateson, M. C., 'Caring For Children, Caring For Earth', *Christ and Crisis*, 40 (1980), 64–76.

Bayles, M. D. (ed.), *Contemporary Utilitarianism* (Doubleday, New York, 1968).

BBC 2, *Close Encounters of the European Kind: Blood Relations*, 24 April 1992.

Beckerman, W., *In Defence of Economic Growth* (Cape, London, 1974).

Beney, G., 'Gaia: The Globalitarian Temptation', in Sachs (1993), 175–85.

Bentham, J., *An Introduction to the Principles of Morals and Legislation* (Russell, London, 1962).

Benton, T., 'The Malthusian Challenge: Ecology, Natural Limits and Human Emancipation', in Osborne (1991), 241–9.

Berkes, F. (ed.), *Common Property Resources: Ecology and Community Based Sustainable Development* (Belhaven, London, 1989).

Berman, M., *The Re-enchantment of the World* (Cornell University Press, Ithaca, 1981).

Bern, M., 'Governmental Regulation and the Development of Environmental Ethics Under the Clean Air Act', *Ecology Law Quarterly*, 17 (1990), 535–68.

Bilderbeck, S., *Biodiversity and International Law: The Effectiveness of International Environmental Law* (IOS, Amsterdam, 1992).

Binder, R., 'Ngugi Wa Thiong'o and the Search for a Populist Landscape Aesthetic', *Environmental Values*, 3 (1994), 47–58.

Birch, C. and Cobb, J., *The Liberation of Life* (Cambridge University Press, Cambridge, 1985).

Birch, T. H., 'The Incarceration of Wilderness: Wilderness Areas As Prisons', *Environmental Ethics*, 12 (1990), 1–24.

Birnie, P., *The International Regulation of Whaling* (Oceana, New York, 1985).

Birnie, P. and Boyle, A. E., *International Law and the Environment* (Clarendon Press, Oxford, 1992).

Blackstone, W. T. (ed.), *Philosophy and the Environmental Crisis* (University of Georgia Press, Athens, 1974).

Blumm, M. C., 'The Fallacies of Free Market Environmentalism', *Harvard Journal of Law and Public and Policy*, 15 (1992), 368–77.

Bodin, J., *On Sovereignty* (Cambridge University Press, Cambridge, 1988).

Bohm, D., *Wholeness and the Implicate Order* (Routledge, London, 1980).

Boman, D. L., 'Recent Developments in Efforts to Enhance the Protection of Animals', *Washburn Law Journal*, 30 (1991), 271–80.

Bonaventura, H., *The Life of Saint Francis* (Cambridge University Press, Cambridge, 1973).

Bookchin, M., *Towards An Ecological Society* (Black Rose, Montreal, 1980).

Bookchin, M., *The Ecology of Freedom* (Cheshire Books, California, 1982).

Bookchin, M., *The Modern Crisis* (Belhaven, London, 1986), 49.

Bookchin, M., *Remaking Society* (Black Rose, Montreal, 1989).

Bookchin, M., *The Philosophy of Social Ecology: Essays on Dialectical Naturalism* (Black Rose Books, Montreal, 1990).

Bookchin, M., 'Deep Ecology Versus Social Ecology: A Challenge For the Ecology Movement', *The Raven*, 1 (1987), 214–24.

Bookchin, M., 'Thinking Ecologically', *Our Generation*, 2 (1987), 3–30.

Bookchin, M., 'Ecology as a Dismal Science', *Green Line*, 96 (1992), 10–16.

Booth, A. L., 'Ties That Bind: Native American Beliefs As A Foundation For Environmental Consciousness', *Environmental Ethics*, 12 (1990), 20–32.

Booth, D. E., 'The Economics of Old-Growth Forests', *Environmental Ethics*, 14 (1992), 43, 60.

Bormann, F. H. and Kettert, S. R. (eds.), *Ecology, Economics, Ethics: The Broken Circle* (Yale University Press, New York, 1991).

Botkin, D. B., *Discordant Harmonies: A New Ecology For the Twenty-first Century* (Oxford University Press, Oxford, 1990).

Bourdeau, P. (ed.), *Environmental Ethics: Man's Relationship to Nature* (Official Publication of the European Community, Brussels, 1989).

Bowden, D. (ed.), *The Satiric Poems Of John Trumbull* (Texas, 1962).

Bowman, M., 'The Protection of Animals Under International Law', *Connecticut Journal of International Law*, 2 (1989), 487–98.

Boyle, F. A., *World Politics and International Law* (Duke University Press, Durham, 1985).

Brady, T. P., 'But Most of it Belongs to Those Yet to be Born', *Environmental Affairs*, 17 (1990), 615–32.

Bramwell, A., *Ecology in the 20th Century: A History* (Yale University Press, New York, 1989).

Brandt Commission, *North-South: A Programme For Survival* (Pan Books, London, 1980).

Brandt Commission, *North-South: Common Crisis* (Oxford University Press, Oxford, 1983).

Bratton, S., 'The Ecotheology of James Watt', *Environmental Ethics*, 5 (1983), 197–209.

Bratton, S., 'Christian Ecotheology and the Old Testament', *Environmental Ethics*, 6 (1984), 200–12.

Bratton, S., 'The Original Desert Solitaire', *Environmental Ethics*, 10 (1988), 25–36.

Brazier, C., 'The Economist's Blind Eye', *New Internationalist*, 232 (1992), 15–18.

Brennan, A., *Thinking About Nature* (Routledge, London, 1988).

British Treasury, *Green Booklet* (London, 1984).

Brophy, B., *The Rights of Animals* (Sphere, London, 1989).

Broughton, R., 'Aesthetics and Environmental Law', *Land and Water Law Review*, 7 (1972), 451–72.

Brown, D., 'James Watt's Land Rush', *Newsweek*, 29 June 1981, 24.

Brown, N. J./UNEP, *Ethics and Agenda 21: Moral Implications of a Global Consensus* (United Nations, New York, 1994).

Brown, P., 'Whalers Steered Towards Tourism', *Guardian*, 14 May 1993, 8.

Brunner, H., *Revelation and Reason* (Switzerland, 1946).

Bryce-Smith, C., 'Ecology, Theology And Humanism', *Zygon*, 12 (1977), 225–30.

Buege, D. J., 'The Ecologically Noble Savage Revisited', *Environmental Ethics*, 18 (1996), 71–88.

Bunyard, P. and Goldsmith, E. (eds.), *GAIA. The Thesis, the Mechanisms and the Implications* (Wadebridge, Cornwall, 1988).

Burch, B., 'The Social Meaning of Forests', *Humanist*, 39 (1979), 39–44.

Burger, J., *The Gaia Atlas of First Peoples* (Gaia Books, London, 1990).

Burke, E., *A Philosophical Inquiry into the Origin of Our Ideas of the Sublime and the Beautiful* (Routledge, London, 1956).

Burke, E., *Reflections On The Revolution In France* (Penguin, Harmondsworth, 1978).

Burnett, G. W., 'Wilderness and the Bantu Mind', *Environmental Ethics*, 16 (1994), 142–53.

Burton, I. and Kates, R. W. (eds.), *Readings in Resource Management and Conservation* (University of Chicago Press, Chicago, 1965).

Button, J. (ed.), *The Green Fuse* (Quartet, London, 1990).

Button, J. (ed.), *The Best of Resurgence* (Devon, 1991).

Cahen, H., 'Against The Moral Considerability of Ecosystems', *Environmental Ethics*, 10 (1988), 201–14.

Cairncross, F., *Costing the Earth* (Economist Books, London, 1991), 32.

Caldwell, L., *Between Two Worlds: Science, the Environmental Movement and Policy Choice* (Cambridge University Press, Cambridge, 1990).

Callicott, J. B., *Companion to a Sand County Almanac: Interpretative Essays* (University of Wisconsin Press, 1987).

Callicott, J. B., *In Defence of the Land Ethic: Essays in Environmental Philosophy* (Random House, New York, 1989).

Callicott, J. B., *The Wilderness Idea Revisited* (Beacon, Boston, 1991).

Callicott, J. B., 'Animal Liberation: A Triangular Affair', *Environmental Ethics*, 2 (1980), 311–28.

Callicott, J. B., 'Traditional American Indian and Western European Attitudes Toward Nature: An Overview', *Environmental Ethics*, 4 (1982), 293–318.

Callicott, J. B., 'Hume's Is/Ought Dichotomy and the Relation to the Land Ethic', *Environmental Ethics*, 4 (1982), 163.

Callicott, J. B., 'The Search for an Environmental Ethic', in Regan (1984), 70–8.

Callicott, J. B., 'Intrinsic Value, Quantum Theory and Environmental Ethics', *Environmental Ethics*, 7 (1985), 270–84.

Callicott, J. B., 'The Metaphysical Implications of Ecology', *Environmental Ethics*, 8 (1986), 294–307.

Callicott, J. B., 'An Eco-holistic Critique of Animal Liberation/Animal Rights', in Regan and Singer (1989) 36–45.

Callicott, J. B., 'The Case Against Moral Pluralism', *Environmental Ethics*, 12 (1990), 95–106.

Callicott, J. B., 'The Wilderness Idea Revisited: The Sustainable Development Alternative', *The Environmental Professional*, 13 (1991), 236–42.

Calvin, J., *Commentaries on the first book of Moses* (London, 1847).

Campiglio, L. et al. (eds.), *The Environment After Rio: International Law and Economics* (Graham and Trotman, London, 1994).

Capra, F., *The Tao of Physics* (Shambhala, London, 1975).

Capra, F., *The Turning Point, Science, Society and the Rising Culture* (Simon and Schuster, London, 1982).

Care, N. S., 'Future Generations, Public Policy, And The Motivation Problem', *Environmental Ethics*, 4 (1982), 205–15.

Carew, G., 'Agenda', *Guardian*, 25 June 1993, 19.

Carley, M. and Christie, I., *Managing Sustainable Development* (Earthscan, London, 1992).

Carpenter, R. A., 'Ecology in Court and Other Disappointments of Environmental Science', *Natural Resources Lawyer*, 15 (1983), 573–93.

Carr, I. M., 'Saving the Environment: Does Utilitarianism Provide a Justification', *Legal Studies*, 12 (1992), 92–9.

Carrol, M., *Puritanism And The Wilderness* (Garden City, New York, 1969).

Casserirer, E. (ed.), *The Renaissance Philosophy of Man* (Chicago University Press, Chicago, 1948).

Castro, F., *Tomorrow is Too Late: Development and the Environmental Crisis in the Third World* (Ocean Press, Melbourne, 1993).

Cavalieri, P. (ed.), *The Great Ape Project: Equality Beyond Humanity* (Fourth Estate, 1993).

Cave, G. P., 'Animals, Heidegger and the Right to Life', *Environmental Ethics*, 4 (1982), 240–51.

Chambers, R., *Sustainable Livelihoods, Environment and Development: Putting Poor Rural People First* (University of Sussex, Brighton, 1987).

Chananie, S., 'Reverence for Life, and Rights for Nature', *Pace Law Review*, 3 (1983), 695–704.

Chase, S. (ed.), *Murray Bookchin and Dave Foreman: Defending the Earth: A Dialogue* (South End, Boston, 1991).

Chase, S., 'Whither the Radical Ecology Movement?', in Chase (1991), 1–20.

Cheng, C. Y., 'On the Environmental Ethics of the Tao and the Ch'i', *Environmental Ethics*, 8 (1986), 353–66.

Chisholm, A., *Philosophers of the Earth: Conversations with Ecologists* (Scientific Book Club, London, 1974).

Chomsky, N., *Cartesian Linguistics* (Harper and Rowe, New York, 1966).

Chopra, S., 'Towards a Developing Right of Survival as Part of an Ecosystem', *Denver Journal of International Law and Politics*, 17 (1989), 250–69.

Chowdhury, S. R. (ed.), *The Right to Development in International Law* (Graham and Trotman, London, 1992).

Churchill, R. and Freestone, P. (eds.), *International Law and Global Climate Change* (Graham and Trotman, London, 1991).

Cicero, *De Finibus* (Penguin, Harmondsworth, 1971).

Clark, W. C. and Mum, R. E. (eds.), *The Sustainable Development of the Environment* (Cambridge University Press, Cambridge, 1986).

Clarke, D., 'Point of Darkness', *Environmental Forum*, 9 (1992), 32–6.

Clarke, J. J. (ed.), *Nature in Question: An Anthology of Ideas and Arguments* (Earthscan, London, 1993).

Clayre, A., *Nature and Industrialisation* (Oxford University Press, Oxford, 1977).

Clements, B., 'Stasis—The Unnatural Value', *Ethics*, 86 (1975–6), 130–44.

Club of Rome/King, A. and Schneider, B., *The First Global Revolution* (Simon and Schuster, London, 1991).

Coarse, R., 'The Problem of Social Cost', *Journal of Law and Economics*, 3 (1960), 201–15.

Cobb, J. B., *Is It Too Late: A Theology of Ecology* (Bruce, Beverley Hills, 1972).

Cohen, J., 'The Bible and Nature in Western Thought', *Journal of Religion*, 65 (1985), 50–62.

Coleridge, S., *Philosophical Lectures* (Pilot Press, London, 1949).

Commission on Global Governance, *Our Global Neighbourhood* (Oxford University Press, Oxford, 1995).

Commoner, B., *The Closing Circle* (Cape, London, 1971).

Commoner, B., *Making Peace With the Planet* (Gollancz, London, 1990).

Commoner, B., 'The Ecological Facts of Life', in Disch (1970), 1–12.

Commoner, B., 'Economic Growth and Environmental Quality: How to Have Both', *Social Policy*, 16 (1985), 18–25.

Conniff, T., 'Fuzzy-Wuzzy Thinking About Animal Rights', *Audubon Magazine* (1990), 120–32.

Connolly, W. E., *Political Theory and Modernity* (Blackwell, 1988).

Cooper, D. and Palmer, J. (eds.), *The Environment in Questions: Ethics and Global Issues* (Routledge, London, 1992).

Cooper, T., *Green Christianity: Caring For the Whole Creation* (Spire, Suffolk, 1990).

Costanza, R. (ed.), *Ecological Economics: The Science and Management of Sustainability* (Colombia University Press, New York, 1991).

Costin, A. B. and Frith, H. J. (eds.), *Conservation* (Penguin, Harmondsworth, 1971).

Costonis, J. L., 'Law and Aesthetics', *Michigan Law Review*, 80 (1982), 355–68.

Cottingham, J., *Rationalism* (Paladin, London, 1984).

Cottingham, R. G., 'A Brute to the Brutes? Descartes' Treatment Of Animals', *Philosophy*, 53 (1978), 543–67.

Cripp, S., 'Environmentalism and Utopia', *Sociological Review*, 24 (1976), 25–37.

Crownfield, D., 'The Curse of Abel: An Essay in Biblical Ecology', *North American Review*, 258 (1973), 54–64.

Curtin, D., 'Dogen, Deep Ecology and the Ecological Self', *Environmental Ethics*, 16 (1994), 122–29.

Daly, H. E. and Cobb, J., *For the Common Good: Redirecting the Economy Towards the Community, the Environment and a Sustainable Future* (Beacon, Boston, 1989).

D'Amato, A. and Chopra, S., 'Whales: Their Emerging Right to Life', *American Journal of International Law*, 85 (1991), 25–60.

Darwin, C. *On the Origin of Species* (Murray, London, 1859).

Darwin, C. *The Descent of Man and Selection in Relation to Sex* (Collier, New York, 1871).

Dascal, M. (ed.), *Cultural Relativism and Philosophy* (Brill, New York, 1991).

Davidson, J., *No Time To Waste: Poverty and the Global Environment* (Oxfam, Wiltshire, 1992).

Dawson, R. K., 'Environmental Policy in the Real World', *Environmental Forum*, 5 (1988).

Day, D., *The Whale War* (London, 1987).

DeBardeleben, U., 'Economic Reform and Environmental Protection in the USSR', *Soviet Geography*, 31 (1990), 222–34.

de Chardin, T., *The Future of Man* (Harper and Row, New York, 1964).

Deeson, H., 'The New Age Rage', *Green Magazine*, April 1991, 40–3.

Deihl, C., 'Antarctica: An International Laboratory', *Boston College of Environmental Affairs Law Reporter*, 18 (1991), 423–32.

Descartes, R., *Discourse on Method and the Meditations* (Penguin, Harmondsworth, 1976).

Descartes, R., *Principles of Philosophy* (Reidel, London, 1983).

Devall, B., *Simple in Means, Rich in Ends: Practising Deep Ecology* (Green Print, Surrey, 1990).

Devall, B., 'The Deep Ecology Movement', *Natural Resources Journal*, 20 (1980), 309–14.

Devall, B., 'Deep Ecology and Radical Environmentalism', *Society and Natural Resources*, 4 (1991), 247–57.

Devall, B. and Sessions, G., *Deep Ecology: Living As If Nature Mattered* (Gibbs Smith, Utah, 1985).

Diamond, C., 'Eating Meat and Eating People', *Philosophy*, 53 (1978), 470–9.

Diamond, J., *The Rise and Fall of the Third Chimpanzee* (Radius, London, 1991).

Diamond, J., 'Overview of Recent Extinctions', in Western and Pearl (1989), 37–41.

Diamond, S., *Spiritual Warfare: The Politics of the Christian Right* (South End, Boston, 1989).

Dias, J. (ed.), *Law And The Ecological Challenge* (Random House, New York, 1971).

Disch, R. (ed.), *The Ecological Conscience* (Spectrum, New Jersey, 1970).

Dobson, A. (ed.), *The Politics of Nature: Explorations in Green Political Theory* (Routledge, London, 1991).

Dobson, A., 'Critical Theory and Green Politics', in Dobson (1991).

Dodds, M. (ed.), *Works of Saint Augustine* (Clark, Edinburgh, 1877).

Dominick, R., 'The Nazis and the Nature Conservationists', *Historian*, 49 (1987) (US), 518–25.

Dooley, P. K., 'The Ambiguity Of Environmental Ethics: Duty Or Heroism', *Philosophy Today*, 30 (1986), 50–9.

Doremus, H., 'Patching the Ark: Improving Legal Protection of Biological Diversity', *Ecology Law Quarterly*, 18 (1991), 265–309.

Dorfman, D. and N. (eds.), *The Economics of the Environment: Selected Readings* (Toronto University Press, Toronto, 1972).

Doubleday, N. C., 'Aboriginal Subsistence Whaling: The Right of the Inuit to Hunt Whales and its Implications', *Denver Journal of International Law and Policy*, 17 (1989), 373, 392.

Douthwaite, R., *The Growth Illusion* (Green Print, Devon, 1992).

Dowdeswell, E., *Symposium on Values for a Sustainable Future*, 2 June 1994. UNEP Speech 1994/10.

Dowdeswell, E., *Speech at the World Summit For Social Development*, 7 March 1995. UNEP Speech 1995/3.

Dubos, R., 'Conservation, Stewardship and the Human Heart', *Audubon Magazine* (1972), 19–25.

Dubos, R., 'Saint Francis Versus Saint Benedict', *Psychology Today* (1973), 544–59.

Durkheim, E., *The Division of Labour Within Society* (Allen and Unwin, London, 1933).

Dworkin, R., *Taking Rights Seriously* (Duckworth, London, 1977).

Ebling, F. (ed.), *Biology and Ethics* (Institute of Biology, London, 1971).

Eckersley, R., *Environmentalism and Political Theory: Towards an Ecocentric Approach* (UCL Press, London, 1992).

Eckersley, R., 'Divining Evolution: The Ecological Ethics of Murray Bookchin', *Environmental Ethics*, 11 (1989), 90–104.

Ecologist, 'Whose Common Future', *Ecologist*, 22 (1992), 179–81.

Edwards, S., 'In Defence of Environmental Economics', *Environmental Ethics*, 9 (1987) 82–97.

Ehrenfeld, D., *The Arrogance of Humanism* (Oxford University Press, Oxford, 1978).

Ehrlich, P. R., 'Paying the Piper', *New Scientist*, 36 (1967), 652–5.

Ehrlich, P. R., 'Playboy Interview', *Playboy Magazine*, August 1970, 53, 55.

Ehrlich, P. R., 'Will Economists Learn to Respect Mother Nature?', *Business and Society Review* (1989), 60–3.

Eidsvik, H. K., 'The Status of Wilderness: An International Overview', *Natural Resources Journal*, 29 (1989), 47–58.

Ekins, P. and Max-Neef, M. (eds.), *Real Life Economics: Understanding Wealth Creation* (Routledge, London, 1992).

Eliade, S., *The Sacred And The Profane* (Harper and Rowe, New York, 1959).

Elliot, R., 'Rawlsian Justice and Non-Human Animals', *Journal of Applied Philosophy*, 1 (1984), 95–103.

Elliot, R. and Gare, A. (eds.), *Environmental Philosophy* (Queensland University Press, Queensland, 1983).

Ely, E. and Wehrwein, G., *Land Economics* (University of Wisconsin Press, Wisconsin, 1984).

Emerson, R. W., *Nature: Addresses And Lectures* (Boston, 1876).

Engel, J. R. and J. G. (eds.), *The Ethics of Environment and Development; Global Challenge, International Response* (Belhaven, London, 1990).

Engel, M., 'Gone With the Wind', *Guardian*, 11 March 1994, 2–3.

Engels, F., 'Dialects of Nature', in Marx, K. and Engels, F., *Collected Works* (Lawrence and Wishart, Oxford, 1987).

Environmental Investigation Agency, *Save the Rhino* (London, 1992).

Environmental Investigation Agency, *Don't Buy The Faroe Pilot Whale Slaughter* (London, 1993).

Environmental Investigation Agency, *CITES: Enforcement Not Extinction* (London, 1995).

Environmental Protection Agency, *EPA's Use of Cost Benefit Analysis* (Washington, 1987).

Epictetus, *Discourses* (Everyman, London, 1910).

Evernden, N., 'Beyond Ecology; Self, Place and the Pathetic Fallacy', *North American Review*, 263 (1978), 12–23.

Fabel, A. J., 'Environmental Ethics and the Question of Cosmic Purpose', *Environmental Ethics*, 16 (1994), 303–7.

Fairlie, S., 'White Satanic Mills?', *Ecologist*, 224 (1994), 85–6.

Farringdon, G., *The Philosophy of Francis Bacon* (New York, 1970).

Feinberg, J., 'The Rights of Animals and Unborn Generations', in Blackstone (1974), 51–5.

Fichte, J. G., *The Vocation of Man* (Routledge, London, 1946).

Fish, A. L., 'Industrialised Countries and Greenhouse Gas Emissions', *International Environmental Affairs*, 6 (1994), 9–21.

Fitzgerald, S., *International Wildlife Trade: Whose Business Is It?* (World Wildlife Fund, New York, 1989).

Fletcher, J., 'Chronic Famine and the Immorality of Food Aid', *Focus*, 3 (1993), 44–51.

Flevares, W. M., 'Ecosystems, Economics and Ethics: Protecting Biological Diversity at Home and Abroad', *Southern California Law Review*, 65 (1992), 2039–59.

Florio, A. (ed.), *Montaigne's Essays*, (Cambridge, 1892).

Foley, G., *Global Warming: Who Is Taking The Heat?* (Panos, London, 1991).

Foley, G., 'Lewis Mumford: Philosopher of the Earth', *Ecologist*, 17 (1987), 108–14.

Foley, G., 'Deep Ecology and Subjectivity', *Ecologist*, 18 (1988), 119–24.

Foreman, D., 'Wilderness Preserve System', *Whole Earth Review*, 53 (1989), 41–8.

Foreman, D., 'Second Thoughts of an Eco-Warrior', in Chase (1991), 107–16.

Foresta, E., *America's National Parks and Their Keepers* (New York, 1984).

Fox, W., *Towards a Transpersonal Ecology: Developing New Foundations for Environmentalism* (Shambhala, London, 1990).

Fox, W., 'Deep Ecology: A New Philosophy of Our Time?', *Ecologist*, 14 (1984), 194–8.

Francis, 'The Canticle of the Sun', in *The Writings of Saint Francis* (Casa Editrice, Assisi, 1989).

Francis, D., 'How to Survive an Attack of New Age Ideology', *Green Line*, 87 (1991), 12–13.

Frankena, W. K., 'Ethics and Environment', in Goodpaster (1976), 12–20.

Freestone, D., *The Road From Rio: International Environmental Law After the Earth Summit* (Hull University Press, Hull, 1992).

French, W. C., 'Against Biospherical Egalitarianism', *Environmental Ethics*, 17 (1995), 38–53.

Frey, R. G., *Interests and Rights: The Case Against Animals* (Clarendon Press, Oxford, 1980).

Freyfogle, E. T., 'The Land Ethic and the Pilgrim Leopold', *University of Colorado Law Review*, 61 (1990), 214–43.

Fridtjof Nansen Institute, *Green Globe Yearbook: 1992* (Oxford University Press, Oxford, 1992).

Fromm, E., *The Sane Society* (Routledge, New York, 1955).

Funk, 'Free Market Environmentalism: Wonder Drug or Snake Oil?', *Harvard Journal of Law and Public Policy*, 15 (1992), 511–19.

Gallileo Gallilei, *The Assayer* (1621).

Gardiner, G., 'Between Two Worlds: Humans in Nature and Culture', *Environmental Ethics*, 12 (1990), 339–47.

Gauthier, D. (ed.), *Morality and Rational Self Interest* (Englewood Cliffs, New Jersey, 1970).

Gauthier, D. 'Morality and Advantage', *Philosophical Review*, 76 (1967), 134–76.

Gelb, F., 'Man and Land: The Psychological Theory of Jung', *Zygon*, 9 (1974), 288–300.

Ghai, D. and Vivian, J. (eds.), *Grassroots Environmental Action: Peoples Participation in Sustainable Development* (Routledge, London, 1992).

Ghazi, P., 'Where Did Our Money Go?', *Observer Life*, 5 June 1994, 14–17.

Ghazi, P., 'U.K. Imports Hasten Ruin of Rainforest', *Observer Life*, 5 June 1994, 15.

Gillespie, A., 'Endangered Species: What they are and the Vexing Question of Why to Save them', *Journal of Wildlife Management, Law and Policy* (forthcoming).

Gillespie, A., *International Environmental Policies: Questions of Politics in International Environmental Law and Policy* (forthcoming).

Gillespie, A., *Burning Follies: The Failure of the New Zealand Response to Climate Change* (Dunmore Press, Palmerston, 1997).

Gillespie, A., 'Are Maori Environmental Guardians?', *Wilderness Magazine*, October 1995, 42.

Gillespie, A., 'The Ethical Question in the Whaling Debate', *Gergetown International Environmental Law Review*, 9 (1996).

Gillespie, A., 'Environmental Politics in New Zealand/Aotearoa: Clashes and Commonality Between Maori and Conservationists', *New Zealand Geographer* (forthcoming).

Gillespie, A., 'Indigenous Environmentalism: Commonality, Clashes and Commitments within Canada, Australia and New Zealand', in Haverman, P. (ed.), *New Frontiers: First Nations' Rights in Settler Dominions* (Oxford University Press, Sydney, 1997 (forthcoming)).

Gleik, J., *Chaos: Making of a New Science* (Viking, Boston, 1987).

Glickman, T. S. and Glough, M. (eds.) *Readings in Risk* (John Hopkins University Press, Washington, 1986).

Godlovitch, D. (ed.), *Animals, Men and Morals* (Random House, New York, 1972).

Golding, A., *The Sermons of John Calvin* (Oxford University Press, Oxford, 1975).

Golding, M. P., 'Obligations To Future Generations', *Monist*, 56 (1972), 97–107.

Goldsmith, E., *The Stable Society* (Green Print, Devon, 1978).

Goldsmith, E., *The Way: Towards an Ecological World View* (Rider, London, 1992).

Golley, F. B., 'Deep Ecology from the Perspective of Ecological Science', *Environmental Ethics*, 9 (1987), 51–2.

Goodin, R. E., *Green Political Theory* (Policy, Cambridge, 1992).

Goodman, D., 'The Theory of Diversity-Stability Relationships', *Quarterly Review Biology*, 50 (1975), 237–51.

Goodpaster, K. E. (ed.), *Ethics And Problems Of the Twenty-first Century* (South End, Notre Dame, 1976).

Goodpaster, K. E., 'On Being Morally Considerable', *Journal of Philosophy*, 75 (1978), 310–22.

Gordan, S. B., 'Indian Religious Freedom and Governmental Development Of Public Lands', *Yale Law Journal*, 94 (1985), 1451–9.

Gore, A. *Earth in Balance: Forging A New Common Purpose* (Earthscan, London, 1992).

Gore, A., 'The Call for a SEI', *New York Times*, 3 April 1990, A. 23.

Goulet, D., 'Biological Diversity and Ethical Development', in Hamilton (1993) 17–30.

Gowdy, J. M., 'Further Problems With Neo-Classical Economics', *Environmental Ethics*, 16 (1994), 161–74.

Gragnocauo, C. and Goldstein, H., 'Law Reform or World Reform: The Problem of Environmental Rights', *McGill Law Journal*, 35 (1990), 346–71.

Greenawalt, K., 'The Limits of Rationality and the Place of Religious Conviction: Protecting Animals and the Environment', *William and Mary Law Review*, 27 (1986), 1011–59.

Greenpeace, *The Whale Catchers* (London, 1992), 10.

Grotius, H., *De Jure Belli Ac* (Cambridge University Press, Cambridge, 1925).

Gruen, L. and Jamieson, D., *Reflecting on Nature: Readings on Environmental Philosophy* (Oxford University Press, Oxford, 1994).

Grumbine, R. E., 'Wilderness, Wise Use and Sustainable Development', *Environmental Ethics*, 16 (1994), 227–39.

Guha, R. 'Radical American Environmentalism and Wilderness Preservation: A Third World Critique', *Environmental Ethics*, 11 (1989), 71–84.

Gundling, L., 'Our Responsibility for Future Generations', *American Journal of International Law*, 84 (1990), 207–24.

Gunn, A., 'Preserving Rare Species', in Regan (1984), 312–31.

Gunn, A., *Ethics and Hazardous Waste Management: Why Should We Care About Future Generations?* (Waikato University, Occasional Paper, 1987).

Guruswamy, L. D., 'Global Warming: Integrating United States and International Law', *Arizona Law Review*, 3 (1990), 222–43.

Hacker, P. M. S. (ed.), *Law, Morality and Society: Essays in Honour of H. L. A. Hart* (Clarendon Press, Oxford, 1977).

Haldane, J., 'Admiring the High Mountains: The Aesthetics of Environment', *Environmental Values*, 3 (1994), 97–109.

Hall, D., 'Sanctioning Resource Depletion: Economic Development and Neo-Economics', *Ecologist*, 220 (1990), 99–107.

Hall, S., Myers, N. and Maganis, P. (eds.), *The Economics of Ecosystem Management* (Netherlands, 1985).

Halligan, P., 'The Environmental Policy Of Saint Thomas Aquinas', *Environmental Law*, 19 (1984), 789–802.

Hamilton, L. S. (ed.), *Ethics, Religion and Biodiversity: Relations Between Conservation and Cultural Values* (White Horse Press, Birmingham, 1993).

Handley, F. J., 'Hazardous Waste Exports: A Leak in the System of International Controls', *Environmental Law Reporter*, 19 (1989), 171–82.

Hanfling, O. (ed.), *Philosophical Aesthetics: An Introduction* (Blackwell, Oxford, 1992).

Hanson, S. (ed.), *Environmental Ethics: Philosophical and Political Perspectives* (Simon Fraser University Press, Toronto, 1986).

Hanula, R. W. and Waverly Hill, P., 'Using Metaright Theory to Ascribe Kantian Rights to Animals Within Nozick's Minimum State', *Arizona Law Review*, 19 (1977), 255–71.

Hardin, G. (ed.), *Managing the Commons* (Freeman, San Francisco, 1977).

Hardin, G., *Stalking the Wild Taboo* (Kaufman, California, 1978).

Hardin, G., 'The Tragedy of the Commons', *Science*, 162 (1968), 1245–51.

Hardin, G., 'Lifeboat Ethics: 'The Case Against Not Helping the Poor', *Psychology Today* (1974), 382–92.

Hardin. G., 'Carrying Capacity As An Ethical Concept', *Soundings*, 59 (1976), 120–7.

Hardin, G., 'Feeding Hungry Countries', *Newsday*, 27 July 1989, 8–13.

Hare, R. M., 'Moral Reasoning About the Environment', *Journal of Applied Philosophy*, 4 (1987), 3–17.

Hargrove, E., *The Foundations of Environmental Ethics* (Englewood Cliffs, New Jersey, 1989).

Hargrove, E. (ed.), *The Animal Rights and Environmental Ethics Debate: The Environmental Perspective* (Sunny, New York, 1992).

Hargrove, E., 'The Role of Rules in Ethical Decision Making', *Inquiry*, 28 (1985), 30–9.

Harris, D., *Animals, Men and Morals* (London, 1983), 163.

Hartmann, T., *Ethics: Moral Values* (Doubleday, New York, 1932).

Hartung, F., 'Cultural Relativism and Moral Judgements', *Philosophy of Science*, 21 (1954), 118–26.

Haught, J. F., 'The Emergent Environment And The Problem Of Cosmic Purpose', *Environmental Ethics*, 8 (1986), 139–49.

Havermann, P. (ed.), *New Frontiers: First Nations' Rights in Settler Dominions* (Oxford University Press, Sydney, 1997 (forthcoming)).

Hawkins, S. M., 'The United States Abuse of the Aboriginal Whaling Exception: A Contradiction in US Whaling Policy and a Dangerous Precedent', *University of California Davis Law Review*, 24 (1990), 489–521.

Hayes, P. and Smith, K. R. (eds.), *The Global Greenhouse Regime: Who Pays?* (Earthscan, London, 1993).

Hays, S. P., *Conservation and the Gospel of Efficiency: The Progressive Conservation Movement* (Harvard University Press, Cambridge, 1959).

Heffernan, J. D., 'The Land Ethic: A Critical Appraisal', *Environmental Ethics*, 4 (1982), 243–61.

Hegel, F., *Lecture on the Philosophy of World History* (Cambridge University Press, Cambridge, 1975).

Heilbroner, R. L., *An Inquiry Into The Human Prospect* (Norton, New York, 1974).

Heinsenberg, W., *The Physicist's Conception of Nature* (Penguin, Harmondsworth, 1958), 29.

Heirs, R., 'Ecology, Theology and Methodology', *Zygon*, 19 (1984), 43–53.

Heisenberg, W., *Physics and Philosophy* (Harper and Rowe, New York, 1962).

Heizer, R. and Elsasser, A., *The Natural World of the Californian Indians* (Los Angeles, University of California Press, 1980).

Helliwell, C., 'Discount Rates and Environmental Conservation', *Environmental Conservation*, 2 (1975), 199–205.

Helm, D. (ed.), *Economic Policy Towards the Environment* (Blackwell, Oxford, 1991).

Hersey, G. (ed.), *Pythagorean Palaces* (Cornell University Press, Ithaca, 1976).

Hettinger, N., 'Valuing Predation in Rolston's Environmental Ethics: Bambi Lovers Versus the Tree Huggers', *Environmental Ethics*, 16 (1994), 2–14.

Hill, T. E., 'Ideals of Human Excellence and Preserving the Natural Environment', in Gruen and Jamieson (1994), 98–108.

Hobbes, T., *Leviathan* (Penguin, Harmondsworth, 1976).

Hoch, D., 'Environmental Ethics and Nonhuman Interests. A Challenge to Anthropocentric License', *Gonzaga Law Review*, 23 (1989), 335–51.

Hoffert, R. W., 'The Scarcity of Politics: Ophuls and Western Political Thought', *Environmental Ethics*, 8 (1986), 5–27.

Holland, A., 'Natural Capital', in Attfield (1994).

Holmberg, J. (ed.), *Policies for a Small Planet* (Earthscan, London, 1992).

Holst, J., 'What is Sustainable Development? The Test Case Over Whaling', *Our Planet*, 5 (1993), 11–21.

Hooker, R., *Laws of Ecclesiastical Policy* (Dent, 1907).

Horkheimer, M., *The Eclipse of Reason* (Oxford University Press. Oxford, 1947).

Hosier, H., 'Energy Planning In Developing Countries', *Ambio*, 11 (1982), 182–97.

Hughes, J. D., 'The Environmental Ethics of the Pythagoreans', *Environmental Ethics*, 2 (1980), 195–212.

Hume, D., *An Enquiry Concerning the Principles of Morals* (Open Court, La Salle, 1946).

Hunt, W. M., 'Are Mere Things Morally Considerable?', *Environmental Ethics*, 2 (1980), 61–76.

Hunton, G. 'Aesthetic Regulation and the First Amendment', *Virginia Journal of Natural Resources Law*, 3 (1984), 237–57.

Hurrell, A. and Kingsbury, B. (eds.), *The International Politics of the Environment* (Oxford University Press, Oxford, 1992).

Huxley, A., *The Perennial Philosophy* (Chatto and Windus, London, 1946).

Indicopleustus, *Christian Topography* (London, 1932).

Indigenous Survival International, *Resolution on Norwegian Whaling*. ISI 7th GA/ Res. 8. 1993. August 18.

International Commission on Peace and Food, *Uncommon Opportunities: An Agenda For Peace and Equitable Development* (Zed, London, 1994).

Ip, P. K., 'Taoism and the Foundations of Environmental Ethics', *Environmental Ethics*, 5 (1983), 338–53.

Irvine, S. and Ponton, A., *A Green Manifesto: Policies For a Green Future* (Optima, London, 1988).

Isaccson, R., 'Big Game Parks: What Future?', *Green Magazine*, June 1991, 40.

IUCN, *World Conservation Strategy* (Switzerland, 1980).

IUCN, *Islamic Principles For The Conservation Of The Natural Environment* (Saudi Arabia, 1983).

IUCN, WWF, WRI, *Conserving the World's Biodiversity* (IUCN, Gland, 1990).

Jacobs, M., *The Green Economy: Environment, Sustainable Development and the Politics of the Future* (Pluto, London, 1991).

Jagger, A. M., *Feminist Politics and Human Nature* (Rodman and Allanhead, Ottawa, 1983).

Janis, M. W. (ed.), *The Influence of Religion on the Development of International Law* (Nijhoff, Netherlands, 1991).

Janis, M. W., 'Religion and International Law', *American Bar Association Journal of International Law*, (1989), 195–207.

Jansen, M., 'The Future of Tropical Ecology', *Annual Review of Ecological Systems*, 17 (1986), 305–21.

Jantzen, G., *God's World: God's Body* (Westminster, Philadelphia, 1984).

Johns, D. M., 'The Relevance of Deep Ecology to the Third World; Some Preliminary Observations', *Environmental Ethics*, 12 (1990), 235–47.

Johnson, L. E., *A Morally Deep World: An Essay on Moral Significance and Environmental Ethics* (Cambridge University Press, Cambridge, 1991).

Johnson, L. E., 'Animal Liberation Versus the Land Ethic', *Environmental Ethics*, 3 (1981), 265–73.

Johnson, L. E., 'Treading the Dirt: Environmental Ethics and Moral Theory', in Regan (1984), 350–79.

Johnson, S.P. (ed.), *The Earth Summit* (Graham and Trotman, London, 1993).

Joseph, L. E., *Gaia: The Growth of an Idea* (Arkana, London, 1990).

Jung, C., 'The Splendour of the World', *Atlantic Naturalist*, 29 (1974) 321–39.

Kant, I., *Critique of Judgement* (Macmillan, London, 1914).

Kant, I., *Lectures on Ethics: Duties Towards Animals and Spirits* (Harper and Rowe, Oxford, 1963).

Kant, I., *Fundamental Principles of Metaphysics And Morals* (Bobbs-Merril, London, 1973).

Kant, I., *Critique of Practical Reason* (Routledge, London, 1981), Book II.

Karp, J. P., 'The Evolving Meaning of Aesthetics in Land Use Regulation', *Colombia Journal of Environmental Law*, 15 (1990), 307–23.

Katz, E., 'Utilitarianism and Preservation', *Environmental Ethics*, 1 (1979) 209–14.

Katz, E., 'Organism, Community, and the Substitution Problem', *Environmental Ethics*, 7 (1985), 243–61.

Kaufman, F., 'Machines, Sentience and the Scope of Morality', *Environmental Ethics*, 16 (1994), 57–68.

Kavka, G., 'The Paradox Of Future Individuals', *Philosophy and Public Affairs*, 11 (1982), 103–21.

Kay, J., 'Concepts of Nature in the Hebrew Bible', *Environmental Ethics*, 10 (1988), 315–29.

Keekok-Lee, *Social Philosophy and Ecological Scarcity* (New York, 1989), 127, 143.

Kegley, C. W. and Wittkopf, E. R., *The Global Agenda: Issues and Perspectives* (McGraw, New York, 1995).

Kelman, M., 'On Democracy-Bashing; A Sceptical Look at the Theoretical and "Empirical" Practice of the Public Choice Movement', *Virginia Law Review*, 74 (1988), 199–217.

Kemp, P. and Wall, D., *A Green Manifesto for the 1990s* (Penguin, Harmondsworth, 1990).

Keniston, K., *The Uncommitted* (Brace and World, New York, 1965).

Kennedy, D., 'Cost-Benefit Analysis: A Critique', *Stanford Law Review*, 33 (1981), 387–403.

Kennick, W. E. (ed.), *Art and Philosophy* (London, 1964).

Kessell, J. L., 'Spaniards, Environment and the Pepsi Generation: An Historian's View', *Historian*, 36 (1973), 87.

Keynes, G. (ed.), *The Complete Writings of William Blake* (London, 1957).

Khachaturov, T., 'Economic Problems of Ecology', *Soviet Review* 20 (1979), 81–93.

Khadduri, A., *The Islamic Conception of Justice* (Cambridge, 1984).

Kiss, A. C. (ed.), *Selected Multilateral Treaties in the Field of the Environment* (UNEP, Kenya, 1982).

Kloppenburg, J. R. (ed.), *Seeds and Sovereignty* (London, 1988), 293, 299.

Kluckholn, C., 'Ethical Relativity', *Journal of Philosophy*, 52 (1955), 663–7.

Koskenniemi, M., *From Apology to Utopia: The Structure of International Legal Argument* (Finnish Lawyers Publishing, Helinski, 1989).

Koskenniemi, P., *From Alienation of Reason: A History of Positivist Thought* (UCL Press, London, 1969).

LaChance, A., *Greenspirit* (Element, Dorset, 1991).

Ladd, J. (ed.), *Ethical Issues Relating to Life and Death* (Oxford University Press, Oxford, 1979).

Lakoff, R., *Women, Fire and Dangerous Things: What Categories Reveal About the Mind* (Random House, New York, 1987).

Lasch, C., *The Culture Of Narcissism: American Life In An Age Of Discriminatory Expectation* (Abacus, London, 1978).

Latin, H., 'Ideal Versus Real Regulatory Efficiency', *Stanford Law Review*, 37 (1985), 1267, 1332.

Lawsdon, H. in David, R., *International Encyclopaedia Of Comparative Law* (International Association of Legal Science, 1992), Chapter 11, § 138.

Lean, G., 'Gorbachev Plots a Green Revolution to Save World', *Observer*, 25 April 1993, 12.

Lee, D. C., 'On the Marxian View of the Relationship Between Man and Nature', *Environmental Ethics*, 2 (1980), 9.

Lehmann, S., 'Do Wildernesses Have Rights?', *Environmental Ethics*, 3 (1981), 130–44.

Leibniz, G. W., *Monadology* (Lowe and Brydone, London, 1898).

Leiss, W., *The Domination of Nature* (Brazillier, New York, 1972).

Lenz, J. W. (ed.), *Hume's Essays* (Bobbs-Merril, Cambridge, 1965).

Leopold, A., *A Sand County Almanac* (Oxford University Press, Oxford, 1949).

Leopold, A., 'Conservation as a Moral Issue', *Environmental Ethics*, 1 (1979) 1–25.

Levine, M. P., 'Pantheism, Ethics and Ecology', *Environmental Values*, 3 (1994), 121–34.

Lewis, M. W., *Green Delusions: An Environmentalist's Critique of Radical Environmentalism* (Duke University Press, London, 1992).

Linder, D. O., 'New Directions for Preservation Law: Creating an Environment Worth Experiencing', *Environmental Law*, 20 (1990), 49–70.

Linzey, R., 'Moral Education and Reverence for Life', in Patterson (1981), 168–79.

Little, C. E., 'Has the Land Ethic Failed in America? An Essay on the Legacy of Aldo Leopold', *University of Illinios Law Review*, 2 (1986), 313–50.

Little, R. and Smith, R., *Perspectives on World Politics* (Routledge, London, 1993).

Livingston, J., *The Fallacy of Wildlife Conservation* (Toronto University Press, Toronto, 1981).

Livingston, J., 'Rightness or Rights?', *Osgoode Hall Law Journal*, 22 (1984), 321–42.

Locke, J., *An Essay Concerning The True Original, Extent And End Of Civil Government* (London, 1969).

Locke, J., *An Essay Concerning Human Understanding*, (Thomas Tegg, London, 1972).

Lockley, D., *New Zealand's Endangered Species* (Auckland University Press, Auckland, 1980).

Logan, B. L., 'An Assessment of the Environmental and Economic Implications of Toxic-Waste Disposal in Sub-Saharan Africa', *Journal of World Trade*, 25 (1991), 61–72.

Lohmann, L., 'Dismal Green Science', *Ecologist*, 21 (1991), 194–203.

Lombardi, L. G., 'Inherent Worth, Respect and Animals Rights', *Environmental Ethics*, 5 (1983), 260–71.

Lovelock, J., *Gaia: A New Look at Life on Earth* (Oxford University Press, Oxford, 1979).

Lovelock, J., 'Discussion on Margalef', in Bourdeau (1989), 233–41.

Lowenthal, P., 'The American Creed of Nature as Virtue', *Landscape*, 9 (1959–60), 21–36.

Lucretius, *On the Nature of the Universe* (Penguin, London, 1951).

Lukes, T., *Individualism* (Harper and Row, New York, 1973).

Lux, K., *Adam Smith's Mistake* (Century, London, 1990).

Lynch, O. J. and Talbott, K., 'Legal Responses to the Philippine Deforestation Crisis', *International Law and Politics*, 20 (1988), 679–706.

Lynge, F., *Arctic Wars: Animal Rights and Endangered Peoples* (Dartmouth, Hanover, 1992).

Lyster, S., *International Wildlife Law* (Grotius, Cambridge, 1985).

Mabbott, G., 'Politics and the Environment', *Texas Quarterly*, 17 (1974), 9–19.

McBurney, S., *Ecology into Economics Won't Go* (Green Print, Devon, 1990).

McClay, W. M., 'Religion in Politics: Politics in Religion', *Commentary*, 86 (1988), 43–54.

McCloskey, H. J., *Ecological Ethics and Politics* (Englewood Cliffs, New Jersey, 1983), 122.

McCloskey, H. J., 'Rights', *Philosophical Quarterly*, 15 (1965), 115–22.

McCloskey, H. J., 'Ecological Ethics and Its Justification', *Australian National University Department of Philosophy*, 2 (1980), 65–76.

McElroy, M. B., 'Change in the Natural Environment of the Earth: A Historical Record', in Clark and Mum (1986), 195–9.

McGinn, T., 'Ecology and Ethics', *International Philosophical Quarterly*, 14 (1974), 155–71.

McGonigle, M., 'The Economising of Ecology: Why Big, Rare Whales Still Die', *Ecology Law Quarterly*, 12 (1980), 120–46.

McHarg, I., *Design With Nature* (Garden City, New York, 1969).

Machiavelli, *The Prince* (Quality Paperbooks, London, 1992).

McLean, A. (ed.), *Values at Risk* (Random House, New York, 1986).

McLean, D. (ed.), *Karl Marx: Selected Writings* (Oxford University Press, Oxford, 1978).

McLuhan, T. C. (ed.), *Touch the Earth* (Abacus, 1971), 129.

McNeely, J. A. (ed.), *National Parks, Conservation and Development: The Role of Protected Areas in Sustaining Society* (IUCN, Geneva, 1982).

MacNeil, J., Winsemius, P., and Yakushiji, T., *Beyond Interdependence: The Meshing Of The World's Economy And The Earth's Ecology* (Oxford University Press, Oxford, 1991).

MacPherson, C. B., *The Political Theory of Possessive Individualism* (Oxford University Press, Oxford, 1962).

Magel, C. R., *Animal Rights* (Mansell, London, 1989).

Maggs, P. B. 'Marxism and Soviet Environmental Law', *Colombia Journal of Transnational Law* 23 (1984–5), 355–84.

Mahar, D. J., 'Fiscal Incentives For Regional Development: A Case Study of the Western Amazonian Basin', *Journal of Interamerican Studies and World Affairs*, 18 (1976), 357–73.

Mahony, R., 'Debt for Nature Swaps: Who Really Benefits?', *Ecologist*, 22 (1992), 97–101.

Majdoff, C., 'Capitalism and the Environment', *Monthly Review*, 41 (1989), 1–5.

Manetti, *The Dignity and Excellence of Man* (Cambridge University Press, Cambridge, 1901).

Manning, S., 'Environmental Ethics and Rawls' Theory of Justice', *Environmental Ethics*, 3 (1981), 155–72.

Mao Tsetung, *Selected Works* (New York, 1954).

Marcuse, H., *One Dimensional Man* (Routledge, London, 1964).

Margalef, E., 'On Certain Unifying Principles in Ecology', *American Naturalist*, 97 (1963), 363–78.

Marsh, G. P., *The Earth As Modified By Human Action* (Scribner, New York, 1874).

Marsh, G. P. 'The Earth As Modified By Human Action', in Burton, I. and Kates, R. W., *Readings in Resource Management and Conservation* (Chicago University Press, Chicago, 1965).

Marshall, P., *Nature's Web: An Exploration of Ecological Thinking* (Simon and Schuster, London, 1992).

Martin, C., *Keepers of the Game: Indian Animal Relations* (University of California Press, Los Angeles, 1978).

Marx, K., *Capital* (Wishart, London, 1972) and (Foreign Publishing, Moscow, 1981).

Marx, K. and Engels, F., *8 Selected Works* (Foreign Publishing, Moscow, 1954).

Marx, K. and Engels, F., *On Religion* (Foreign Publishing, Moscow, 1955).

Mark, K. and Engels, F., *Collected Works* (Lawrence and Wishart, Oxford, 1987).

Massey, S. C., 'UNCED Will Not Culminate in a Successful Preventive Global Warming Treaty Without the United States Support', *Georgia Journal of International and Comparative Law*, 22 (1992), 175–93.

Mathews, F., 'Conservation and Self Realisation: A Deep Ecology Perspective', *Environmental Ethics*, 10 (1988), 351–83.

Mellor, M., *Breaking the Boundaries: Towards A Feminist Green Socialism* (Virago, London, 1992).

Mellos, K., *Perspectives on Ecology* (Macmillan, London, 1988).

Merchant, C., *The Death of Nature: Women, Ecology and the Scientific Period* (Wildwood, London, 1982).

Merchant, C., *Radical Ecology: The Search for a Livable World* (Routledge, London, 1992).

Michaelsen, R. S, 'American Indian Religious Freedom Litigation: Promises and Perils', *Journal of Law and Religion*, 3 (1985), 47–58.

Midgley, M., *The Beast and Man: The Roots of Human Nature* (Harvester, London, 1980).

Midgley, M., 'Is the Biosphere a Luxury?', *Hastings Centre Report*, (1992), 7–15.

Midgley, M., 'Towards a More Humane View of Beasts', in Cooper and Palmer, (1992), 28–39.

Mill, J. S., *Nature, The Utility of Religion and Theism* (London, 1858).

Mill, J. S., *Utilitarianism, Liberty and Representative Government* (Dent, London, 1910).

Mill, J. S. *Collected Works* (University of Toronto Press, Toronto, 1986).

Miller, F. (ed.), *Living In The Environment* (London, 1975).

Mishan, E., 'How Valid are Economic Evaluations of Allocative Changes?', *Journal of Economic Issues* 14 (1980), 29–47.

Miss Ann Thropy, 'Population and Aids', *Earth First!*, 1 May 1987.

Mitchell, B., *Law, Morality and Religion in a Secular Society* (Oxford University Press, Oxford, 1970).

Mitchell, W. J. T. (ed.), *Landscape and Power* (University of Chicago Press, Chicago, 1994).

Molesworth, D. (ed.), *The English Works of Thomas Hobbes of Malmsbury* (John Bohn, London, 1841).

Moline, J. N., 'Aldo Leopold and the Moral Community', *Environmental Ethics*, 6 (1986), 113–21.

Moment, J., 'Bears: The Need For A New Sanity in Wildlife Conservation', *Bioscience*, 18, 1105–14.

Monbiot, G., 'Supplying the Demand', *Guardian*, 23 March 1992, 27.

Montefiore, D., 'Man And Nature: A Theological Assessment', *Zygon*, 12 (1977), 211–23.

Moore, G. E., *Principa Ethica* (Cambridge University Press, Cambridge, 1903).

Moore, G. E., *Philosophical Studies* (Routledge, London, 1922).

Moore, J., 'The Future Looks Bad For Ugly Species Too', *Daily Telegraph*, 23 March 1992, 8.

Morgenthau, H., 'Positivism, Functionalism and International Law', *American Journal of International Law*, 34 (1940), 261–83.

Morito, B., 'Value, Metaphysics and Anthropocentricism', *Environmental Values*, 4 (1995), 31–45.

Moroni, A., Mamiani, M., and Zurlini, G., 'From Domination Over Nature to Environmental Ethics: Scientific and Philosophical Foundations', in Bourdeau (1989), 141–54.

Morris, B., 'Reflections on Deep Ecology', in *Deep Ecology and Anarchism* (Freedom Press, London, 1993), 37–46.

Morris, R. (ed.), *On The Fifth Day: Animal Rights and Human Ethics* (Acropolis, Washington, 1978).

Muir, J., *Our National Parks* (Houghton Mifflin, Boston, 1901).

Mumford, L., *The Culture of Cities* (Secker and Warberg, London, 1938).

Munasinghe, M., *Environmental Economics and Sustainable Development* (World Bank, Washington, 1993).

Myers, N., 'An Introduction To Environmental Thought', *Indiana Law Journal*, 50 (1975), 432–63.

Myers, N., 'A Major Extinction Spasm: Predictable or Inevitable?', in Western and Pearl (1989), 42–9.

Myrdal, S., 'Institutional Economics', *Journal of Economic Issues*, 12 (1978), 6–17.

Naess, A., *Ecology, Community and Lifestyle* (Cambridge University Press, Cambridge).

Naess, A., 'The Shallow and the Deep, Long Range Ecology Movement', *Inquiry*, 16 (1973), 90–100.

Naess, A., 'Spinoza and Ecology', *Philosophy*, 7 (1977), 46–61.

Naess, A., 'Self Realisation in Mixed Communities', *Inquiry*, 22 (1979), 201–17.

Naess, A., 'A Defence of the Deep Ecology Movement', *Environmental Ethics*, 6 (1984), 265–73.

Naess, A., 'Identification as a Source of Deep Ecological Attitudes', in Tobias (1985), 48–62.

Naess, A., 'The Deep Ecology Movement: Some Aspects', *Philosophical Inquiry*, 8 (1986), 14–24.

Naess, A., 'Deep Ecology and the Ultimate Premises', *Ecologist*, 18 (1988), 128–35.

Naess, A., 'The Basics of Deep Ecology', in Button (1990), 130–35.

Narveson, J., 'Utilitarianism and Future Generations', *Mind*, 76 (1967), 64–82.

Narveson, J., 'Animal Rights', *Canadian Journal of Philosophy*, 7 (1977), 177–89.

Nash, J. A., 'The Case for Biotic Rights', *Yale Journal of International Law*, 18 (1993), 235–51.

Nash, R., 'The American Invention of National Parks', *American Quarterly*, 22 (1970), 726–35.

Nash, R., 'Do Rocks Have Rights', *Centre Magazine*, 10 (1977), 32–43.

Nasr, S. H., *Man and Nature: The Spiritual Crisis in Modern Man* (Unwin, London, 1968).

Navrud, S. (ed.), *Pricing the European Environment* (Oxford University Press, Oxford, 1992).

Nelson, J. G. (ed.), *International Experience With National Parks and Related Reserves* (University of Waterloo Press, 1978).

Nelson, M. P., 'A Defence of Environmental Ethics', *Environmental Ethics*, 15 (1993), 245–57.

Niang, C. I., 'From Ecological Crisis in the West to Energy Problems in Africa', *International Social Sciences Journal*, 42 (1990), 226–40.

Nietzsche, F., *The Gay Science* (Penguin, Harmondsworth, 1975).

Nietzsche, F., *A Nietzsche Reader* (Penguin, Harmondsworth, 1977).

Nietzsche, F., *Human, All Too Human* (Penguin, Harmondsworth, 1978).

Nisbet, F., *Kant's Political Writings* (Cambridge University Press, Cambridge, 1970).

Nordhaus, W. D., 'To Slow, or Not to Slow: The Economics of the Greenhouse Effect', *Economic Journal*, 101 (1991), 921–38.

Norgaard, R., *Development Betrayed* (Routledge, London, 1994).

Norton, B. G. (ed.), *The Preservation of Species* (Princeton University Press, New York, 1986).

Norton, B. G. 'Environmental Ethics and Non-human Rights', *Environmental Ethics*, 4 (1982), 35–49.

Norton, B.G., 'Environment l Ethics And The Rights Of Future Generations', *Environmental Ethics*, 4 ('982), 322–35.

Norton, B.G., 'Environmental Ethics and Weak Anthropocentricism', *Environmental Ethics*, 6 (1984), 141–57.

Norton, B. G., 'Sand Dollar Psychology', *The Washington Post Magazine*, 1 June 1986, 11–14.

Norton, B.G., 'Conservation and Preservation: A Conceptual Rehabilitation', *Environmental Ethics*, 8 (1986), 195–211.

Norton, B. G., 'Why Environmentalists Hate Mainstream Economists', *Environmental Ethics*, 13 (1991) 335–51.

Norton, B. G., 'Economists' Preferences and the Preferences of Economists', *Environmental Values*, 3 (1994), 311–30.

Nozick, R., *Anarchy, State, Utopia* (Oxford University Press, Oxford, 1974).

Nozick, R., *Philosophical Explanations* (Clarendon Press, Oxford, 1981).

Oddie, G. and Perrett, R. (eds.), *Justice, Ethics and New Zealand Society* (Oxford University Press, Oxford, 1992).

Odum, E. P., *Fundamentals of Ecology* (Saunders, Philadelphia, 1978).

Oelschlaeger, M., *The Idea of Wilderness: From Prehistory to the Age of Ecology* (Yale University Press, New York, 1991).

Omran, A. R., *Family Planning and the Legacy of Islam* (Routledge, London, 1992).

O'Neill, J., *Ecology, Policy and Politics: Human Well-Being and the Natural World* (Routledge, London, 1993).

Ophuls, W., *Ecology and the Politics of Scarcity* (Freeman, San Francisco, 1977).

Ophuls, W., 'Scarcity Society', *Harpers*, 248 (1974), 25–51.

Ophuls, W., 'The Politics of the Sustainable Society', in Pirages (1977), 161–219.

O'Riordan, T., *Environmentalism* (Pion, London, 1981).

O'Riordan, T., 'The Ever Changing Politics of Nature Conservation in the United Kingdom', *Environment and Planning* 22 (1990), 143–52.

Orr, D. W. (ed.), *The Global Predicament* (Duke University Press, North Carolina, 1979).

Orr, D. W., 'Leviathan, the Open Society, and the Crisis of Ecology', in Orr (1979), 308–18.

Orr, D. W., 'Economics in a Hotter Time', *Ecologist*, 22 (1992), 42–5.

Osborne, P. (ed.), *Socialism and the Limits of Liberalism* (Verso, London, 1991), 241, 249.

O'Sullivan, M., *The Four Seasons of Greek Philosophy* (Efstathiadis, Cyprus, 1982).

Paehlke, R. C., *Environmentalism and the Future of Progressive Politics* (Yale University Press, New York, 1989).

Paehlke, R. C., 'Development, Bureaucracy and Environmentalism', *Environmental Ethics*, 10 (1988), 291–312.

Palme Commission, *Disarmament and Security Issues* (Oxford University Press, Oxford, 1980).

Palmer, G., *Environmental Politics: A Greenprint for New Zealand* (McIndoe, Dunedin, 1990).

Panjabi, R. K. L., 'Idealism and Self-Interest In International Law: The Rio Dilemma', *Californian Western International Law Journal*, 23 (1992), 189–211.

Parfit, D., *Reasons and Persons* (Oxford University Press, Oxford, 1984).

Parker, K., 'The Values of a Habitat', *Environmental Ethics*, 12 (1990), 353–64.

Parson, H., *Marx and Engels on Ecology* (Greenwood Press, Connecticut, 1977).

Partridge, E. (ed.), *The Rights Of Future Generations* (Prometheus, New York, 1981).

Pascal, B., *Lettres Provincials*, (Cambridge University Press, Cambridge, 1928).

Pascal, B., *Pensees* (Penguin, Harmondsworth, 1975).

Passmore, J., *Man's Responsibility For Nature* (Duckworth, London, 1974).

Passmore, J., 'Removing the Rubbish: Reflections on the Ecological Craze', *Encounter*, (1974), 19–31.

Patten, B. C. and Odum, E. P., 'The Cybernetic Nature of Ecosystems', *American Naturalist*, 118 (1981), 886–97.

Patterson, C. H. (ed.), *Humanistic Education: A Symposium* (Sussex, 1981).

Pearce, D. W. (ed.), *Blueprint 2: Greening the World Economy* (Earthscan, London, 1991).

Pearce, D. W. and Barbier, E. B., *Sustainable Development: Economics and the Environment in the Third World* (Earthscan, London, 1990).

Pearce, D. W., Markandya, A., and Barbier, E. B., *Blueprint for a Green Economy* (Earthscan, London, 1989).

Pearce, D. W. and Turner, K., *The Economics of Natural Resources and the Environment* (Harvester, Hempstead, 1990).

Pearce, D. W. and Warford, J. J., *World Without End: Economics, Environment and Sustainable Development* (World Bank, Washington, 1993), 65–80.

Pearce, F., *Green Warriors: The People and Politics Behind the Environmental Revolution* (London, Bodley Head, 1991).

Pearson Commission, *Partners in Development* (Pall Mall Press, London, 1969).

Penning-Rowsell, E. C., *Landscape Meanings and Values* (Allen & Unwin, London, 1986).

Pepper, D., *The Roots of Modern Environmentalism* (Routledge, London, 1984).

Pepper, D., *Eco-Socialism: From Deep Ecology to Social Justice* (Routledge, London, 1993).

Pepper, D., 'New Economics and the Deficiencies in Green Political Thought', *Political Quarterly*, 58 (1987), 334–48.

Percival, R. V., 'Back to Basics: An Environmental Policy for the 1990s', *Environmental Forum*, 5 (1988), 21–33.

Peterson, J. J. and T. R., 'A Rhetorical Critique of Non-Market Economic Valuations for Natural Resources', *Environmental Values*, 2 (1993), 47–59.

Pierce, C. and Van De Veer, D., (eds.), *People, Penguins and Plastic Trees: Basic Issues in Environmental Ethics* (Wadsworth, London, 1995).

Pinchot, G., *The Fight For Conservation* (Harcourt Brace, New York, 1910).

Pinchot, G., *Breaking New Ground* (Harcourt Brace, New York, 1947).

Pirages, D. C. (ed.), *The Sustainable Society* (Praeger, New York, 1977).

Plant, C. and J. (eds.), *Green Business: Hope or Hoax?* (Green Books, Devon, 1991).

Plato, *Phaedo* (Penguin, Harmondsworth, 1969).

Plato, *The Republic*, trans. F. Conford (Oxford University Press, Oxford, 1974).

Pleumaron, A., 'The Political Economy of Tourism', *Ecologist*, 24 (1994), 142–9.

Plotinus, *Enneads* (Penguin, London, 1981).

Polak, F. L. *The Image of the Future* (Oceana, New York, 1961).

Polunin, N and Burnett, J. H. (eds.), *Maintenance of the Biosphere. Proceedings of the Third International Conference on Environmental Future* (Edinburgh University Press, Edinburgh, 1990).

Ponting, C., *A Green History of the World* (Sinclair Stevenson, London, 1991).

Pope, A., *An Essay on Man* (Macmillan, Indianapolis, 1965).

Porritt, J., *Seeing Green* (Blackwell, Oxford, 1984).

Porritt, J., 'Halting the G-7 Juggernaut', *Guardian*, 16 July 1991.

Porritt, J., 'Comment', *Green Magazine*, 11 May 1992.

Porritt, J. and Winner, D., *The Coming of the Greens* (Fontana, London, 1988).

Porter, G. and Brown, J. W., *Global Environmental Politics* (Westview, Colorado, 1996).

Posner, R., 'Utilitarianism, Economics and Legal Theory', *Journal of Legal Studies*, 8 (1979), 103–13.

Potter, B., *Bioethics: The Bridge to the Future* (London, 1971).

Potter, R. B., 'The Simple Structure of the Population Debate: The Logic of the Ecology Movement', in Scherer (1983), 177–90.

Press, K., 'Kosher Ecology', *Commentary*, 79 (1985), 58–68.

Priestly, T. (ed.), *Collected Works of J. S. Mill* (Oxford University Press, Oxford, 1954).

Primatt, H., *A Dissertation on the Duty of Mercy and the Sin of Cruelty to Animals* (Constable, Edinburgh, 1834).

Prins, G. (ed.), *Threats Without Enemies: Facing Environmental Insecurity* (Earthscan, London, 1993).

Pufendorf, S., *The Law of Nature and of Nations* (Oceana, New York, 1931), vol. II.

Rachels, J., 'Darwin, Species and Morality', *Monist*, 70 (1987), 98–114.

Rachels, J., 'Created From Animals', in Pierce and Van Der Veer (1995), 59–72.

Ragsdale, J. W., 'Ecology, Growth and Law', *Ecology Law Quarterly*, 16 (1980), 214–45.

Ramphal, S., *Our Country the Planet* (Lime Tree, London, 1992).

Ransom, D., 'Green Justice', *New Internationalist*, 230 (1992), 5–9.

Rawls, J., 'The Sense of Justice', *Philosophical Review*, 72 (1963), 284–311.

Rawls, J. *A Theory of Justice* (Oxford University Press, Oxford, 1972).

Rawls, J., 'Justice as Fairness: Political Not Metaphysical', *Philosophy and Public Affairs*, 14 (1985), 223–47.

Ray, J., *The Wisdom God Manifested in the Works of Creation* (Oxford University Press, Oxford, 1958).

Reagan, R., 'Presidential Address on Environmental Issues', *Environmental Protection Agency Journal*, 10 (1984), 35.

Redclift, M., *Sustainable Development: Exploring the Contradictions* (Routledge, London, 1987).

Redclift, M., 'Sustainable Development: Needs Values, Rights', *Environmental Values*, 2 (1993), 1–28.

Rees, W. F., 'The Ecology of Sustainable Development', *Ecologist*, 20 (1990), 18–24.

Regan, T. (ed.), *Ethics And Problems Of The Twenty-first Century* (Random House, New York, 1976).

Regan, T. (ed.), *All That Dwell Within: Essays on Animal Rights and Environmental Ethics* (University of California Press, Berkeley, 1982).

Regan, T. (ed.), *Earthbound: New Introductory Essays in Environmental Ethics* (Random House, New York, 1982).

Regan, T. (ed.), *An Introduction to Modern Moral Philosophy* (Random House, New York, 1984).

Regan, T., *The Case for Animal Rights* (Routledge, London, 1988).

Regan, T., 'The Moral Basis of Vegetarianism', *Canadian Journal of Philosophy*, 5 (1975), 181–202.

Regan, T., 'The Nature And Possibility Of An Environmental Ethic', *Environmental Ethics*, 3 (1981), 25–38.

Regan, T. and Singer, P. (eds.), *Animal Rights and Human Obligations* (Englewood Cliffs, New Jersey, 1989).

Reinhart, P., 'To Be Christian Is To Be Ecologist', *Epiphany*, 6 (1985), 17–24.

Reinhart, P., 'The Eleventh Commandment: Access to Christian Environmentalism', *Whole Earth Review*, 50 (1986), 85–99.

Renteln, A. D., *International Human Rights: Universalism vs Relativism* (Sage, California, 1990).

Rescher, T., *Welfare: The Social Issues in Philosophical Perspective* (1972).

Robbins, T. (ed.), *Cults, Culture and the Law: Perspectives on New Religious Movements* (Scholars Press, California, 1985).

Roberts, R., 'Law, Morality and Religion in a Christian Society', *Religious Studies*, 20 (1984), 79–85.

Robinson, J. M. (ed.), *John Stuart Mill: Essays on Ethics, Religions and Society* (Routledge, London, 1969).

Rodgers, W., 'Benefits, Costs and Risks: Oversight of Health and Decision Making', *Harvard Environmental Law Review*, 4 (1980), 191–213.

Rodman, J. 'The Dolphin Papers', *North American Review* (1974), 12–27.

Rodman, J., 'The Other Side of Ecology In Ancient Greece', *Inquiry*, 19 (1976), 111–24.

Rodman, J., 'The Liberation of Nature?', *Inquiry*, 22 (1977), 83–96.

Rodman, J., 'Four Forms of Ecological Consciousness Reconsidered', in Scherer (1983), 82–90.

Rolston, H., *Environmental Ethics: Duties and Values in the Natural World* (Temple University Press, Philadelphia, 1988).

Rolston, H., 'Is There an Ecological Ethic?', *Ethics*, 85 (1974), 93–117.

Rolston, H., 'Values Gone Wild', *Inquiry*, 26 (1983), 193–211.

Rolston, H., 'Valuing Wetlands', *Environmental Ethics*, 7 (1985), 38–54.

Rolston, H., 'Biology Without Conservation: An Environmental Misfit and Contradiction in Terms', in Western and Pearl (1989), 232–40.

Rolston, H., 'Values and Duties to the Natural World', in Bormann and Kettert (1991), 73–80.

Rolston, H., 'Challenges in Environmental Ethics', in Cooper and Palmer (1992), 135–8.

Rolston, H., 'The Wilderness Idea Reaffirmed', *The Environmental Professional*, 13 (1992), 370–7.

Rolston, H., 'Rights and Responsibilities on the Home Planet', *Yale Journal of International Law*, 18 (1993), 251–61.

Rolston, H., 'Value in Nature and the Nature of Value', in Attfield (1994).

Ross, A., *The Chicago Gangster Theory of Life: Nature's Debt To Society* (Verso, London, 1994).

Ross, J. (ed.), *The Portable Renaissance Reader* (Harmonsdworth, Penguin, 1977).

Rousseau, H., *The Social Contract and Discourses* (Dent, London, 1913).

Rousseau, J. J., *Discourse on the Origins of Inequality Among Men* (Everyman, London, 1961).

Rousseau, J. J., *The Social Contract* (Dent, 1973).

Routley, R., 'Critical Notice of Passmore's Man's Responsibility for Nature', *Australasian Journal of Philosophy*, 53 (1975), 177–83.

Routley, R. and V., 'Against the Inevitability of Human Chauvinism', in Goodpaster (1976), 41–52.

Routley, R. and V., 'Nuclear Energy and Obligations to the Future', *Inquiry*, 21 (1978), 128–37.

Rowe, H., 'Kakadu Man's Concession', *Green Magazine*, April 1991, 61.

Royal Norwegian Ministry of Foreign Affairs, *Information on Whaling* (Norway, 1993).

Ruckelshaus, N., 'Risk, Science and Democracy', *Issues in Science and Technology*, 3 (1985), 28–41.

Ruitenbeek, H. J., *The Economic Analysis of Tropical Forest Conservation Initiatives: Examples From West Africa* (World Bank, Washington, 1992).

Rummel-Bulska, I. (ed.), *Selected Multilateral Treaties in the Field of the Environment* (Grotius, Cambridge, 1991).

Russell, B., *A History of Western Philosophy* (Allen and Unwin, London, 1946).

Russell, B., *The Principles of Human Experimental Technique* (Allen and Unwin, London, 1959).

Rusta, B. and Simma, B. (eds.), *International Protection of the Environment* (New York, 1976).

Sabine, G. H. and Thorson, T. L., *A History of Political Theory* (Dryden, Illinois, 1973).

Sachs, W. (ed.), *Global Ecology: A New Area of Political Conflict* (Zed, London, 1993).

Sadler, B., *Environmental Aesthetics: Essays in Interpretation* (Sadler & Carlson, Toronto, 1982).

Sagoff, M., *The Economy of the Earth* (Cambridge University Press, Cambridge, 1990).

Sagoff, M., 'On Preserving the Natural Environment: A Non-utilitarian Rationale For Preserving the Natural Environment', *Yale Law Journal*, 84 (1974), 234–67.

Sagoff, M., 'On The Preservation Of Species', *Colombia Journal of Environmental Law*, 7 (1980), 52–74.

Sagoff, M., 'At The Shrine Of Our Lady Fatima or Why Not All Political Questions Are Not All Economic', *Arizona Law Review*, 23 (1981), 1290–319.

Sagoff, M., 'We Have Met the Enemy and He is Us, or Conflict and Contradiction in Environmental Law', *Environmental Law*, 12 (1982), 383–404.

Sagoff, M., 'Animal Liberation and Environmental Ethics: Bad Marriage, Quick Divorce', *Osgoode Hall Law Journal*, 22 (1984), 304–25.

Sagoff, M., 'Fact and Value in Ecological Science', *Environmental Ethics*, 7 (1985), 99, 105.

Sagoff, M., 'Reason and Rationality in Environmental Law', *Ecology Law Quarterly*, 14 (1987), 265–73.

Sagoff, M., 'Integrating Science and Law', *Tennessee Law Review*, 56 (1988), 159–68.

Sagoff, M., 'Four Dogmas of Environmental Economics', *Environmental Values*, 3 (1994), 285–303.

Salt, H., *Animal Rights Connected in Relation to Social Progress* (George Bell, London, 1987).

Sandbrook, R., 'Development for the People and the Environment', *Journal of International Affairs*, 41 (1991), 403–18.

Sanders, B. L. (ed.), *Contemporary International Politics: Introductory Readings* (Wiley, New York, 1971).

Sands, P. (ed.), *Greening International Law* (Earthscan, London, 1993).

Santayana, G., *The Sense of Beauty* (Dover, 1955).

Sapontzis, S. F., 'The Moral Significance of Interests', *Environmental Ethics*, 4 (1982), 347–64.

Saunders, P. M. (ed.), *The Legal Challenge of Sustainable Development* (Canadian Institute of Resource Law, Calgary, 1990).

Scharlemann, R. P., 'A Theological Model of Nature', *Bucknell Review*, 20 (1972), 104–15.

Scherer, D. (ed.), *Ethics and the Environment* (Prentice Hall, New Jersey, 1983).

Scherer. D., 'Anthropocentricism, Atomism and Environmental Ethics', *Environmental Ethics*, 4 (1982), 115–28.

Scherer, D., 'A Disenthropic Ethic', *Monist*, 71 (1988), 6–19.

Schmidt, A., *The Concept of Nature in Marx* (New Left, London, 1971).

Schopenhaur, A., *The World as Will and Representation* (Kegan Paul, New York, 1969).

Schumacher, F., *Small is Beautiful* (Abacus, London, 1973).

Schumacher, F., *A Guide for the Perplexed* (Abacus, London, 1980).

Schwartz, W. and D., *Breaking Through* (Green Books, Devon, 1987).

Schwartzchild, S., 'The Unnatural Jew', *Environmental Ethics*, 6 (1984), 347–67.

Schwarz, W., 'Anatomy of an Eco–Anarchist', *Guardian*, 15 May 1992.

Schwarzenberger, G., *Power Politics* (Stevens, London, 1964).

Schweitzer, A., *Civilisation and Ethics* (Black, London, 1929).

Schweitzer, A., *Out of My Life and Thought* (Henry Holt, New York, 1961).

Scott, W., *The Conflict Between Atomism and the Conservation Theory* (MacDonald, London, 1970).

Seelman, H., 'Towards Ecological Justice', *Christ and Crisis*, 38 (1978), 250–63.

Sellers, W., 'Science or Scenery? A Conflict in Values in National Parks', *Wilderness*, 52 (1989), 29–38.

Sergeant, E., *The Spectrum of Pain* (London, 1969).

Sessions, G., 'Anthropocentricism and the Environmental Crisis', *Humboldt Journal of Social Relations*, 2 (1974), 73–89.

Sessions, G., 'Spinoza and Jefferson Man in Nature', *Inquiry*, 20 (1977), 481–92.

Sessions, G., 'The Deep Ecology Movement: A Review', *Environmental Review*, 11 (1987), 107–21.

Shaddow, T. H., 'Religious Ritual Exemptions: Sacrificing Animal Rights for Ideology', *Loyola of Los Angeles Law Review*, 24 (1991), 1367–78.

Shaiko, R. G., 'Religion, Politics and Environmental Concern: A Powerful Mix of Passions', *Social Sciences Quarterly*, 68 (1987), 244–58.

Sheldrake, R., *The Rebirth of Nature: The Greening of Science and God* (Rider, London, 1990).

Shepard, P., 'Ecology and Man', in Disch (1970), 52–8.

Sherrard, P., *The Rape of Man and Nature* (Golgonooza, Suffolk, 1987).

Shields, A., 'Wilderness: Its Meaning and Value', *Southern Journal of Philosophy*, 11 (1973), 240–56.

Short, J. R., *Imagined Country: Society, Culture and Environment* (Routledge, London, 1991).

Siddwick, H., *The Methods of Ethics* (Macmillan, London, 1893) and (Routledge, London, 1962).

Singer, B., 'An Extension of Rawls' Theory of Justice to Environmental Ethics', *Environmental Ethics*, 10 (1988), 211–24.

Singer, P., *Animal Liberation: Towards an End to Man's Inhumanity to Animals* (Cape, London, 1976).

Singer, P. *Animal Liberation: A New Ethic for Our Treatment of Animals* (Paladin, Sydney, 1977).

Singer, P., *Practical Ethics* (Cambridge University Press, Cambridge, 1993).

Singer, P., 'All Animals are Equal', *Philosophic Exchange*, 1 (1974), 103–16.

Singer, P., 'Not for Humans Only: The Place of Non-humans in Environmental Issues', in Regan (1976), 199–216.

Singer, P., 'Killing Humans and Killing Animals', *Inquiry*, 22 (1979), 152–64.

Singer, P., 'Utilitarianism and Vegetarianism', *Philosophy and Public Affairs*, 9 (1979–80), 327–48.

Singleton, J., 'Do the Greens Threaten the Reds?', *World Today*, 46 (1986), 160–74.

Skare, M., 'Whaling: A Sustainable Use of Natural Resources or a Violation of Animal Rights?', *Environment*, 36 (1994), 12–31.

Skolimowski, H., *Eco-Philosophy: Designing New Tactics for Living* (Boyars, London, 1981).

Skolimowski, H., *Living Philosophy: Eco-Philosophy as a Tree of Life* (Arkana, London, 1992).

Skolimowski, H., 'Eco-Philosophy and Deep Ecology', *Ecologist*, 18 (1988), 124–9.

Smart, N., *The Philosophy of Religion* (Random House, New York, 1970).

Smith, A., *The Theory of Moral Sentiments* (Methuen, London, 1904).

Smith, A., *An Enquiry Into the Nature and Causes of the Wealth of Nations* (Methuen, Book 1, 1904).

Smith, D., 'Ecological Genesis Of Endangered Species: The Philosophy Of Preservation', *Annual Review Of Ecological Systems*, 7 (1976), 43–56.

Smith, E. M., 'The Endangered Species Act and Biological Conservation', *Southern California Law Review*, 57 (1984), 361–89.

Smith, L., 'A Hurricane Whipped Up By Windmills', *Independent*, 25 January 1992, 15.

Smith, S. 'The Messes Animals Make In Metaphysics', *Journal of Philosophy*, 46 (1949), 150–65.

Sober, E., 'Philosophical Problems For Environmentalism', in Gruen and Jamieson (1994), 345–54.

Soderbaum, P., 'Economics, Evaluation and Environment', in Hall, Myers and Maganis (1985), 215–27.

Soderbaum, P., 'Neoclassical and Institutional Approaches to Environmental Economics' *Journal of Economic Issues*, 24 (1991), 481–98.

Solomon, R. C., *Introducing Philosophy* (Harcourt, London, 1993).

Sophocles, *Theban Plays* (Harmondsworth, 1947).

South Commission, *The Challenge of the South* (Oxford University Press, Oxford, 1990).

Spindle, G. S., 'A Response to Elliot Richardson', *John Marshall Law Review*, 25 (1991), 33–53.

Spinoza, *Ethics* (Dent and Sons, London, 1959).

Spitler, G., 'Justifying a Respect for Nature', *Environmental Ethics*, 4 (1982), 256–69.

Splash, C. L., 'Economics, Ethics and Long Term Environmental Damage', *Environmental Ethics*, 15 (1993), 117–33.

Spretnak, C., *The Spiritual Dimension of Green Politics* (Bear, New Mexico, 1986).

Spretnak, C. and Capra, F., *Green Politics* (Bear, New Mexico, 1986).

Stambor, H., 'Manifest Destiny and American Indian Religious Freedom', *American Indian Law Review*, 10 (1982), 59–86.

Stanley, G. (ed.), *Characteristics* (Bobbs-Merril, New York, 1964).

Starke, L. (ed.), *Signs of Hope: Working Towards Our Common Future* (Oxford University Press, Oxford, 1990).

Stephen, C., 'Varieties of Individualism', *Berkeley Journal of Sociology*, 28 (1983), 115–23.

Sterba, J. P. 'The Welfare Rights Of Distant People And Future Generations: Moral Side-Constraints On Social Policy', *Social Theory and Practice*, 7 (1981), 110–27.

Sterba, J. P., 'Reconciling Anthropocentric and Non-Anthropocentric Ethics', *Environmental Values*, 3 (1994), 229–40.

Sterba, J. P., 'From Biocentric Individualism to Biocentric Pluralism', *Environmental Ethics*, 17 (1995), 191–205.

Sterling, S., 'Culture, Ethics and the New Environment: Towards a New Synthesis', *Environmentalist*, 5 (1990), 197–208.

Sterling, S., 'Towards an Ecological World View', in Engel (1990), 72–81.

Stevenson, C. P., 'A New Perspective on Environmental Rights After the Charter', *Osgoode Hall Law Journal*, 21 (1983), 390–9.

Stirling, A., 'Environmental Valuation: How Much is the Emperor Wearing?', *Ecologist*, 23 (1993), 97–108.

Stone, C., 'Moral Pluralism and the Course of Environmental Ethics', *Environmental Ethics*, 10 (1988), 147–65.

Stretton, H., *Capitalism, Socialism and the Environment* (Cambridge University Press, Cambridge, 1978).

Sullivan, A., *Greening the Tories* (Centre For Policy Studies, London, 1985).

Sumi, K., 'The Whale War Between Japan and the United States: Problems and Prospects', *Denver Journal of International Law and Policy*, 17 (1989), 317–50.

Summers, L., 'Why the Rich Should Pollute the Poor', *Guardian*, 14 February 1992, 29.

Susskind, L. E., *Environmental Diplomacy: Negotiating More Effective Environmental Agreements* (Oxford University Press, Oxford, 1994).

Swardson, A., 'Canada to Boost Seal Hunting', *Guardian International*, 19 March 1995, 3.

Sykes, S., 'The Cutting Edge', *Green Magazine*, April 1992, 34, 37.

Sylvan, R., 'A Critique of Deep Ecology', *Radical Philosophy*, 40. 2, 7.

Sylvan, R., 'On the Value Core of Deep Green Theory', in Oddie and Perrett (1992), 222–39.

Taliaferro, C., 'The Environmental Ethics of an Ideal Observer', *Environmental Ethics*, 10 (1988), 233.

Tarlock, D., 'Earth and Other Ethics: The Institutional Issues', *Tennessee Law Review*, 56 (1988), 43–62.

Taylor, A., *Choosing Our Future: A Practical Politics of the Environment* (Routledge, London, 1992).

Taylor, P., *Respect for Life: A Theory of Environmental Ethics* (Princeton University Press, Princeton, 1986).

Taylor, P., 'Frankena On Environmental Ethics', *Monist*, 64 (1981), 375–95.

Taylor, P., 'The Ethics of a Respect for Nature', *Environmental Ethics*, 3 (1981), 201–20.

Taylor, P., 'Are Humans Superior to Animals and Plants?', *Environmental Ethics*, (1984), 157–69.

Thomas, K., *Man and the Natural World: Changing Attitudes in England 1500–1800* (Penguin, Harmondsworth, 1984).

Thompson, J., 'Aesthetics and the Value of Nature', *Environmental Ethics*, 17 (1995), 291–314.

Thoreau, H. J., *Excursions and Poems* (Houghton, Boston, 1906).

Thucydides *History of the Peloponnesian War* (Penguin, Harmondsworth, 1954).

Tietenberg, T., 'The Poverty Connection to Environmental Policy', *Challenge*, 33 (1990), 23–9.

Timmerman, P., 'Mythology and Surprise in the Sustainable Development of the Biosphere', in Clark and Mum (1986), 430–8.

Tobias, D., *Deep Ecology* (San Diego, 1985).

Tokar, B., 'Social Ecology, Deep Ecology and the Future of Green Political Thought', *Ecologist*, 18 (1988), 132–49.

Tolman, C. 'Karl Marx, Alienation and the Mastery of Nature', *Environmental Ethics*, 3 (1981), 63–78.

Toulmin, S., 'The Case For Cosmic Purpose', *Tennessee Law Review*, 56 (1988), 37–50.

Travis, J. L., 'Progressivism and the Human Supremacy Argument', *Philosophical Forum*, 3 (1972), 208–21.

Trechman, E. J., *Essays of Montaigne* (Oxford University Press, Oxford, 1927).

Tribe, L., 'Trial By Mathematics: Precision and Ritual In Legal Process', *Harvard Law Review*, 84 (1971), 1361–94.

Tribe, L., 'From Environmental Foundations To Constitutional Structures: Learning From Nature's Future', *Yale Law Journal*, 84 (1974), 548–89.

Tribe, L., 'Ways Not to Think About Plastic Trees: New Foundations For Environmental Law', *Yale Law Journal*, 83 (1975), 1325–50.

Tuan, Y., *A Study of Environmental Perception, Attitudes and Values* (Prentice Hall, New Jersey, 1974).

Turnbull, C., *The Forest People* (Triad Paladin, London, 1962).

Turner, R. K., *Sustainable Environmental Economics: Management, Principles and Practice* (Belhaven, London, 1993).

Turner, R. K., 'Environment, Economics and Ethics', in Pearce, D. (1991), 167–89.

Udall, S., *The Quiet Crisis and the Next Generation* (Gibbs Smith, Utah, 1988).

UNEP, *Poverty and the Environment: Reconciling Short-Term Needs and Long-Term Sustainable Goals* (Nairobi), 1995).

UNEP/Brown, N. J., *Ethics and Agenda 21: Moral Implications of a Global Consensus* (United Nations, New York, 1994).

UNICEF, *State of the World's Children* (Oxford University Press, Oxford, 1993).

Vallance, P. (ed.), *A Hundred English Essays* (Macmillan, London, 1950).

Van De Veer, D., 'Of Beasts, Persons and the Original Position', *Monist*, 62 (1979), 371–85.

Varner, G. E. 'Do Species Have Standing', *Environmental Ethics*, 9 (1987), 71–89.

Vidal, J., 'Earth Soundings', *Guardian*, 3 April 1992.

Vidal, J., 'Drawing the Poison', *Guardian*, 23 April 1992, 8.

Vidal, J., 'Weeping and Whaling', *Guardian*, 7 May 1993, 18.

Vidal, J. 'America Versus The World', *Guardian*, 15 May 1992.

Vig, N. J. and Kraft, M. E. (eds.), *Environmental Policy in the 1990s* (Washington, 1990).

Waddel, H., *Beasts and Saints* (Constable, London, 1949).

Waitari, G., *The Roots of Heaven* (London, 1958).

Walker, B., 'Diversity and Stability in Ecosystem Conservation', in Western and Pearl (1989), 121–30.

Walker, K. J., 'The Environmental Crisis: A Critique of Neo-Hobbesian Responses', *Polity*, 21 (1988), 67–88.

Wall, D. (ed.), *Green History: A Reader in Environmental Literature, Philosophy and Politics* (Routledge, London, 1994).

Warren, K. J., 'Feminism and Ecology: Making Connections', *Environmental Ethics*, 9 (1987), 3–14.

Watkins, K., 'Trade Route of Almost All Evils', *Guardian*, 6 March 1992, 29.

Watson, R. A., 'A Critique of Anti Anthropocentric Biocentrism', *Environmental Ethics*, 5 (1983), 253–68.

Watson, R. A., 'Challenging The Underlying Dogmas Of Environmentalism', *Whole Earth Review*, 45 (1985), 9–19.

Weale, A., *The New Politics of Pollution* (Manchester University Press, Manchester, 1992).

Webb, B. and S., *Soviet Communism: A New Civilisation* (Longman, London, 1941).

Weber, W., 'Morality and National Power in International Politics', *Review of Politics*, 26 (1964), 31–62.

Weiss, E. B., *In Fairness To Future Generations* (United Nations University, Japan, 1989).

Weiss, E. B., 'The Planetary Trust: Consequences and Intergenerational Equity', *Ecology Law Quarterly*, 11 (1984), 453–572.

Wenz, P. S., *Environmental Justice* (State of New York University Press, Albany, 1988).

Wenz, P. S., 'Minimal, Moderate and Extreme Pluralism', *Environmental Ethics*, 15 (1993), 61–74.

Wenzel, J., *Animal Rights, Human Rights: Ecology, Economy and Ideology in the Canadian Arctic* (Belhaven, London, 1991).

Western, D. and Pearl, M. (eds.), *Conservation for the Twenty-first Century* (Oxford University Press, Oxford, 1989).

Westfall, R., *A Biography of Isaac Newton* (Cambridge University Press, Cambridge, 1980).

Weston, A., 'Beyond Intrinsic Value: Pragmatism In Environmental Ethics', *Environmental Ethics*, 7 (1985), 331–48.

Weston, A., 'Forms Of Gaian Ethics', *Environmental Ethics*, 9 (1987), 220–32.

Westra, A., 'Let It Be: Heideggger And Future Generations', *Environmental Ethics*, 7 (1985), 348–62.

Wheelwright, H., *The PreSocratics* (Indianapolis, 1960).

Whewell, W., *Lectures on the History of Moral Philosophy of England* (Parker, London, 1852).

White, J., 'Native American Religious Issues', *The Indian Historian*, 13 (1980), 39–64.

White, L., 'The Historical Roots of the Environmental Crisis', *Science*, 155 (1967), 1205–21.

Whitehead, A. N., *Science and the Modern World* (Macmillan, London, 1925).

Wiggins, A., 'Indian Rights and the Environment', *Yale Journal of International Law*, 18 (1993), 345, 349–51.

Williams, D., 'Subjectivity, Expression and Privacy: The Problems of Aesthetic Regulation', *Minnesota Law Review*, 62 (1977), 1–57.

Williams, G., *Wilderness and Paradise in Christian Thought* (Harper, New York, 1962).

Wilson, A., *The Culture of Nature: North American Landscape from Disney to the Exxon Valdez* (Blackwell, London, 1992).

Wilson, E. O., *Biophilia* (Harvard University Press, Massachusetts, 1984).

Wilson, E. O. (ed.), *Biodiversity* (National Academy Press, Washington, 1988).

Windelband, W., *An Introduction to Philosophy* (Fisher Unwin, London, 1921).

Wittgenstein, L., *Philosophical Investigations* (Blackwell, Oxford, 1953).

Wolfrum, D. (ed.), *The Antarctica Challenge* (Oxford University Press, Oxford, 1988).

Wood, H. W., 'Modern Pantheism As An Approach To Environmental Ethics', *Environmental Ethics*, 7 (1985), 159–76.

Wood, H. W., 'The United Nations Charter for Nature', *Ecology Law Quarterly*, 12 (1985), 977–90.

Woodbury, S. E., 'Aesthetic Nuisance: The Time Has Come to Recognise It', *Natural Resources Journal*, 27 (1987), 877–82.

World Bank, *World Development Report 1992: Development and the Environment* (Oxford University Press, Oxford, 1992).

World Bank, *Malaysia: Forestry Subsector Report* (Oxford University Press, Oxford, 1992).

World Commission on Environment and Development, *Our Common Future* (Oxford University Press, Oxford, 1987).

Worster, D., 'The Shaky Grounds of Sustainability', in Sachs (1993), 132–44.

Wynne-Tyson, J. (ed.), *The Extended Circle: An Anthology of Humane Thought* (Cardinal, Sussex, 1990).

Yaffee, S. L., *Prohibitive Policy: Implementing the Federal Endangered Species Act* (MIT Press, Massachusetts, 1982).

Young, J., *Post Environmentalism* (Belhaven, London, 1990).

Young, O., 'Natural Resources Policy: A Modest Plea for Political Analysis', *Ocean Development and International Law Journal*, 8 (1980), 183–93.

Zak, S., 'The Case for Animal Rights', *Loyola of Los Angeles Law Review*, 20 (1987), 1236–45.

Zimmerman, M. E., 'Towards a Heideggerean Ethics for Radical Environmentalism', *Environmental Ethics*, 5 (1983), 123–35.

Zimmerman, M. E., 'Beyond Humanism: Heidegger's Understanding of Technology', *Listening*, 12 (1977), 81–94.

Index

aesthetics
  collective 90–1
  conservation 85
  endangered species 89
  inherent value 84
  international environmental law 82–91
  motivation 84
  natural beauty 83–4, 87
  national parks 82, 89
  Nature 82–91
  objectivity 90
  problems 91
  seals 85–6, 177
  subjectivity 87–9
  treaties and conventions 82
  UNESCO 82
  World Charter for Nature 83
African Convention on the Conservation of
    Nature and Natural Resources 1972 15,
    103
Agrippa 73
agreements *see* treaties and conventions
alienation 118
animals *see also* endangered species, Nature
  contractualism 144
  cruelty 74, 93
  ecosystems 147–8
  equality 70
  ethics 136, 137–49
  extinction 101, 140, 165
  farming 139
  holistics 148
  hunting 146
  indigenous cultures 146
  inherent value 141–3
  land ethic 167
  mentally disabled 144
  pets 128
  plants 146
  predators 147
  rationality 144
  rights 147
  sacrifices 68
  sentience 137–40, 145–7
  slaughter 76
  suffering 138–41, 155
  utilitarianism 137–41
  value 123, 142
  wild 146
anthropocentricism 2, 4–18
  Atomism 6, 7, 8
  Christianity 7
  conservation 16
  definition 4–5
  economics 9
  environmental policy 15, 17, 44, 176
  foundations 5–15
  future generations 124–6
  humanity 9–11
  individual nature of existence 6–9
  intrinsic value 6, 18
  international environmental law 15–18
  land ethic 159, 161
  liberalism 7
  mental 5–6
  natural resources 17
  Nature 9–15, 17
  physical 5–6
  positions 5–15
  rationality 9
  religion 66, 75, 176
  respect for life 150, 165
  self-interest 19, 21, 22–3
  theories 5–15
  value 6, 18, 43–4
Aquinas, St Thomas 74
Aristotle 5, 88
Atomism 6, 7, 8
Augustine 7, 74, 88, 177–8

Bacon, Sir Francis 12–13
Baumgarten, Alexander Gottlieb 87
Bentham, Jeremy 137
Bergen Ministerial Declaration on
    Sustainable Development 1990 31, 43,
    109
Bible 67–76, 81
biosphere
  land ethic 162, 166, 167–8
  misanthropy 170, 171
  self-interest 22
biodiversity
  Convention 64
  culture 93
  endangered species 132
  international environmental law 134
  religion 64
  value 49, 129
Bodin, Jean 62
Brandt Reports 16, 19–20

Cairo Conference 1994 78
Calvin, John 74
capital 57–8
Cartagena Commitment 1992 32
Chaos theory 159
chauvinism 5
Christianity
  anthropocentricism 7
  God 14
  Nature 14
  religion 7, 14, 69–76
climate change
  economics 34, 35
  emissions 16–7
  Framework Convention 1992 25
  precautionary principle 26
  self-interest 25–7
  United Nations 25
Club of Rome 169
Commission on Global Governance 20, 32
Communism 14
community 50, 52
competition
  economics 53, 60
  land ethic 168
  self-interest 24
conservation
  aesthetics 85
  anthropocentricism 16
  economics 29, 33, 54, 59
  ethics 44
  future generations 110
  international environmental policy 16
  recreation 103
  religion 71–81
  value 44, 48, 127, 131
contractualism 144
Convention concerning the Protection of the
  World Cultural and Natural Heritage
  1972 108
Convention on the Conservation of
  Antarctic Marine Living Resources 1988
  17
conventions *see* treaties and conventions
cost-benefit analysis 29–31, 33–5, 38, 51, 55,
  57, 60
  endangered species 39
  value 39, 41
Council of Europe 15–16
culture
  biodiversity 93
  cruelty 98
  endangered species 97–8, 100–1
  environmental protection 92–102
  environmentally destructive cultures
    99–102
  ethics 101–2

exploitation 97–101
extinction 101
food 97
future generations 108
imperialism 100
indigenous peoples 93–5, 98
  Maoris 94–5, 99
national identity 96
Nature 95, 101
'noble savage' 96
recreation 105
rhinocerous 97–8, 177
Rio Summit 93
sustainable development 99
symbolisation 96
treaties and conventions 92–3
whaling 100–1
World Commission on Environment and
  Development 93

Darwin, Charles 160
Declaration of Fontainbleau 1986 128
Declaration of the UN on the Right to
  Development 1986 16
Democritus 6
Descartes, Rene 6–9, 14
Dewey, John 13
Diamond, Cora 141
discounting 57–8
dominion, 67–8, 74
Dorbis Conference 129
Durkheim, Emile 90

ecology
  deep 1–2, 164–8, 174, 178
  land ethic 164–8, 174
  radical 1–2
  social 1
economics
  anthropocentricism 9
  background 28–32
  capital 57, 58
  climate change 34, 35
  community 50, 52
  competition 53, 60
  conservation 29, 33, 54, 59
  cost-benefit analysis 29–31, 33–5, 38, 51,
    55, 57, 60
  decision-making 56–7, 60
  discounting 57–8
  emissions 34
  environmental policy 31, 33–7
  environmental protection 28–61, 176
  ethnocentricity 50–1
  exploitation 54, 57
  financial incentives 29

forestry 36–7, 59–61
individualism 51–2
interest rates 57–8
market problems 57–61
natural resources 56
Nature 54–5
political problems 54–7
polluter pays 32, 35–6, 38
poverty 56
Rio Summit 35
self-interest 50, 52–3
social problems 50–3
sustainable development 29, 31
taxation 32
Total Economic Value 36–7, 43
treaties and conventions 28
United States 30–1, 61
valuation 29–30, 33, 54
value 30, 31–2, 36–51, 53–5, 57, 176
whaling 58–9
World Commission on Environment and
    Development 1987 29, 34, 60
Emerson, Ralph Waldo 79
emissions 25–6, 34
endangered species
  aesthetics 89
  biodiversity 132
  convention 89, 132
  cost-benefit analysis 39
  culture 97–8, 100–1
  extinction 101, 140
  food 97
  philosophical consideration if protecting
    131–3
  respect for life 156
  suffering 141
  value 127, 131–3
  whaling 100–1
Engels, Friedrich 13
environmental policy
  anthropocentricism 15, 17, 44, 176
  economics 31, 33–7
  international environmental law 15
  religion 63–4
  value 44
environmental protection
  culture 91–102
  economics 28–61, 176
  religion 62–81
  self-interest 19–27, 176
ethics
  animals 136, 137–49
  basis 159–62
  conservation 44
  culture 101–2
  future generations 110–14, 122–3
  international environmental law 135

land ethic 135, 159–75, 178
  objective 159–62
  religion 66–71, 76, 79
  respect for life 150–8
  value 42, 44, 130
ethnocentrism 50–1
evolution 160, 166–7
exploitation
  culture 101
  economics 54, 57
  recreation 103
  religion 73
extinction 101, 140, 165

family planning 77, 78
farming 139
financial incentives 29
food 97
forestry
  economics 36–7, 59–61
  United States 61
  value 36–7, 49–51
Framework Convention on Climate Change
    1992 25
Francis of Assisi 70
Freud, Sigmund 116
fundamentalism 72
future generations
  alienation 118
  anthropocentricism 124–6
  charters 109–10
  community 115–16
  conservation 110
  cost 119
  cross-temporal argument 115–16
  culture 108, 115
  decision-making 112
  distance 119–21
  environmental protection 107–26
  ethics 110–14, 122, 123
  existence 122–4
  future generations 125
  Ideal Observer 114–15
  interest 122–4
  international law 107–10
  justice 125
  knowledge 119–21, 124–5
  motivation 117–19, 121
  natural heritage 108
  natural resources 121
  Nature 107
  necessities 121
  nuclear waste 112–13
  ombudsman 110
  practical problems 117–26
  problems 117–126
  rationality 125

future generations (*cont.*):
　Rawls 114–15, 121, 124–5
　religion 111
　Rio Summit 1992 109
　self-interest 114, 118
　sustainable development 110
　treaties and conventions 107
　United Nations 108–9
　United States 107
　whaling 107

Gaia 79, 81, 156, 160, 163, 170
Galileo Galilei 7, 8
global warming *see* climate change
God 66–76, 81
　Christianity 14
　Nature 14, 65, 67–9
Grotius, Hugo 62

Hardin, Garrett 24
Hobbes, Thomas 7, 24
homeostasis 167–8
humanity
　anthropocentricism 9–11
　land ethic 185–7
　misanthropy 170, 173
　Nature, dichotomy between 9–11, 19,
　　142, 146
　religion 73
　self-interest 19
Hume, David 162, 163
hunting 146

Ideal Observer 114–15
indigenous people
　culture 92–5, 98
　hunting 146
　Maoris 94–5
individualism
　anthropocentricism 6–9
　economics 51–2
　misanthropy 169
　value 42
inherent value
interest rates 57–8
International Convention for the Regulation
　of Whaling 1946 17
international environmental law 127–36
　aesthetics 82–91
　animals 135–6
　anthropocentricism 15–18
　biodiversity 134
　conservation 16, 17
　ecosystems 133–4
　environmental policy 15, 17
　ethics 135–6
　future generations 107–10

land ethic 135
natural resources 16, 17
Nature 17
　value 15, 18
　objectives, changing 133–5
　pluralism 135–6
　self-interest 19–20, 23–9
　treaties and conventions 134
　values 127–33
international organisations 64
International Tropical Timber Agreement
　1983 17
International Whaling Commission 45
intrinsic value
　aesthetics 84
　animals 141–3
　anthropocentricism 6, 18
　land ethic 161, 164–5
　misanthropy 172–3
　religion 80
　respect for life 152

justice
　future generations 12
　rationality 125
　self-interest 23, 24

Kant, Immanuel 5, 7, 13, 22, 86, 115, 142
Kepler, Johann 9
Kierkegaard, Søren 7

land ethics 1–2, 135, 159–75, 178
　animals 167
　anthropocentricism 159, 161
　basis 159–62
　biosphere 162, 166, 167–8
　Chaos theory 159
　competition 168
　ecological theory 164–8, 174
　ecosystems 160, 164, 168
　ethics 163, 166–7
　evolution 160, 166–7
　extinction 165
　Gaia 160, 168
　holistics 160–2, 167
　homeostasis 167–8
　humanity 165–7
　inherent value 161, 164–5
　misanthropy 168–173, 178
　natural law 163
　Nature 164–7
　objectives 159–62
　philosophical problems 162–4
　poverty 174–5
　problems 162–8
　progress 174–5
　quantum theory 159

values 161, 162, 164–5
Leucippus 6
liberalism 7, 12
liberties 169, 170
Locke, John 7, 12, 13
Lovelock, James 81, 170
Lucerne Declaration 1993 36
Lucretius 6

Machiavelli, Nicolo 23–4
machinery 154–5
Maoris 94–5, 99
Marx, Karl 11, 12, 14, 90, 116
Maslow, Abraham 116
mentally disabled 144
Mill, John Stuart 14, 80
misanthropy
    biosphere 170, 171
    democracy 168–9
    Gaia 170
    humanity 170, 173
    individualism 169–70
    inherent value 172–3
    land ethic 168–73, 178
    liberties 169–70
Montaigne, Michel de 86
Moore, G.E. 84, 90, 141, 151
morality *see* ethics

national identity 96
national parks 82, 89, 102
natural beauty 83–4, 87
natural law 163
natural resources
    anthropocentrism 17
    economics 56
    future generations 121
    poverty 56
    religion 73
Nature
    aesthetics 82–91
    anthropocentrism 9–15, 17
    Christianity 14
    Communism 14
    control 12–15, 75
    culture 95, 101
    economics 54–5
    God 14, 65, 67–9
    humanity, dichotomies between 9–11, 19, 142, 146
    Labour 11–12
    land ethic 164–7
    liberalism 12
    morality 10
    property 11
    rationality 10
    religion 11, 14, 67–76, 79, 81

respect for life 151, 152
self-interest 19, 47
theriophobia 10
use 11–12
value 2, 11–12, 15, 43, 47, 54–5, 130, 143, 164
nature reserves 103
necessity 158
New Age 79
Newton, Isaac 7–8
Nietzsche, Friedrich 7, 14, 24, 86
Nozick, Robert 139
nuclear waste 112–13

Palme Commission on Disarmament and Security Issues 19
Pantheism 65, 79
Parfit, David 123
Pearson Commission 19
pets 128
Pinchot, Gifford 119
plants 146, 153
Plato 5, 6, 22, 88
Plotinus 86
polluter pays 32, 35–6, 38
population 63, 77–8
    Cairo Conference 1994 78
    family planning 77, 78
    International Conference 63, 77
    Rio Summit 1992 78
poverty
    economics 56
    land ethic 174–5
    natural resources 56
precautionary principle 26, 46
predators 147
Protagoras 87
public policy 23
Puritans 72
Pythagoras 5, 6

quantum theory 159

radical ecology 1–2
rationality
    animals 144
    anthropocentrism 9
    future generations 125
    justice 125
    Nature 10
    value 44
Rawls, John 114–15, 121, 124–5
Ray, John 70
recreation
    conservation 103
    culture 105
    environmental protection 102–6

recreation (*cont.*):
  exploitation 103
  national parks 102
  nature reserves 103
  tourism 105–6, 177
  treaties and conventions 102–3
  wilderness 103–4
Regan, Tom 141, 142–3, 144–7, 150, 154
religion
  animal sacrifices 68
  anthropocentricism 66, 75, 176
  Bible 67–76, 81
  biodiversity 64
  Christianity 7, 14, 69–76
  conservation 71–81
  cruelty 74
  dominion 67–8, 74
  environmental policy 63–4
  environmental protection 62–81
  equality of living creatures 70
  ethics 66–71, 76, 79
  exploitation 73
  fundamentalism 72
  future generations 111
  Gaia 79, 81, 156
  God 66–76, 81
  hostility 76–80
  humanity 73
  indifference 76–80
  inherent value 80
  international law 62
  international organizations 64
  motivation 76–80
  natural resources 73
  Nature 11, 14, 67–76, 81
  New Ageism 79
  Pantheism 65, 79
  population 63, 77–8
  problems 71–81
  Puritans 72
  respect for life 152
  Rio Summit 1992 63–4
  role in a secular society 80–1
  self-interest 80
  slaughter 76
  spiritual value system 65–6
  stewardship 68–71
respect for life 150–8, 178
  anthropocentricism 150, 155
  aversive behaviour 150
  ecosystems 157
  endangered species 156
  ethics 150–8
  Gaia 156
  intrinsic value 152
  machinery 154–5
  Nature 151, 152

  necessity 158
  plants 153
  problems 152–8
  proposal 150–1
  religion 152
  reverence 152
  self-interest 157
  sentience 153
  suffering 155
  trees 152–5, 158
  utilitarianism 157–8
  value 151–2
reverence 152
rhinos 87–8, 177
Rio Summit 1992 17
  economics 35
  future generations 109
  religion 63–4
  value 129

sacrifices 68
Salt, Henry 138
Schweitzer, Albert 152, 158
seals 85–6, 177
self-interest
  anthropocentricism 19, 21, 22–3
  biosphere 22
  climate change 25–7
  community 50
  competition 24
  economics 50, 52–3
  environmental protection 19–27, 176
  future generations 118
  holistic approach 21
  humanity 19
  international environmental law 19–20,
    23–7
  justice 23–4
  Nature 19, 22, 47
  public policy 23
  religion 80
  respect for life 157
  United Nations 19
  utilitarianism 22–3
  value 39, 47
sentience 137–40, 145–7, 153
shallow environmentalism 2
Sidgwick, Henry 119
Singer, Peter 137, 139, 144–7, 150
slaughter 76
Smith, Adam 12, 22, 39, 52–3
South Commission *Challenge of the South*
    report 20, 109
Spinoza, Benedict 65
spiritual value system 65–6
Statement of Principles on a Global
    Consensus on the Management,

Conservation and Sustainable
Development of Forests 1992 31
stewardship 68–71
suffering 138–41, 155
Sumner, John 14
sustainable development
  conservation 110
  culture 99
  economics 29, 31
  value 45–7
  whaling 45–7, 58
Sutich, Antony 116

taxation 32
Thatcher, Margaret 7–8
theriophobia 10
Thucydides 23
tourism 105, 106, 177
treaties and conventions *see also* Particular
  treaties and conventions
  aesthetics 92
  culture 92–3
  economics 32
  future generations 107
  international environmental law 134–5
  recreation 102–3
Trumball, John 117

United Nations
  future generations 108–9
  self-interest 19
  UNESCO 82
  value 130
United States
  economics 30–1, 61
  forestry 61
  future generations 107
utilitarianism
  animals 137–41, 158–9
  respect for life 157–8
  self-interest 22–3

value
  anthropocentricism 6, 18, 43–4
  biodiversity 49, 129
  conservation 44, 48, 127, 131
  cost-benefit analysis 39, 41
  economics 29–30, 31–3, 36–51, 53–5, 57,
    176

endangered species 39–40, 127, 131–3
environmental policy 44
ethics 42, 130
forestry 36–7, 49–50
individualism 42
international environmental law 127–33
intrinsic 6, 18
land ethics 161, 162, 164–5
location 47–50
Nature 2, 11–12, 15, 43, 47, 54–5, 130,
  143, 164
pets 128
precautionary principle 48–9
problem 38–47
rationality 44
respect for life 151–2
right to life 131
Rio Summit 129
self-interest 39, 47–8
sustainable development 45–7
Total Economic Value 36, 43
Unit Nations 130
whaling 45–7, 50, 131
World Commission on Environment and
  Development 128

Weiss, Edith 120–1
whaling
  culture 100–1
  economics 58–9
  endangered species 100–1
  International Convention on the
    Regulation of Whaling 45, 107
  International Whaling Commission 45
  Norway 46–7
  precautionary principle 46
  right to life 131
  sustainable development 45–7, 58
  value 45–7, 50, 131
wilderness 103–6
World Charter for Nature 1980 16, 20, 83,
  108, 128, 130
World Commission on Environment and
  Development 1987 16, 20
  culture 93
  economics 29, 34, 60
  future generations 108
  value 44, 128
World Conservation Strategy 16